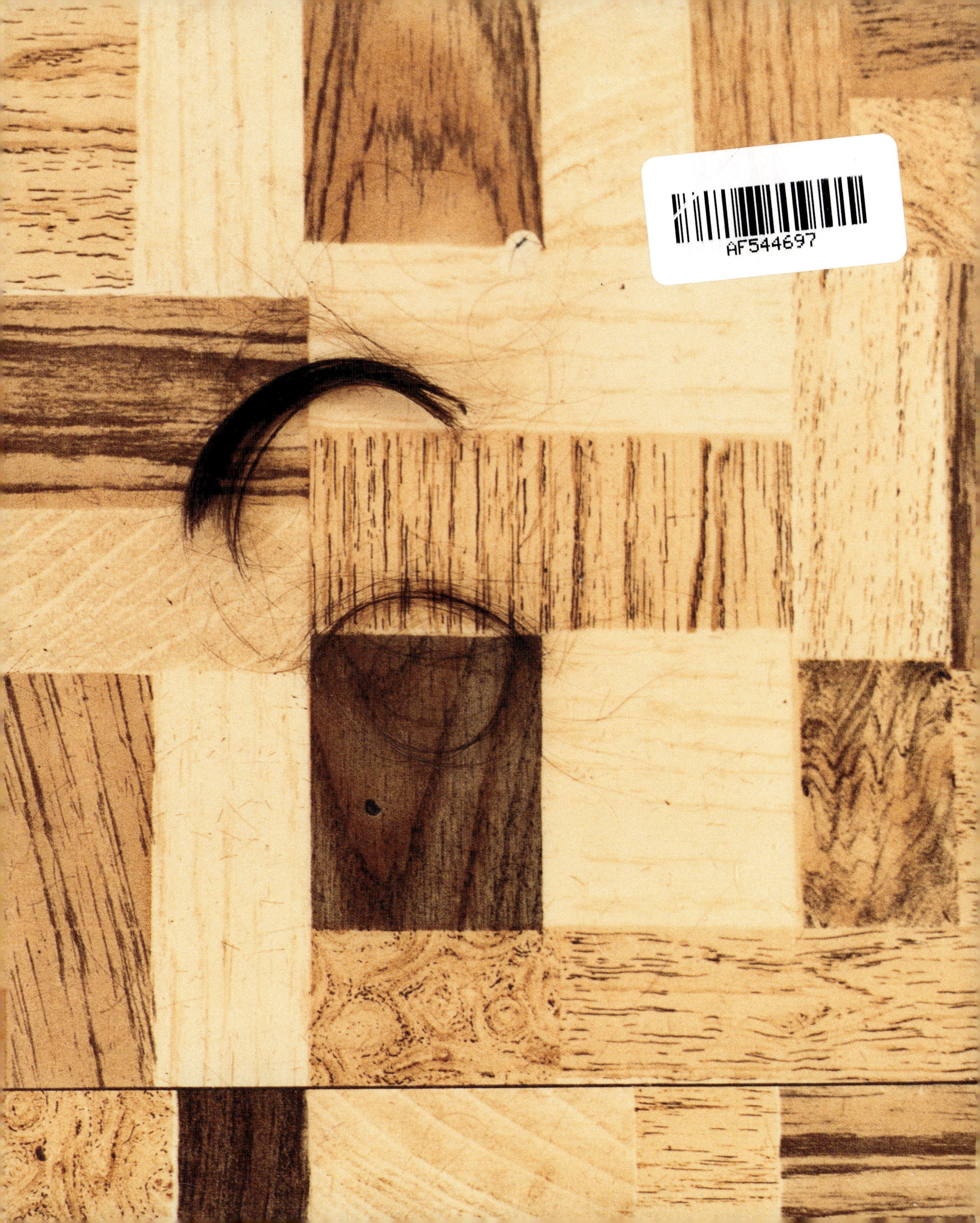

BARBERSHOPS

TALLY ABECASSIS & CLAUDINE SAUVÉ

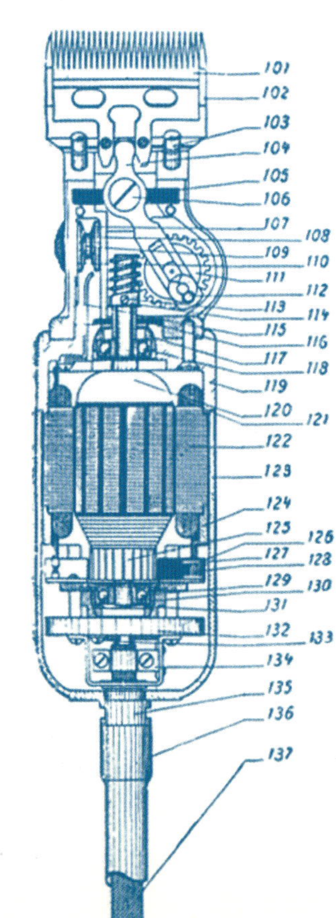

101. Upper cutting plate
102. Lower cutting plate
103. Detachable pins for small cut heads
104. Lever
105. Felt packing
106. Pivot screw
107. Insulating disc for switch
108. Switch button
109. Contact disc for switch
110. Switch spring
111. Worm wheel
112. Cotter and disc
113. Worm screw
114. Worm
115. Contact spring for switch
116. Felt packing
117. Tumbler bearing sleeve
118. Ball bearing
119. Motor head
120. Rotor
121. Magnet coils
122. Stator
123. Insulating covering
124. Bearing bracket
125. Commutator
126. Carbon brush-holder
127. Carbon
128. Carbon spring
129. Ball bearing
130. Tumbler bearing sleeve
131. Ball bearing compression sprin
132. Connecting plate
133. Connecting screw
134. Tension balancing clamp
135. Fixing sleeve of covering
136. Protecting rubber tube
137. Cable

FIG. 110
SECTIONAL DIAGRAM—
KOH-I-NOOR 2 MODEL

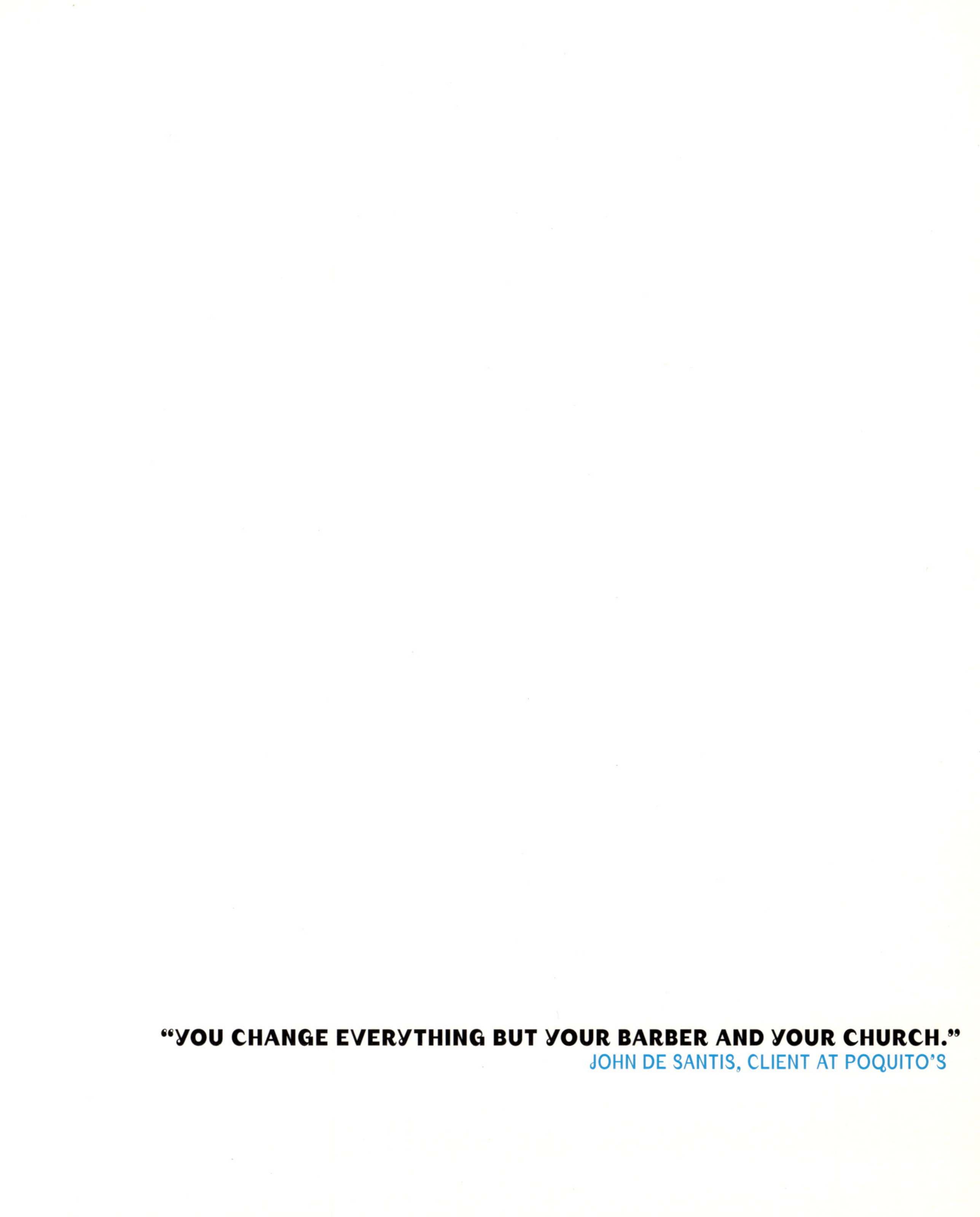

"YOU CHANGE EVERYTHING BUT YOUR BARBER AND YOUR CHURCH."
JOHN DE SANTIS, CLIENT AT POQUITO'S

CONTENTS

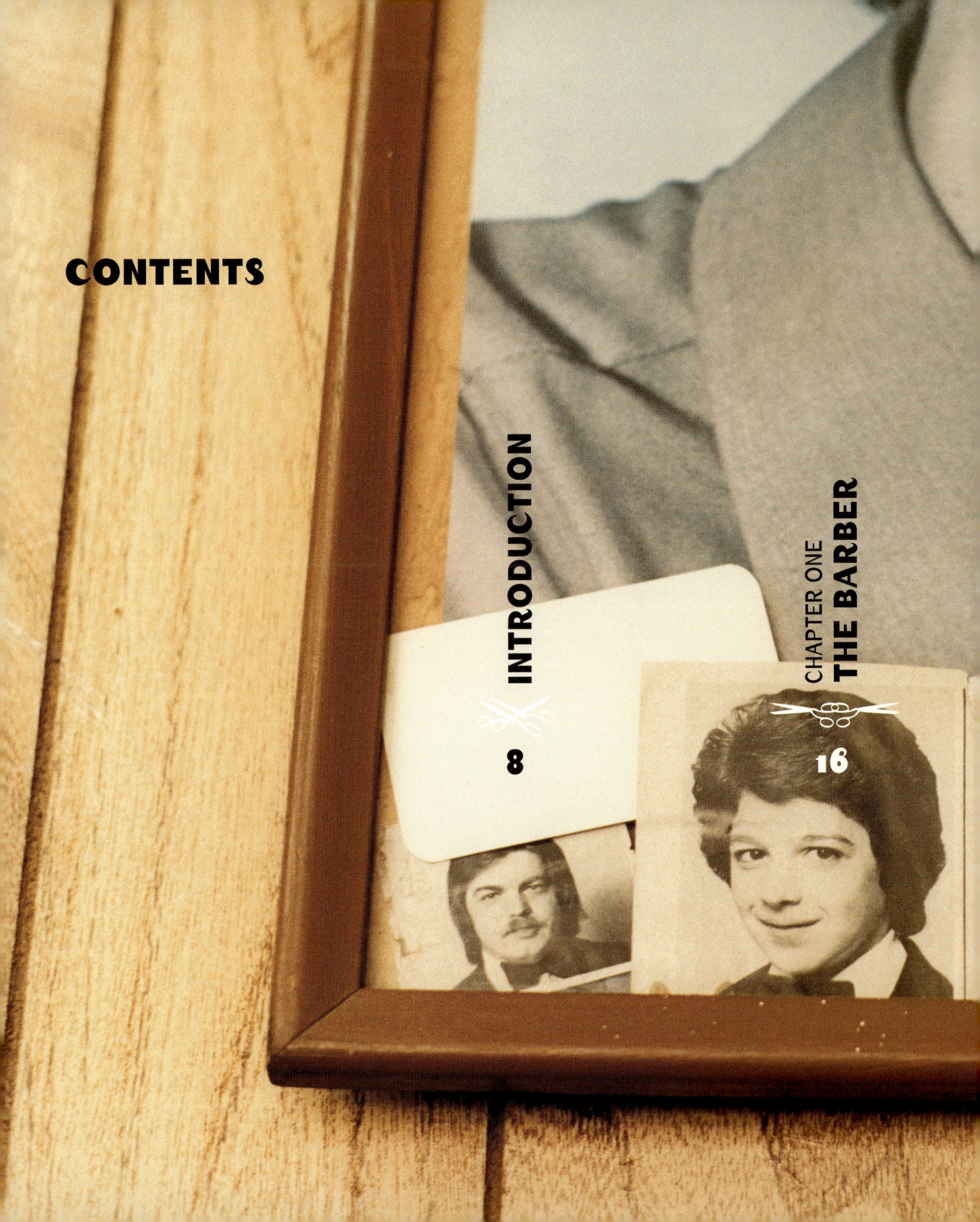

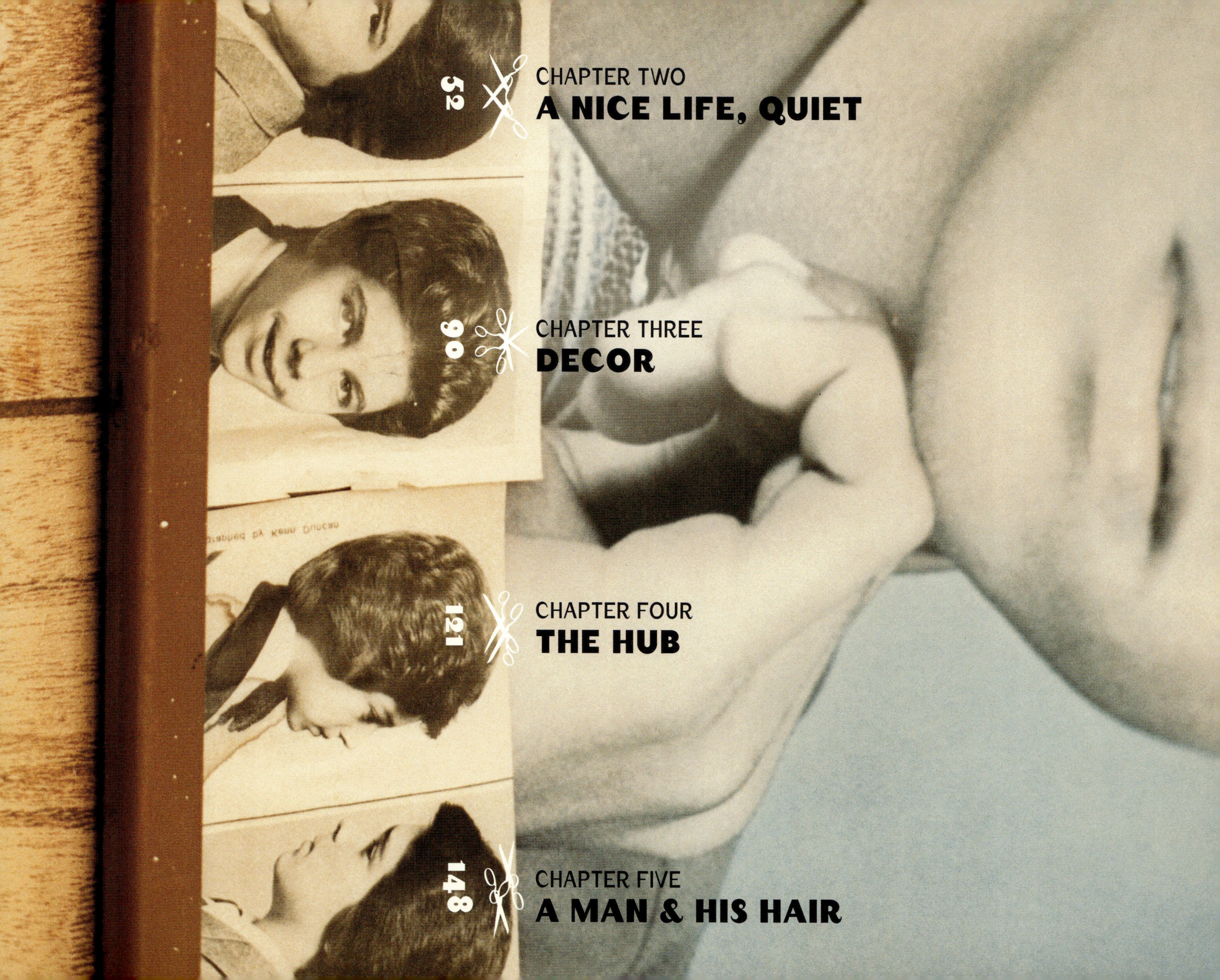

Sir, will you have your worship's hair cut after the Italian manner, short and round, and then frounst with the curling irons to make it look like a half-moon in a mist; or like a Spaniard, long at the ears and curled like the two ends of an old cast periwig; or will you be Frenchified with a love-lock down to your shoulders, whereon you may wear your mistress's favour?

A BARBER TO HIS COURTIER CLIENT, 1592

Same as last week – a little off the back, long on the top, but not quite no shag, slope to the left like Gumby, some Eddie Mustard in the front, a little Wyclef to the right.

A CLIENT TO HIS BARBER, *BARBERSHOP* THE MOVIE, 2002

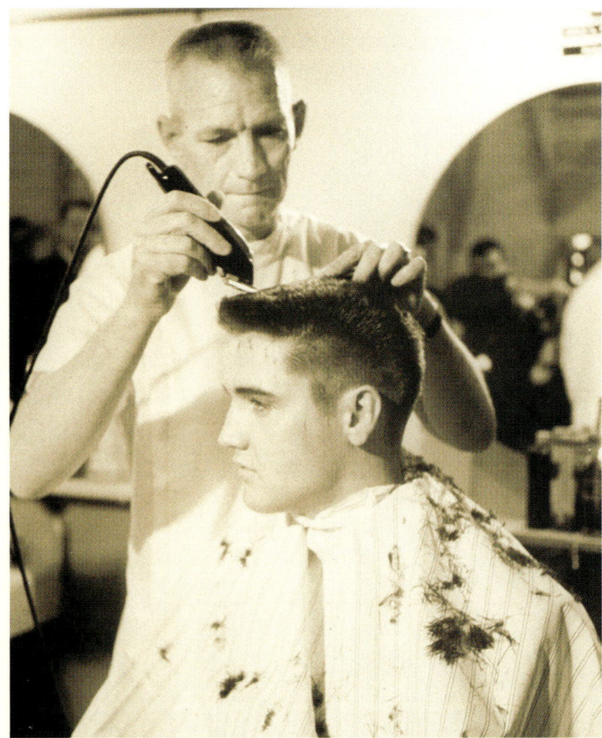

Army barber James Peterson brush cuts Elvis Presley's mane.
Photo by Don Cravens/Times Life Pictures/Getty Images

HOLLYWOOD DREAMS

The relationship between a man and his hair has generally seemed to me to be a straightforward one. It wouldn't be entirely inaccurate to say that until working on this book, my personal appreciation of men's hairstyling had never really gone beyond "long", "short", and noticing whether a man had any hair at all.

Popular folklore has always upheld that a man takes pleasure in the familiarity of his signature hairstyle, involving a minimum of preparative steps. Certainly my father's generation never made it seem otherwise. Gentlemen of a certain age put a premium on personal appearance and grooming, but ease of procedure is fundamental. Today's man may struggle with a few more thorny issues in his styling (mousse or gel?) but by and large it seems that hairstyle is not a subject for discussion, it is an unchanged given. The less said about it, the better.

Once Claudine Sauvé and I entered the world of men's barbershops, however, we realized that this is not entirely the case. The cutting of a man's hair is a ritualistic event that will determine the image he presents to the world around him. A hairstyle is but one of the myriad visual codes that bombard us on a day to day basis. The right hairstyle is a powerful identifying marker. It says: "I am strong, I am virile, I play hockey." The man responsible for making it happen can only be one of his most important allies.

Spend time with a man getting his hair cut by his barber and this all becomes evident. Theirs is a relationship laced with subtlety and a certain invisible design. Beneath the hairstyle, beneath the hair and how it is cut, is the rapport between a man, his barber, and the barbershop – that temple of manhood where it all takes place – that is the most meaningful of all.

My interest in these curious spaces was sparked in 2001. I noticed a barbershop in my neighborhood in Montreal. The Hollywood Barbershop is an homage to cinema, decorated with jazzy striped chairs and posters of the familiar icons of classic Hollywood cinema: Clark Gable, Greta Garbo, Marlon Brando, and Lassie. I watched as every day a little scene would

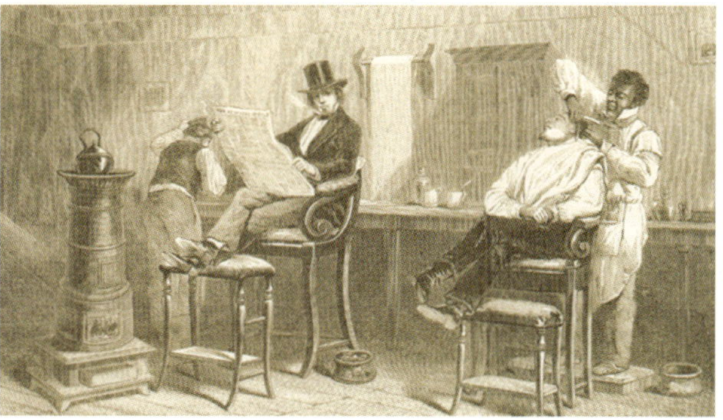

A Barbershop in Richmond, Virginia, circa 1850. Photo by Hulton Archive/Getty Images

unfold in the window. The barber, cloaked in what appeared to be an iridescent purple satin robe, would move deftly about the barber chair, cutting the hair of another loyal client – a vision of cinematic glamour incarnate. It was too beautiful.

In talking about the Hollywood Barbershop with Claudine, my frequent partner in crime, we realized that the barbershop was a world that was foreign to us, a seemingly-closed microcosm. We decided to indulge our curiosity and dig a little deeper into this male-beauty space and create a book of photographs and interviews.

We set out to find other barbershops for the book, each with a remarkable shop to photograph and barber to interview. The research was not without its challenges. It is no simple thing to walk into a barbershop and casually browse around, chatting up the barber and scrutinizing the furnishings. Never mind two women. Women who have been known to cut their own hair. We ended up doing much of the reconnaissance at night when no-one was around to see us staring into the brightly-lit shops, dictating scrupulous notes to one another, assessing whether the shop under surveillance merited a day-time visit.

Often, when approaching the shops during operating hours, we could see that lively conversations were taking place inside. Inevitably, as the door opened and we set foot inside, an uncomfortable silence would fall over the room like so much dandruff. Words hung suspended in mid-sentence, cigarettes dangled from open mouths. After some explanation, we were welcomed with a mixture of suspicion and incredulity: "A book on barbershops? This is a project for school? Who gave you those haircuts?"

Jimmy, the owner of Salon Outremont, in particular needed coaxing; he was concerned that we would disrupt the fraternal atmosphere that reigns in his shop. In the end, we stayed for several hours, listening to the regulars' hold a dizzyingly circular debate about the politics of hunting – a performance that must take place on a daily basis. By the time we left, we had shared shots of Ouzo and anecdotes about our respective families.

BARBERSHOP BEGINNINGS

Grooming, my friend, is the most important thing in business, after personality.

CREIGHTON TOLLIVER,
***THE MAN WHO WASN'T THERE*, 2001**

Men have been removing the hair on their faces since the proverbial dawn of time. Since its days as a scraping tool in the Stone Age, the device we now know as a straight razor has turned out to be one of the most perfect and simple instrument designs ever made. The strange paradox is that the removing of beards in the Stone Age was actually practiced by a painful plucking process and not via the stone precursor to the razor.

The word "barber" comes from the Italian *barba*, meaning beard. However the barber profession actually originated from Ancient Egypt where barbering services were performed by the Egyptian nobility. In Ancient Greece the barbershop would become a social center for daily exchanges of philosophical views and sporting news. It was only around 300 BC that barbering made its way to Rome (via Sicily) where it was developed into a refined artform that included everything from shaving to massaging and manicuring. From the time of Alexander the Great, men in Rome shaved their beards for one of two recognized reasons: to imitate the fashion of the leader (as we are wont to do) or by decree of Alexander the Great himself, to prevent soldiers being gripped by their beards and thrown to the ground during battle.

Barbers throughout the eleventh century were primarily phlebotomists (dressers of wounds) and assistants to the clergy, who were responsible for performing surgery in most parts of Europe back then. In 1163, the top church brass decided that surgery was not a suitable activity for men of the cloth – probably a wise move. They decreed that monks would be forbidden from performing surgery and barbers were more than happy to pick up the slack, becoming "barber-surgeons" in an effortlessly bestowed career promotion.

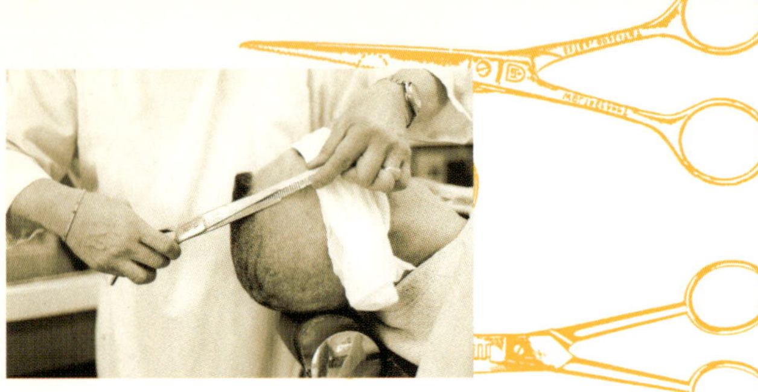

There were still "real" surgeons from institutions such as the Royal College in London, but barber-surgeons were the men to see for leeching, bleeding, minor surgery, and of course a smooth shave.

Often at that time barbers would also do shaves in public – at churchyard fairs where merchandise and services were sold. Shaving had its own rules and, apparently, a code of honor – as witnessed by a notice from the meeting of the barber-surgeons in Newcastle-on-Tyne in 1742, England, when it was ordered that no shaves were to take place on a Sunday and that "no brother should shave John Robinson till he pays what he owes to Robert Shafto".

Eventually, barbers were relieved of their duties as surgeons and the barbershops returned to being the less gory, but no less social environments that we now know them to be. The move was made official in England by an Act of Parliament in 1745 and many other countries followed suit. But losing their right to perform surgery meant that by the end of the eighteenth century barbers were on a downward spiral. Relegated to the status of mere laborers their barbershops became rather shady establishments where only the very brave or very foolish dared to enter.

In spite of this gloomy outlook, the art of barbering experienced a revival in the late nineteenth century which saw the opening of the first school for barbers in Chicago by AB Moles and the foundation of the Barbers' Protective Union in Columbus, Ohio, which, in 1887, became the Journeymen Barber's International. Around the same time the State of Minnesota passed legislation for a barber licence and finally, the world wars solidified the barber's new standing in bringing about the short hair fashion, especially the flat top, butch, crew cut and the Princeton cut.

As barbershops gained cultural importance, the most prosperous proprietors proudly displayed their success to their clientele, and the world. The barbershop in the Palmer House hotel in Chicago, elaborately rebuilt in 1872 just after the Great Chicago Fire, featured a floor tiled with 300 dollars worth of silver dollars. In the 1930s, the New Yorker Hotel, the largest hotel in New York City with 2,500 rooms, had a barbershop with 42 barber chairs and 20 manicurists.

Attend the tale of Sweeney Todd
His skin was pale and his eye was odd
He shaved the faces of gentlemen
Who never thereafter were heard of again
He trod a path that few have trod
Did Sweeney Todd
The Demon Barber of Fleet Street.
...
He kept a shop in London Town
Of fancy clients and good renown
And what if none of their souls were saved?
They went to their maker impeccably shaved.

THE BALLAD OF SWEENEY TODD,
MUSICAL BY STEPHEN SONDHEIM, 1982

The oldest barber that most of us have ever heard of is Sweeney Todd, the Demon Barber of Fleet Street. Sweeney Todd notoriously slit the throats of unsuspecting clients with his straight-razor. As if that wasn't awful enough, his wife would then use the ground up remains to make meat pies, serving them up to equally-unsuspecting diners. The story has long been considered legend, but in *Sweeney Todd: The Real Story of the Demon Barber of Fleet Street*, author Peter Haining proved that the basis of the story was indeed – shockingly – true.

Sweeney Todd aside, even to the initiated the idea of getting a shave – lying in a chair as the barber slides a sharp razor blade up and down your jugular – may seem unwise. The relationship between shaver and "shavee" is necessarily one of absolute trust. In exchange, the customer is indulged and pampered with steaming towels, waxy creams, and peaks of perfect foam. It is an inherently slow and utterly sensual experience – quite different from the hasty job most men do today on their own faces as they run out the door in the morning.

It was a traveling salesman named King Camp Gillette who was responsible for sealing the fate of the professional barber shave. In the early 1900s, he called to his wife one morning while shaving with a blade and announced that he had thought up an ingenious invention – the original disposable razor, then called the safety razor. 30 years later, Colonel Jacob Schick followed up with the first consumer electric shaver. Of course, the market war was intense. The typewriter manufacturer

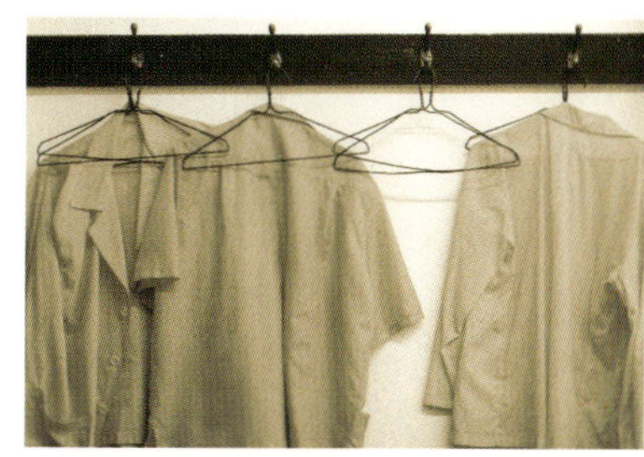

Remington joined the race in 1937 when it introduced its first electric dry shaver, the "Closer Shave", which was presented to millions of Americans at the New York World's Fair of 1939.

> ***Is your beard black as pitch and hard as nails, or blonde as hay and nearly as light? Is your skin leather-tough or tender as a child's? Just name it... and get the Gillette Super-Speed Razor that's matched to your face. What a difference in the shaves you get... easy, refreshing!***
>
> GILLETTE ADVERTISEMENT, 1955

> ***A Master Barber – In the Palm of Your Hand The All New Remington 60 Electric Shaver***
>
> REMINGTON ADVERTISEMENT, 1952

The professional jurisdiction of the barber evoked in the second ad is a clear testament to the expertise still attributed to the barber. But the barbershop shave is fast becoming a thing of the past. A ritual that is so time-consuming and much costlier than the home job is losing its allure for the modern man, besides the few who go once for the novelty of the experience. It is even unappealing for some of the barbers we met. As Marcel told us: "I don't feel like doing shaves anymore. It's a waste of time. It costs eight dollars – for that price a guy can buy a razor and shaving cream for a month. Guys can shave their beards themselves nowadays! We do stuff that they can't do themselves, like their hair."

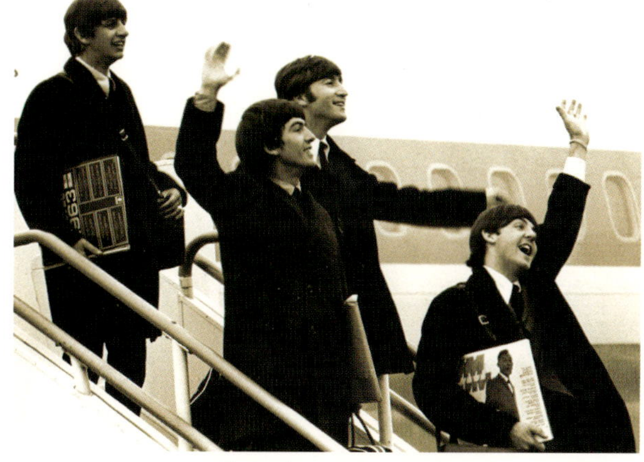

The Beatles step off the aeroplane which brought them back from their tour of the United States, 22nd February 1964. Photo by Hulton Archive/Getty Images

THE BEATLES NEARLY KILL THE BARBER

Barbering's trajectory is deeply intertwined with the dictates of fashion and the whims of popular taste. In 1971, the magazines *Men's Hair Stylist* and *Canadian Barber* began profiling a change brewing in men's hairstyling. Long hair was sweeping North America. The magazine's editors tried to downplay the problematic nature of the new fashion to the industry. They provided some enthusiastic yet vague tips for the concerned barber: "Men are seeking other ways to express their personalities – most personal expression of self is in the hair style. Keep up with the image in fashion. When you work in a fashion field, you really can't afford not to." The trend persisted and, one by one, barbershops began to close.

In 1974, a group of five enthusiastic sociologists set out to assess the state of the barber and barbershop. The resulting study paints a picture of a vocation in the twilight of its life. A variety of potential factors were cited, the most convincing of which was the dreaded, omnipresent trend of the long-haired man.

In their study, the sociologists cited a barber's typical reaction to long hair: "My first reaction when faced with it: give the kids a good kick in the ass." When asked about their preference for long hair, the young people surveyed were similarly unambiguous in their reasoning: "I hate the way my ears look," "A guy with short hair looks straight-laced," and poetically, "I like chaos and feeling the wind in my hair."

The study concluded that a new attitude towards hair rather than a negative attitude towards barbers was accounting for the declining frequency of barbershop visits in the male population. This new way of thinking was empirically clear as 52.5 per cent of the respondents were so concerned with their hair's appearance that they reported to "regularly" keeping a comb on their person every day.

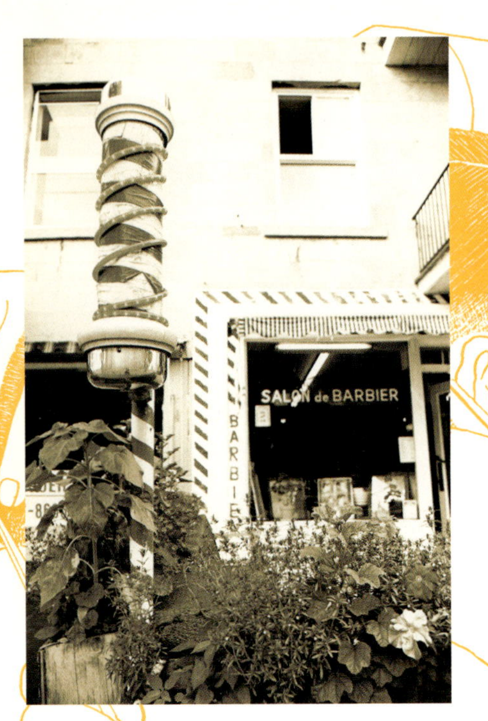

POLES, CHAIRS & ALL THE TRIMMINGS

Claudine and I heard a lot about the "long hair crisis" in our encounters. Barbers told us that more than half of the barbershops in Montreal closed in the early 1970s. The numbers are similar across North America. In Vince Staten's book *Do Bald Men Get Half-Price Haircuts? In Search of America's Great Barbershops*, Staten claims that in the United States the number of barbershops went from 106,000 in 1963 to 69,000 in 1978.

Many of the barbers we met spoke with unabashed disdain for the fad that amounted to a virtual death knell for the profession. Stronger still was their resentment for the Beatles, blamed by most self-respecting barbers for the cursed trend. I have since heard of the Beatles being blamed for the crisis from Alaska to Florida. Not the Monkees, not the Rolling Stones, not The Who. It was the Beatles. It is unclear if this sentiment was extended to their music.

In more recent times, the craft of the barber has been further diminished by another development: the electric hair-clipper, lovingly nicknamed "the mower" in our hometown. Billed as "progress," depending on who you ask this is either the most wonderfully efficient device to hit barbering or the final step in its inevitable demise. Naysayers not only criticize its pedestrian nature but also the lack of skill required for its operation. Bob from Salon Bob expressed his concerns rather nicely when he told us: "You can buy the clippers at any pharmacy. Now the girlfriend can butcher the guy's hair at home – and say it was the barber!" The clippers have annihilated any finesse of cut and sadly, the barber's delicate dance of comb and scissors moving rhythmically over the client's head.

The origin of the barber's pole is the subject of much speculation. Early conjecture indicates that barber-surgeons used to affix a pole outside their shops on which to hang bandages. The red and white bandages blowing in the wind would make up the swirling beacon. The blue stripe is what most historians disagree on – most say that the blue represents the veins, but in the United States, some claim that it was later added as a sign of patriotism.

Vince Staten tells the story of another innovative businessman who made his mark on barbering: William Marvy, the creator of the Marvy pole in the 1950s. Until Marvy showed up, barber poles were made of wood that splintered and metal that rusted, and also needed to be wound up manually for turning action. Marvy produced his own futuristic protoype of lucite, aluminum, and stainless steel that ran with an electric motor. Orders poured in and barbers lined up to buy them. The new poles were so successful that most barbers only needed to buy one in their lifetime and Marvy basically put himself out of business.

Once inside a barbershop, the focal point is surely the chairs. The first thing you will notice are either the relatively unremarkable chairs of a newer barbershop (or unisex salon) or the classic-model chrome and leather chairs of an old-school authentic barbershop. The latter don't so much resemble chairs; they are like the driver's seat on a spaceship of the past. They turn 360 degrees, raise, lower, and recline required versatility for the various positions a barber needs to attain the perfect shave. The classic models didn't come cheap but they too could last a lifetime. According to Staten's book, his own barber's chair cost approximately $1,200 in the mid 1930s. The author's father bought a house in the mid 1940s for $1,700.

Another gentlemanly accoutrement of a barbershop is the coat-hanger, the spot where a man hangs his hat and coat, announcing his arrival to all. It struck us as eerie that the coat-hanger in almost every shop we visited was the same

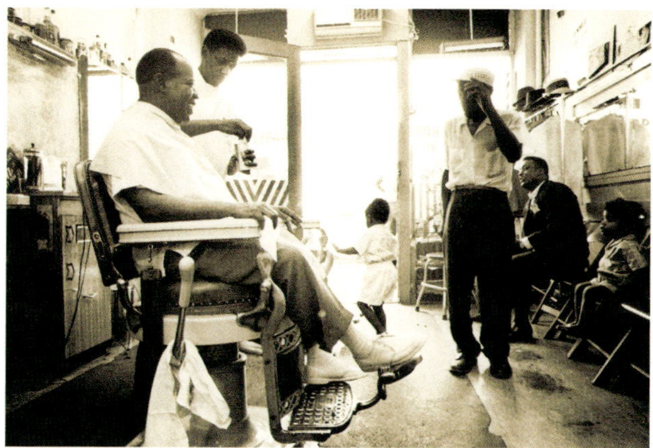

Louis Armstrong in his neighborhood barber shop, Queens, New York, 1965. Photo by John Loengard/Time Life Pictures/Getty Images

metal model. In trying to track down the provenance of the coat-hanger, I met with confused responses from the barbers as to my interest, "You want one? This is not a modern style – you should get something better. They have nicer ones now at Home Depot."

HIP-HOP, CADILLACS & HUNTING RABBITS

Few places today maintain the gender restrictions once favored by taverns and many private clubs. The barbershop, however, has in large part remained immune to the feminine touch. Unless researching a book, women have little if any reason to visit a barbershop – an arrangement that seems to suit both parties just fine thank you. "Don't let them fool you," Jason of Fades barbershop told us, "men talk just as much as women! And especially in a barbershop. The only reason why it's quiet now is because there are two women in here."

The barbershop is a "safe" male space, where men can be among men in a comfortably familiar and uniquely male environment; the décor is haphazard, the conversations are uncensored, and the coffee is black. According to Jimmy, "My wife says I have to clean this place up and to leave just the bottles with the perfume and the tools. In Greece they have a special place in downtown Athens, a bazaar, they call it Monastiraki. She said it's like that. But she's at home and I'm here. This is my place to do what I want. Here each one expresses his ideas, some are politicians, for others it's sports. I knew from the beginning the barbershop is a public place. I love it!"

The conversation at barbershops mostly revolves around "male" topics. As a result, the barbershop becomes a shrine to those eternal signifiers of maleness: hunting, fishing, gambling, shaving, cars, and sports. For the clients and hangers-on, it is of equal or perhaps greater value. Each of the clients may not have his own private refuge were it not for this unofficial clubhouse where membership is lax and dues are tallied in haircuts. The barber is the club's leader and head honcho. Jimmy told us that there was a virtual mutiny when he announced that he was going to reduce the opening hours of his barbershop, "I want to go, but my friends say: 'No, you can't close, you have to keep open.' It's like the politician who stays in office too long and when people ask why he stays, he answers: 'the people are voting for me!'"

> ***In my day, a barber was a counselor, a fashion expert, style coach, just general all-around hustler.***
>
> EDDIE, *BARBERSHOP* THE MOVIE, 2002

From what we saw, the barber is also confidante, psychologist, bookie, financial analyst, automotive advisor, real-estate broker, personal conscience, and shoulder to lean on. But more than the advice and entertaining conversation, the culture of the barbershop also allows for serious political and social debate. There was a story in Ancient Greece of a barber accused by the leaders of letting political discussions become too rowdy in his barbershop, sowing disorder among the public. Demosthenes, the celebrated orator of the time, is reported to have risen to the defense of the barber, calming those who were upset by all the open discourse. And though it may not have taken place in the barbershops, the original Journeymen Barbers' Protective Union played a defining role in the foundation of the American Federation of Labor in 1886.

> ***This is the barbershop. The place where a black person means something. The cornerstone of the neighborhood. Our own country club.***
>
> EDDIE, *BARBERSHOP* THE MOVIE, 2002

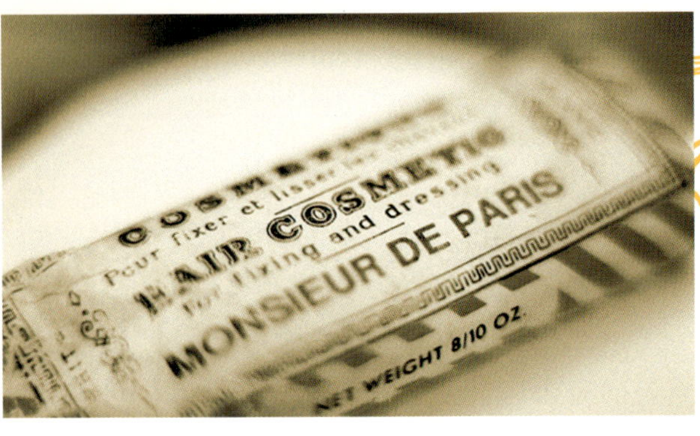

In North America, barbershops hold a privileged position in African-American communities. According to Laurence A Glasco, professor at Pittsburgh University:

> Blacks coped with job discrimination partly by setting up their own businesses. In doing so, they developed their own status hierarchy, with self-employed service businesses at the top of the ladder.... Barbering was [one of] their most prestigious occupation[s], and community leaders often were barbers who operated downtown barbershops that catered to the city's elite.

In *Barbershop* the movie, the barbershop is a "safe" male space, but also a "safe" space for the African-American neighborhood. Friends wander in and out, salesmen come and go, and the characters in the film make controversial statements about leaders of the black community – ideas that would only be uttered in a comfortable setting out of an outsider's earshot. In her book, *Barbershops, Bibles, and BET: Everyday Talk and Black Political Thought*, Melissa Victoria Harris-Lacewell suggests that "Barbershops are the archetype of the black public space.... The one constant is that black people in these spaces believe themselves to be free to talk to one another beyond the gaze of racial others." Whether the comments in the film are true or not, the viewer has the vantage point of a fly on the wall witnessing the sort of uncensored conversation that takes place in an African-American barbershop.

The atmosphere at Fades, a hip-hop/Caribbean barbershop that we visited, is reminiscent of the conviviality in the shop of the *Barbershop* movie. Frequented by locals and some professional baseball players, it has the aura of a neighborhood hub. At Fades you can buy tickets to a local rap show or reggae party; women call for their husbands and friends come looking for each other. "This place is like a community center, a hangout," says Jason the owner, "A place to see the people that you don't see all the time. A place to have a conversation. Half the time people come in here and don't even get a haircut. They come in – 'how you doing', 'what's up.' A lot of people know that lots of times it's not so busy so we're just sitting in here relaxing. We're bored too!"

Many of the barbershops we saw that double as local drop-in centers are those of various immigrant communities. Immigrants have always gravitated to the manual trades due to their situation; not yet comfortable in the language of the new country and low on financial capital. Barbering is a vocation that allows near-total mobility. A barber needs but a pair of scissors, a blade and a comb to be able to work. Barbers have come in large numbers from countries like Italy and Greece, both places where the barbershop played an important role in society. Here, their barbershops have become an integral part of the cultural landscape, where stories are told and histories are remembered.

Jimmy's salon is not only the meeting place for local Greeks to talk about news from "back home," but also headquarters for some Armenians, Jews, and a few Italians. The legendary Astor Place barbershop in Manhattan may be the most culturally diverse ever. At one point, it employed a whopping 73 barbers from outside the United States. Or take Rafael Barber Shop in Long Island, run entirely by Bukharian Jews from central Asia. A Washington Post article on Rafael Barber Shop cites Rakhmin Izgelov, a barber since 1968 who sums up the situation: "The customers are different. But hair is hair."

Beyond offering haircuts, fades, and beard trims, barbershops like Fades and Jimmy's Salon Outremont help foster a sense of community and civic value. Society's social structure is evolving and we are finding new places to impart meaning in our built-up environment. In neighborhoods where urban sprawl hasn't taken hold but where church groups have lost their grip, the barbershops has the distinction of being one of the few places where men go on a regular basis and can feel a sense of connection with the other clients; a kind of cultural nexus.

In the American south, barbershops are often gathering spaces for other purposes. The most successful barbershops have been those where the owners found alternate ways to make extra money. Often, barbershops would have a back room where clients could come to gamble. The owner of the shop would regulate the gambling and take a cut of the pot. Marcel told us a "back-room" story reminiscent of this: in the days when pornography was not the readily-available commodity it is today, Marcel would occasionally invite his friends to come to the barbershop at night and watch an

8mm or 16mm porno reel he got his hands on. They would pile into the shop basement with a case of beer, spilling up onto the stairs. "We didn't get to see them very often, so it was really a big deal. It would empty the bar across the street!"

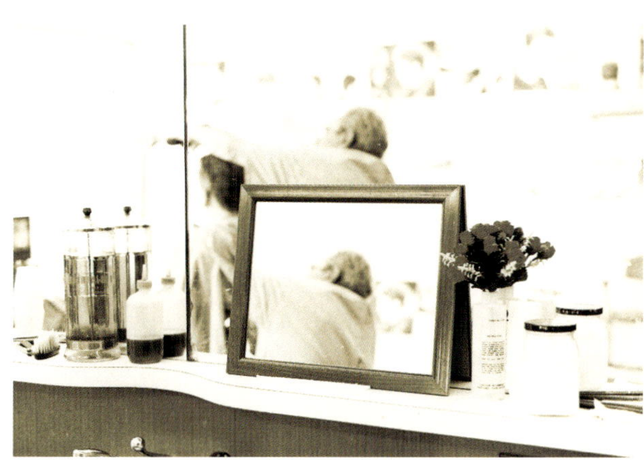

AND THE BARBER KEPT ON SHAVING...

There is a certain mythology to the barbershop experience that is quite beautiful; a man's loyalty to his haircut is outweighed only by his loyalty to his barber. Once the relationship is forged, the bond can remain intact for years, outlasting friendships and some of the strongest marriages. The security of a barber who can make a man look and feel his personal best can't be overstated. As Jimmy told us: "I have customers that come from far away who make the trip because they have been coming here for 20 years. They come for every haircut – once every five weeks. For some of them it's a one-hour drive." Another barber told us of a customer who was 85 years old and had never had a haircut at a different barbershop his whole life.

Every barbershop holds a mythic position for some man somewhere. Modern day barbershops run the gamut from ordinary to odd. I recently walked by a medieval-themed barbershop in New York City, replete with full iron armor and swords (for a friendly duel, not for shearing hair). In a suburban Toronto strip mall I was told of a one-eyed barber who waves his scissors around dangerously but cuts at lightning speed. In Montreal we saw several brightly-painted African barbershops that also sell CDs, long-distance phone cards, t-shirts, crucifixes, and cellphones. One summer in London, my husband routinely got his hair "Number Two-ed" at a barbershop in Covent Garden run by identical twin barbers. There is the ten-foot by ten-foot barbershop in Myers Flat, California, a free-standing blue house in the middle of a field by the side of the road. And then there are the roadside barbershops in East Asia – a chair, a piece of mirror, a canvas tarp for a roof, and a pair of scissors.

The sad reality of our adventures in barberland is that these bastions of ritual and relationships exist in a rapidly changing world; a world where all things authentic are swallowed up, re-packaged and sold to the masses as the new pink. All without anyone noticing that it has even happened. The Salon Pierre and Salon Bob are two barbershops that have closed since we started work on the book. As rent went up and business went down, Bob the barber and bric-a-brac salesman reluctantly moved on to other things. His shop is now a private apartment in a saturated tenant's market. For its part, the Salon Pierre is now an art gallery. Perhaps Panagis, the owner, poet, singer, philosopher, and avid reader of classics, can find some solace in the fact that his little sanctuary has become a venue for the dissemination of art.

When Claudine and I initially approached the barbershops, we thought of them as romantic, nostalgic, visually beautiful locations, but not much more than that. We didn't imagine the potential richness of meaning they harbored. As barbershops slowly disappear from our urban landscape, the few that remain have become time-machines in which certain traditional aspects of manhood remains encapsulated in a few well-worn chairs, a taxidermied moosehead, sports banners, and a soft-drink dispenser. The earnestness of the décor hides an authenticity hard to find in the world of franchise boutiques and chain restaurants. It is this experience that the clients of traditional barbershops covet as part of this near-sacred relationship, essential to the proper execution of haircut and style. The relationship between a man and this magical place, community hub, sacred male space, replete with history both public and private, is what keeps him coming back and looking good.

As you will see in this collection of photos and interview excerpts, the old-school barbershops that remain today are each a venue for an authentic bit of unscripted theater and spontaneous urban beauty.

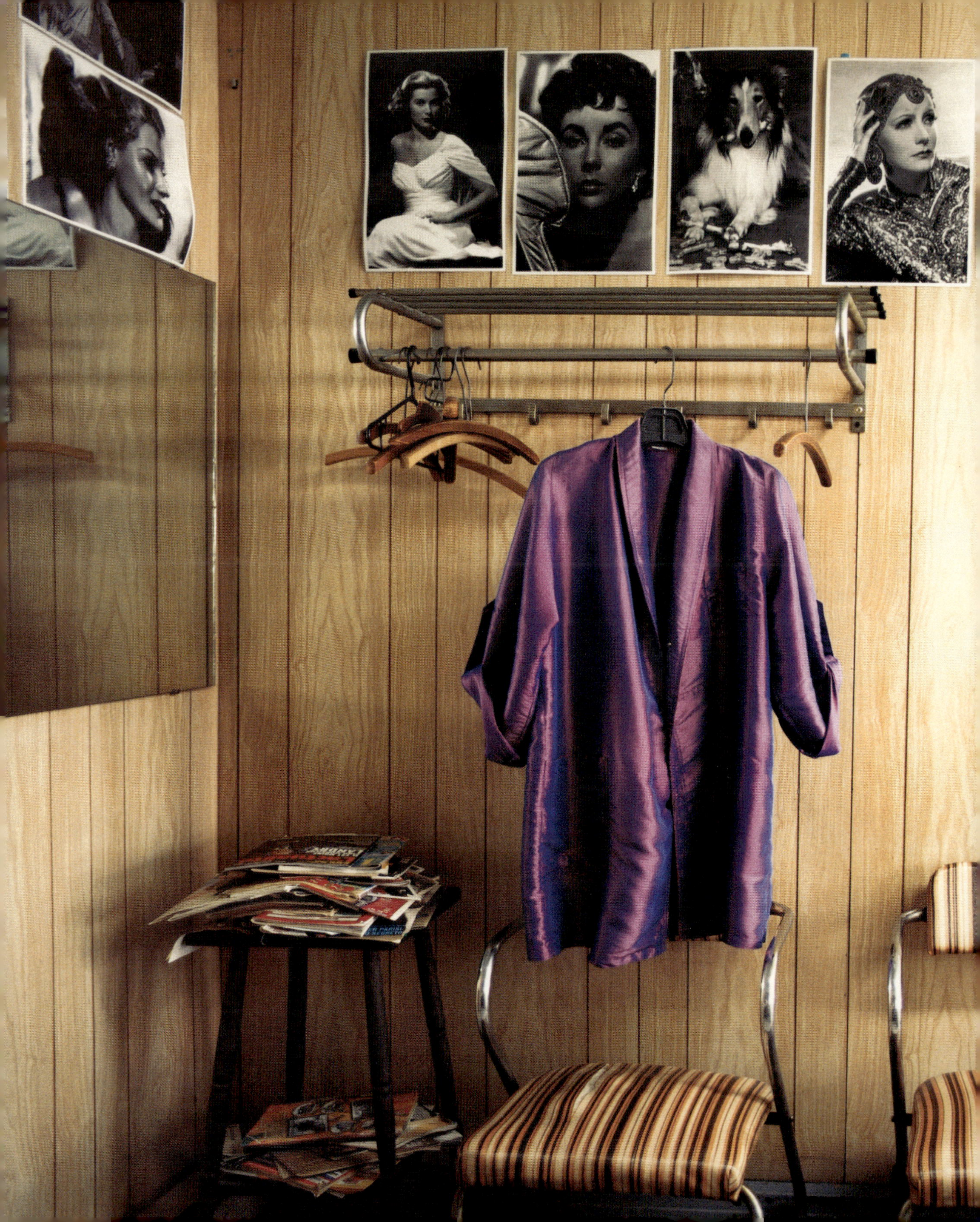

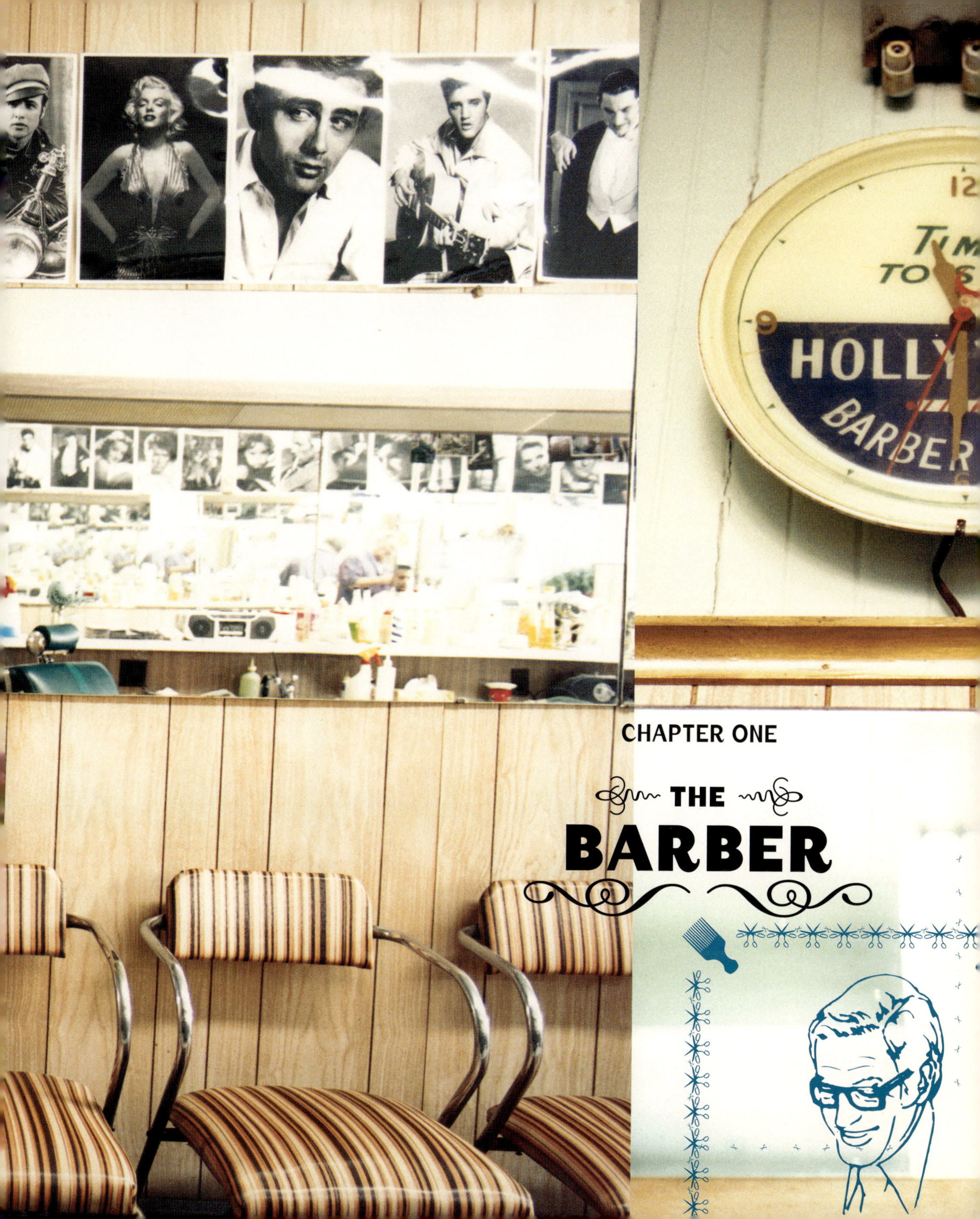

CHAPTER ONE

THE BARBER

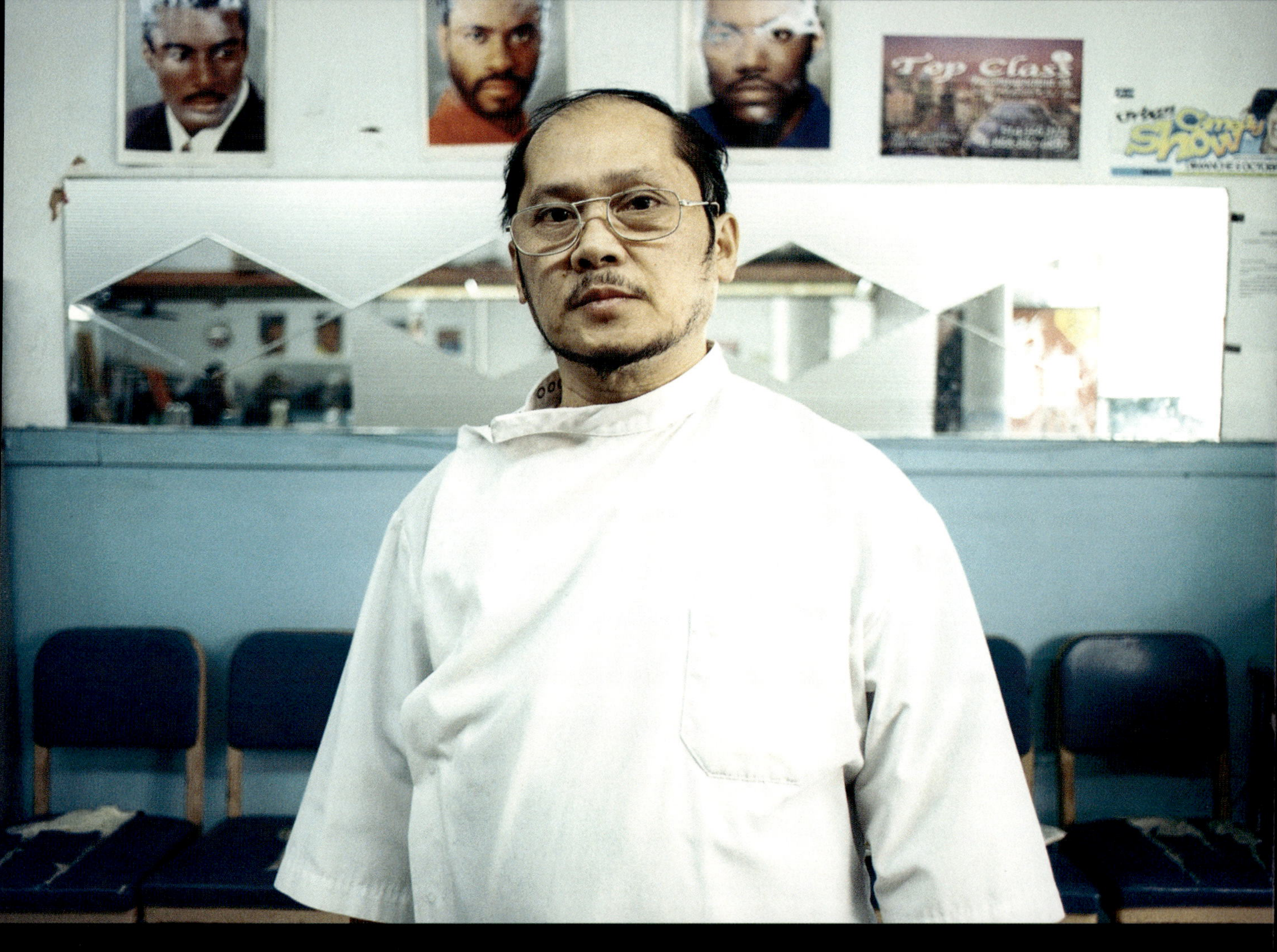

Poquito

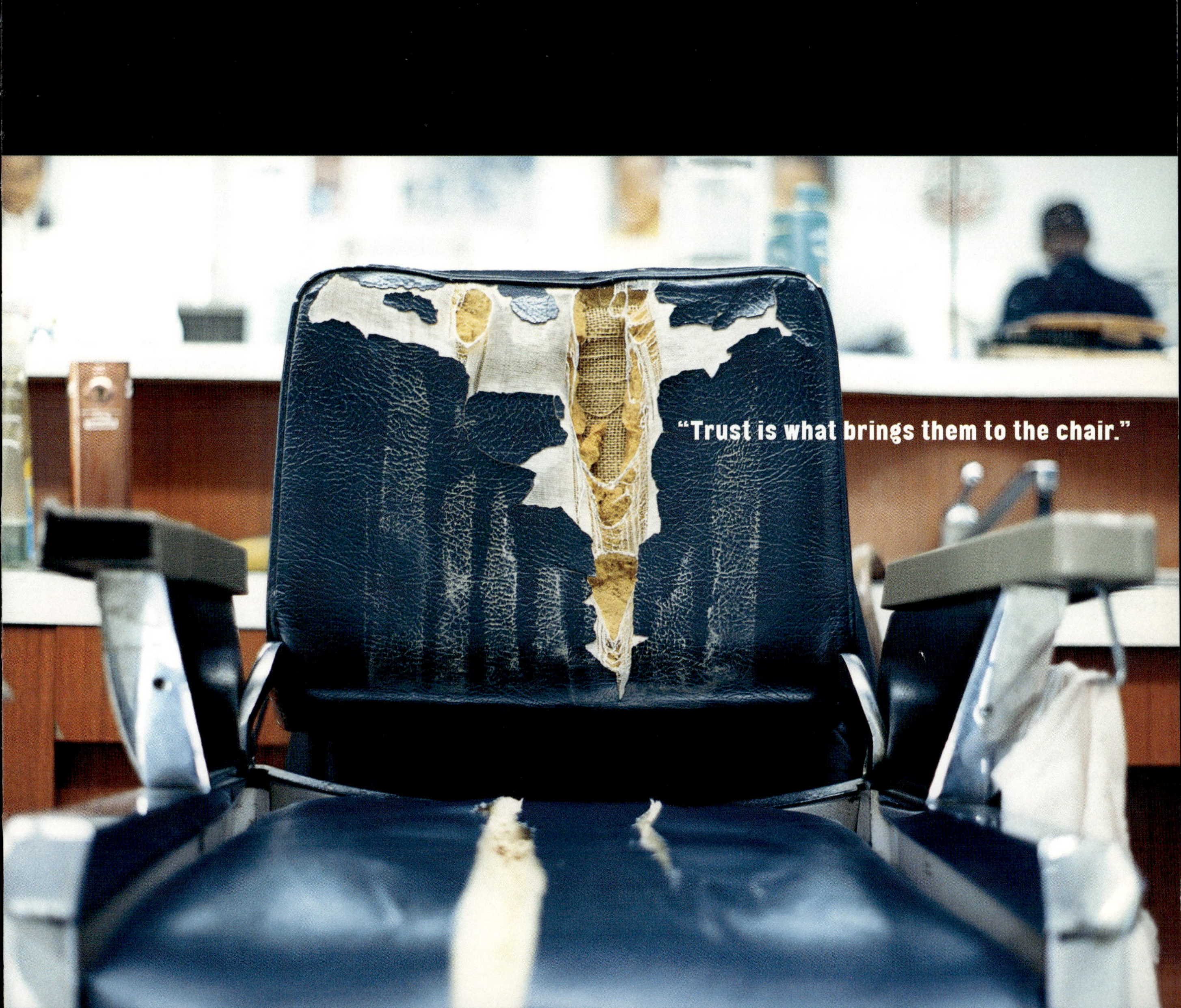
"Trust is what brings them to the chair."

"I carry my tools everywhere I go. They are a part of my life.
They're always in the trunk of my car, 24-7.
You meet me at a party and you need a haircut, I can do it."

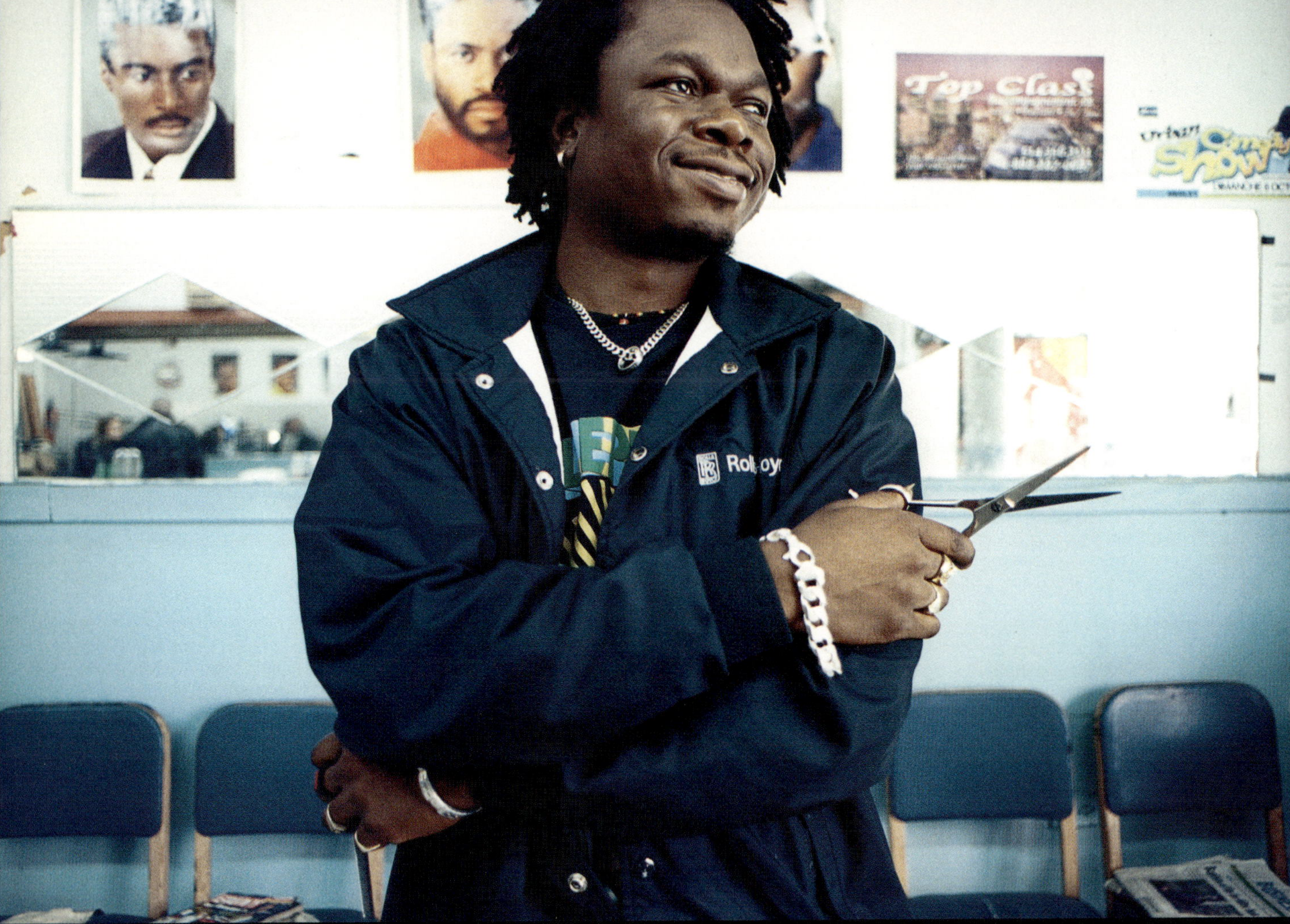

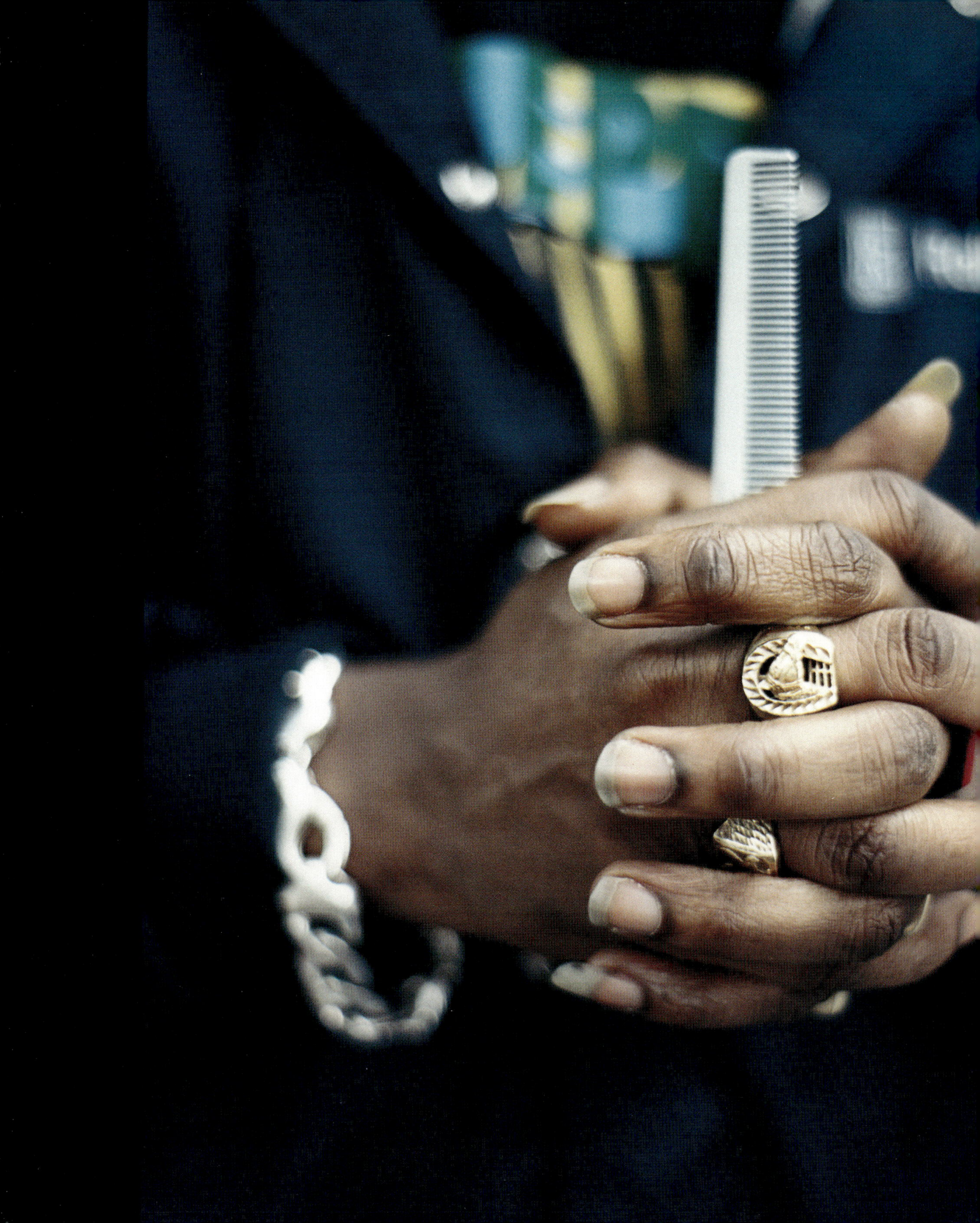

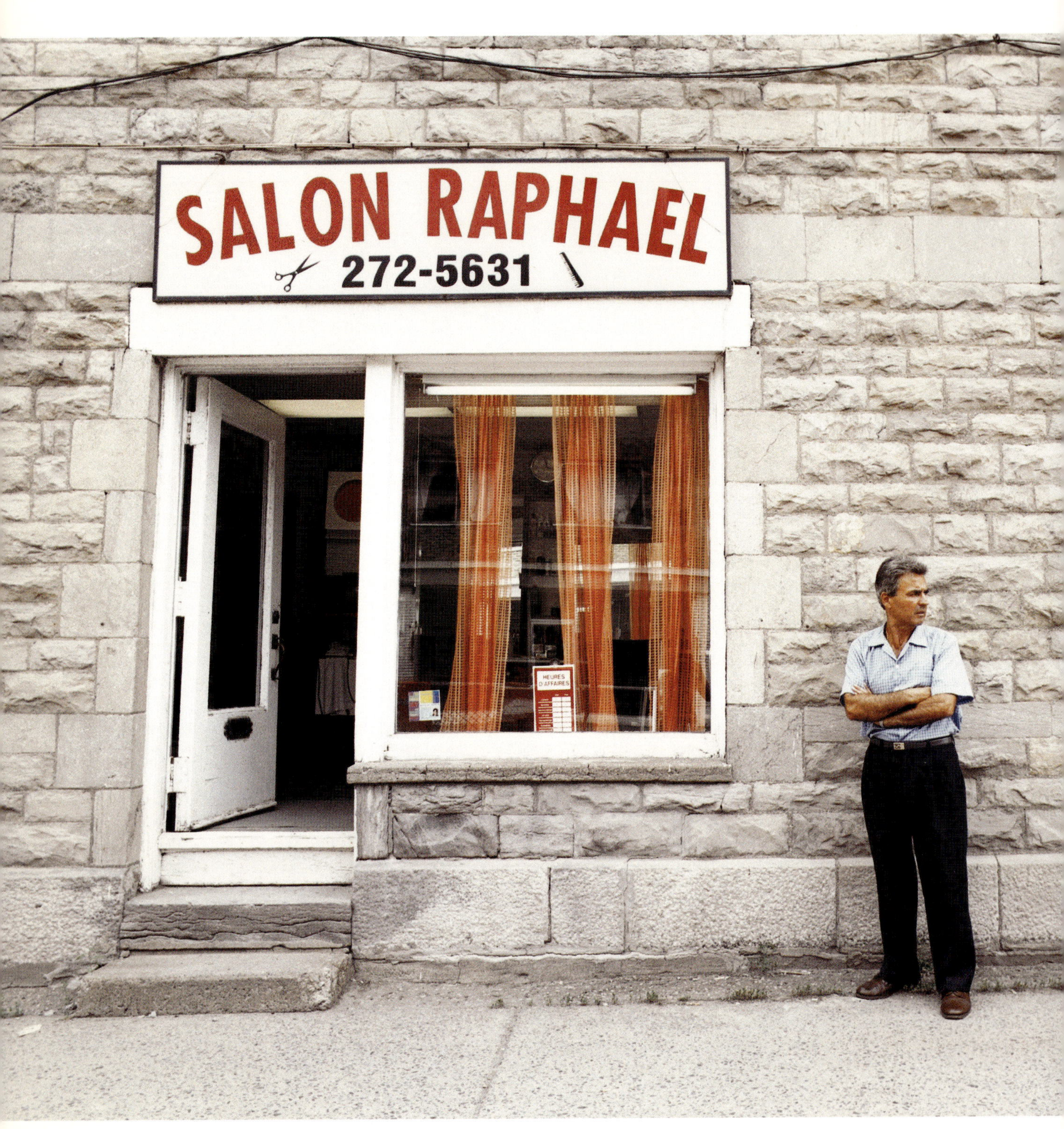
SALON RAPHAEL
272-5631
HEURES D'AFFAIRES

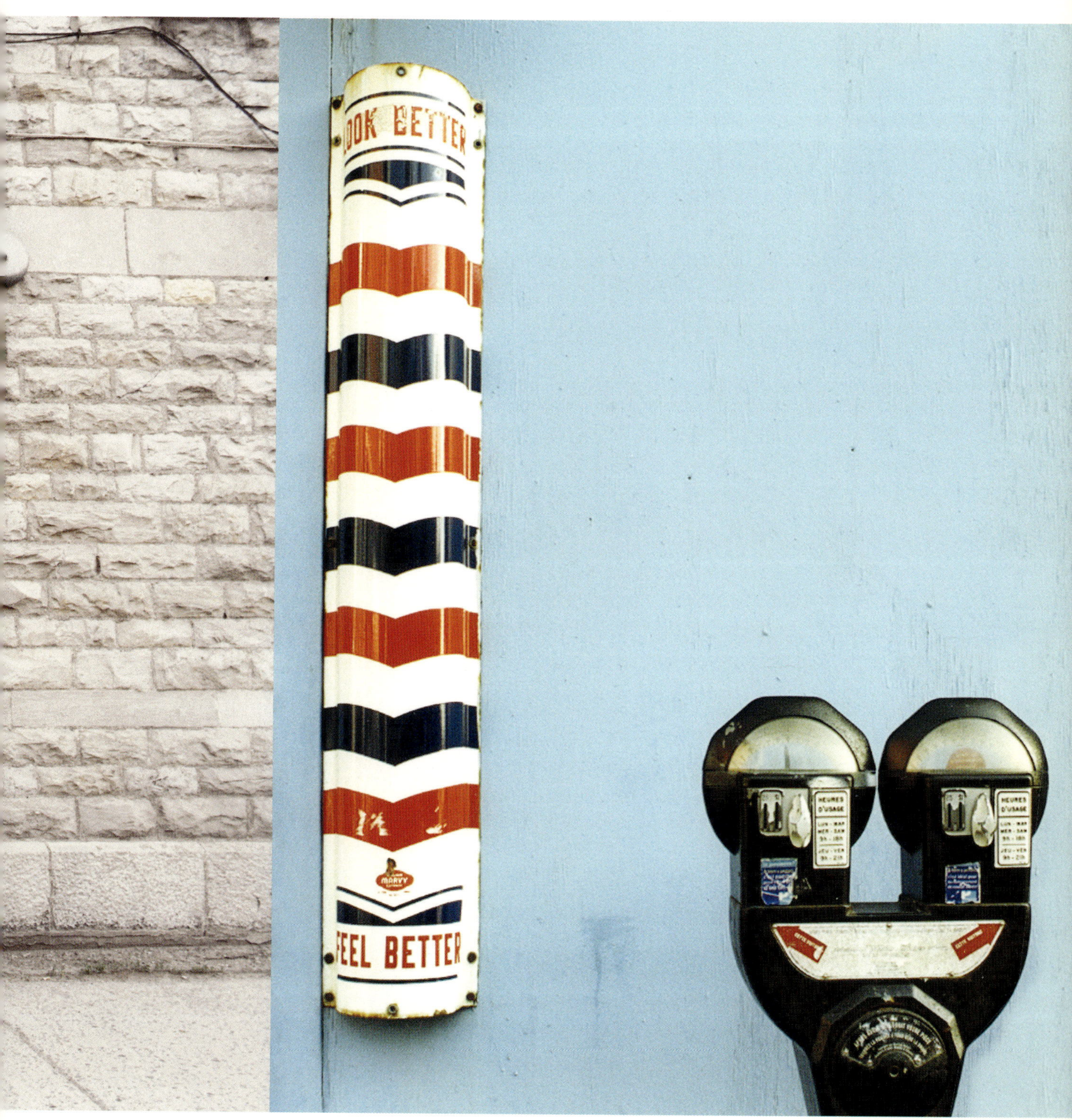
LOOK BETTER
FEEL BETTER
HEURES D'USAGE
HEURES D'USAGE

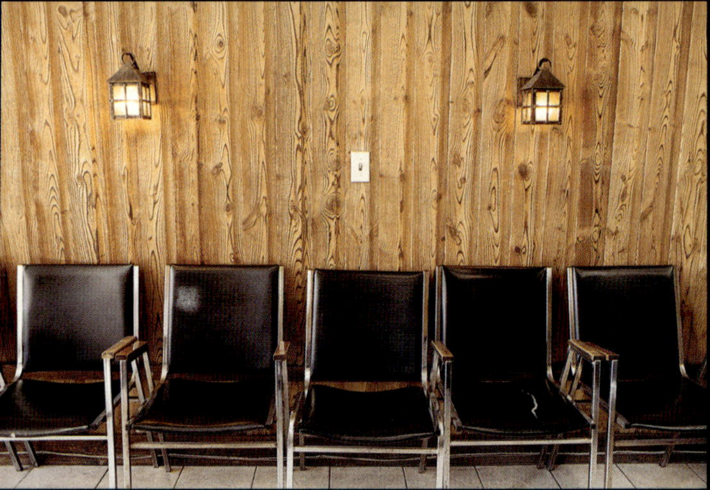

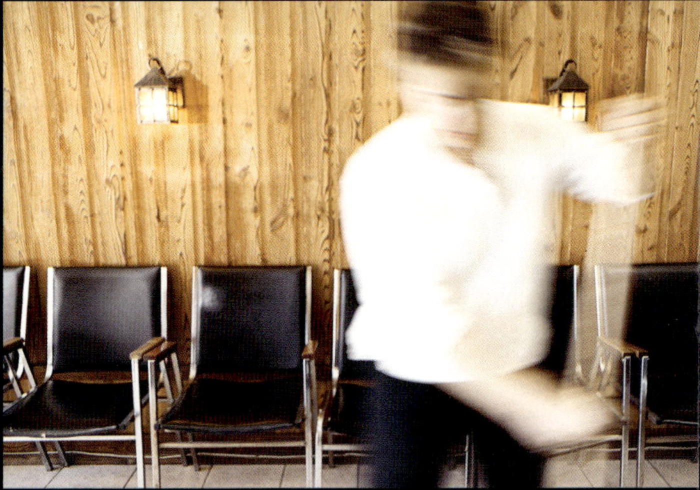

"When I see a man I know what's good for him, what style suits him. You get that thing, you feel it. I don't know, it's this thing I have."

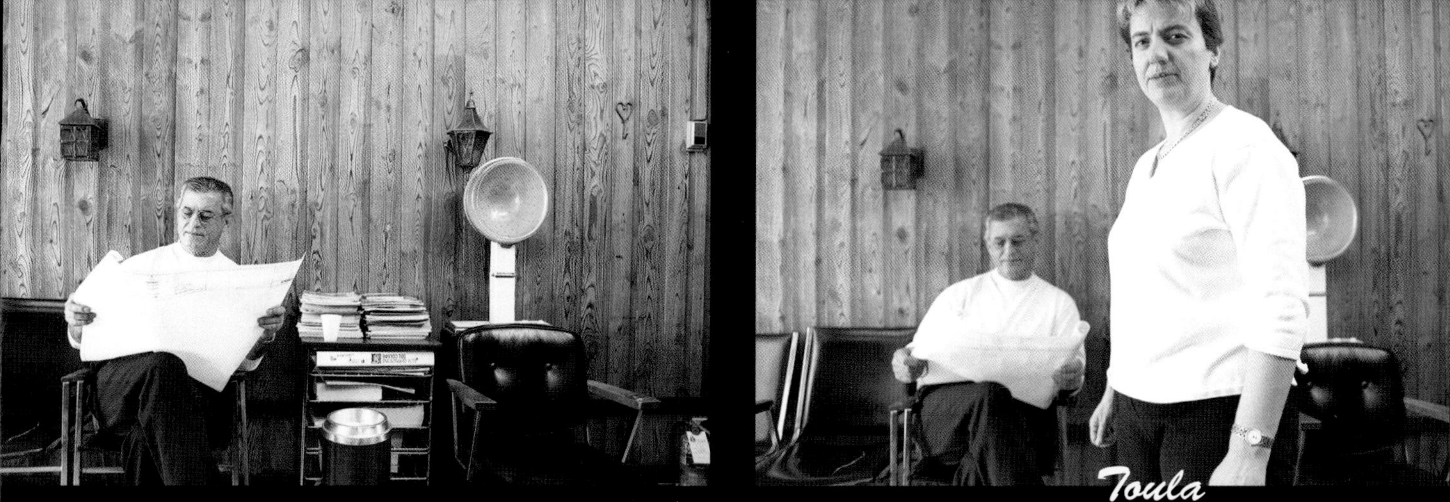

Toula

"I LEARNT IN THE BACKYARD AT MY GRANDMOTHER'S HOUSE, MESSING UP MY FRIEND'S HAIR.

That's the truth, that's the honest-to-god truth!

SHE GAVE ME THE CLIPPERS, SHE SAID JUST DO A LITTLE TRIM AND I WENT

'ZZZZ

MESSED IT UP, AFTER THAT LEARNED HOW TO FIX IT AND THAT'S HOW I STARTED."

Jason

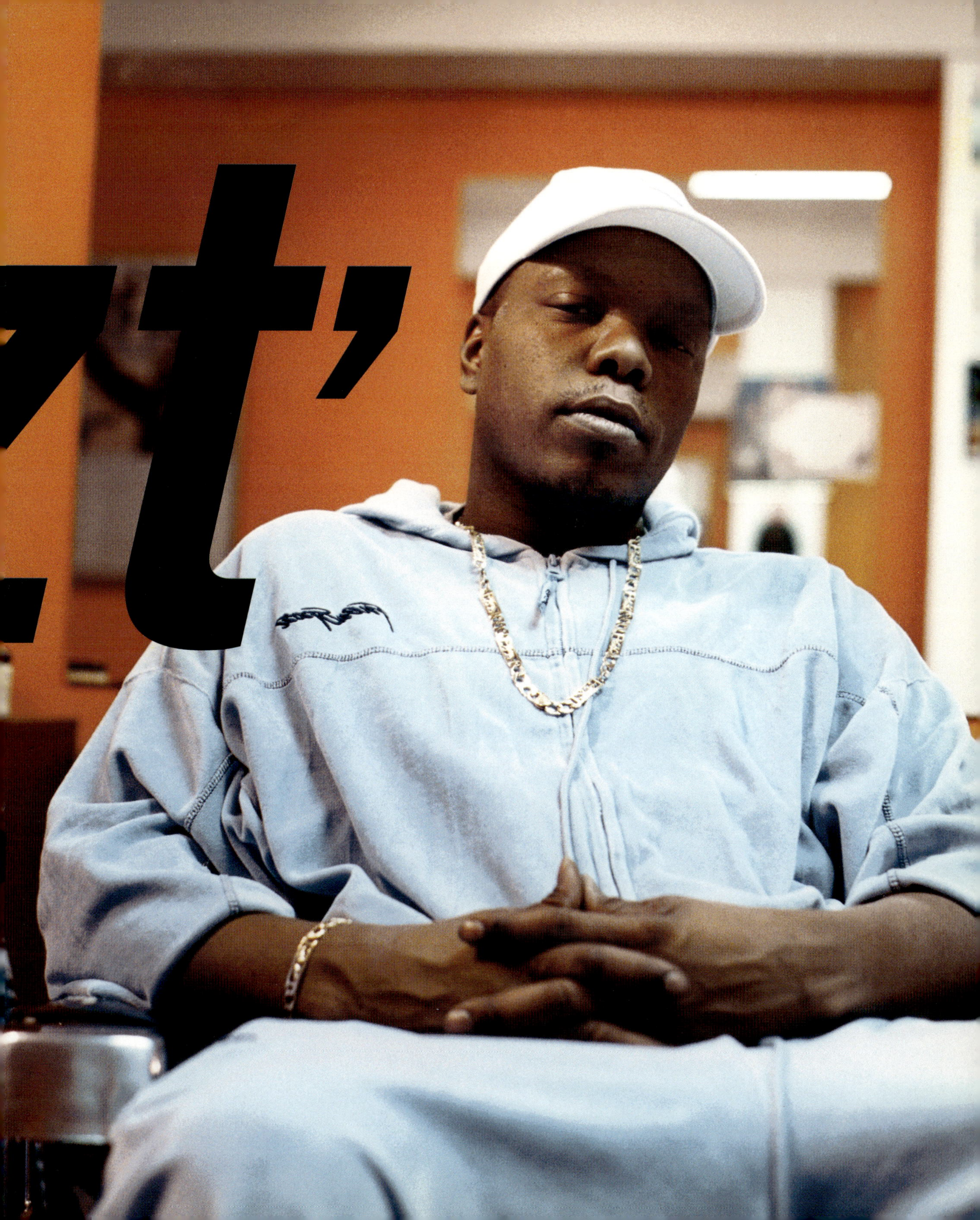

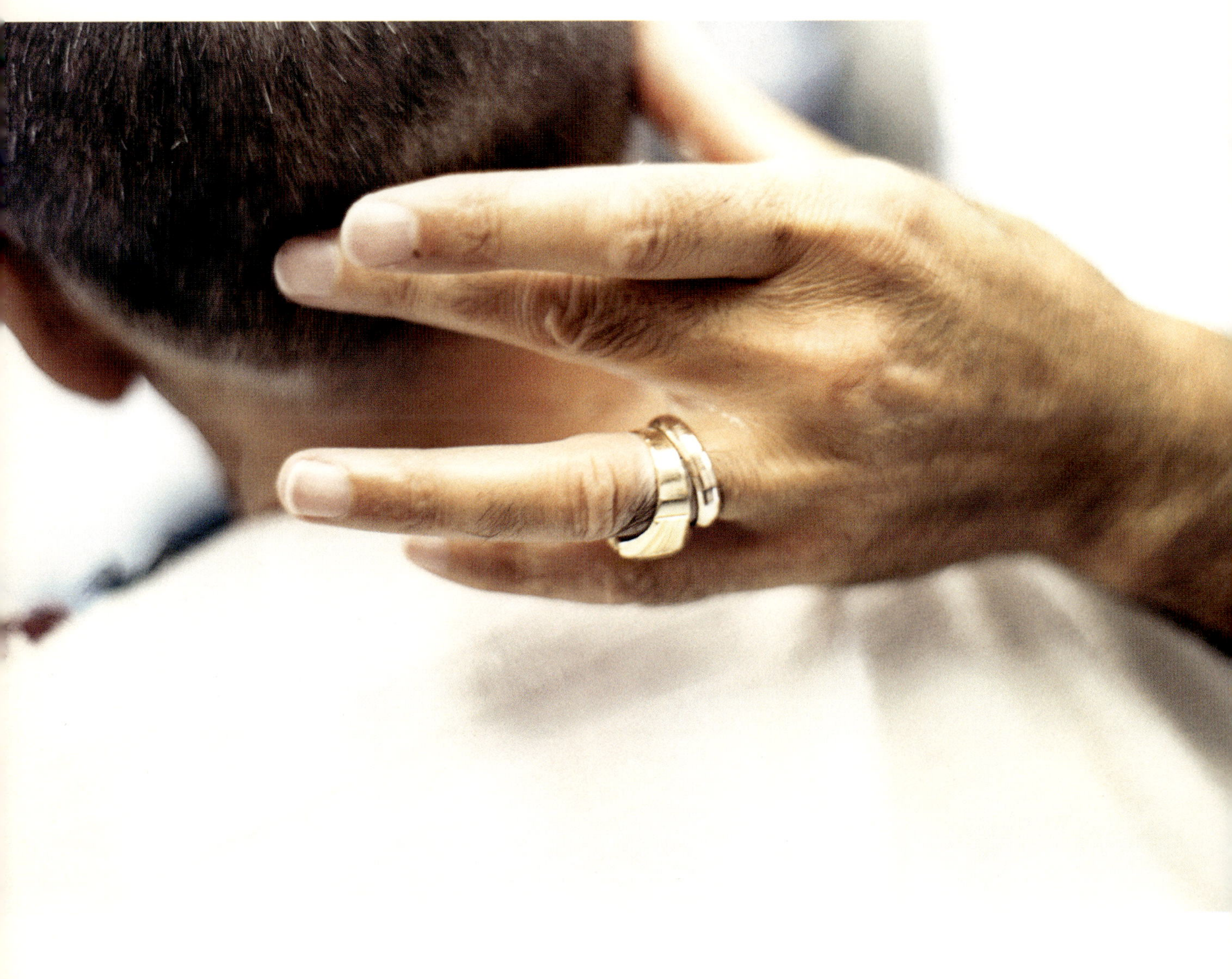

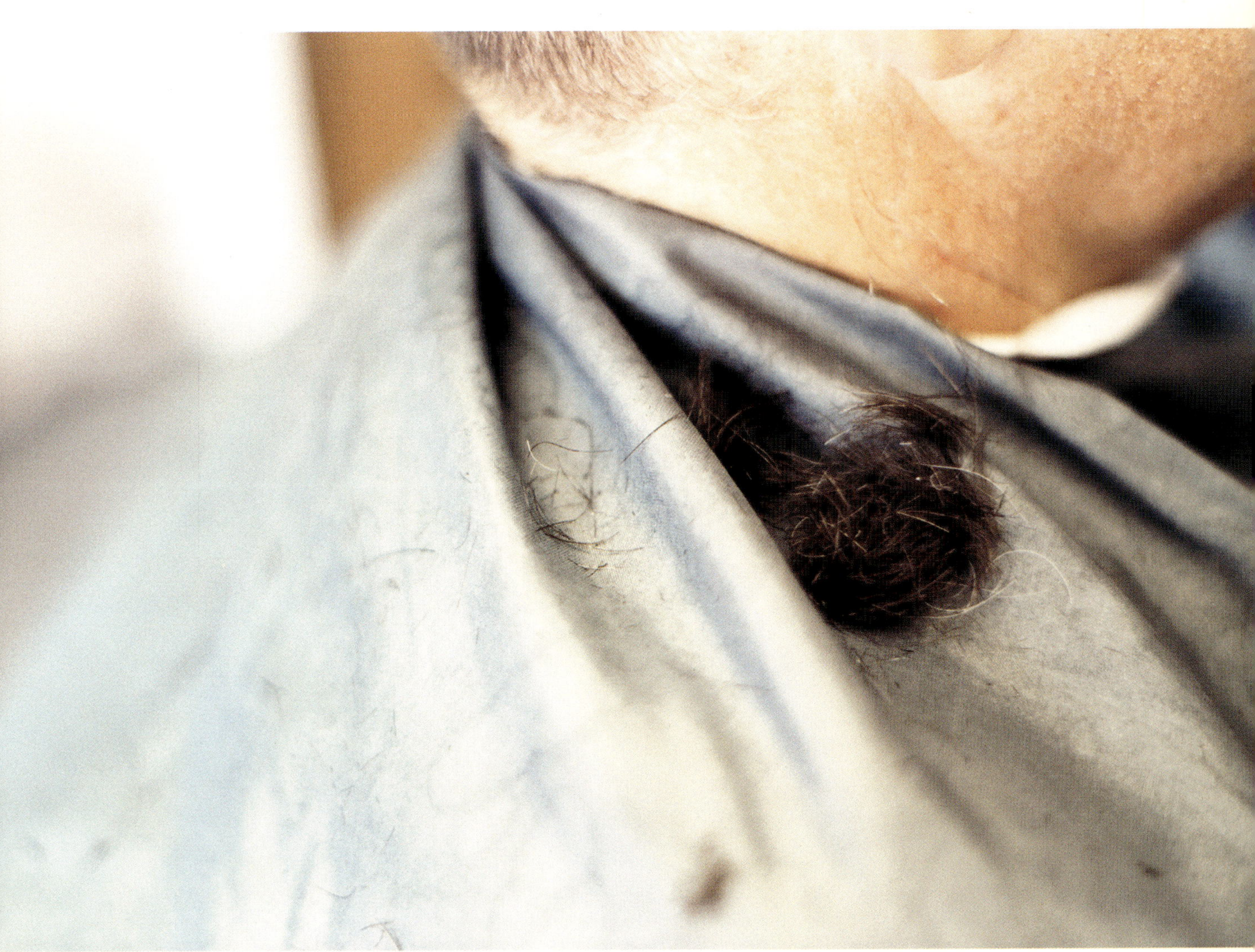

"I was always passionate about working with my hands. In this line of work, your hands are always clean, that's what's nice. Like doctors and pharmacists, your hands are always clean."

Raffaele

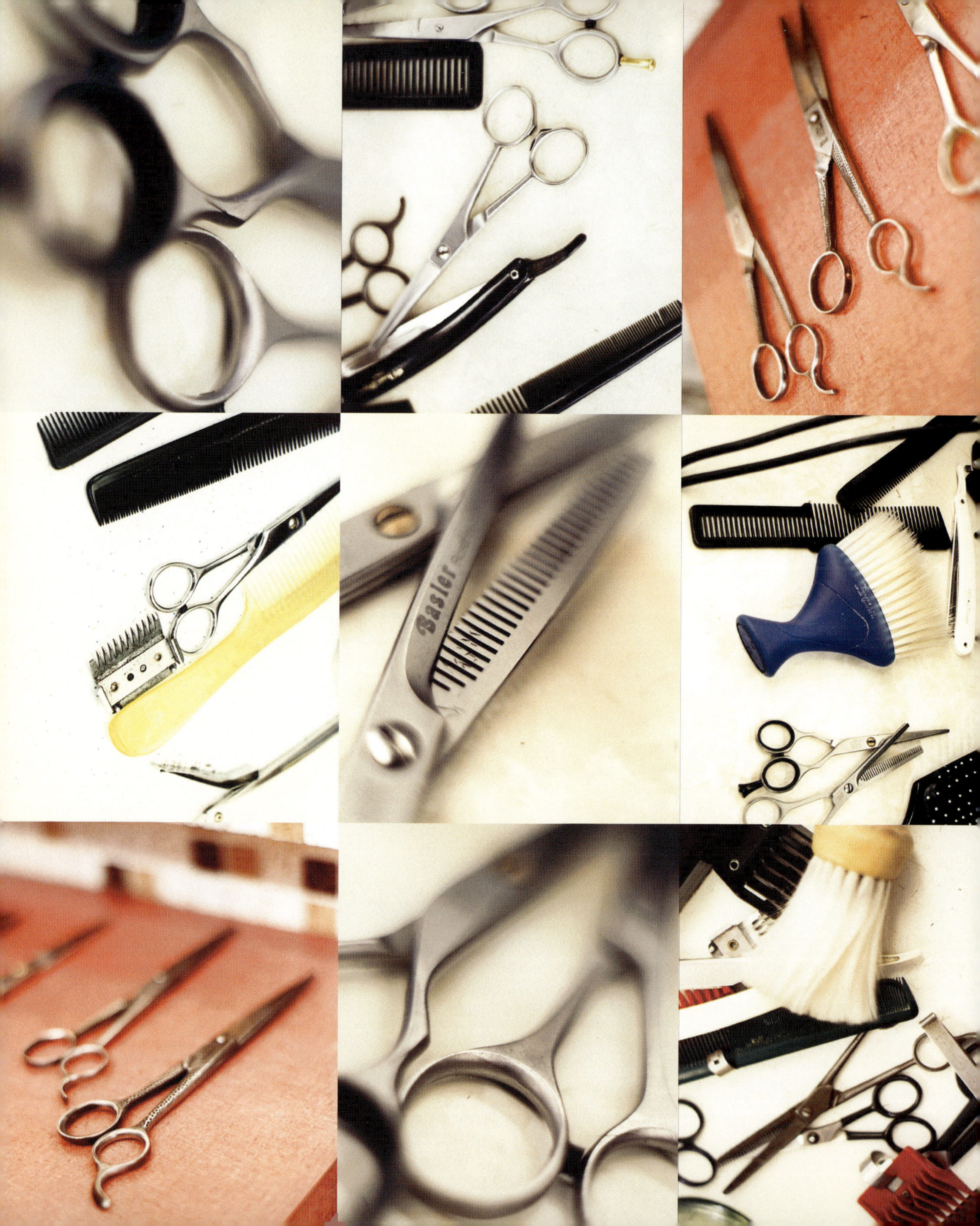
Basler

"My old boss in Belgium said to me: 'I'm not going to teach you to cut hair. Any imbecile can cut hair – he takes the scissors and cuts – it's not exactly hard. I'm going to teach you how to make a man handsome.'

But to make him handsome you can't change his facial features. You have to harmonise the cut, the movement of the hair with his natural facial features. You have to learn to draw, it's almost like drawing.

If one day you have a young man, or a gentleman, or an old man, or a baby, even the ugliest in the world – there will always be someone to look at him. And if that person looks at him and says: 'well, he has a nice haircut!' maybe you've made a customer for life."

Mike

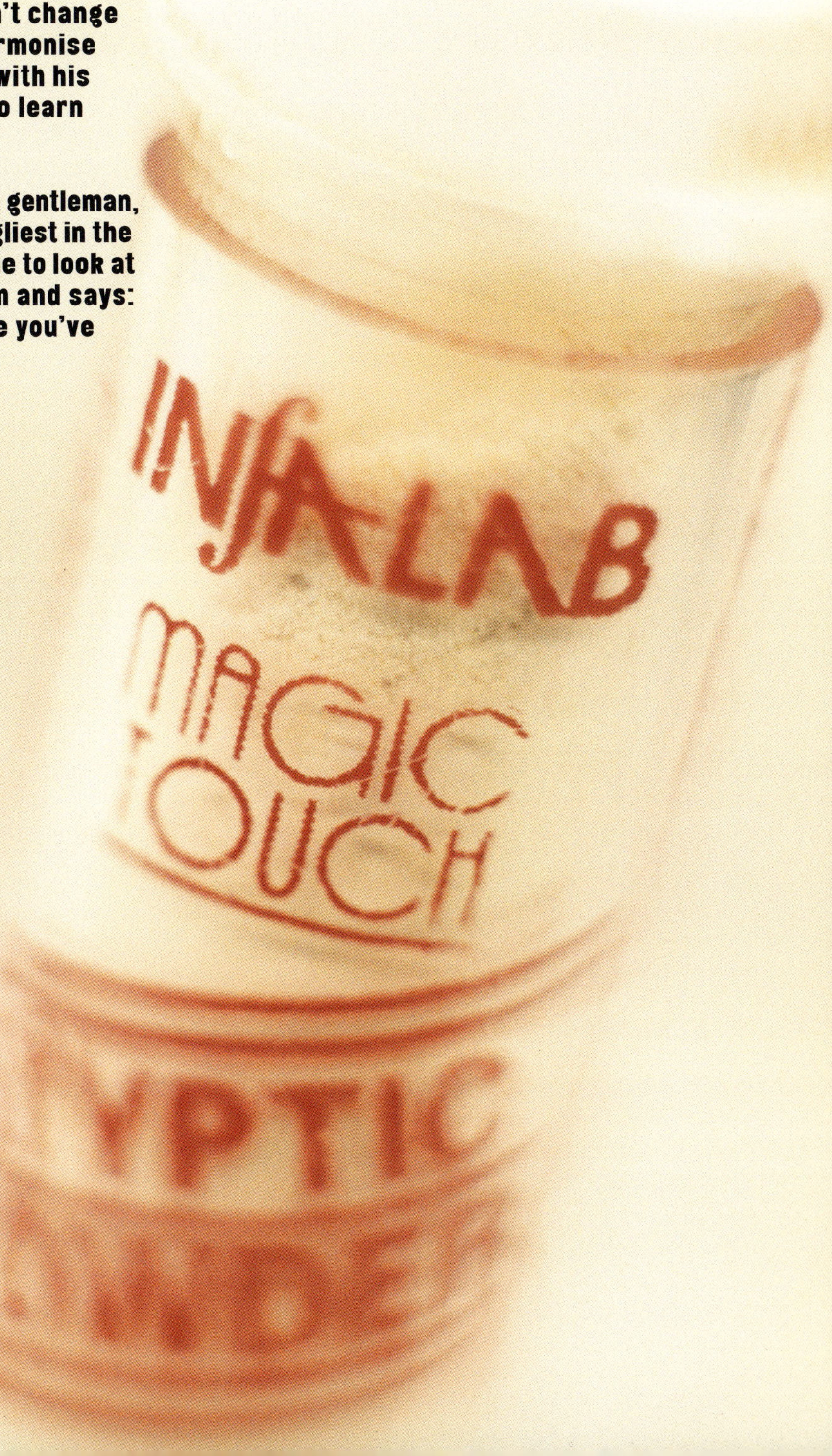

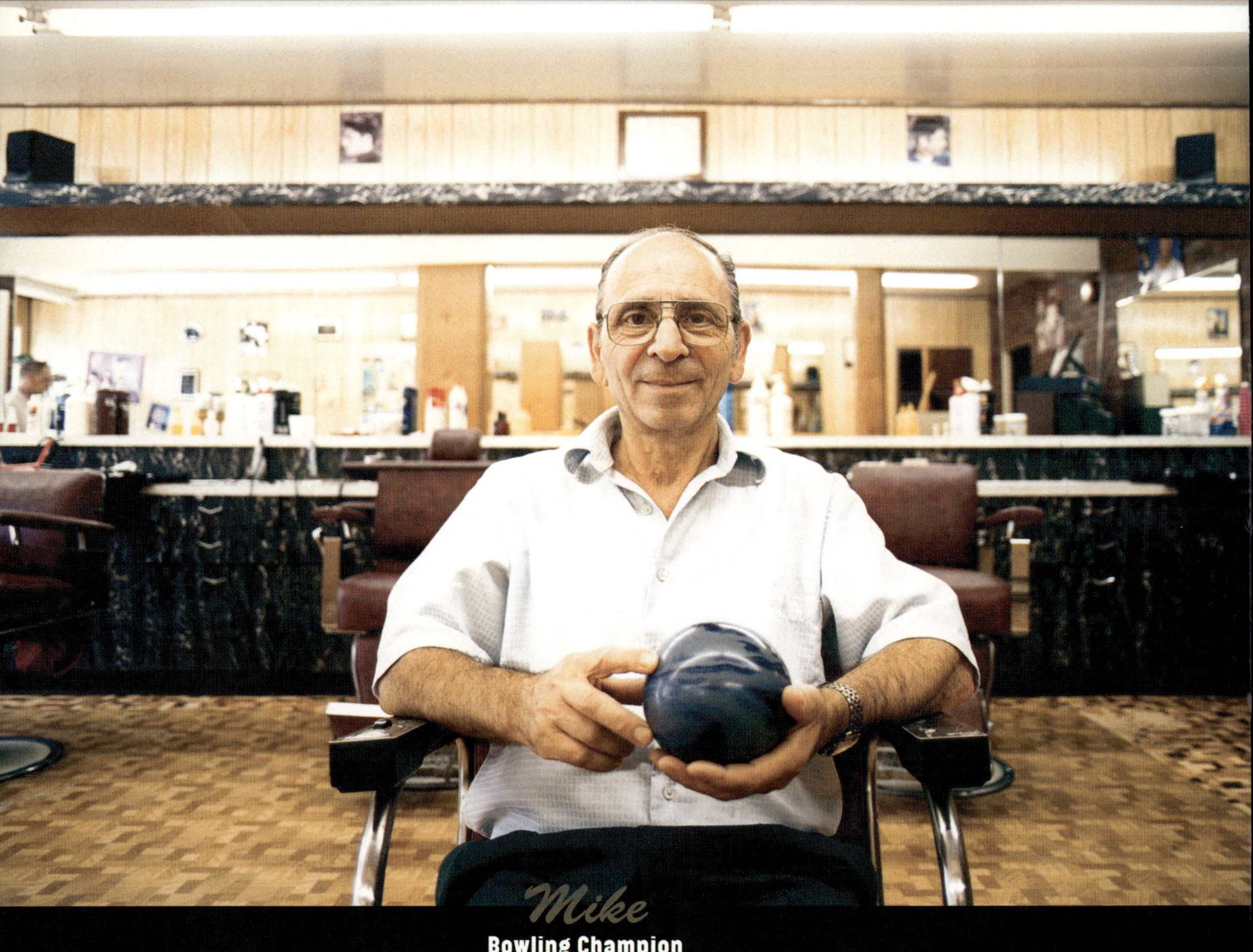

Mike

Bowling Champion

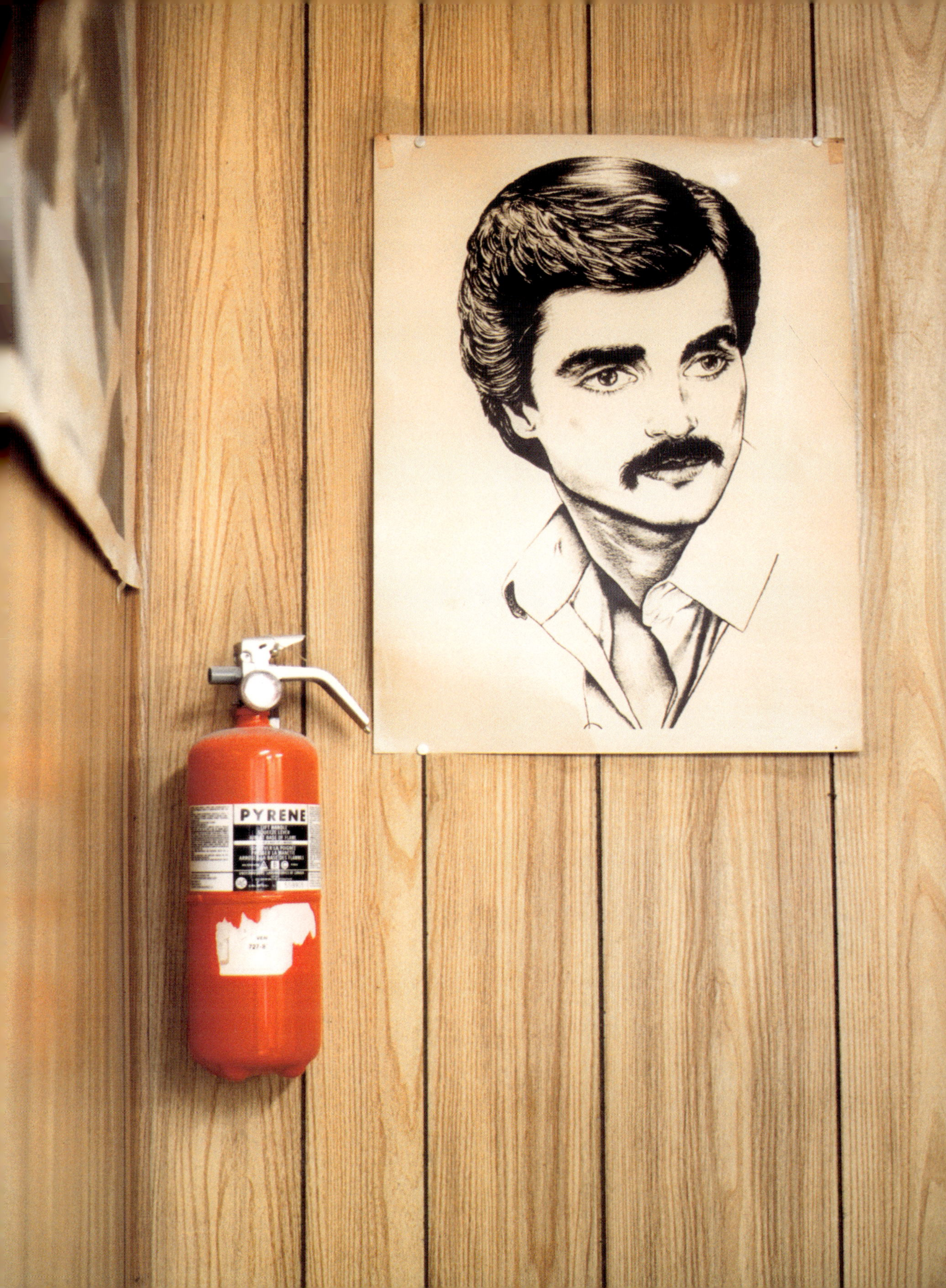
PYRENE

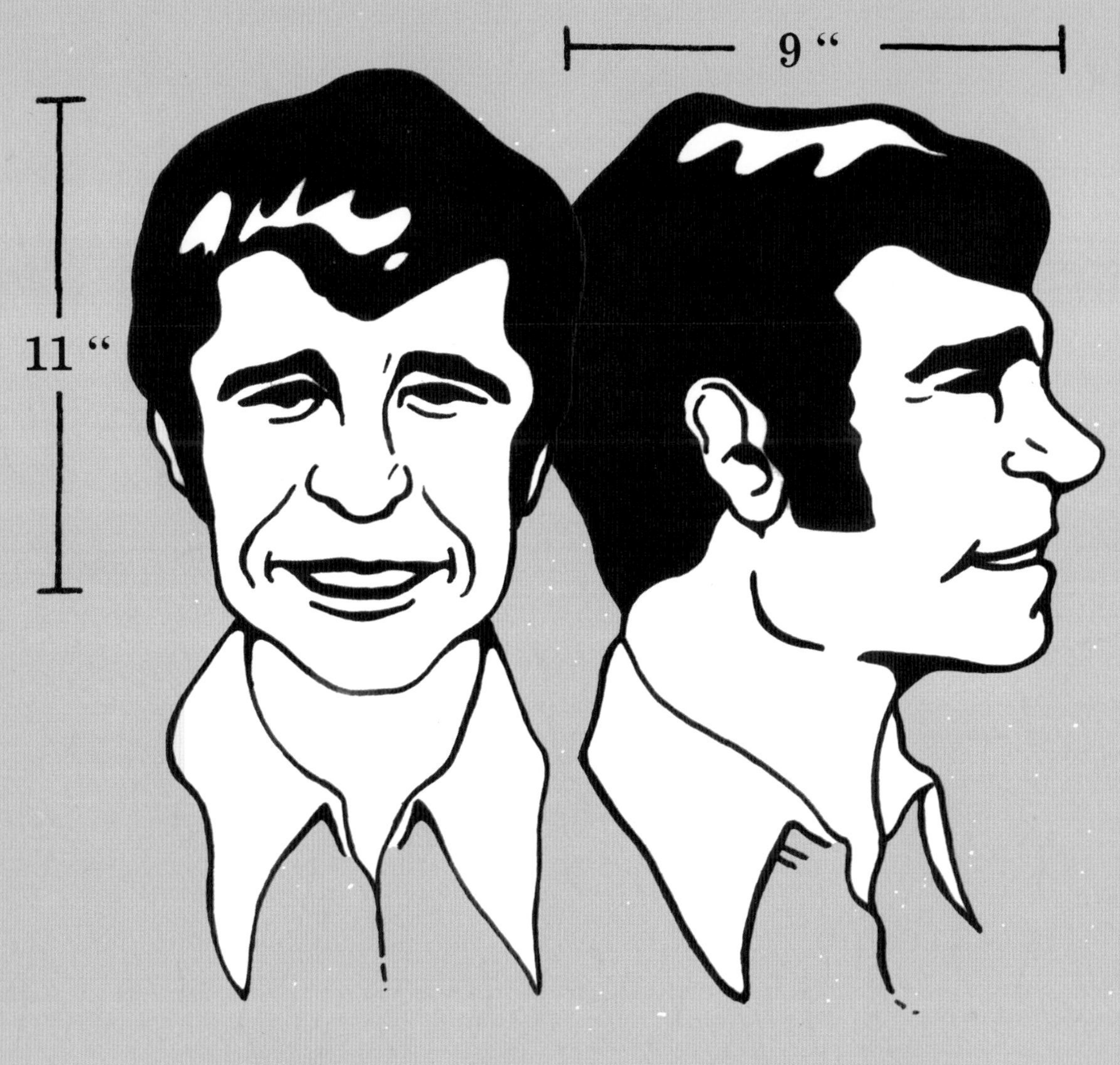

Face A *Face B*

SCALE: 1" = 1'3"	129" *Imperial crow haircut*

"I can see the haircut in my mind before starting. It's like the plans for a house - you know where you're going and how it will look in the end. You make the plans before you build the house." *Mike*

SPECIFICATIONS

-Aerodynamic features to improve wind-control
-Provides increased acceleration and positive feminine response
-Reduced hair thickness for enhanced cooling systems

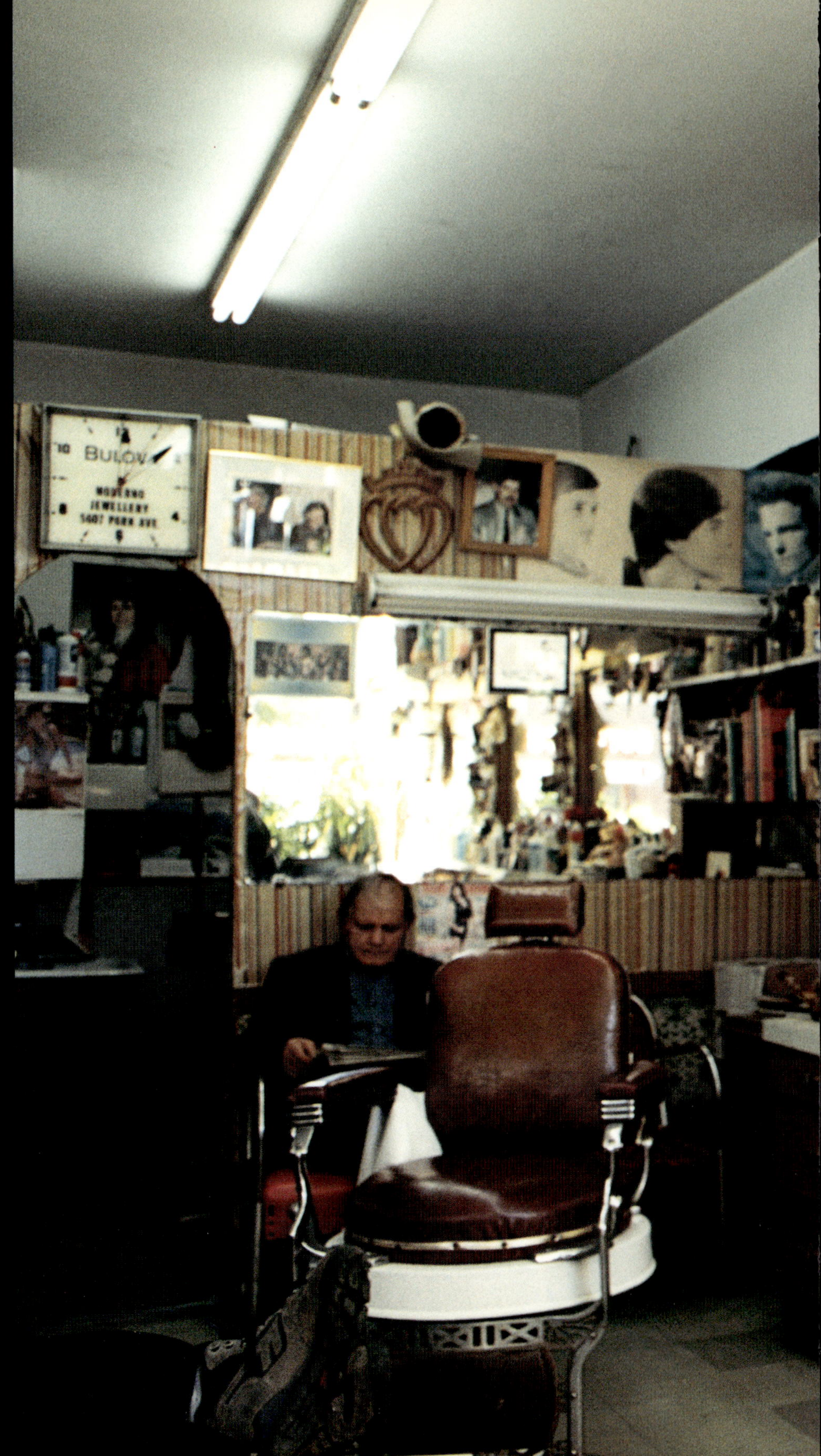

"Clean the moustache to kiss the wife."

Jimmy

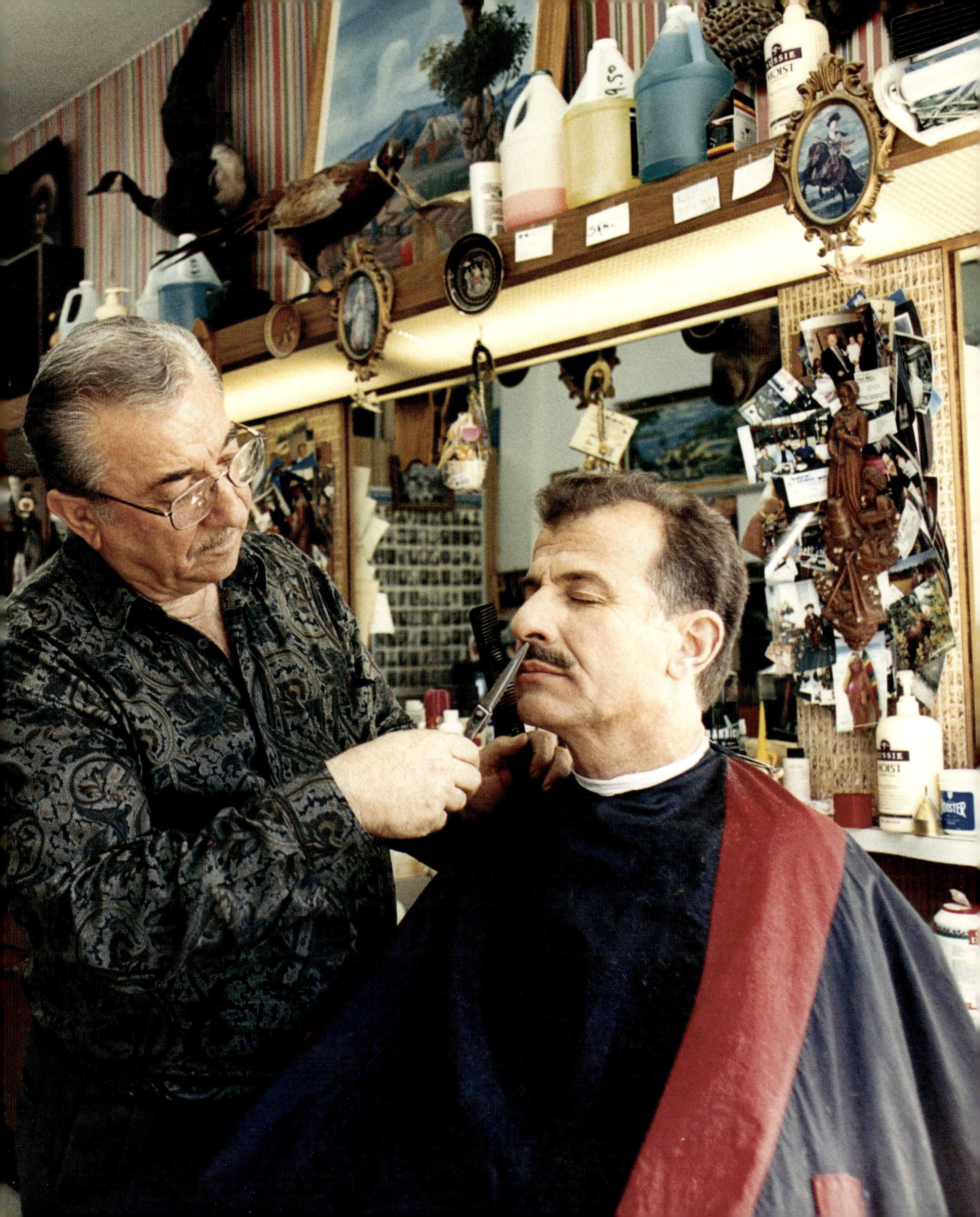
MOIST

Genevieve

Barber at Menick the Sports Barber

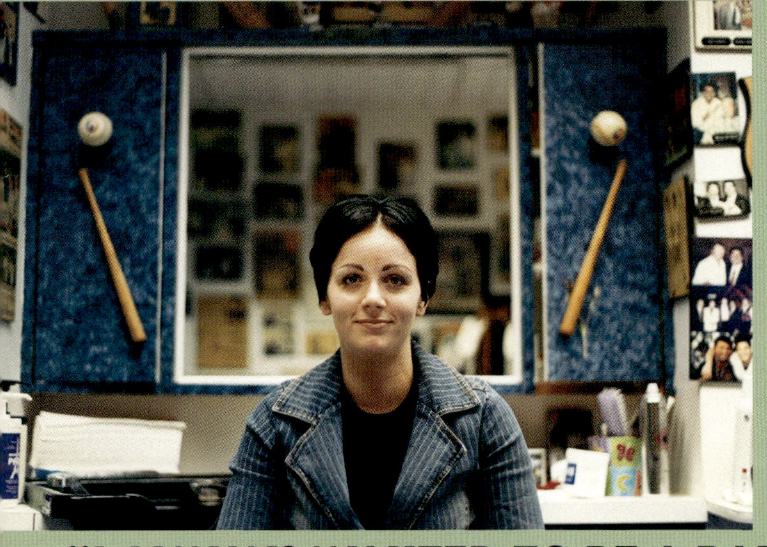

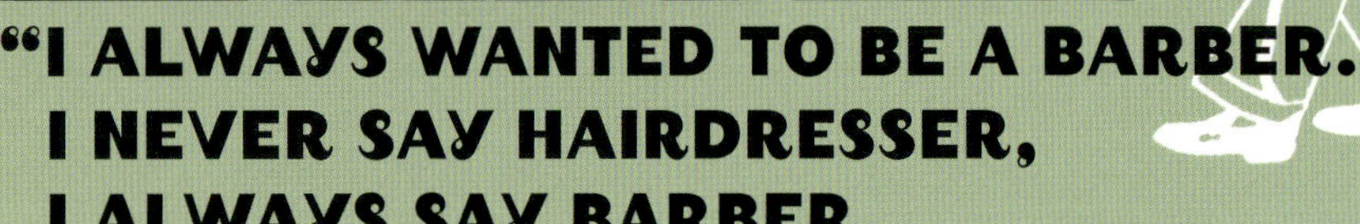

"I ALWAYS WANTED TO BE A BARBER. I NEVER SAY HAIRDRESSER, I ALWAYS SAY BARBER.

I told myself that it was modern for my age that it was 'in' to work in a barbershop. What I liked were the old chairs. I think they have cachet. And the shaving cream, the razor finish, it's all so romantic. I didn't have a lot of customers when I started out but where I worked there was an old Italian barber and I would watch him work all day long. He cut hair so fast! His hands were moving so fast you could barely make out the scissors and comb! It was scary – I thought I would never be able to do that.

Now, I'm pretty good at layering. Men like to get their hair cut by a woman. They're more open-minded now, it's less old-fashioned than before. The generation is changing so you can have more interesting conversations. Before men would talk about cars, baseball, hockey but now, you can talk about recipes, even exchange recipes with the customers."

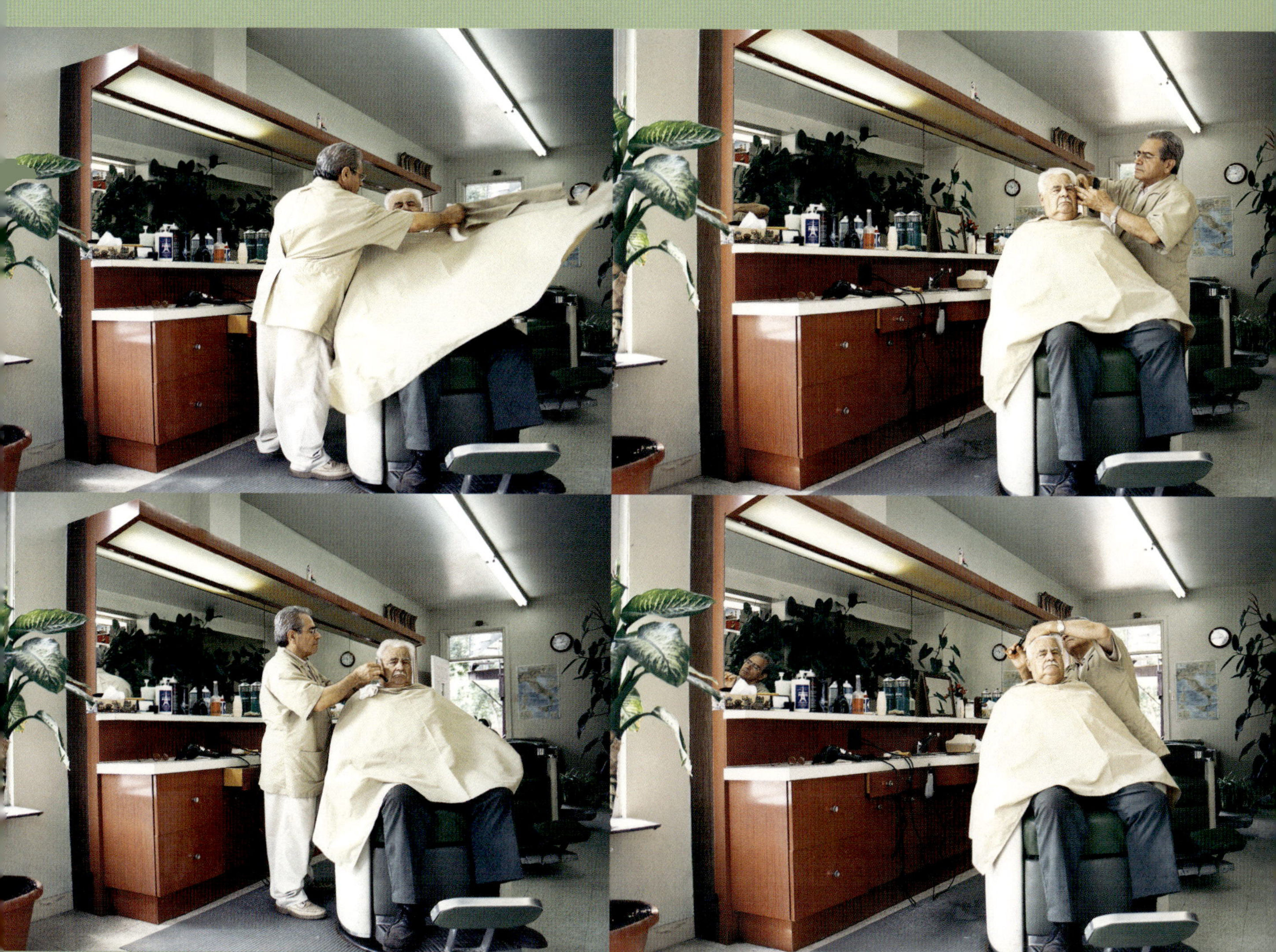

Giuseppe

“I used to cut soldiers’ hair
when I was in the military in Rome.
Not their heads, just the hair!”

Giuseppe

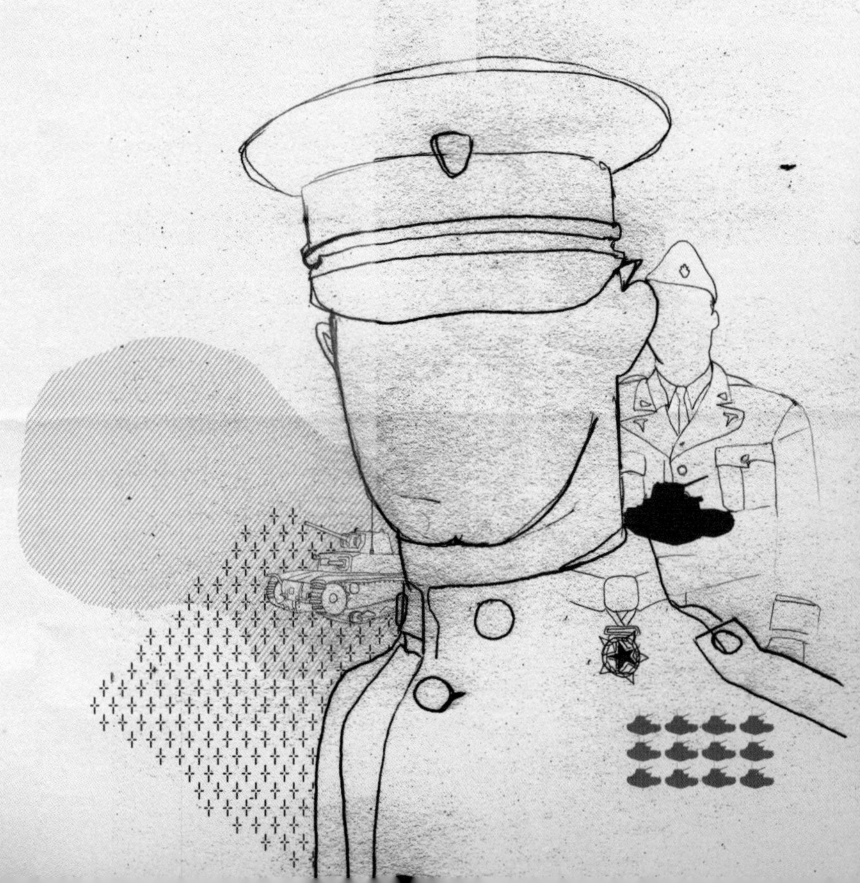

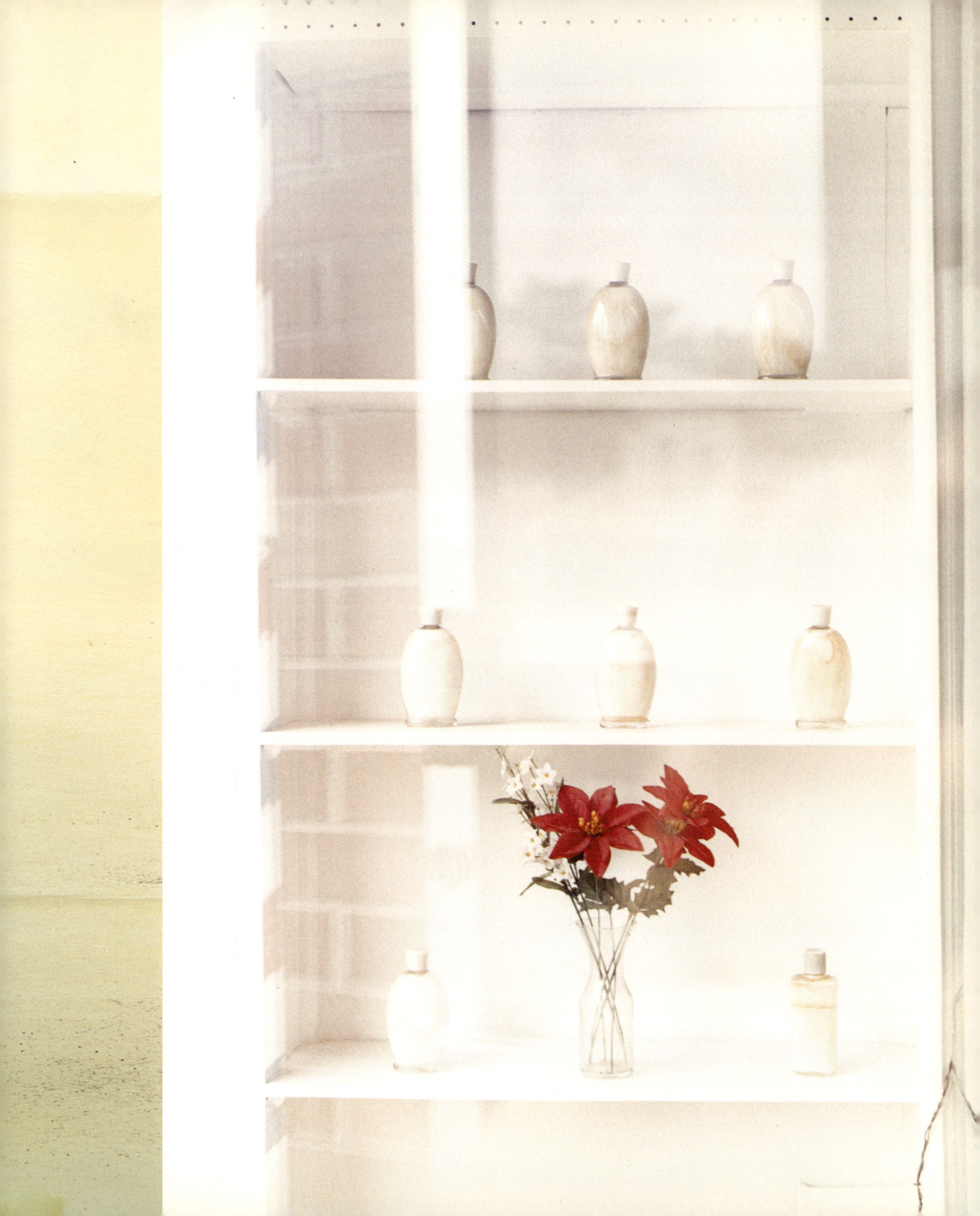

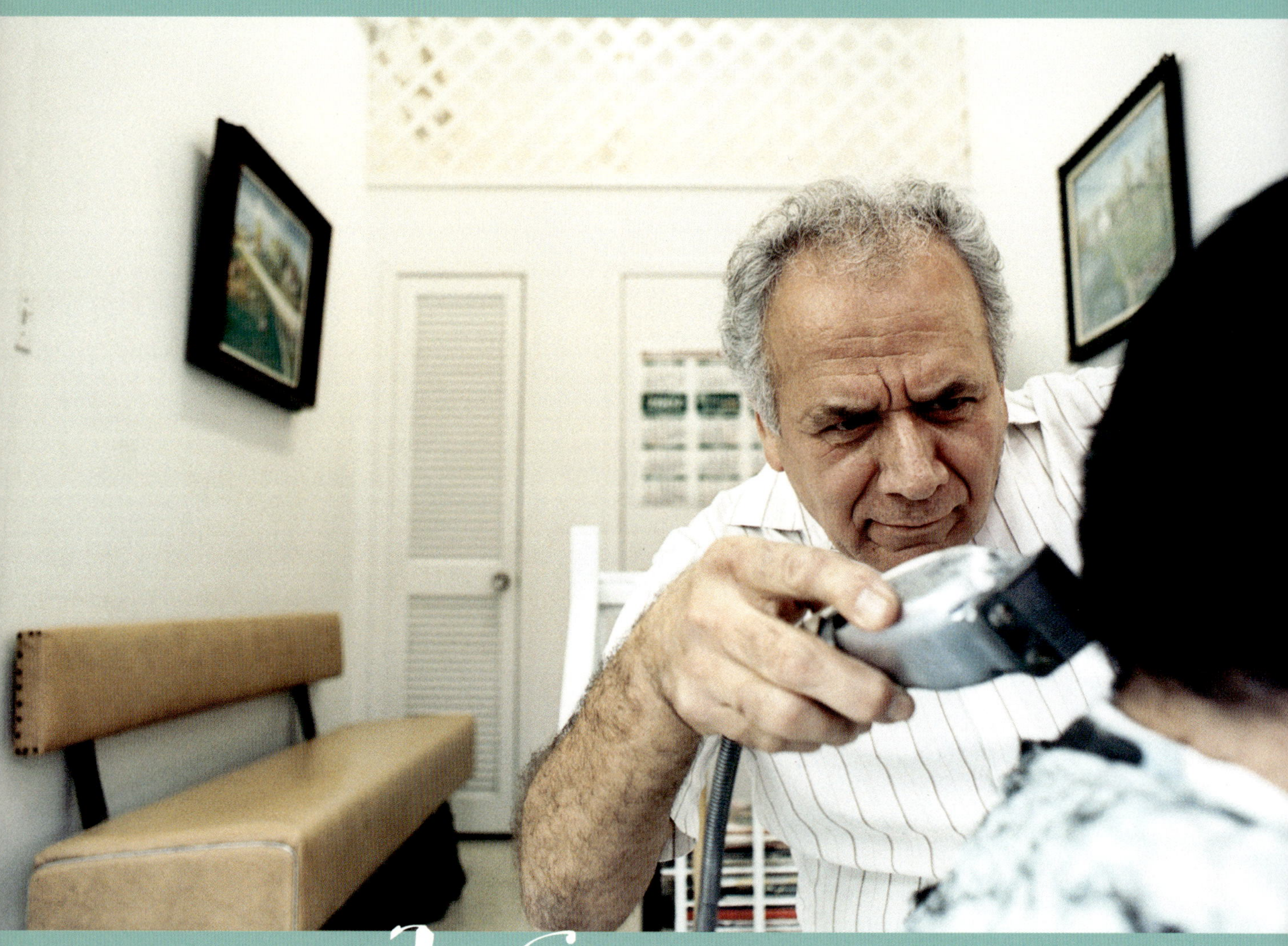

Jean-Guy
Owner of JG Bacon's Salon
Son of a hospital barber

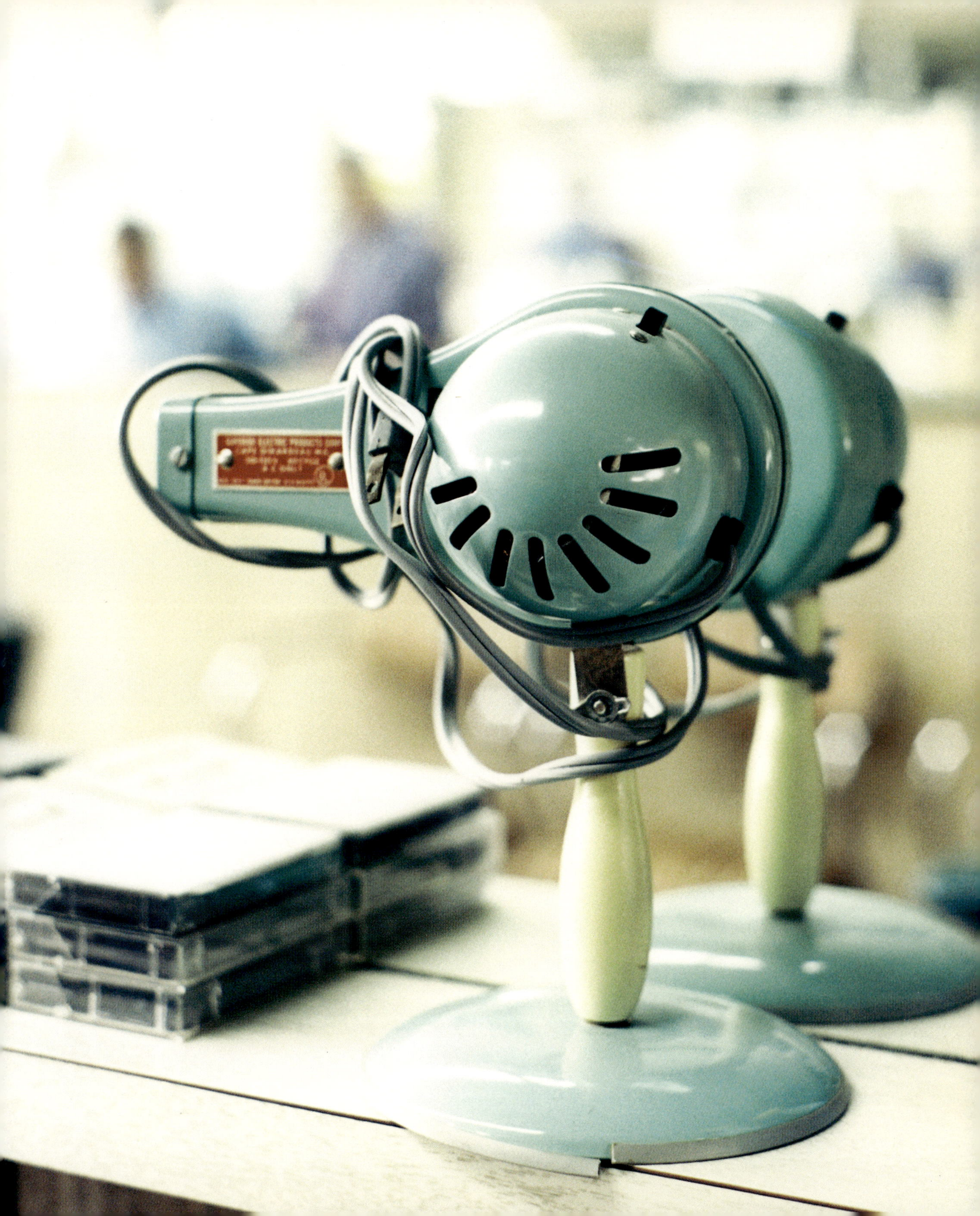

"I don't come here crying every morning. I love doing this. It's the best job. Because when the customers come in, they're all messed up and when they leave, they're fixed. It's a finished job every time. That's the feeling. You fix them and it gives you this *feeling*. I would never have been good at bodywork for cars but I would have loved to paint them. Because painting is the finishing work. Like when I was painting my boat – I would paint fine lines and when I pulled off the masking tape, it gave me this *feeling*."

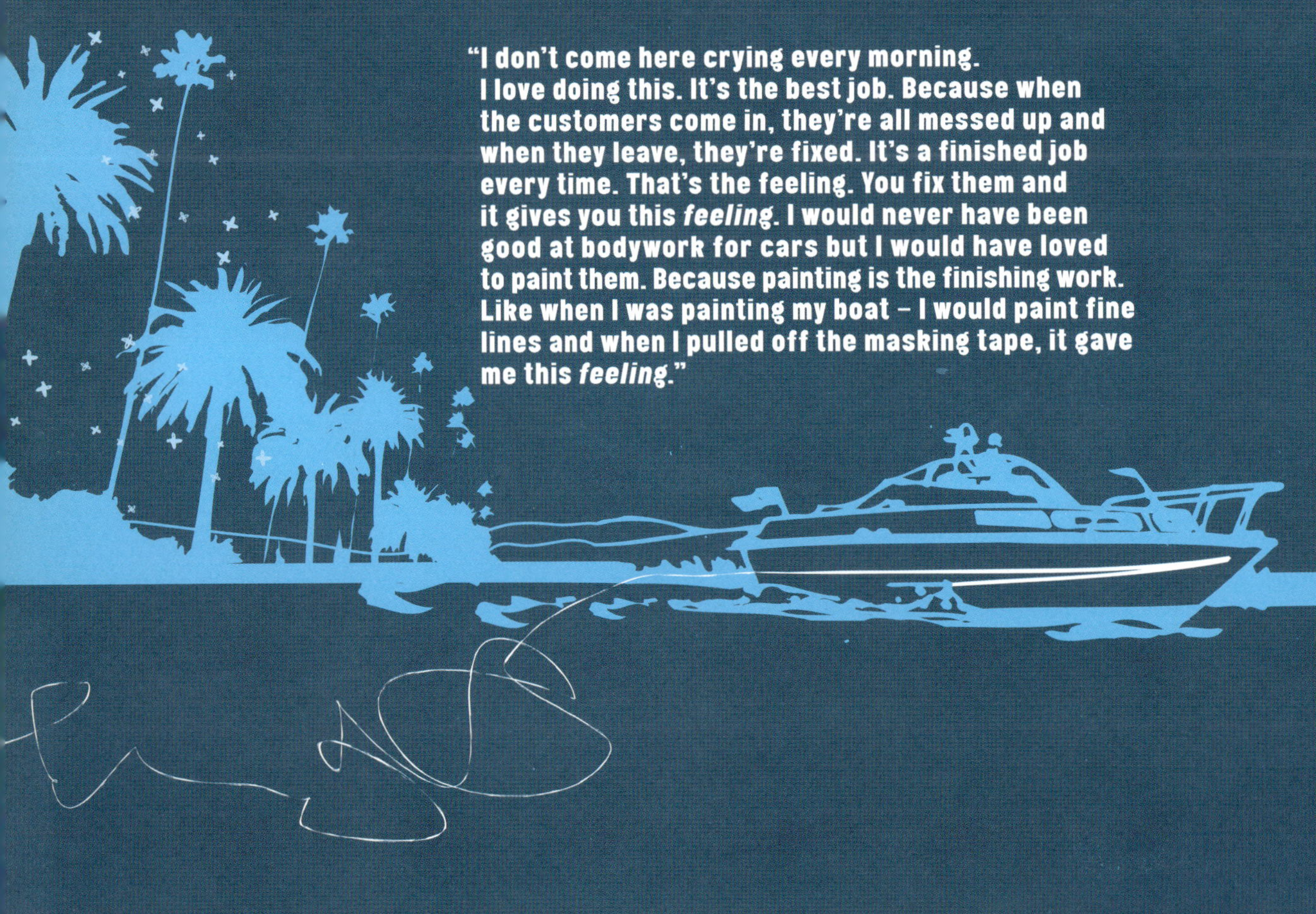

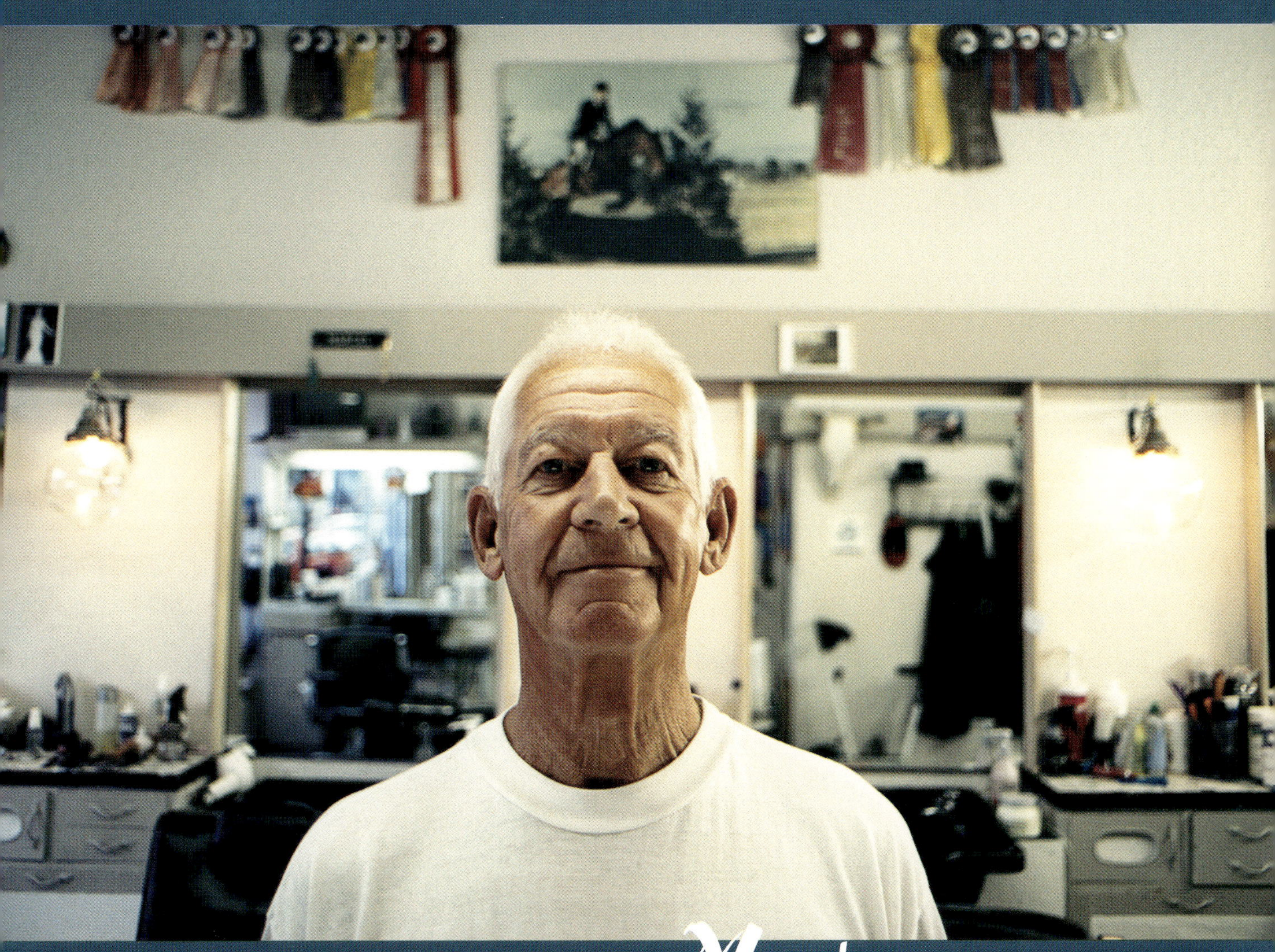

Marcel

Accomplished horseback rider
Least favorite haircut: the bowl cut

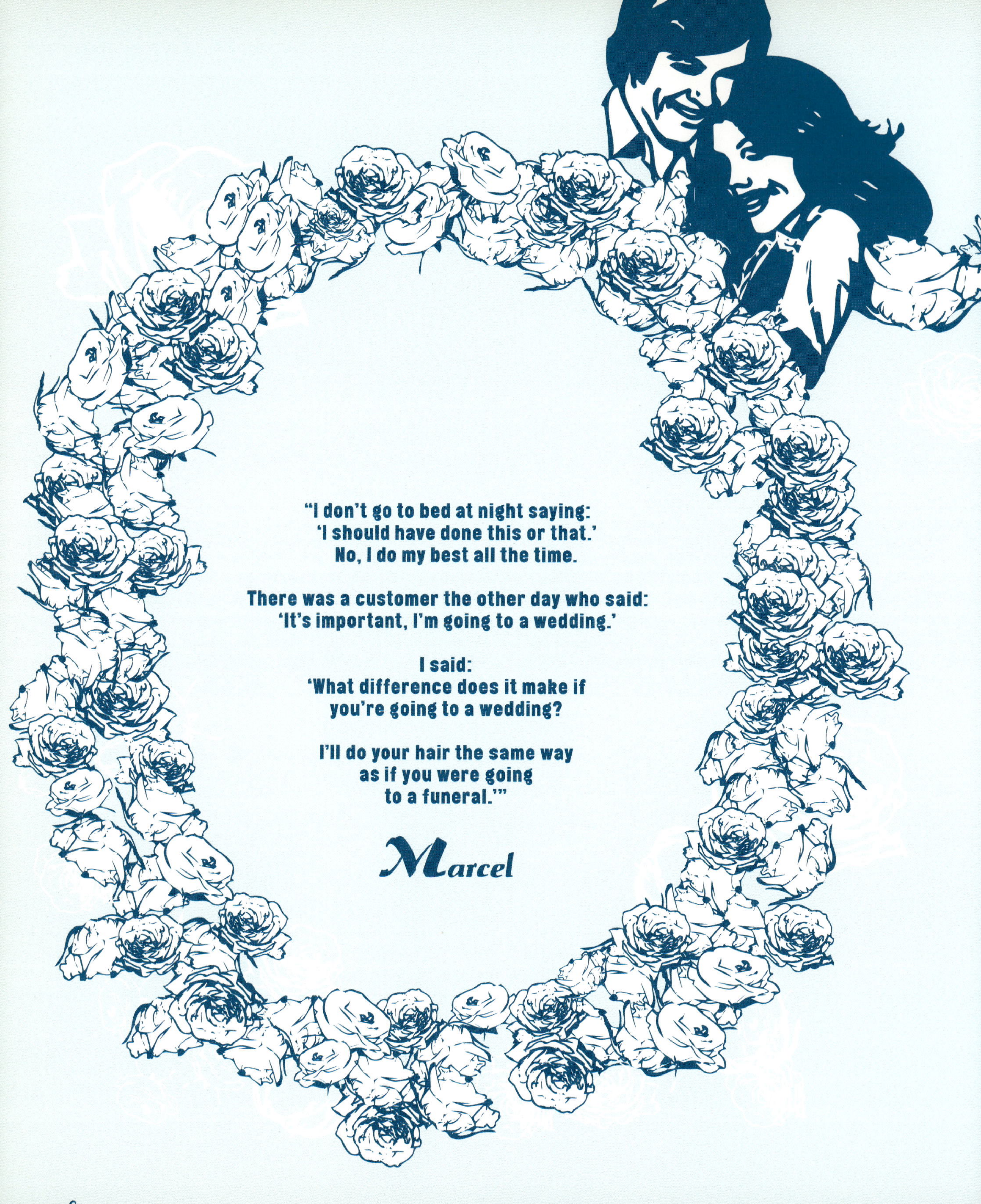

"I don't go to bed at night saying:
'I should have done this or that.'
No, I do my best all the time.

There was a customer the other day who said:
'It's important, I'm going to a wedding.'

I said:
'What difference does it make if
you're going to a wedding?

I'll do your hair the same way
as if you were going
to a funeral.'"

Marcel

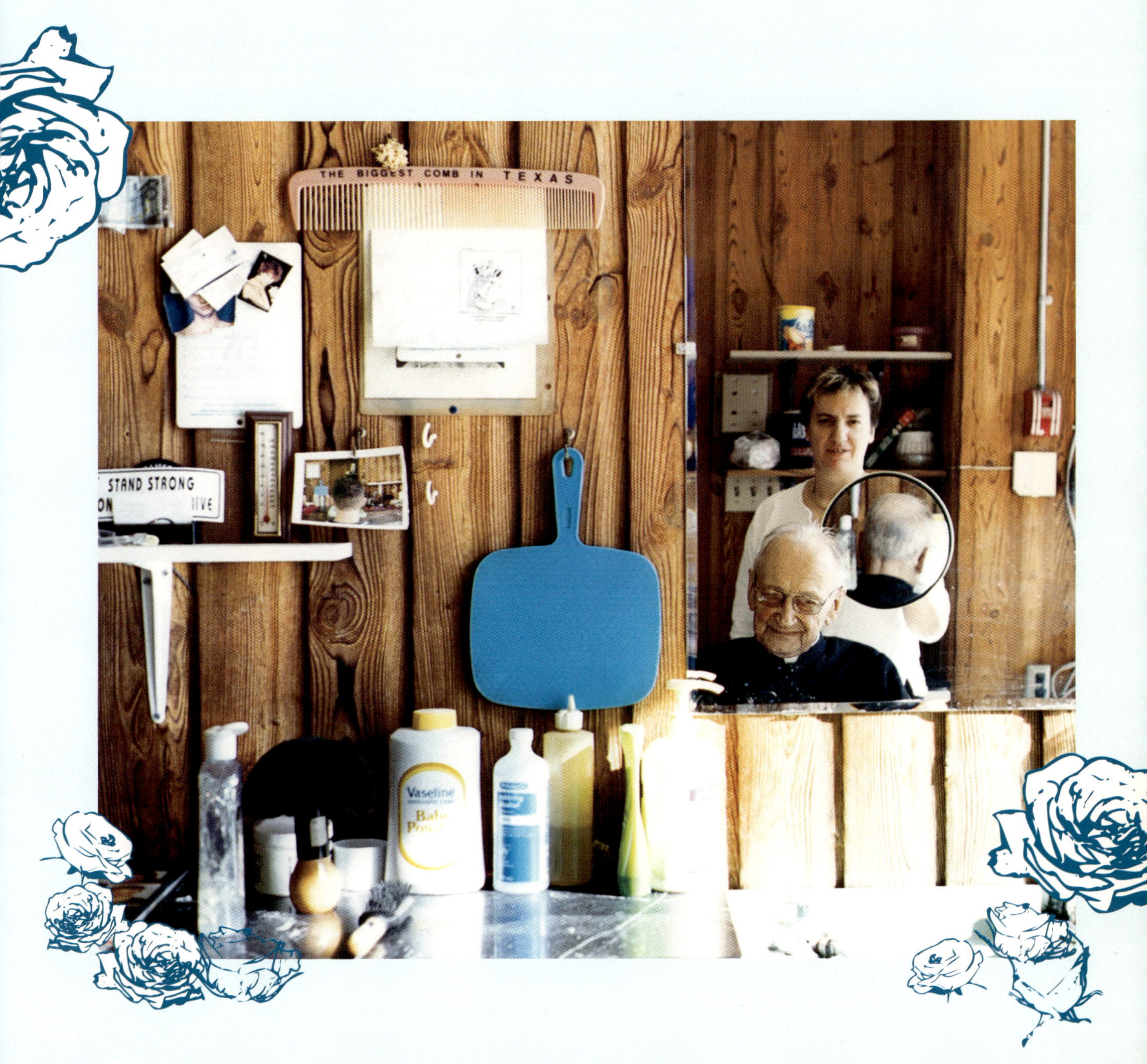
THE BIGGEST COMB IN TEXAS
STAND STRONG
Vaseline
Baby

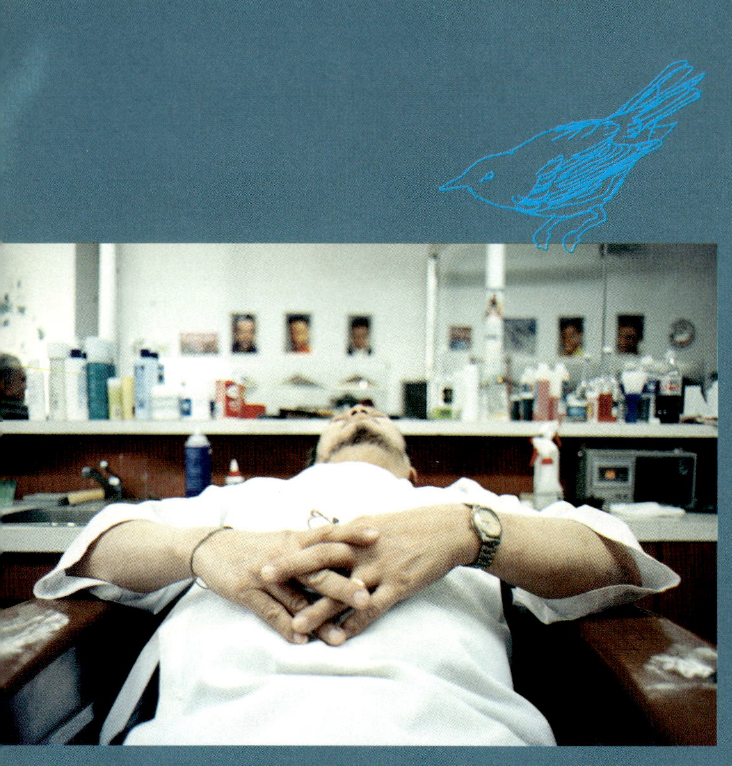

Customer:
"No matter what time of day you come here you'll always wait. You come Saturday morning 6 o'clock, there's people waiting outside. Saturday morning a quarter to six there are people knocking on the door! He's that popular. Sometimes he sleeps here on a Friday night!"

Ricky:
"You pass here Friday night at 11 or 12 at night, you see him walking around in his briefs."

Customer:
"Yeah – my girlfriend told me she saw him in his briefs!"

Ricky:
"He's not a shy guy."

Customer:
"It's true, and Saturday morning, he's lying down in his chair."

Poquito:
"I sleep in any of the chairs, I can even sleep in the blue chairs against the wall. It's all my bed. If my eyes are closed that's comfortable already. I don't care about my position. I turn off the light and you can't see anything inside. It's my little room. When I open my eyes I feel strong. In the morning, the customers look in the window, they see me and they knock on the window."

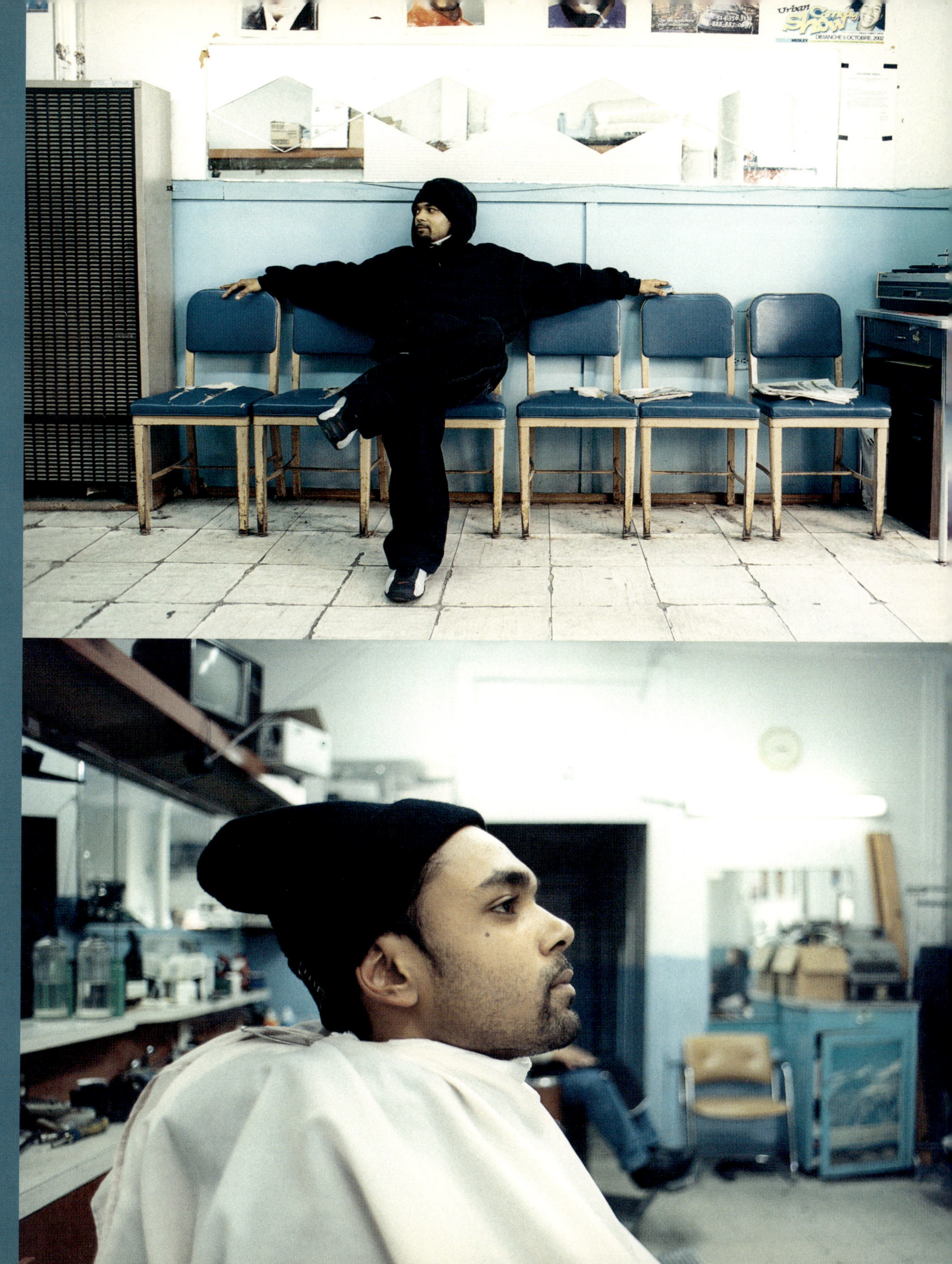
Urban Comedy Show
DIMANCHE 6 OCTOBRE, 2002
MEDLEY
514-356-3111
888-887-0697

"The name of the previous owner of the barbershop was Abner, it wasn't Gilbert. Before him, I'm talking maybe 30 years ago, even that guy's name wasn't Gilbert. I have no idea who Gilbert is."

Toula

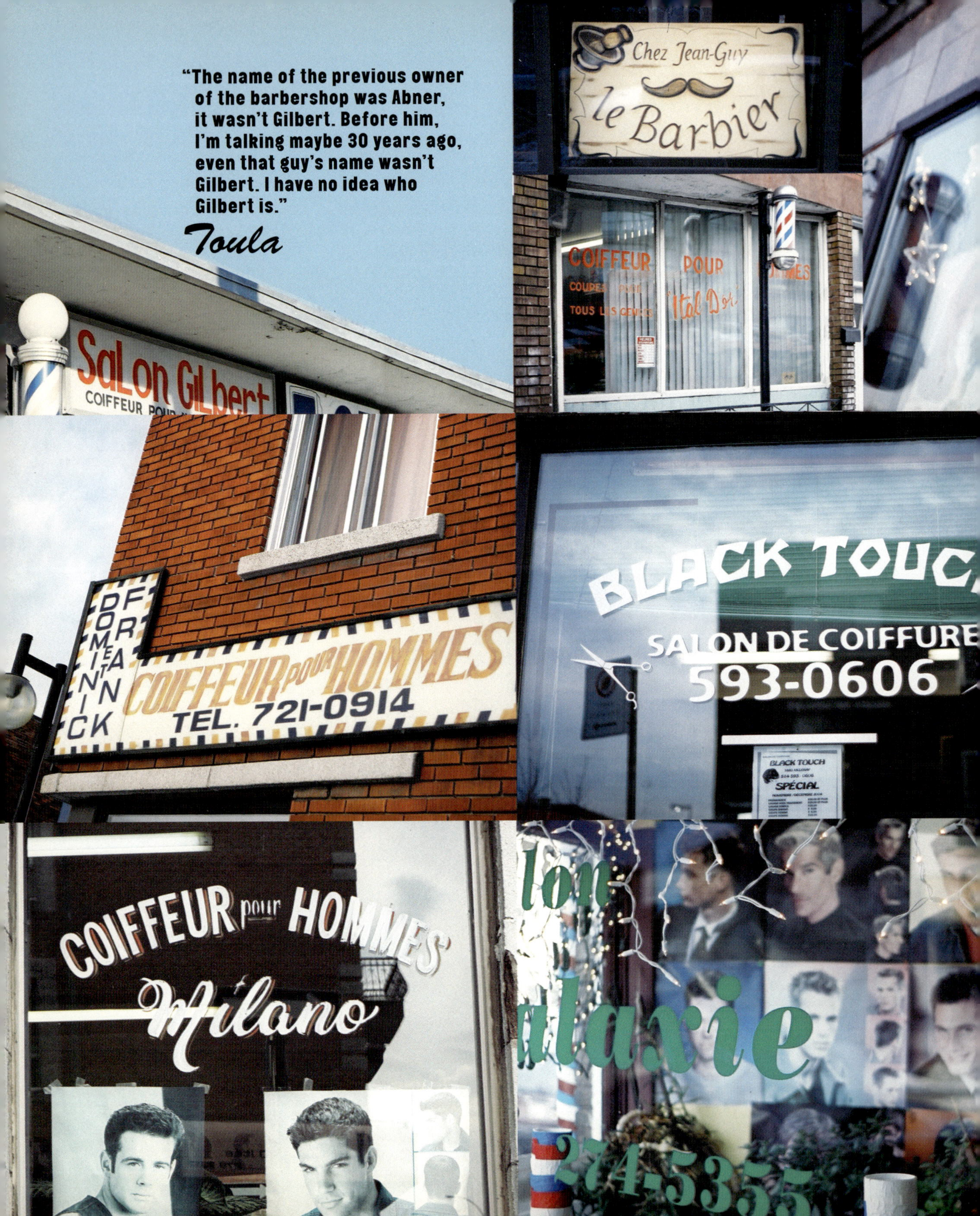

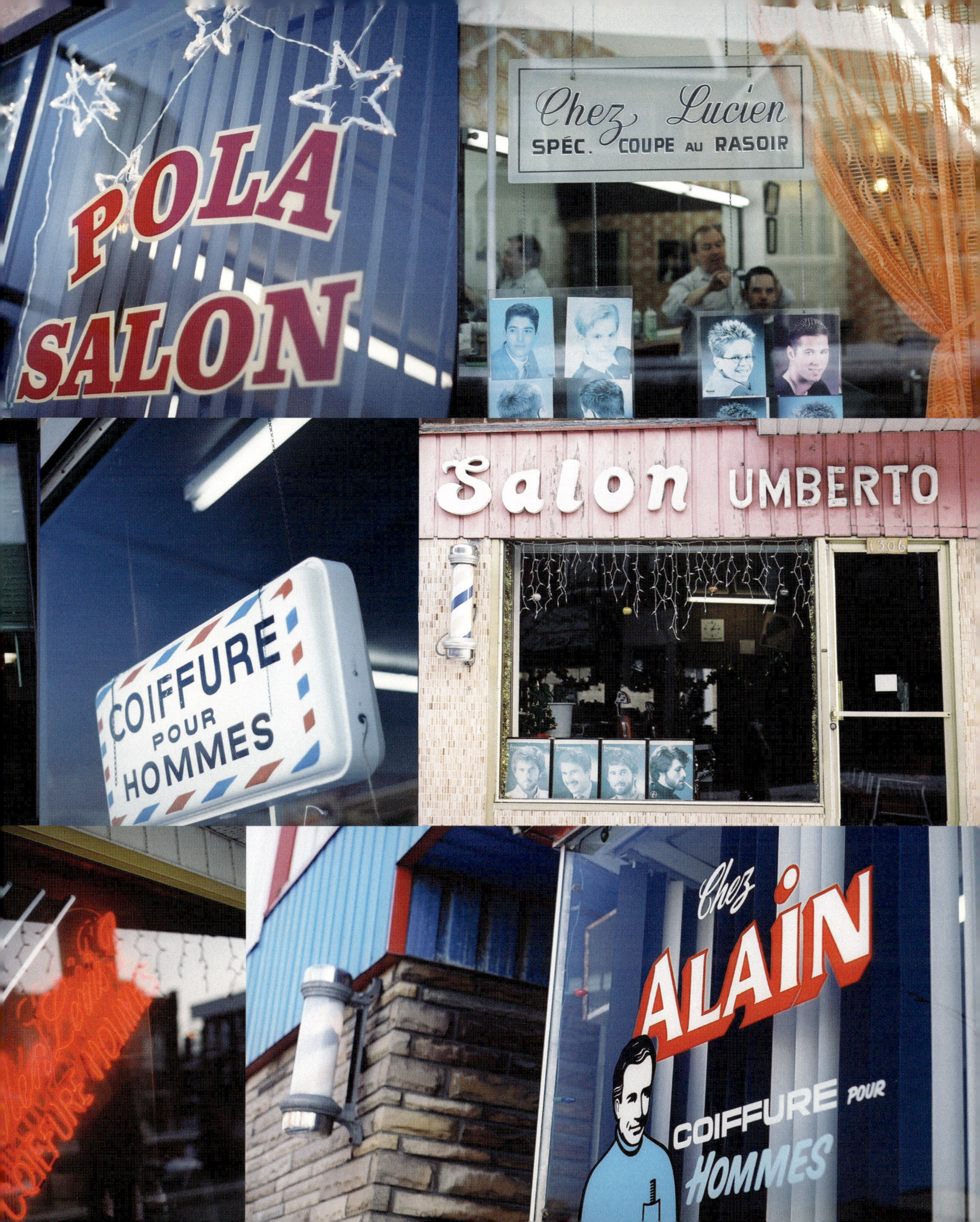
POLA
SALON
Chez Lucien
SPÉC. COUPE AU RASOIR
COIFFURE
POUR
HOMMES
Salon UMBERTO
Chez
ALAIN
COIFFURE POUR
HOMMES

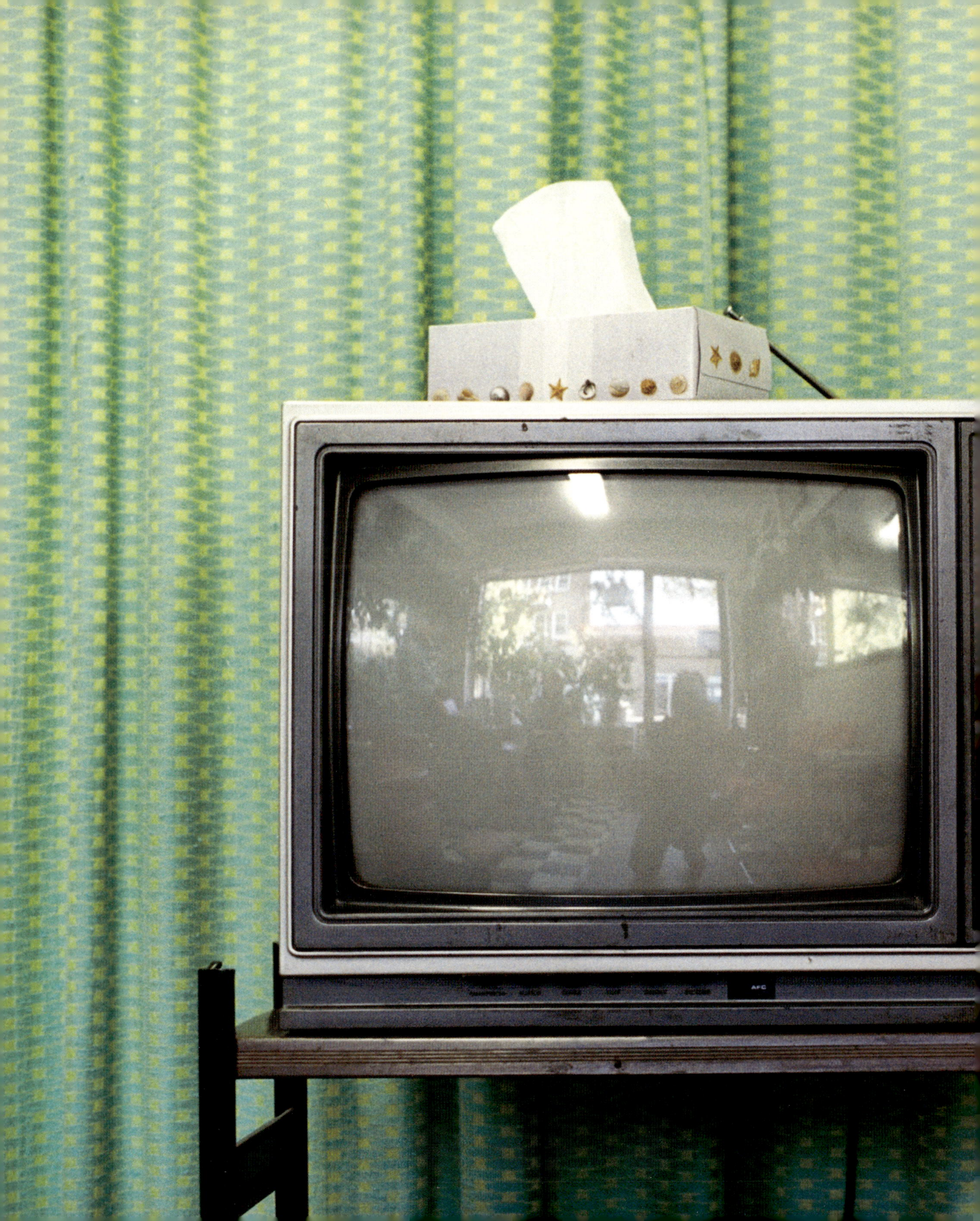

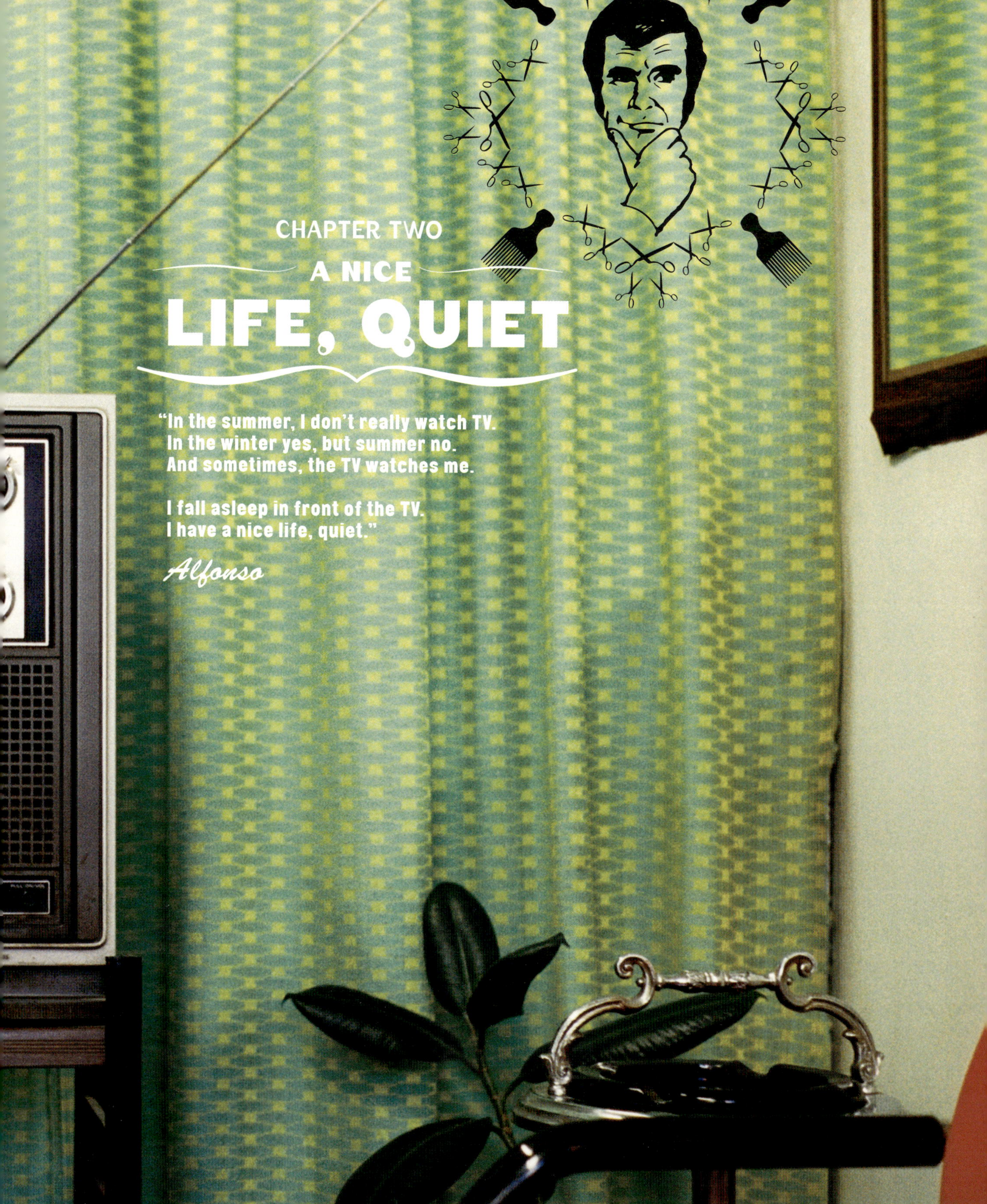

CHAPTER TWO

A NICE LIFE, QUIET

"In the summer, I don't really watch TV.
In the winter yes, but summer no.
And sometimes, the TV watches me.

I fall asleep in front of the TV.
I have a nice life, quiet."

Alfonso

"A TYPICAL DAY:

I wake up, I shave, I have a shower every morning, I get changed. After coffee, I come here and prepare all the tools. After that, I wait for people to come and I work.Then, when I'm not working, I watch the women go by."

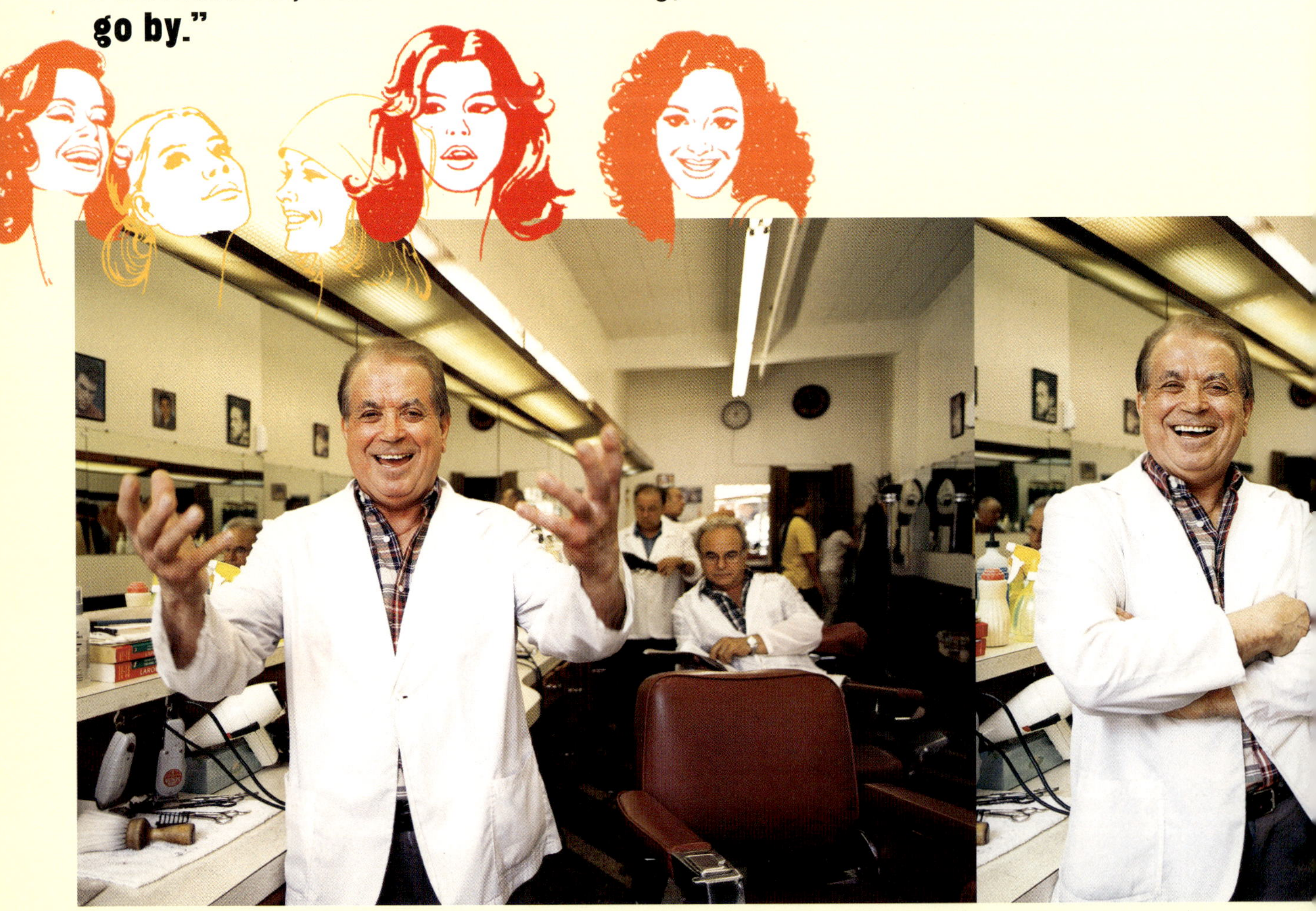

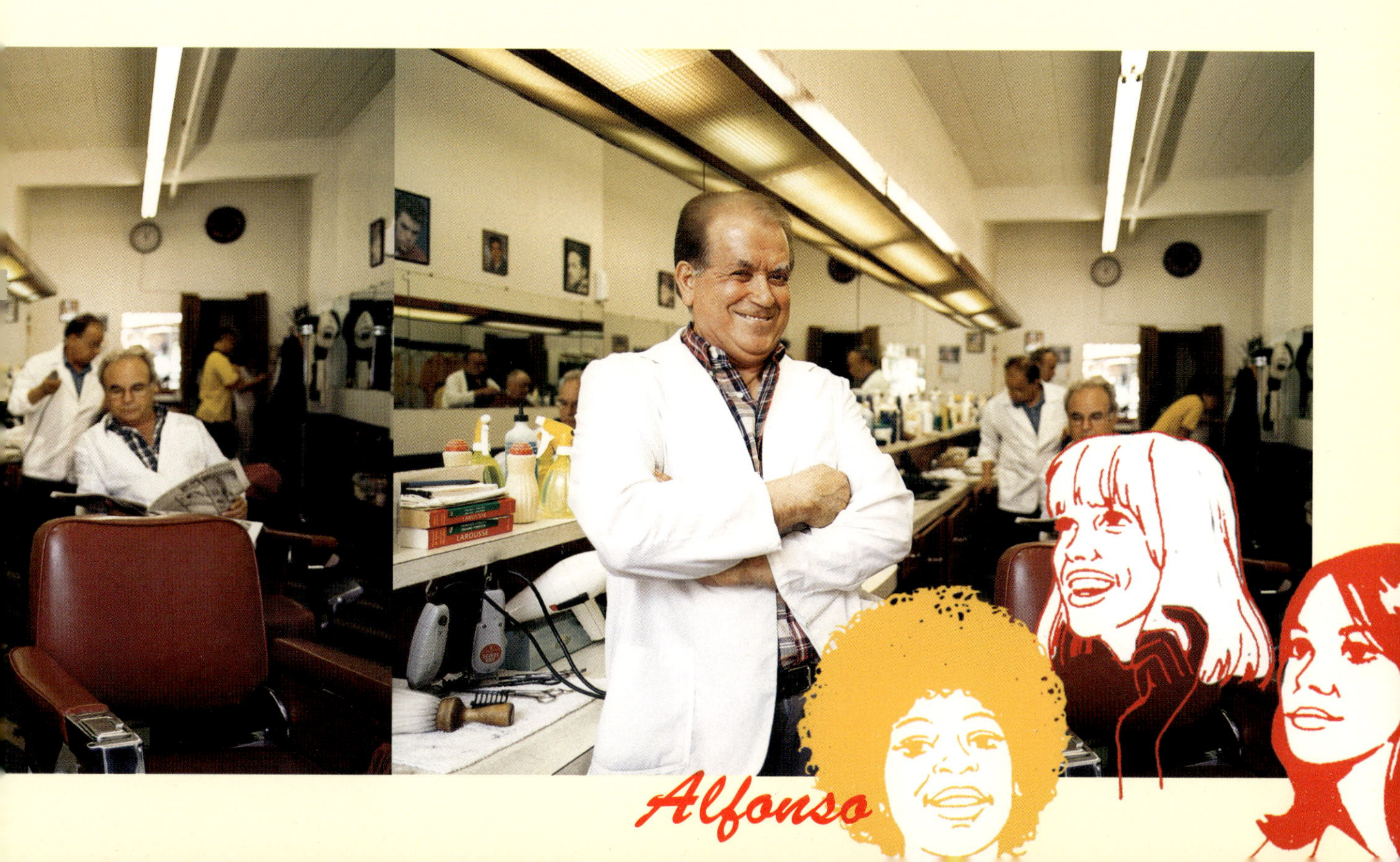
LAROUSSE
LAROUSSE
Alfonso

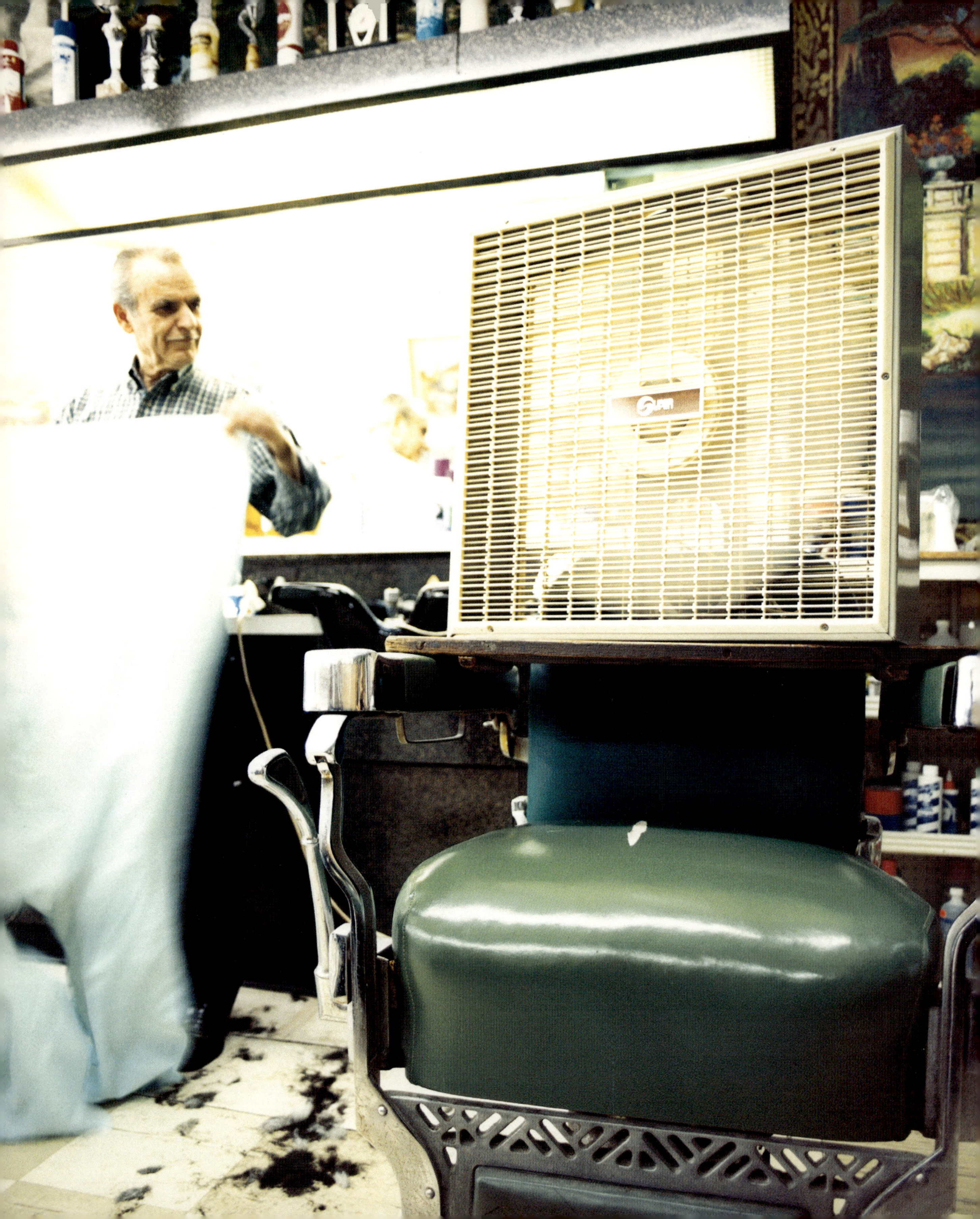

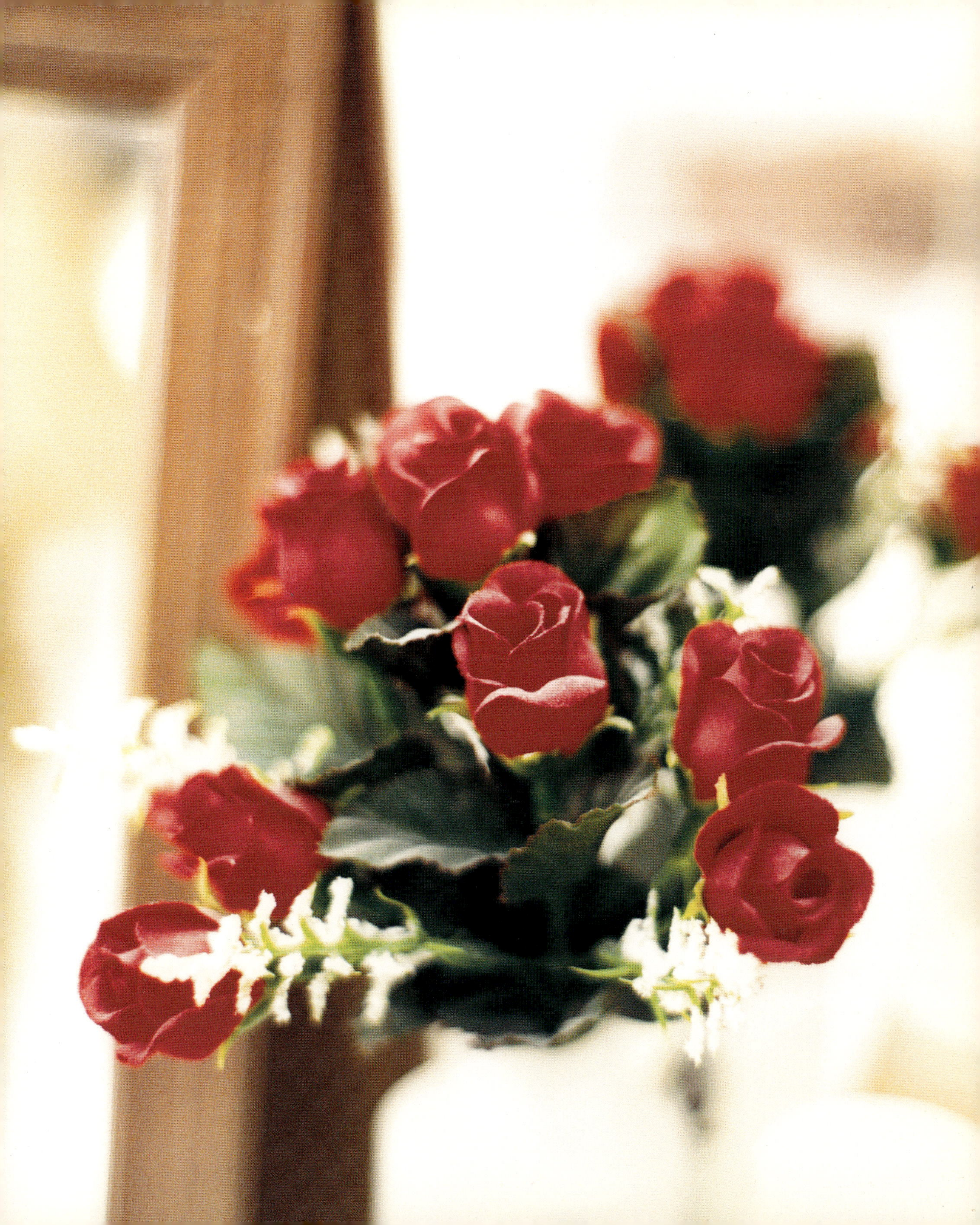

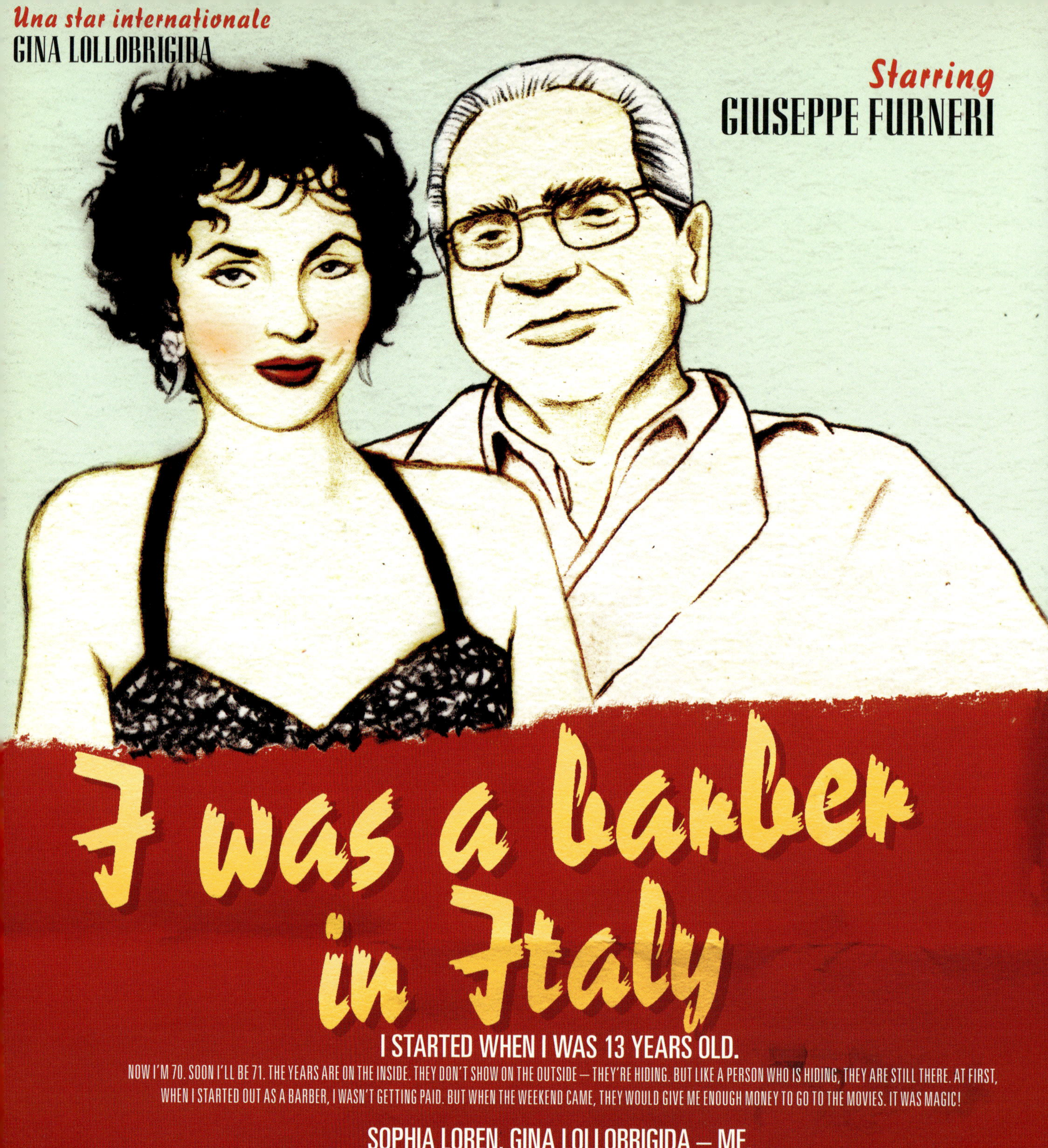
Una star internationale
GINA LOLLOBRIGIDA
Starring
GIUSEPPE FURNERI
I was a barber in Italy
I STARTED WHEN I WAS 13 YEARS OLD.
NOW I'M 70. SOON I'LL BE 71. THE YEARS ARE ON THE INSIDE. THEY DON'T SHOW ON THE OUTSIDE – THEY'RE HIDING. BUT LIKE A PERSON WHO IS HIDING, THEY ARE STILL THERE. AT FIRST, WHEN I STARTED OUT AS A BARBER, I WASN'T GETTING PAID. BUT WHEN THE WEEKEND CAME, THEY WOULD GIVE ME ENOUGH MONEY TO GO TO THE MOVIES. IT WAS MAGIC!
SOPHIA LOREN, GINA LOLLOBRIGIDA – ME,
TO BE HONEST, I LIKED GINA LOLLOBRIGIDA. SHE WAS BEAUTIFUL! I SAW HER ONCE WHEN I WAS IN ROME, SHE WAS TWO FEET AWAY FROM ME.
EVERY NIGHT THE ACTORS HUNG OUT AT THE VIA VENETO. SHE WAS SO BEAUTIFUL BACK THEN. WHEN I WALKED IN FRONT OF HER, I DID A LITTLE PIROUETTE AND THEN I FELL TO THE GROUND.
I BELIEVE IN HEAVEN ON EARTH. FOR ME,
HEAVEN WAS MY YOUTH.
PANORAMA

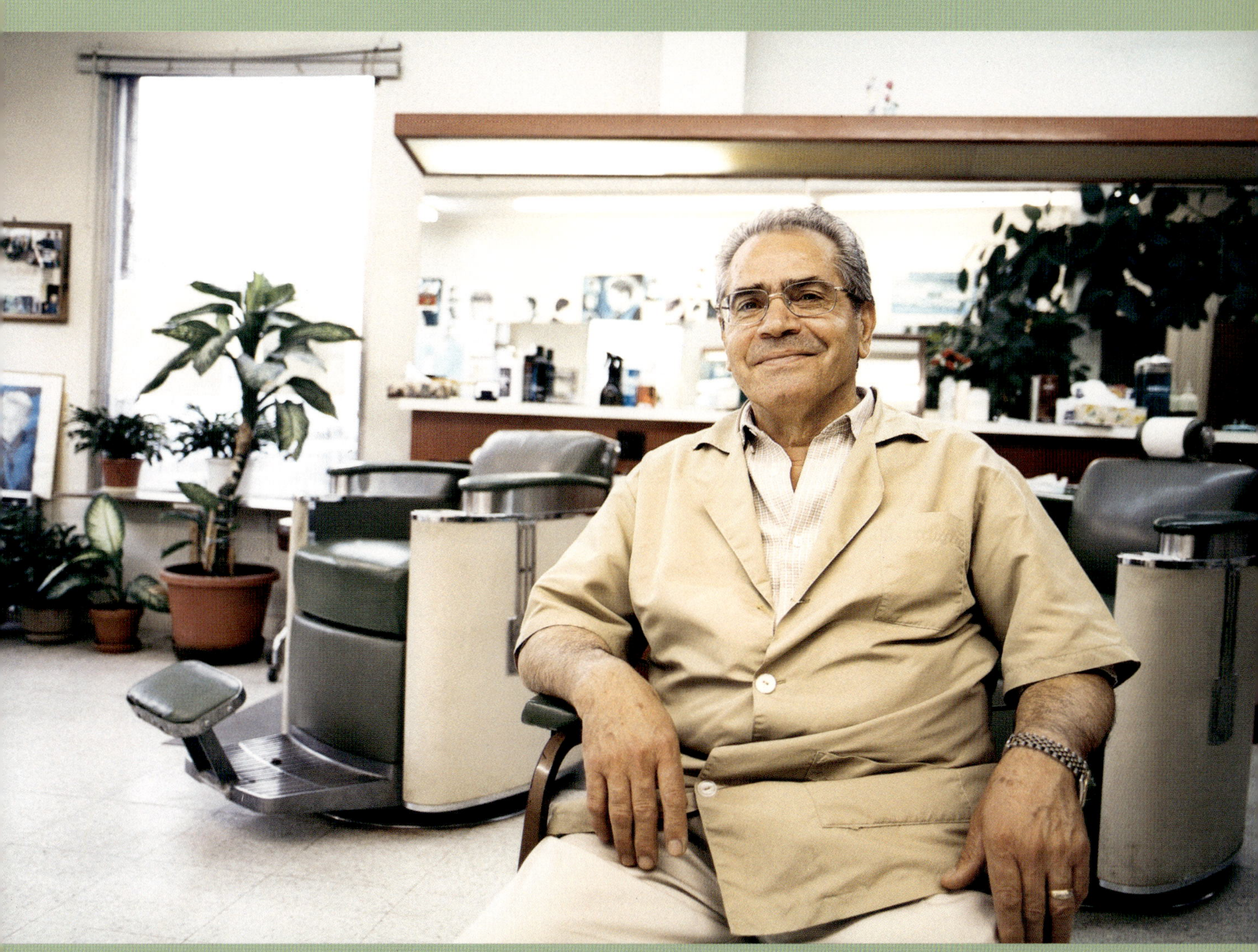

Giuseppe

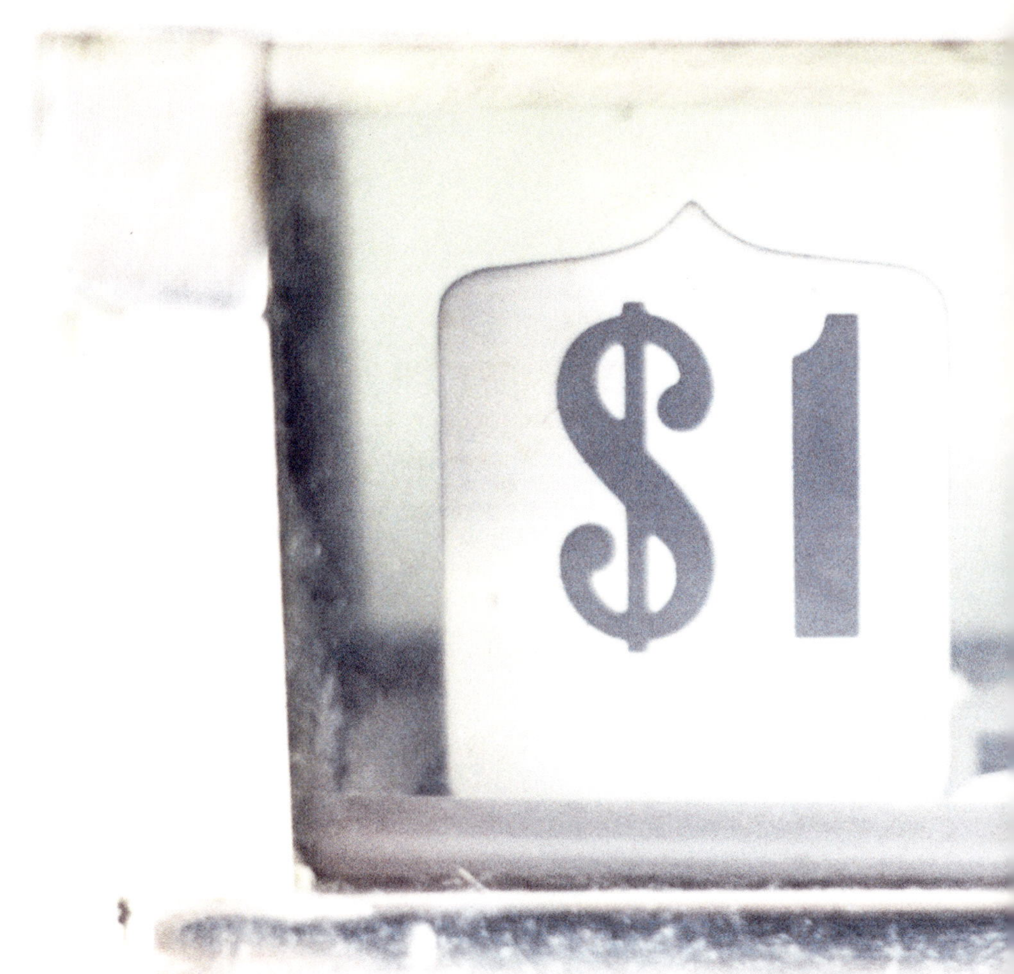
$1

"The barber will never be rich, but he will have a good life.

Not one barber is rich, but they have money all the time. It's something you can do until you are 70 years old and even more than that. It's not very hard. It's not too busy so you don't feel tired all the time. It's quiet."

Antonios

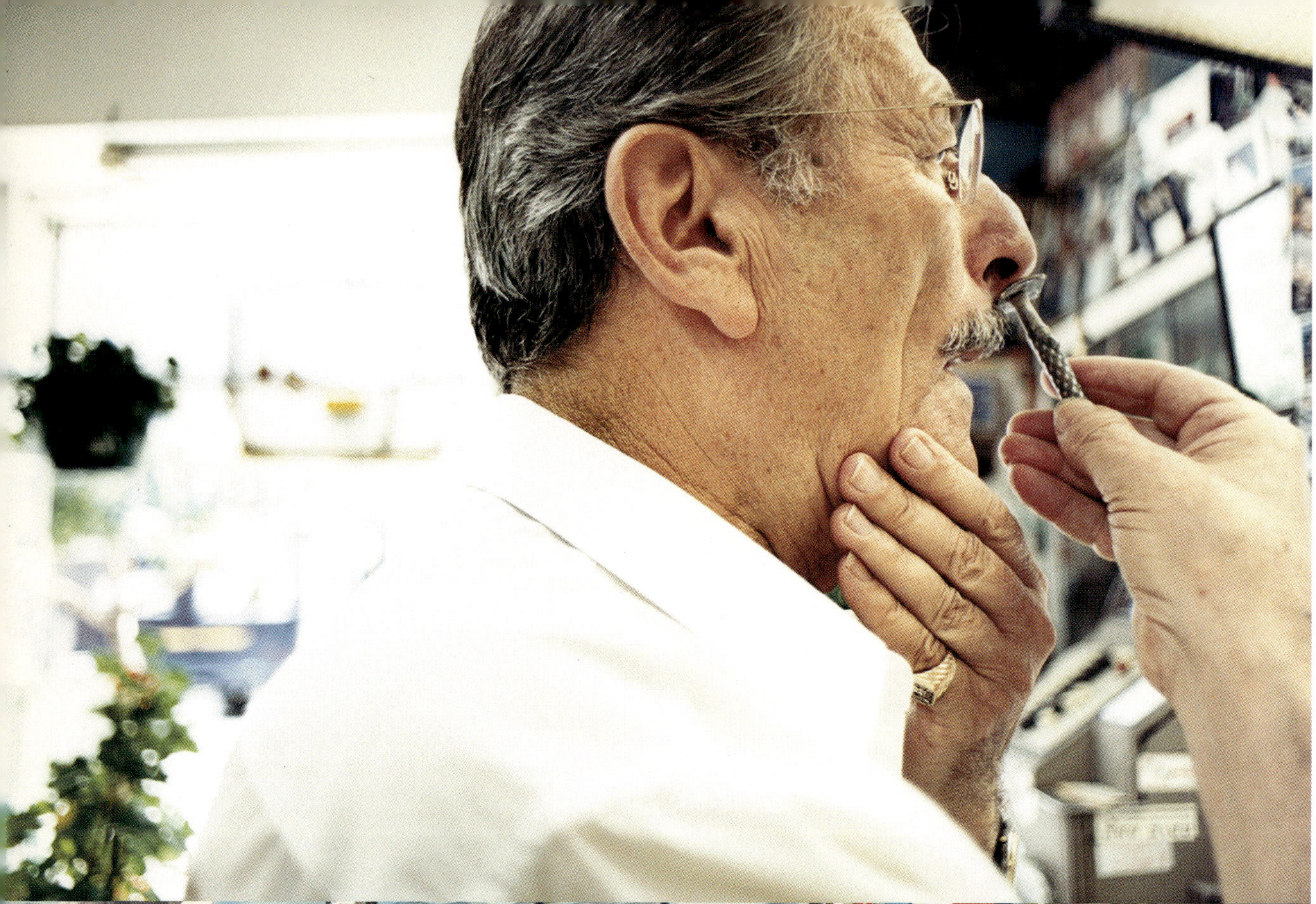

Antonios

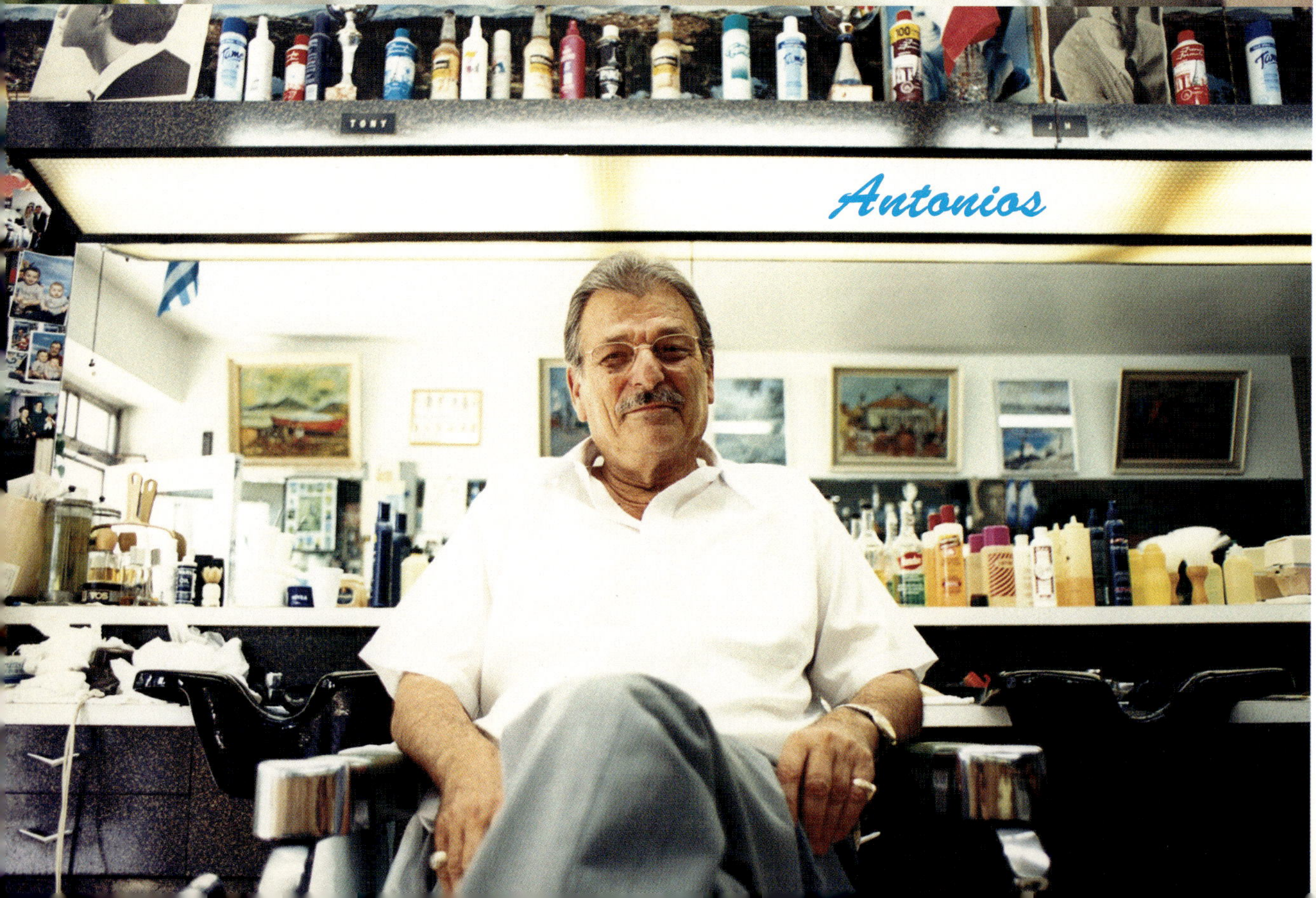

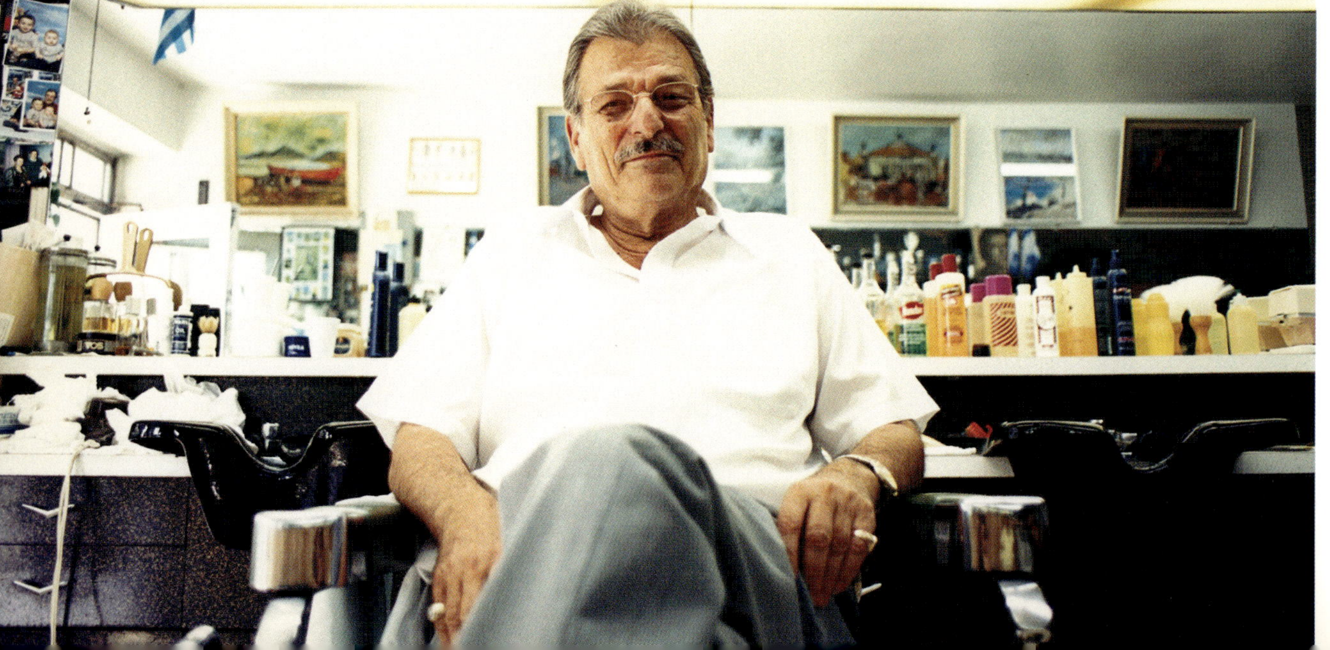

I never eat a sandwich for lunch. If you don't eat it on a plate, it's not a meal.

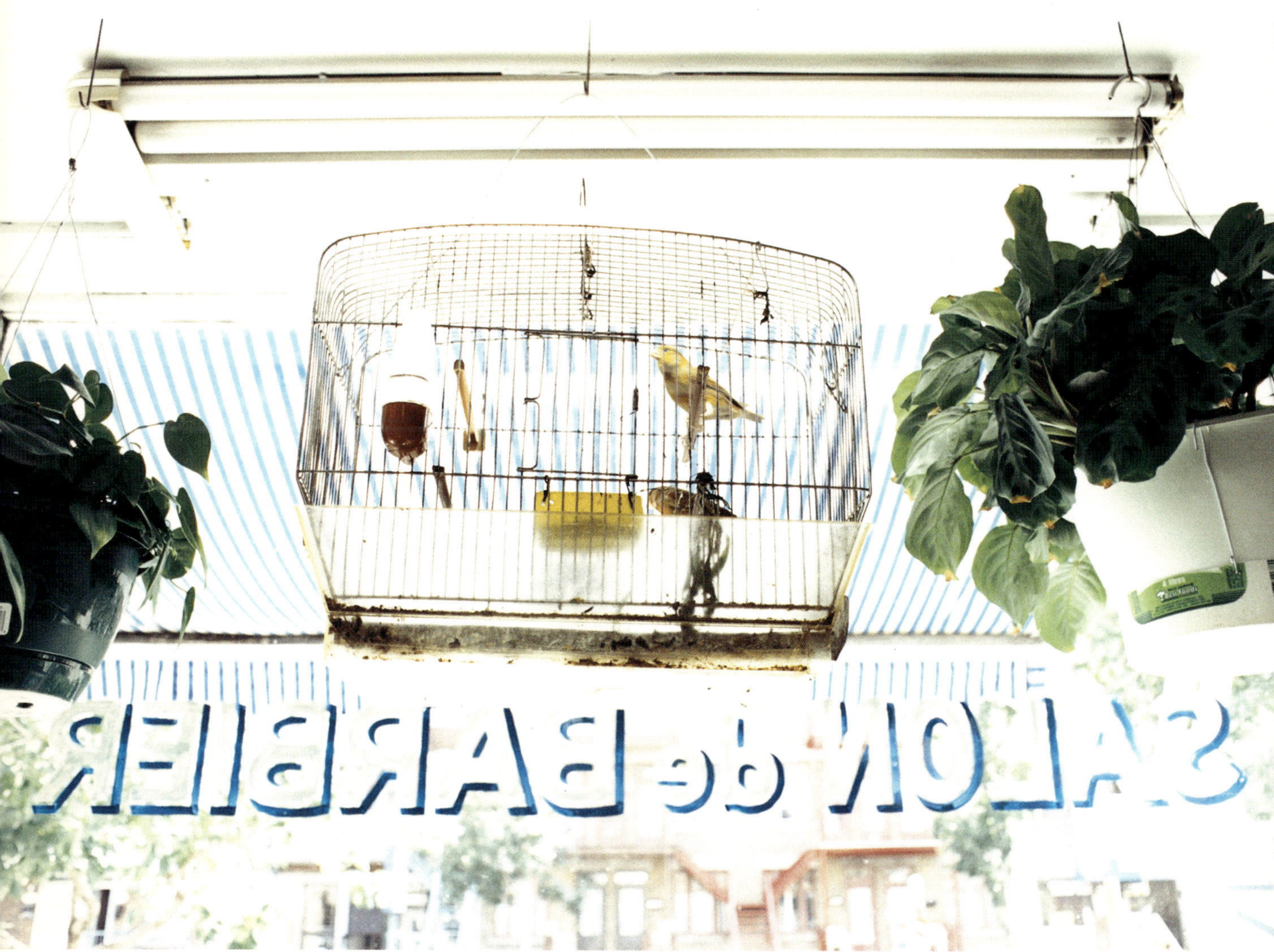

"This is not noise, this is nice to hear. It used to be common to have a bird in a barbershop in Greece. Because in barbershops in my country, after the War, they didn't have a radio or TV or something like that, so they had the birds to sing."

Antonios

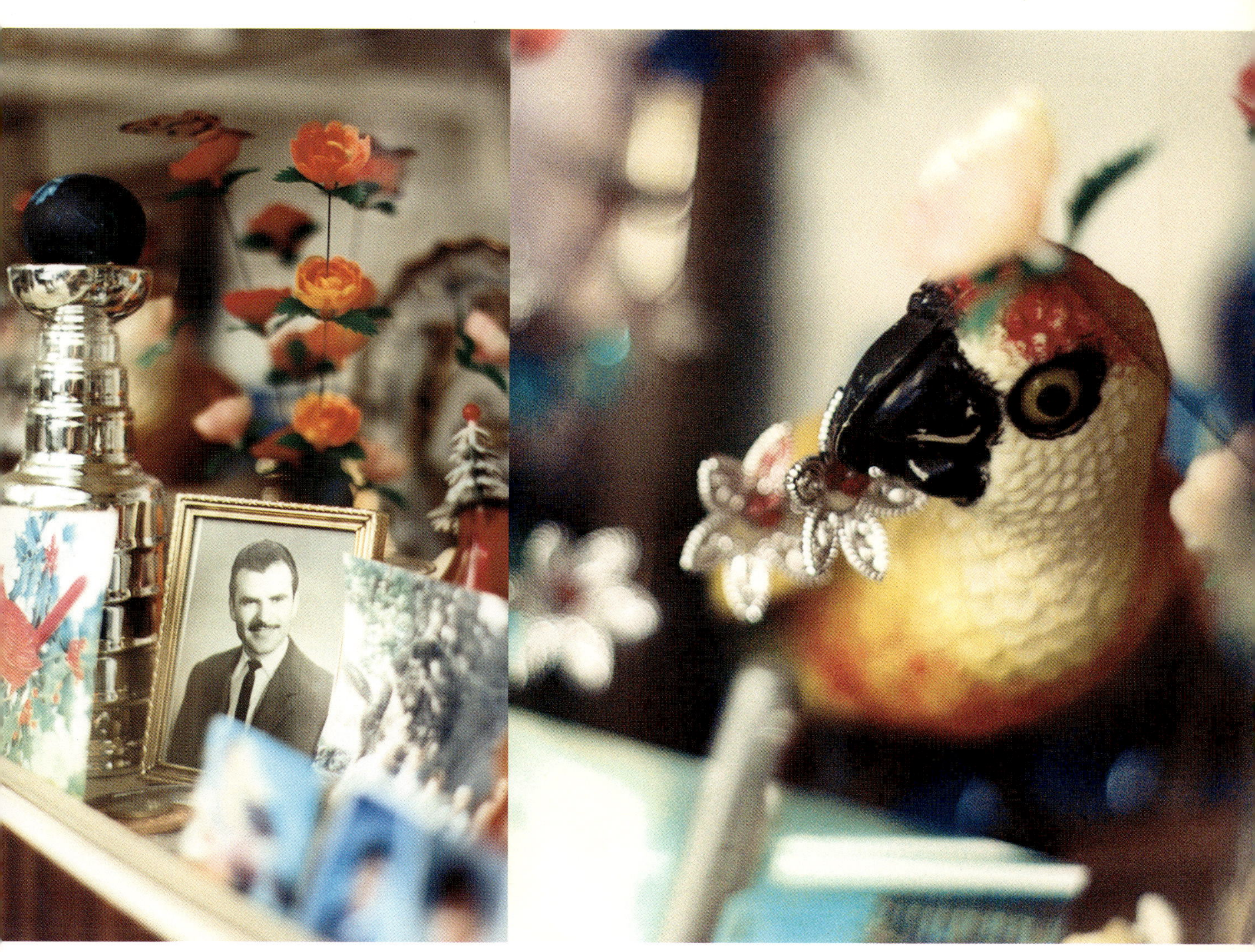

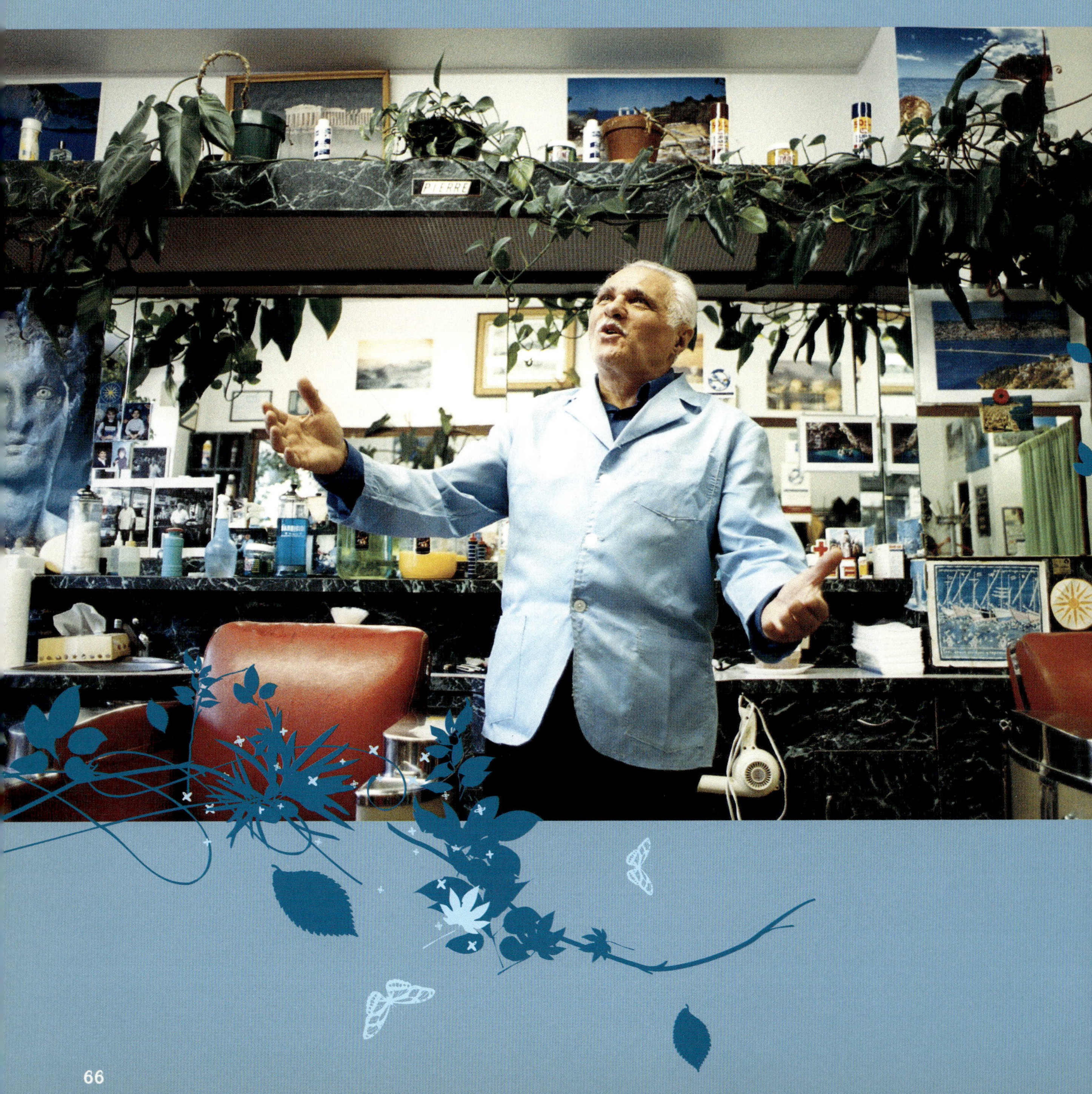
PIERRE

"I write poems. They are in Greek.
I started a long time ago.
I have over 300 poems.
On anything, politics,
my island, everything.
One of the best ones
I wrote is about the mother.
For any mother. It goes:

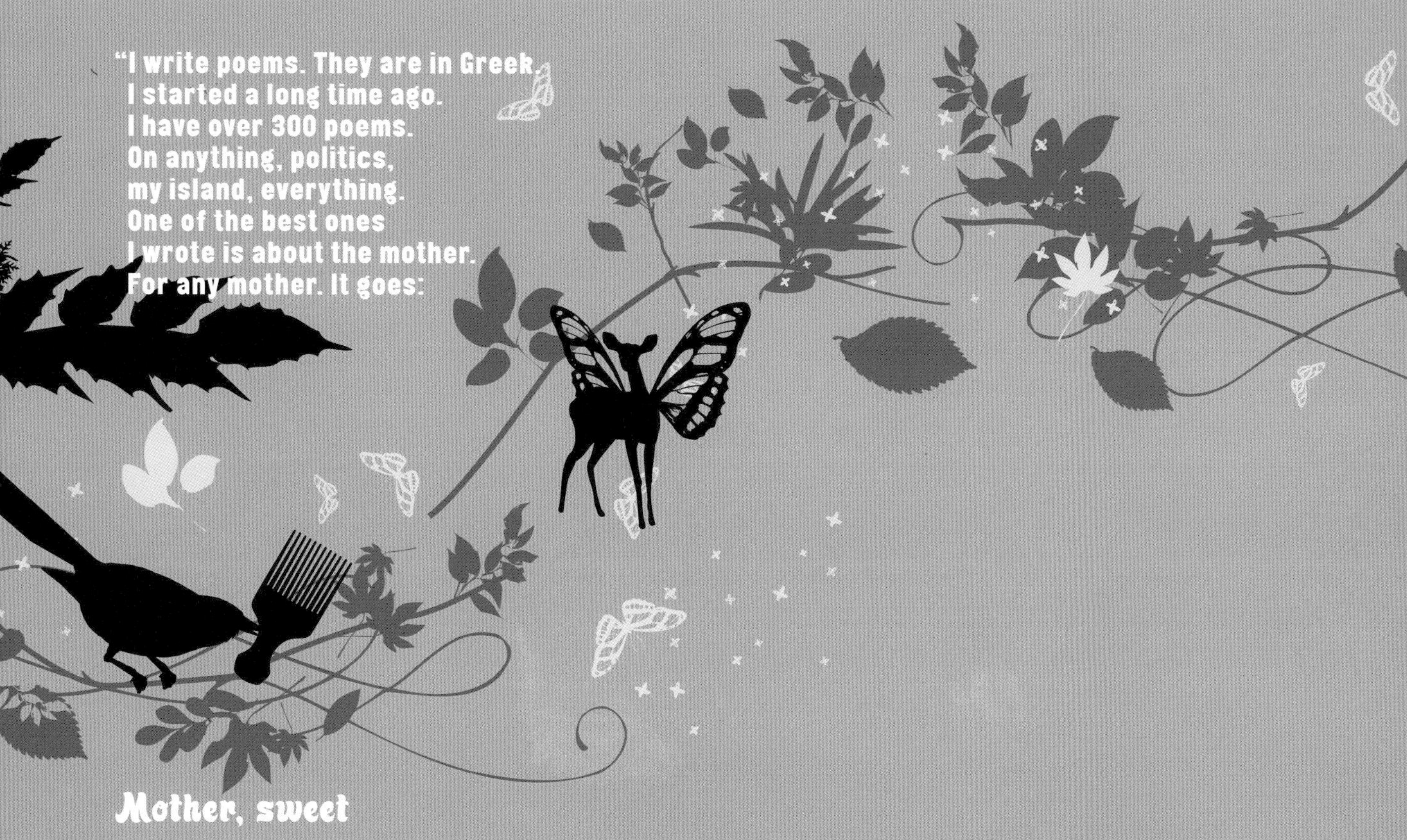

Mother, sweet
Are you really a garden that blooms
Your flower makes beauty
You make the nest, we birds fly
You, mother earth, when you plant seeds in the ground
You make peace with your embrace

(He sings.)

I have the part for the piano somewhere.
They played it on the radio."

Panagis

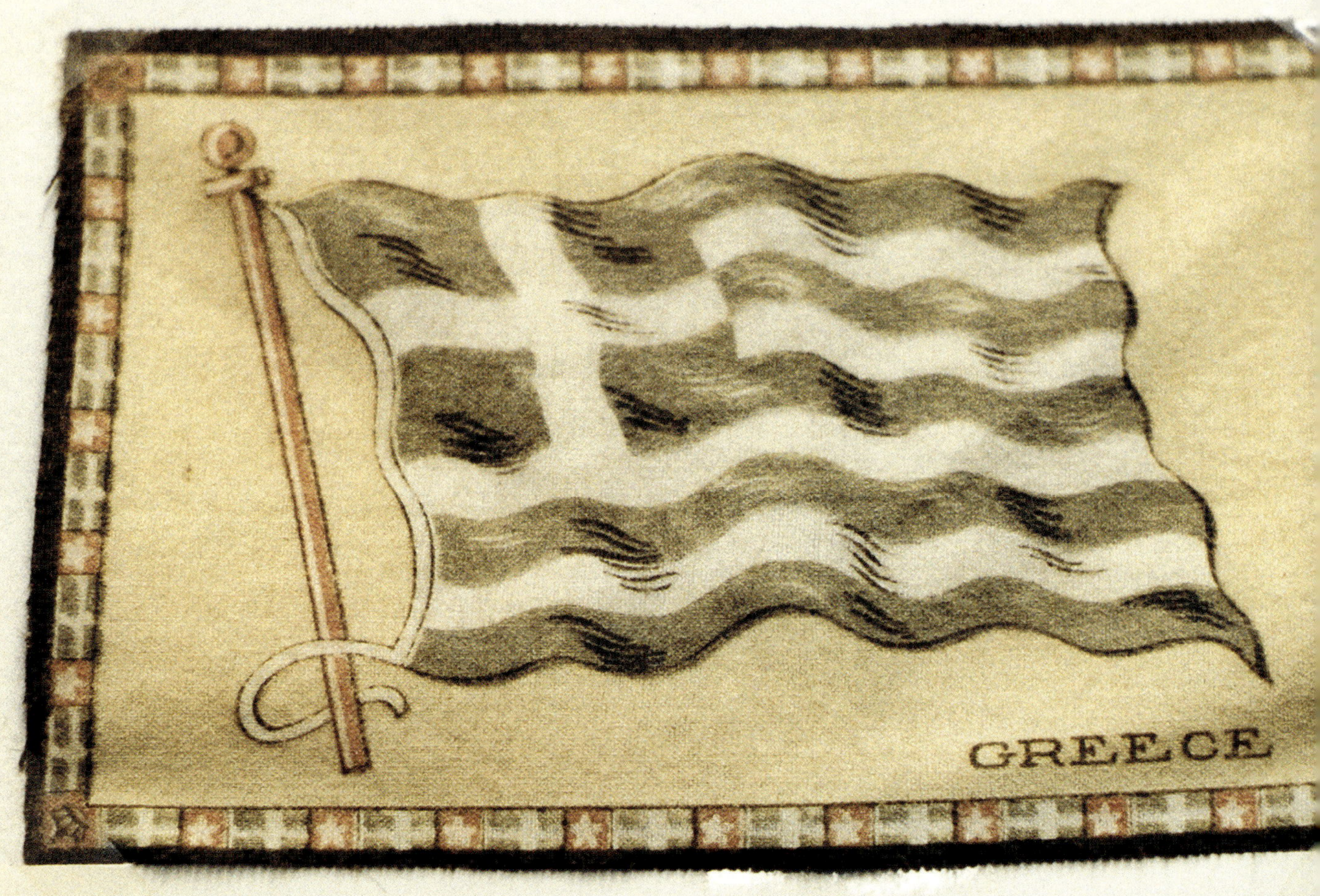

"My two girls were born in Greece, they left when they were three and five. People say that you must have something to remember it by. When we went to visit a few years ago I said: 'Cathy, turn around, what do you see?' She said: 'What do you mean, what do I see, just sea and sky.' I asked her: 'Do you want to stay forever here?'"

Panagis

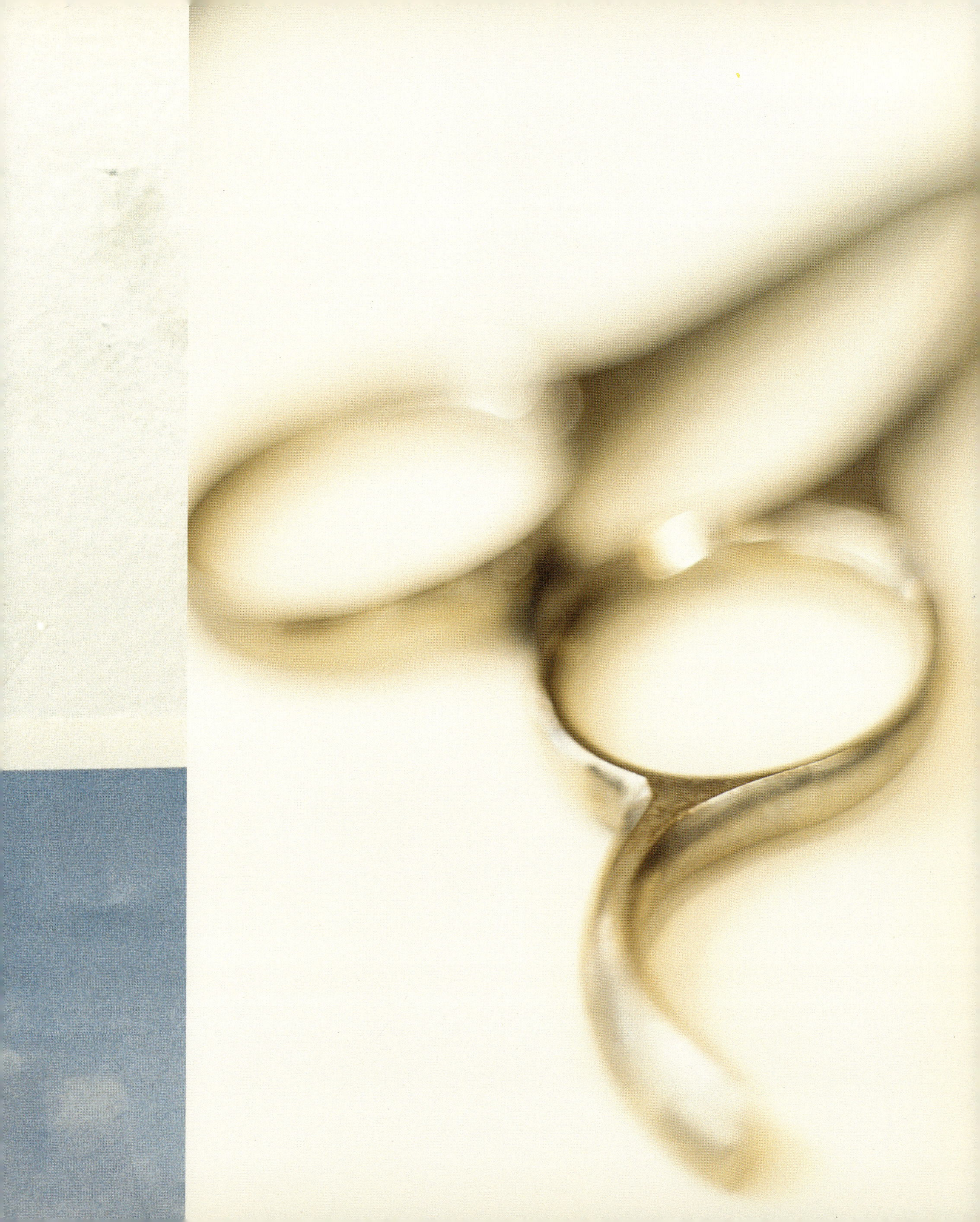

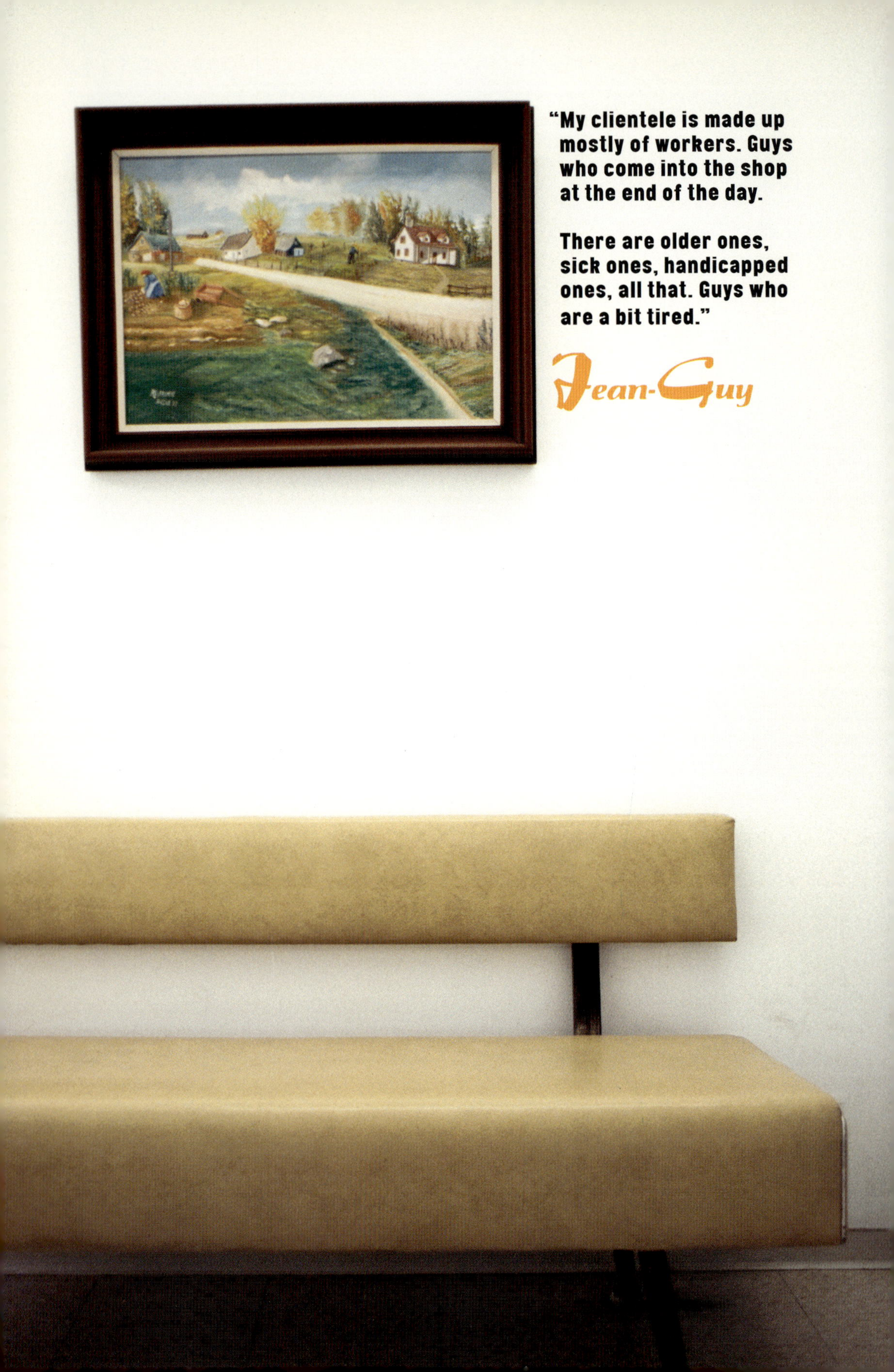

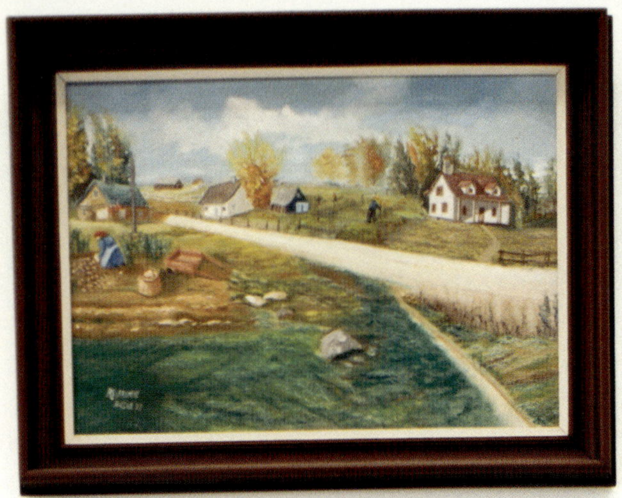

"My clientele is made up mostly of workers. Guys who come into the shop at the end of the day.

There are older ones, sick ones, handicapped ones, all that. Guys who are a bit tired."

Jean-Guy

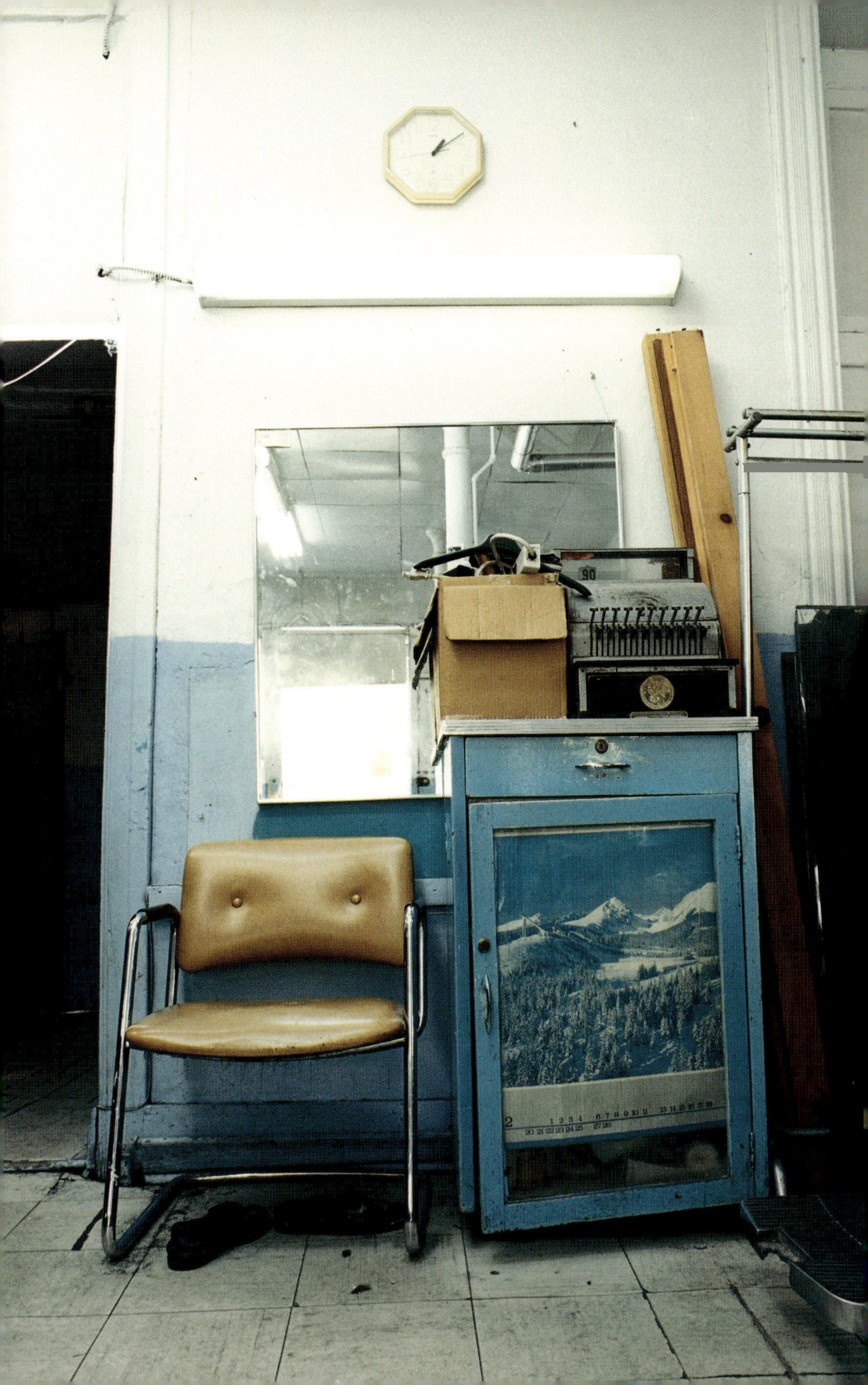

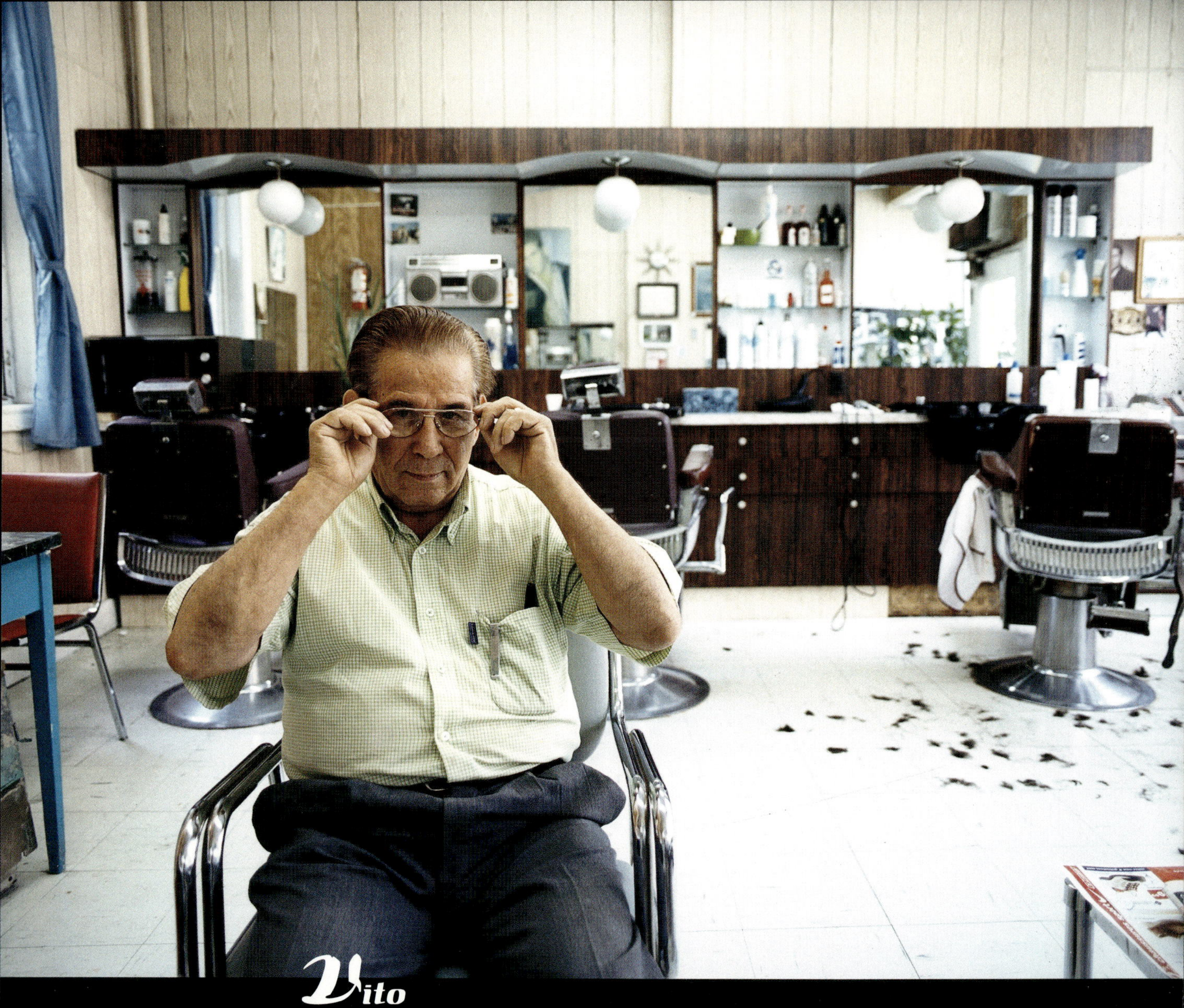

Vito

Amateur gardener
Grows orange blossoms, figs, rosemary, and ferns in his barbershop

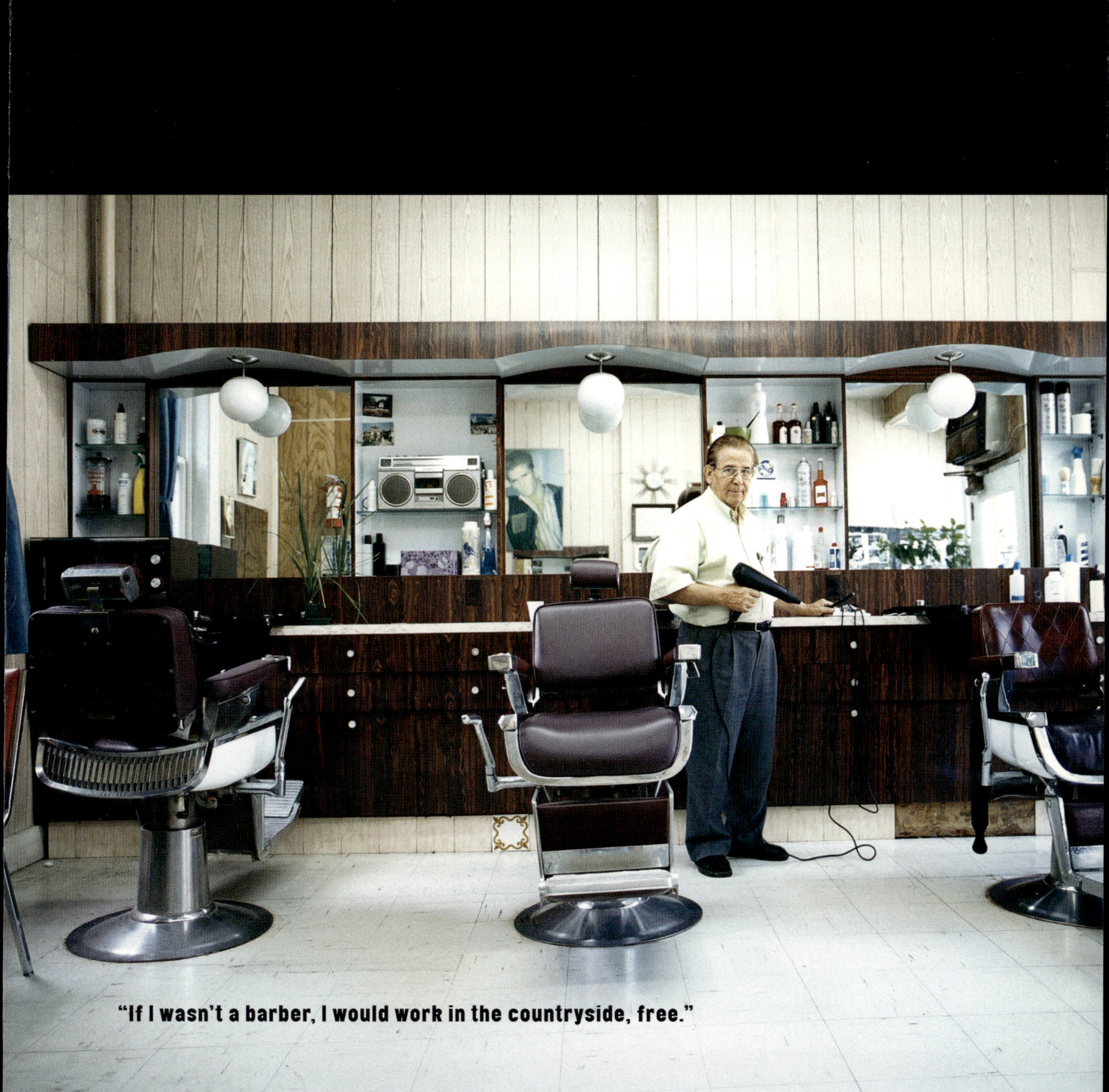

"If I wasn't a barber, I would work in the countryside, free."

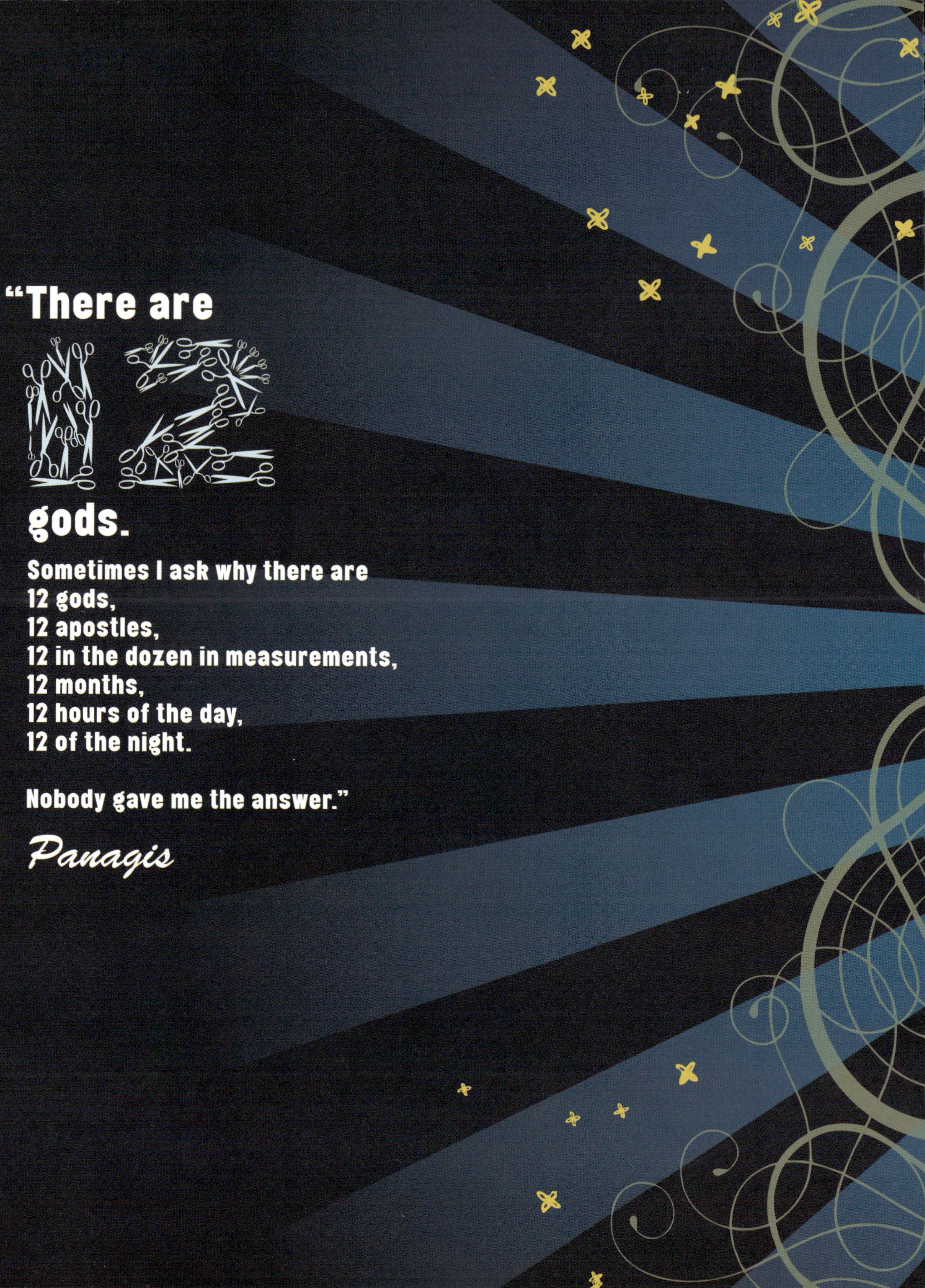
"There are
12
gods.
Sometimes I ask why there are
12 gods,
12 apostles,
12 in the dozen in measurements,
12 months,
12 hours of the day,
12 of the night.

Nobody gave me the answer."
Panagis

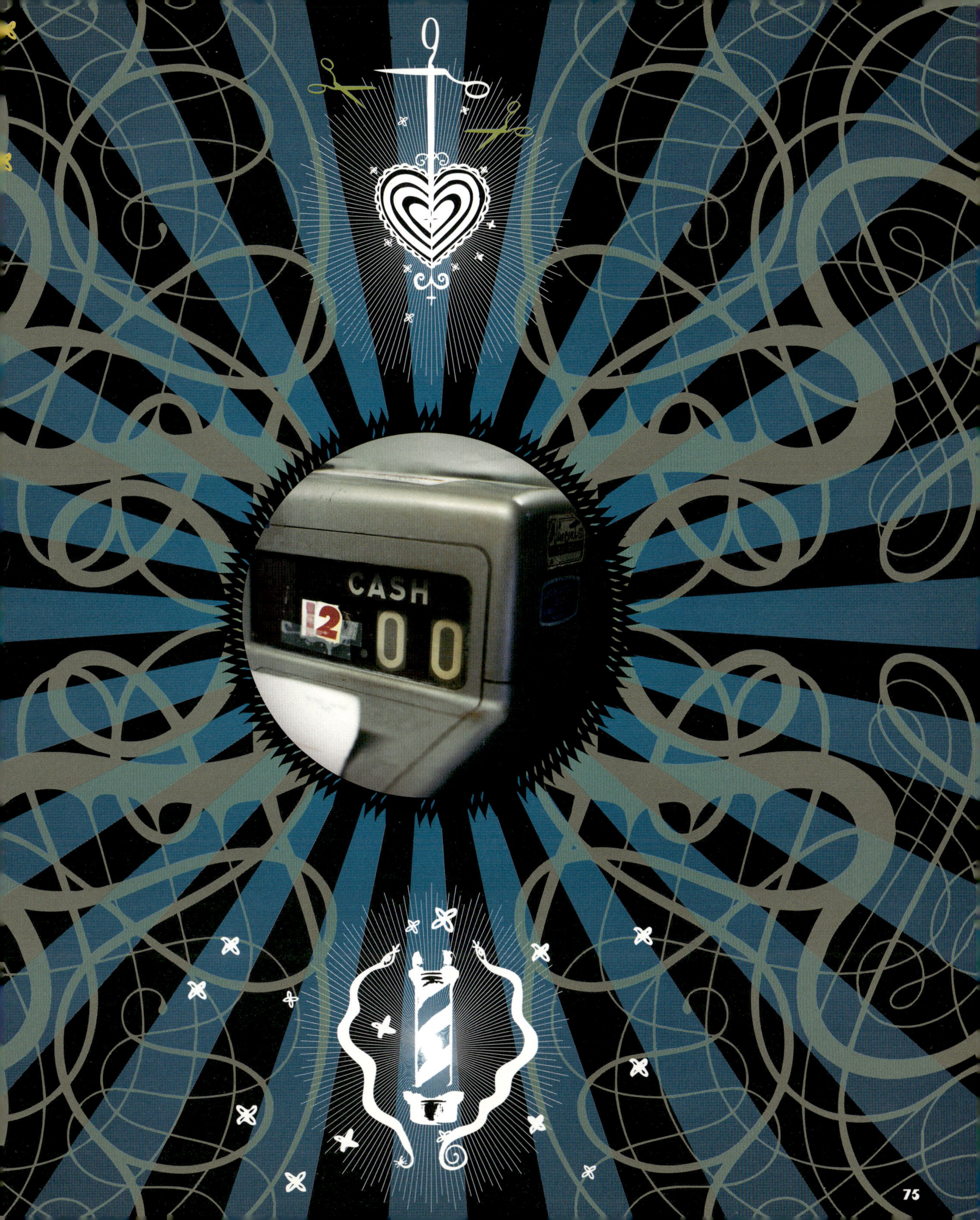
CASH
12.00

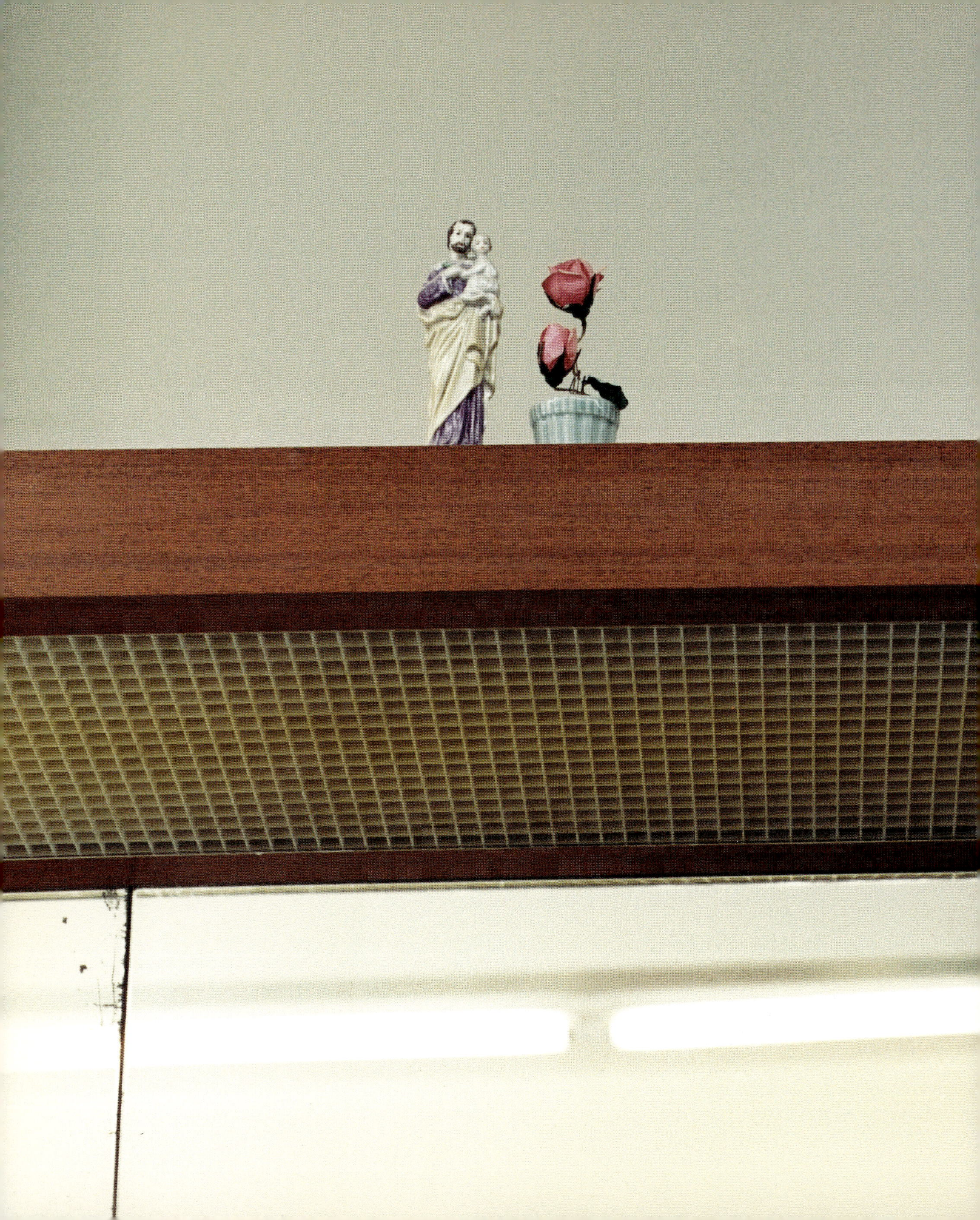

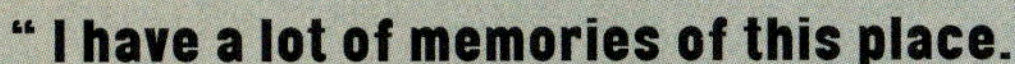

" I have a lot of memories of this place.

FOR A BARBER, MEMORIES ARE SOMETHING VERY POPULAR,

you remember people. For 40 years you have a lot of people to remember, friends who have been coming here for 40 years. We remember the bad times, the friends who left life, who passed away. Sometimes they enter my memory and I ask myself: 'where is this guy, where is that guy?' So many have died."

Jimmy

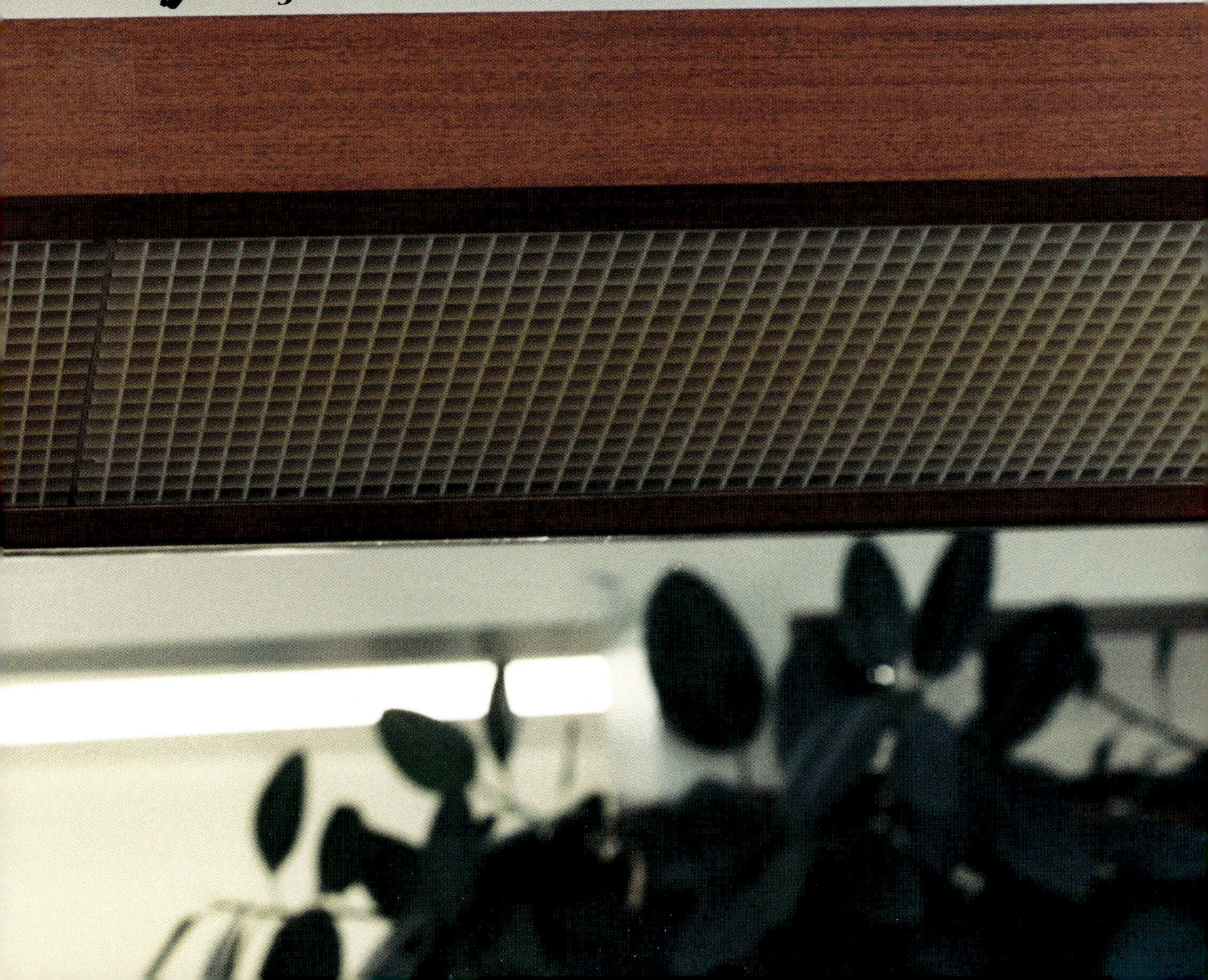

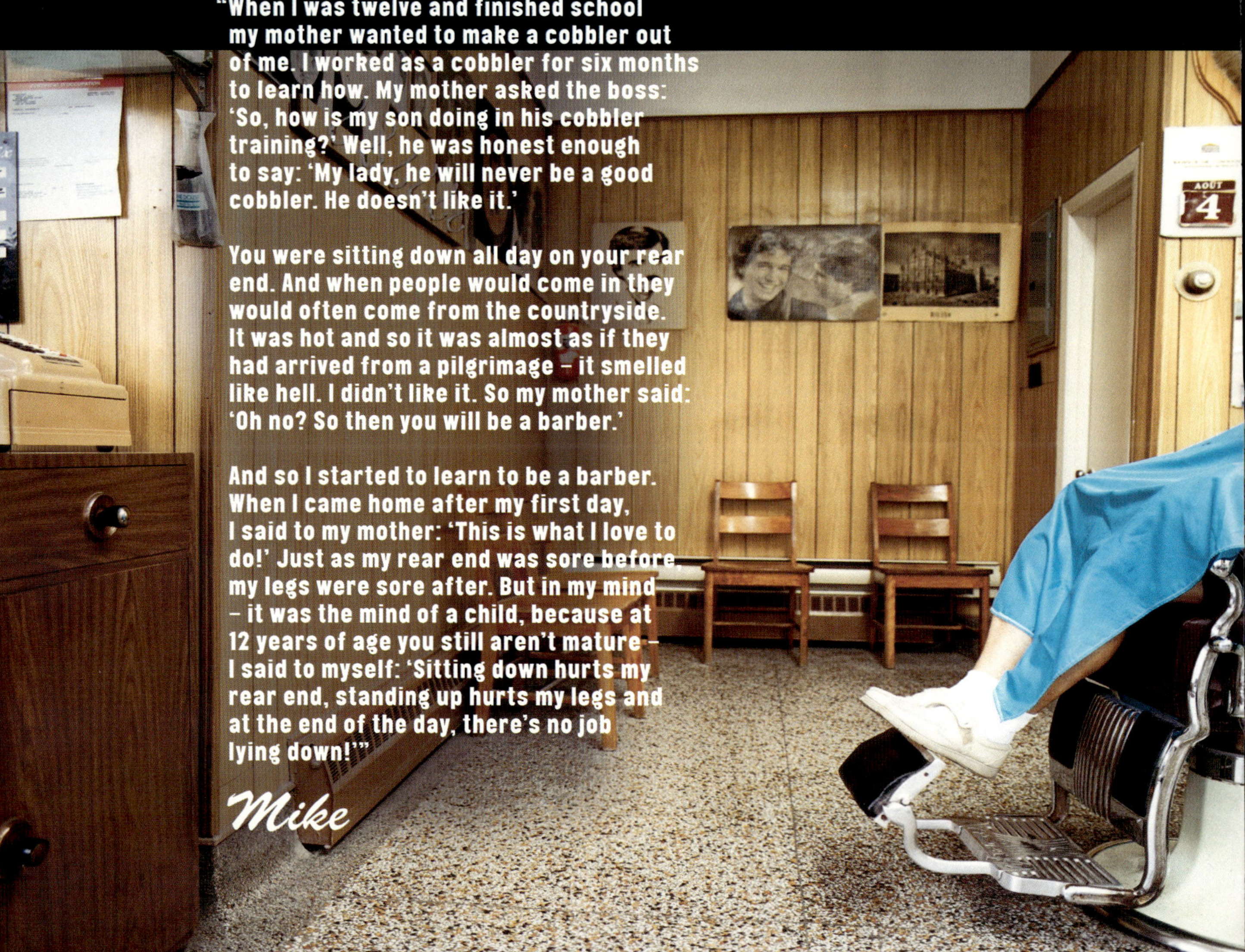

"When I was twelve and finished school my mother wanted to make a cobbler out of me. I worked as a cobbler for six months to learn how. My mother asked the boss: 'So, how is my son doing in his cobbler training?' Well, he was honest enough to say: 'My lady, he will never be a good cobbler. He doesn't like it.'

You were sitting down all day on your rear end. And when people would come in they would often come from the countryside. It was hot and so it was almost as if they had arrived from a pilgrimage – it smelled like hell. I didn't like it. So my mother said: 'Oh no? So then you will be a barber.'

And so I started to learn to be a barber. When I came home after my first day, I said to my mother: 'This is what I love to do!' Just as my rear end was sore before, my legs were sore after. But in my mind – it was the mind of a child, because at 12 years of age you still aren't mature – I said to myself: 'Sitting down hurts my rear end, standing up hurts my legs and at the end of the day, there's no job lying down!'"

Mike

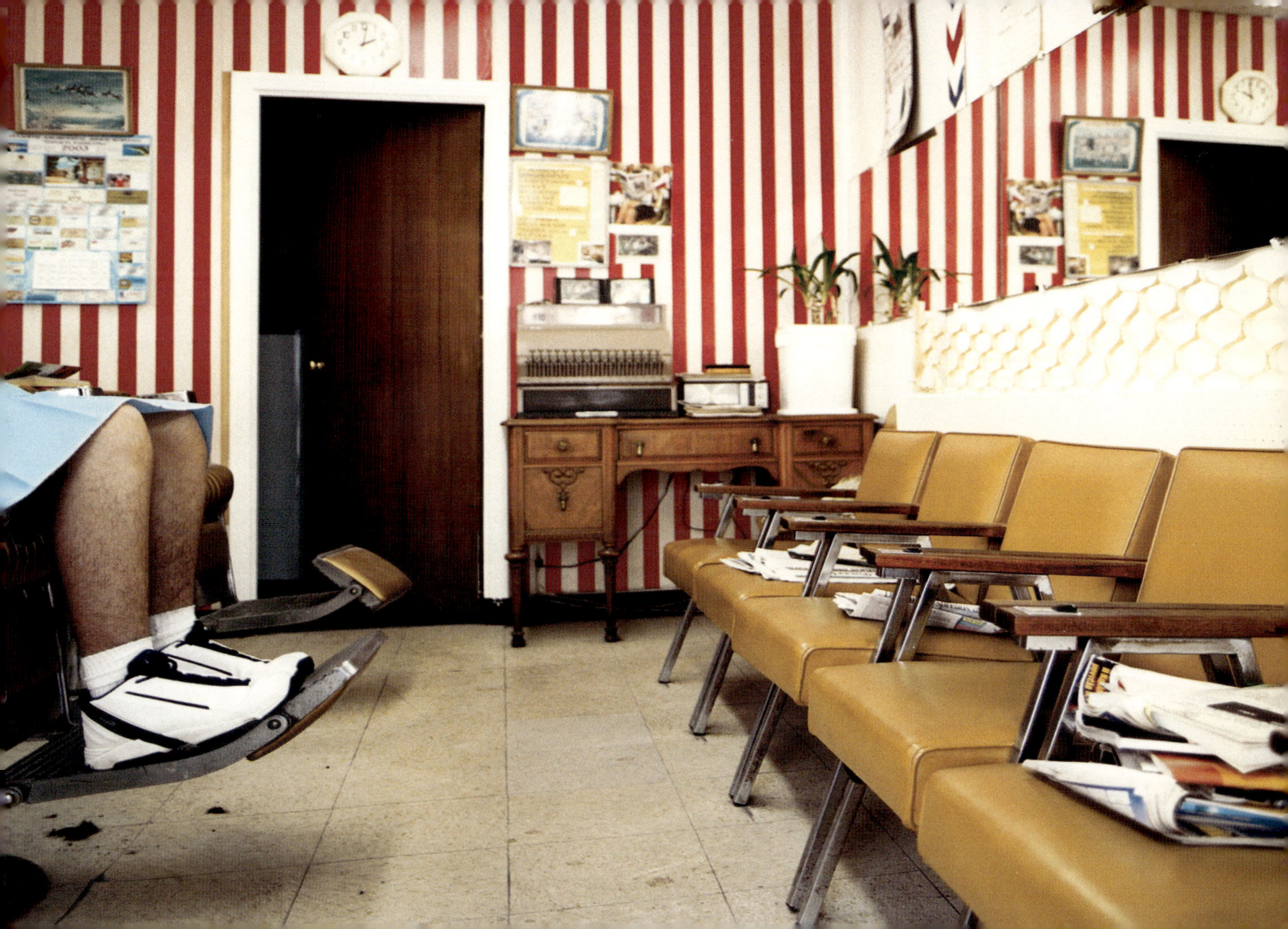

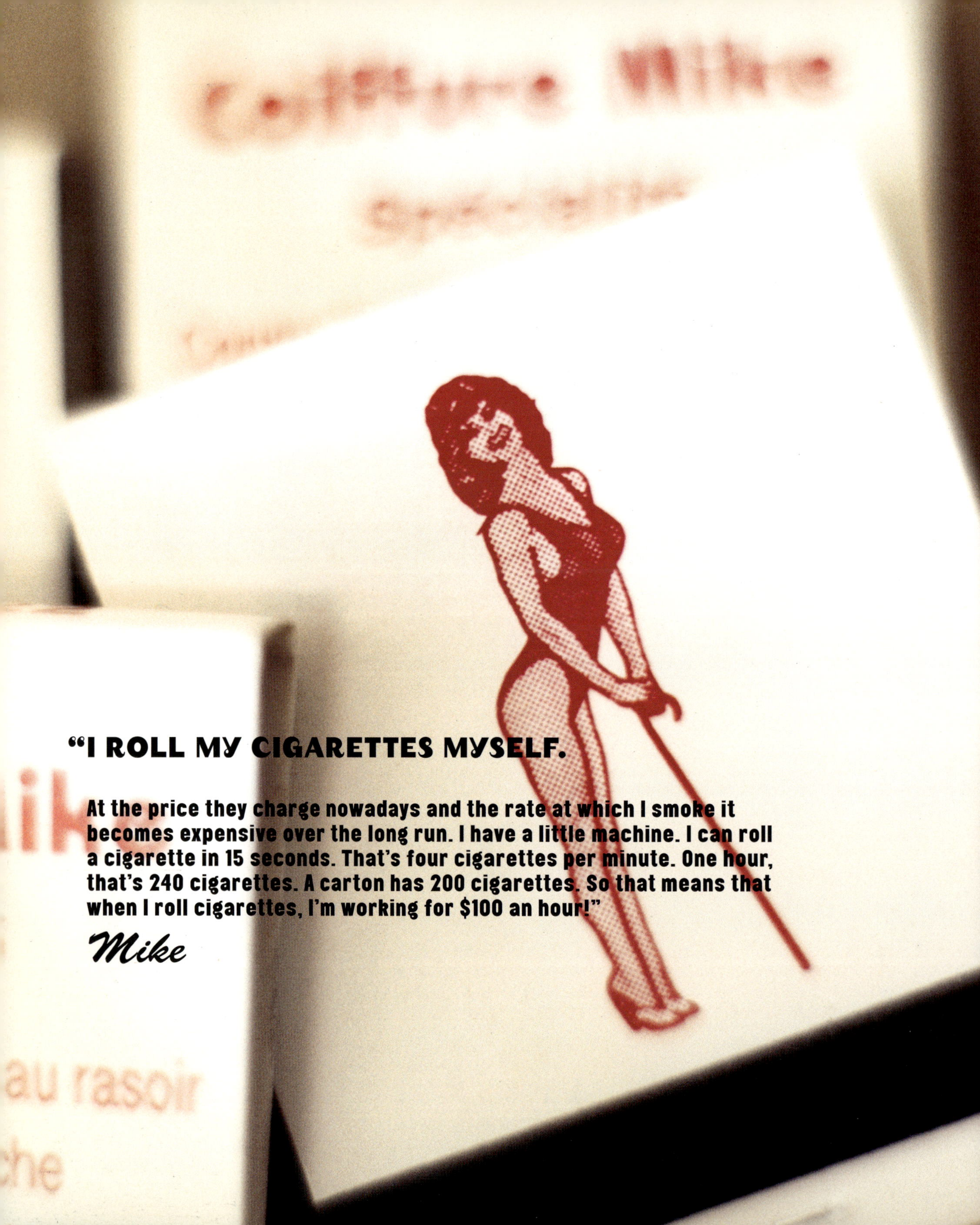

"I ROLL MY CIGARETTES MYSELF.

At the price they charge nowadays and the rate at which I smoke it becomes expensive over the long run. I have a little machine. I can roll a cigarette in 15 seconds. That's four cigarettes per minute. One hour, that's 240 cigarettes. A carton has 200 cigarettes. So that means that when I roll cigarettes, I'm working for $100 an hour!"

Mike

"I NEVER HAD A PHONE IN HERE.

I was never interested. The phone rings, you're in the middle of doing a haircut... I don't work by appointment. Anyway, there are always customers, there's always someone around. So I'm never alone."

Bob

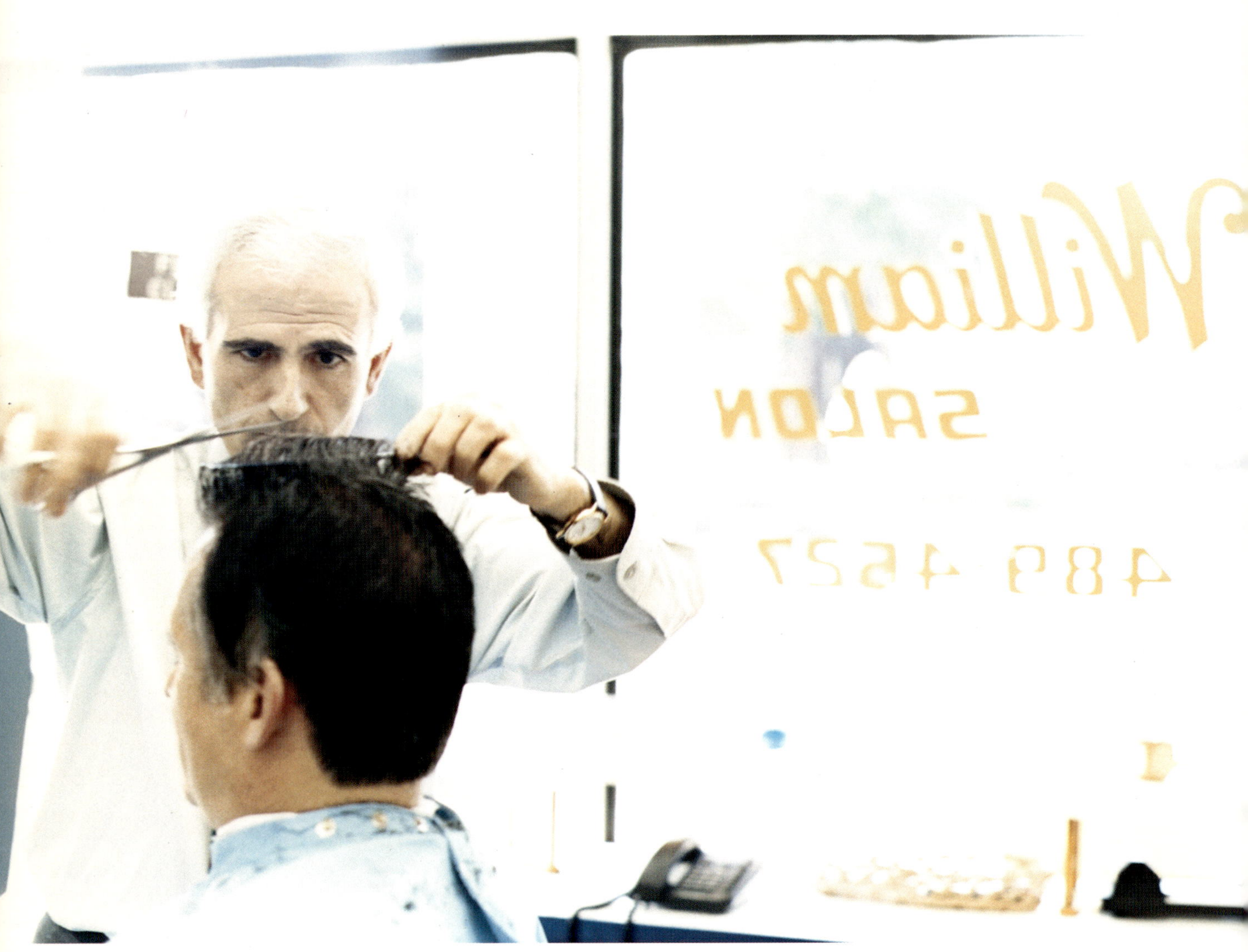

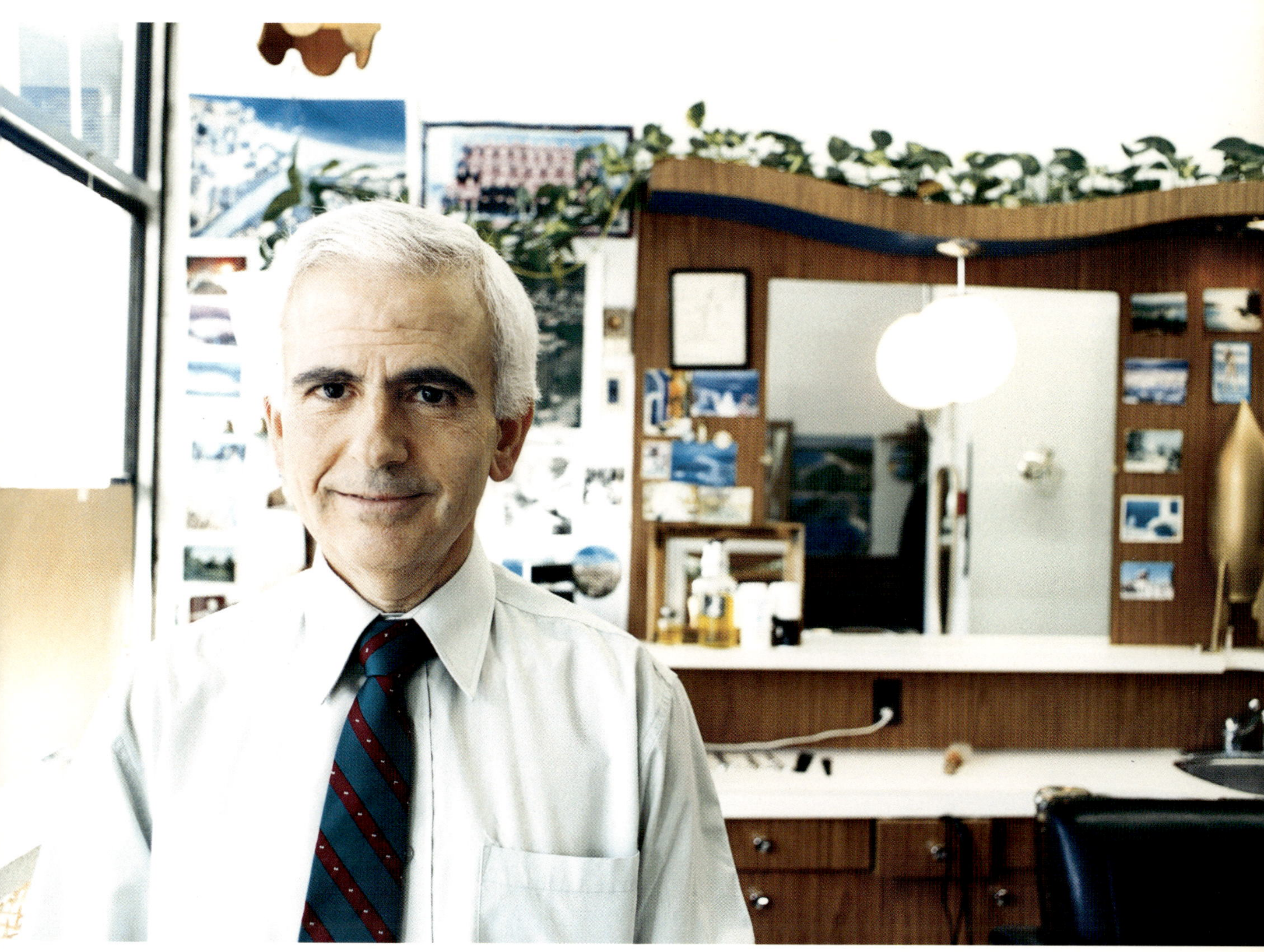

"Sometimes I give people free haircuts.
People need them."

Zacarias

Giuseppe, Ademar

Alfred,

Sigmund, Henry, George

ubert, Humphrey, Richard, Julius

Joseph, Armand, Arthur, Roger, Jack, Bernard, Ricardo,

Leon, Herman, Emile, Paul, Peter, Byron, Nigel, Adrian, Je

Cheniston, Roland, Bertolt, Christopher, Ronald, Gary, Conan

s, Jacob, Harry, Jeffrey, Alfonso, Joshua, Benson,

rnold, Alexander, David, Daniel, Ralph, Hugh, Dennis,

e, Nicolas, Milton, Brian, Mark, James, Michael, Robert, Ke

Duncan.

homas, Delphis, Philip, E

and, Boris, Charlie, Reynold, Victor, Wilfrid, Leo-

Giuseppe, Ademar, Sean, Domenico, Alfred, Ken-

Godfried, Saul, Louis, Auguste, Simon, Jerome,

n, William, Niles, Heinrich, Pierre, Jesus, Maurice,

Werner, Ernest, Evan, Ch

Karl, Judas, Nikos, Ba

Godfried,

Simon,

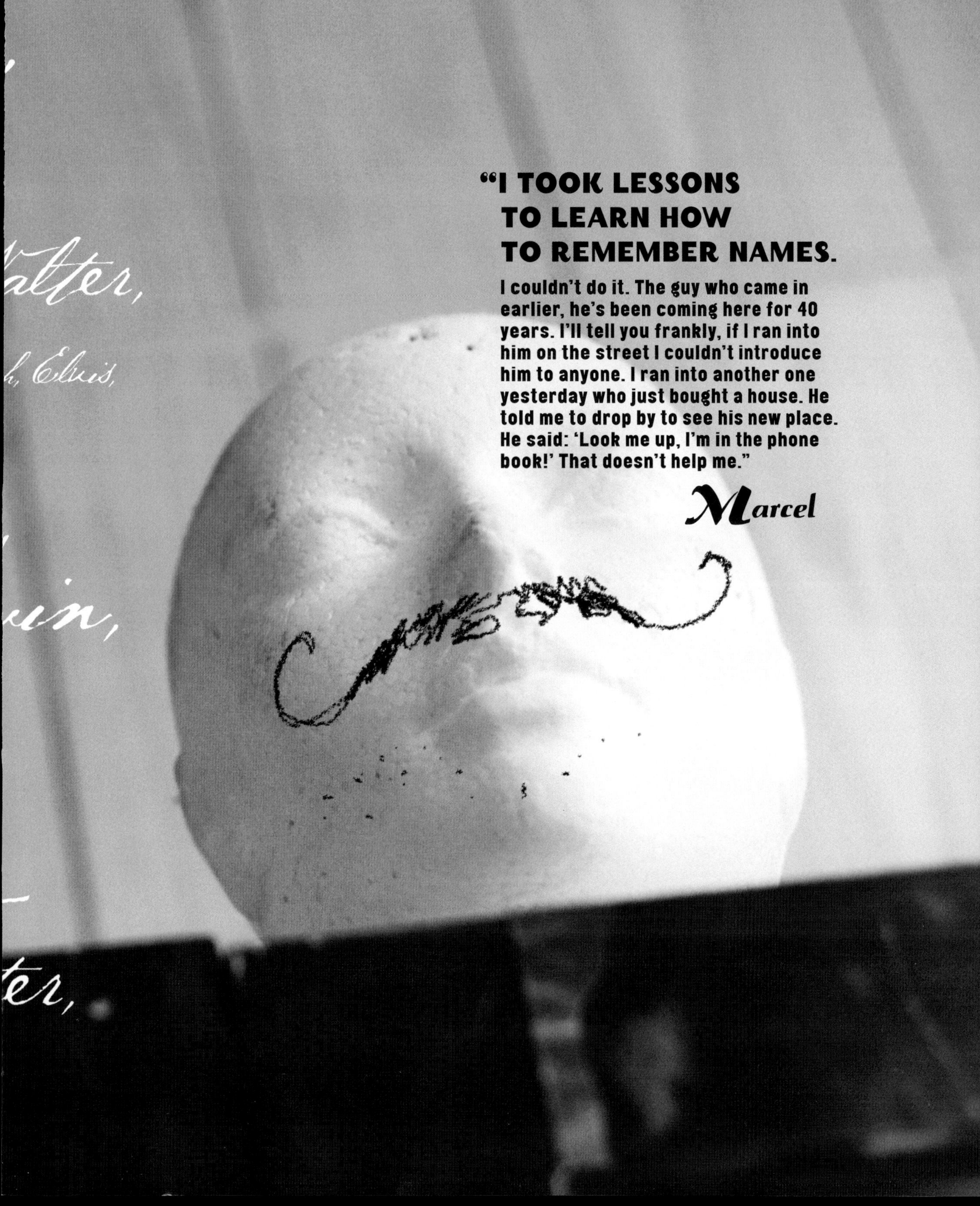

"I TOOK LESSONS TO LEARN HOW TO REMEMBER NAMES.

I couldn't do it. The guy who came in earlier, he's been coming here for 40 years. I'll tell you frankly, if I ran into him on the street I couldn't introduce him to anyone. I ran into another one yesterday who just bought a house. He told me to drop by to see his new place. He said: 'Look me up, I'm in the phone book!' That doesn't help me."

Marcel

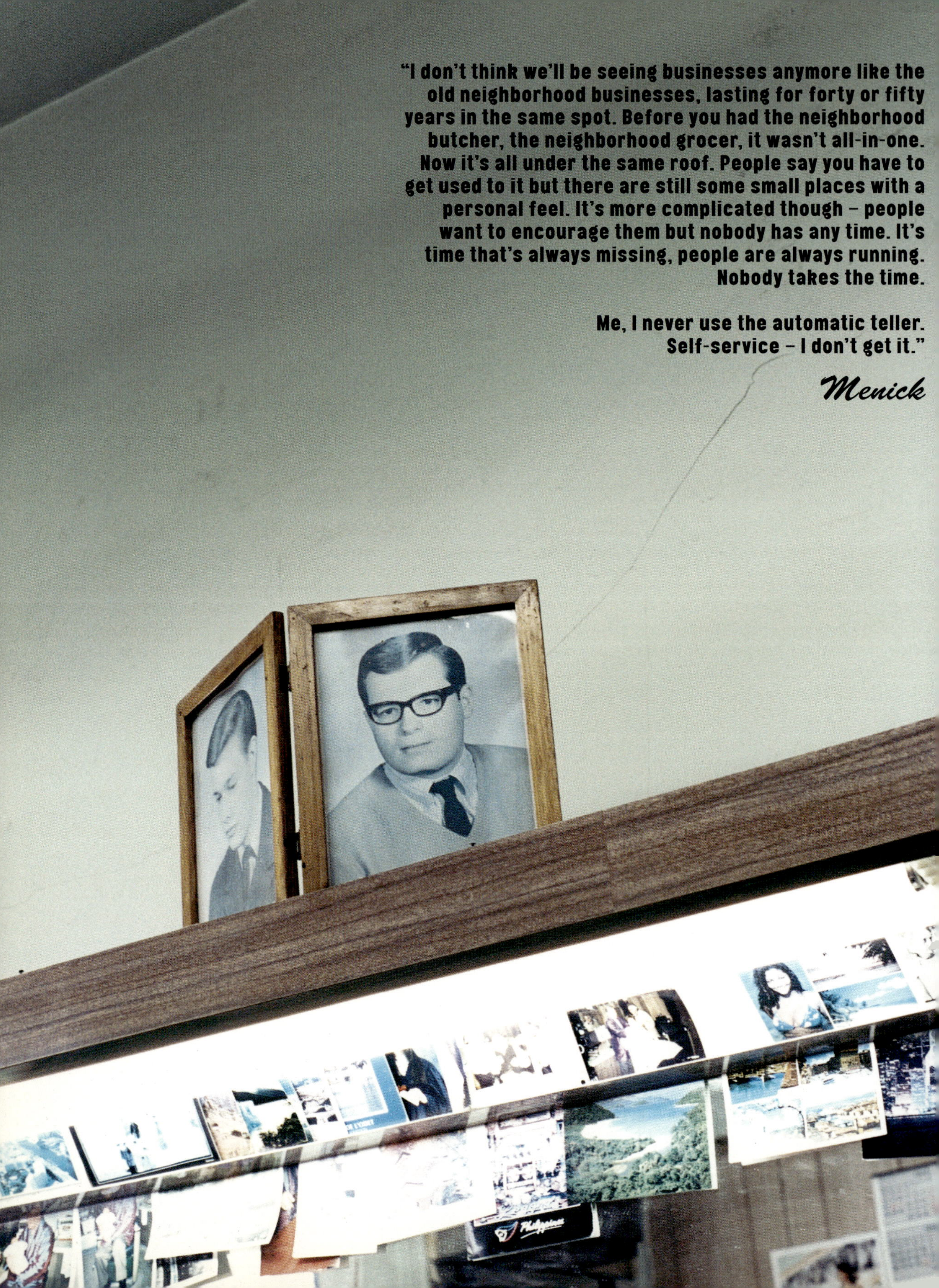

"I don't think we'll be seeing businesses anymore like the old neighborhood businesses, lasting for forty or fifty years in the same spot. Before you had the neighborhood butcher, the neighborhood grocer, it wasn't all-in-one. Now it's all under the same roof. People say you have to get used to it but there are still some small places with a personal feel. It's more complicated though – people want to encourage them but nobody has any time. It's time that's always missing, people are always running. Nobody takes the time.

Me, I never use the automatic teller. Self-service – I don't get it."

Menick

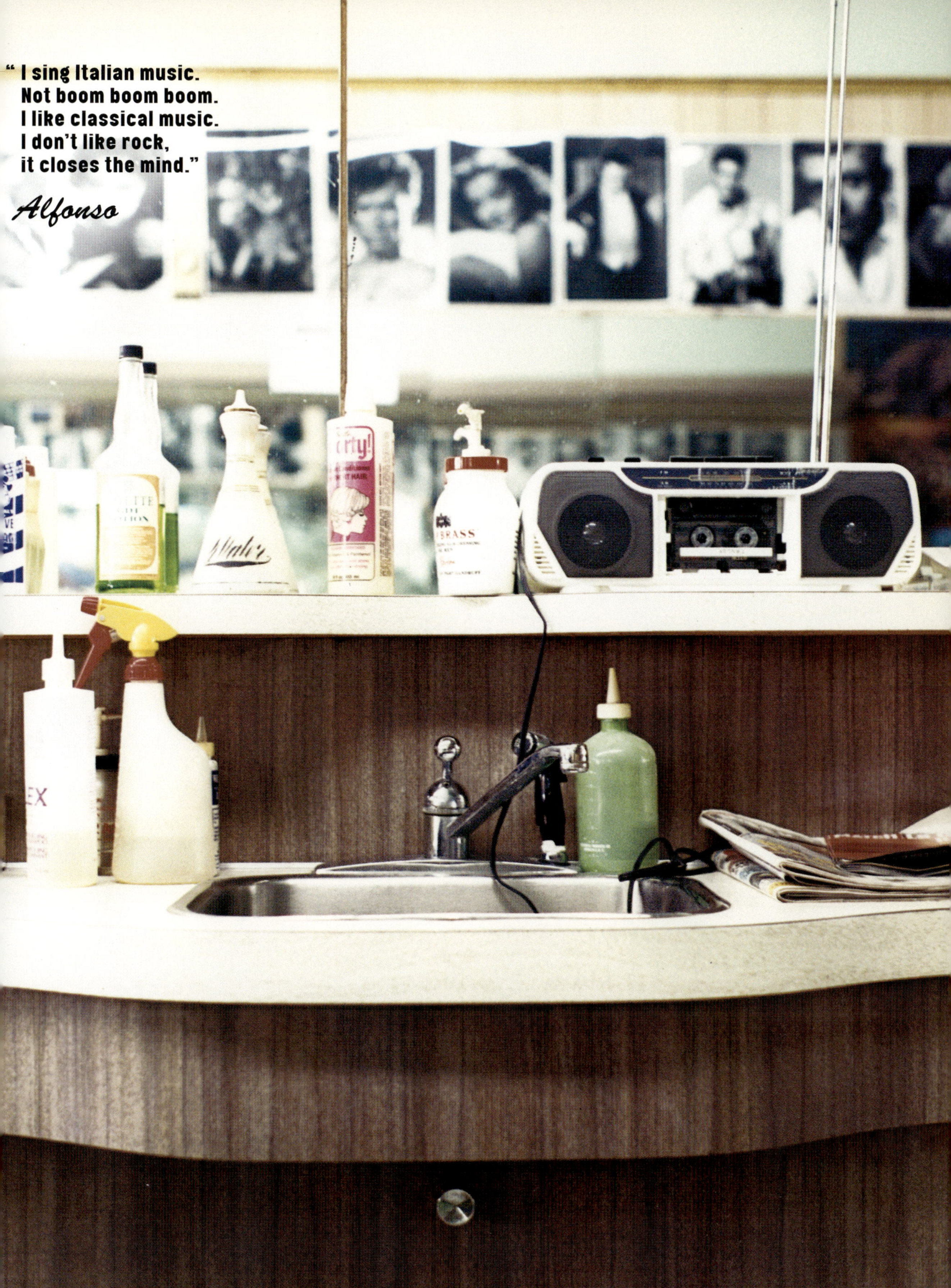
" I sing Italian music.
Not boom boom boom.
I like classical music.
I don't like rock,
it closes the mind."
Alfonso

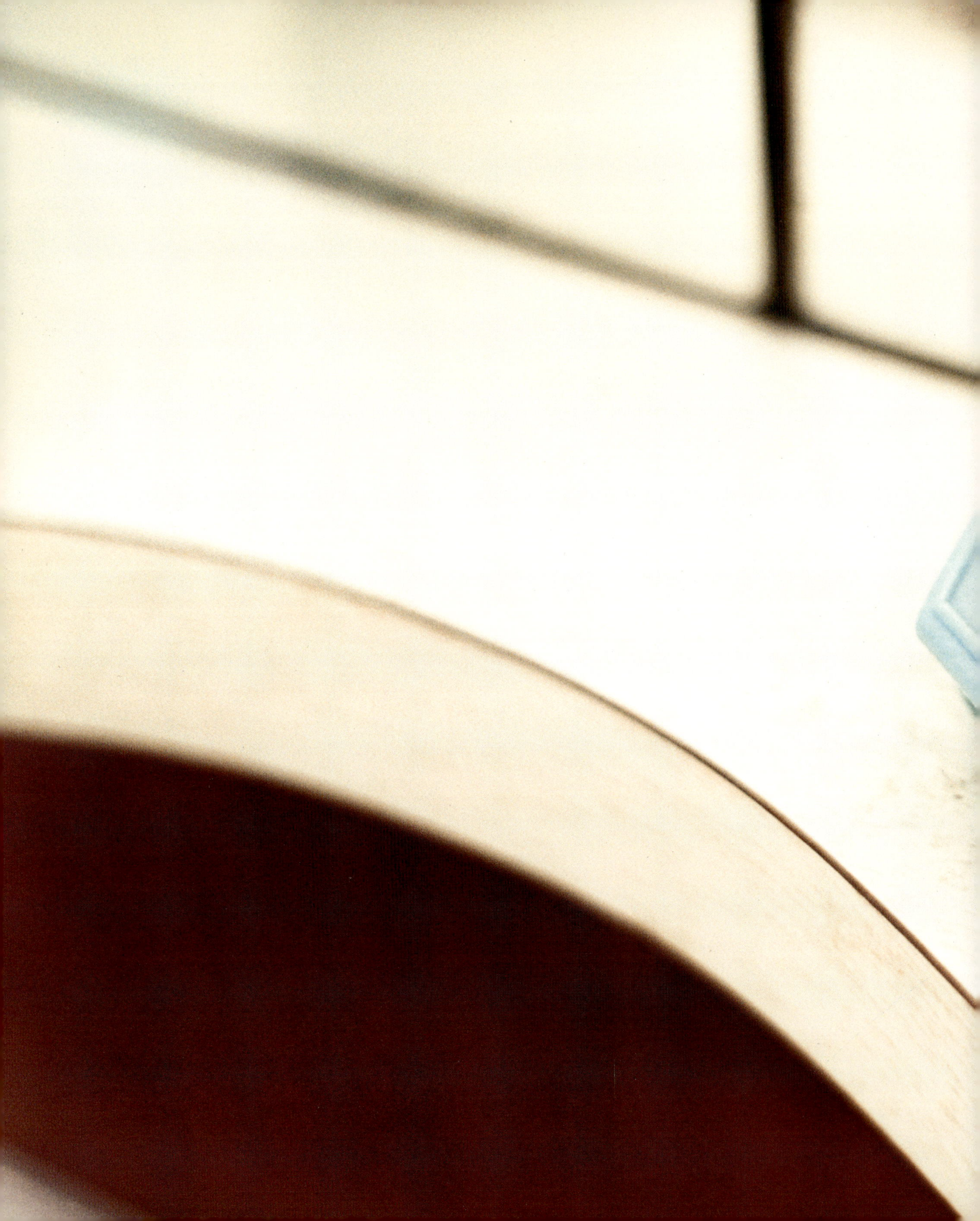

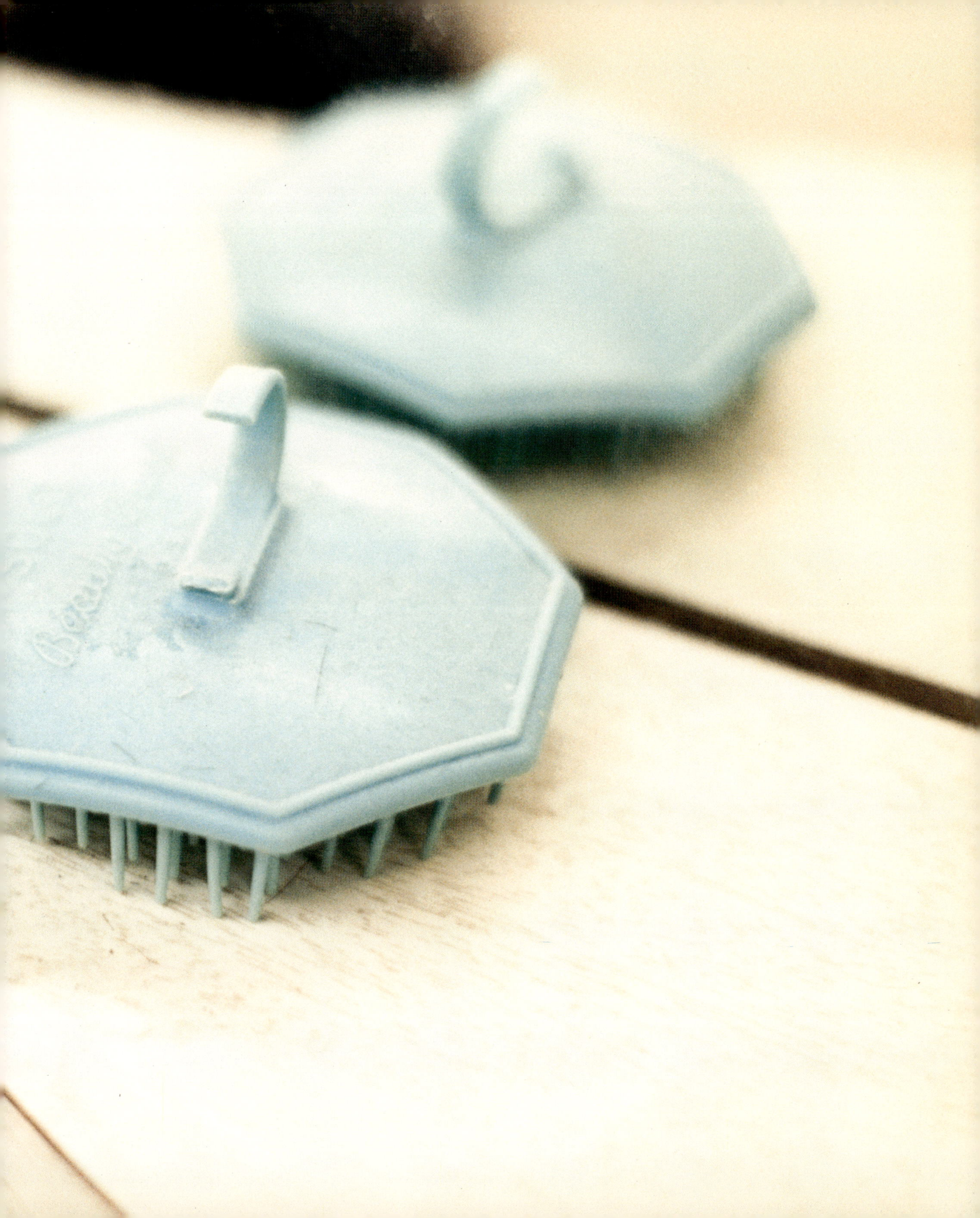

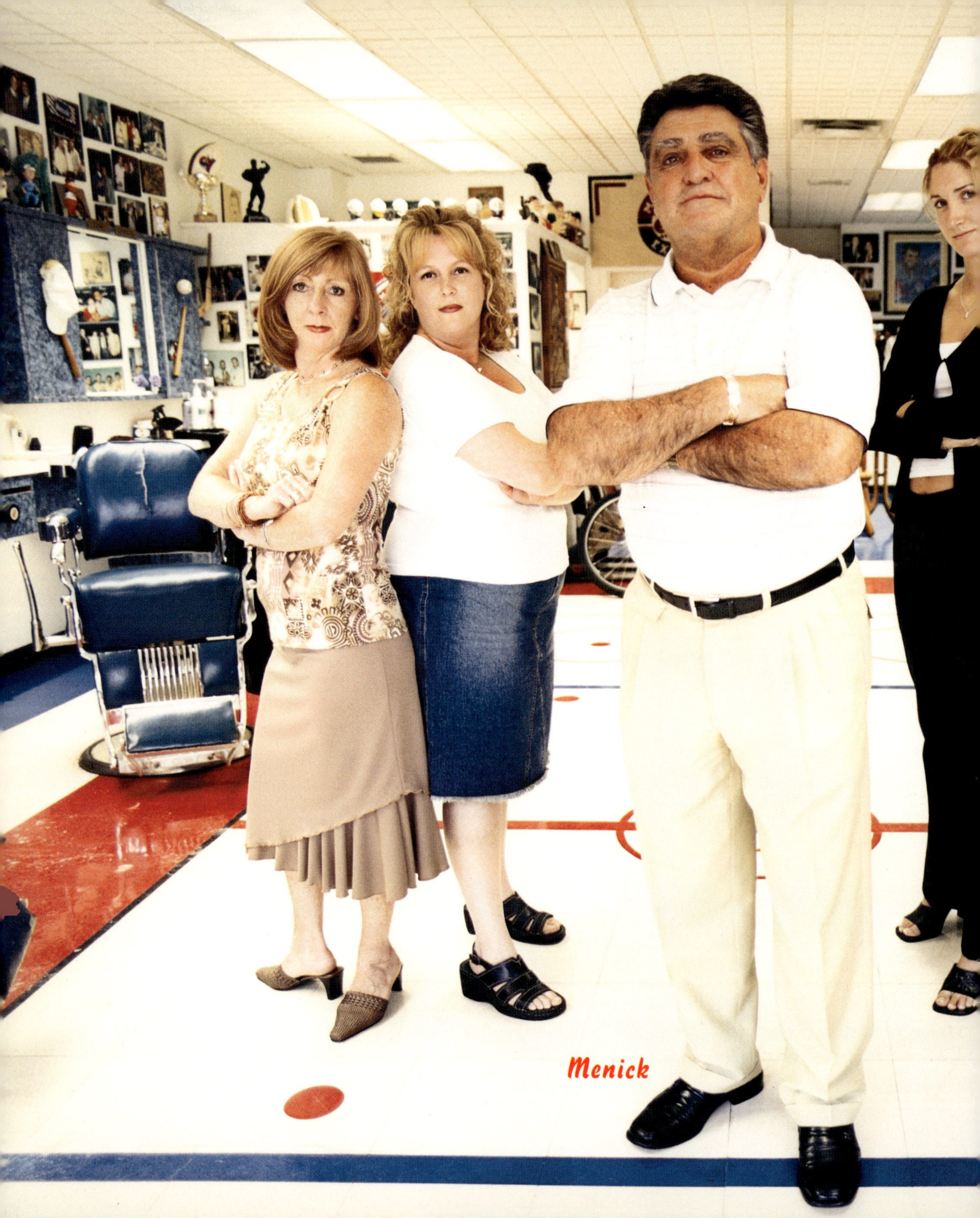
Menick

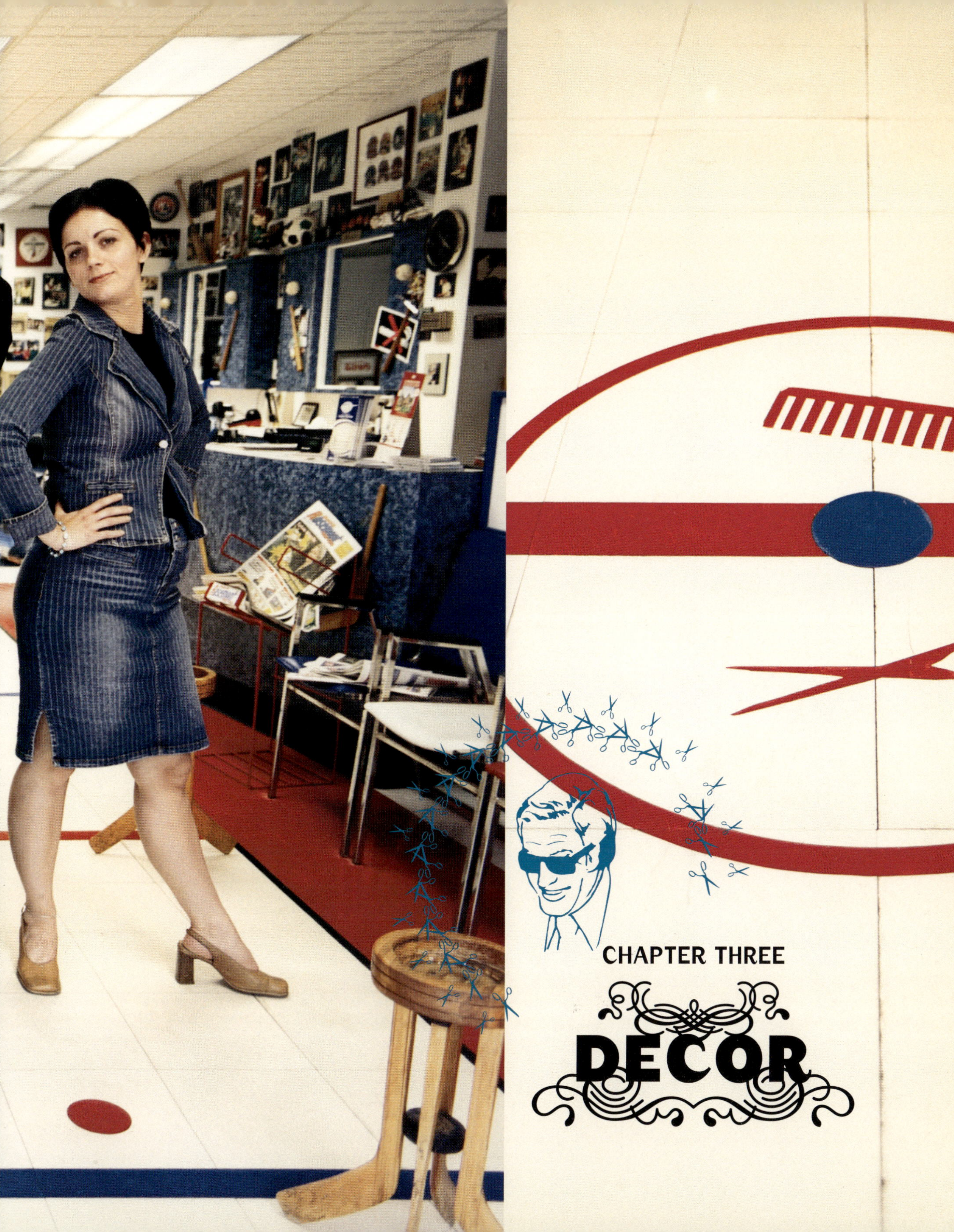

CHAPTER THREE

DECOR

"I started out with the name

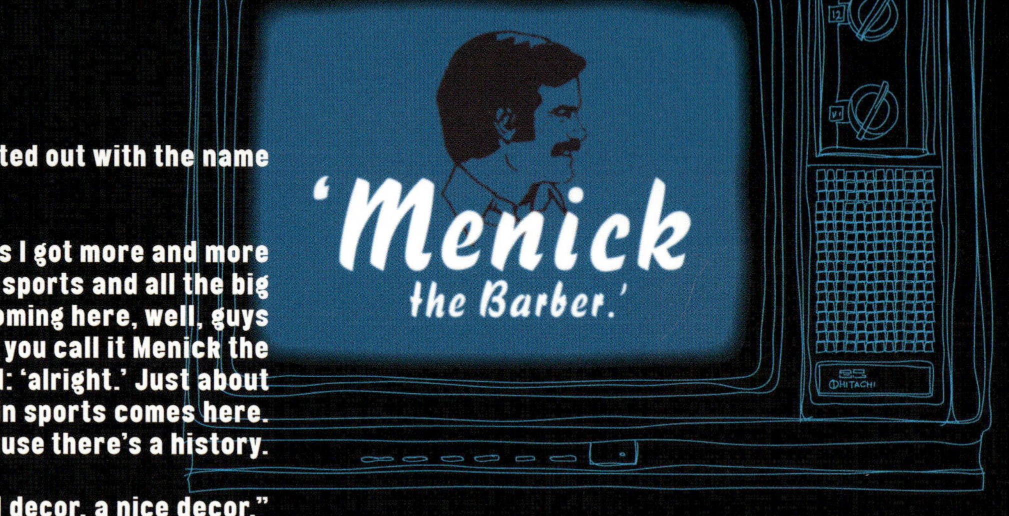

As years went by, as I got more and more involved in the world of sports and all the big names in sports started coming here, well, guys started to say: 'Why don't you call it Menick the Sports Barber?' So I said: 'alright.' Just about everything and everyone in sports comes here. Because there's a history.

And decor, a nice decor."

Menick

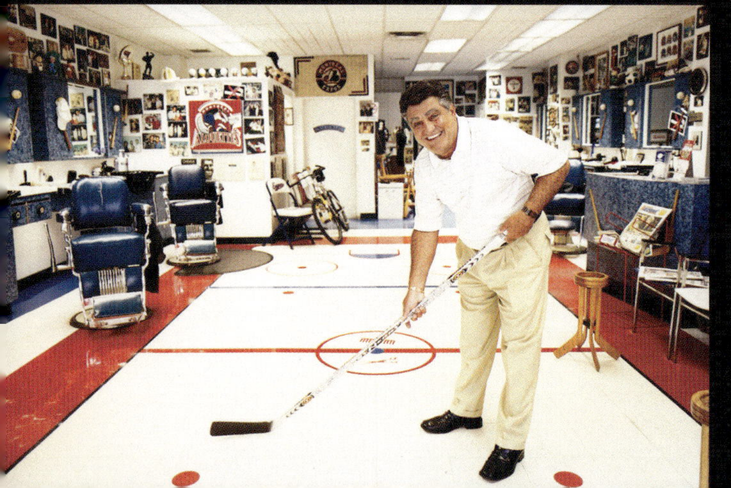

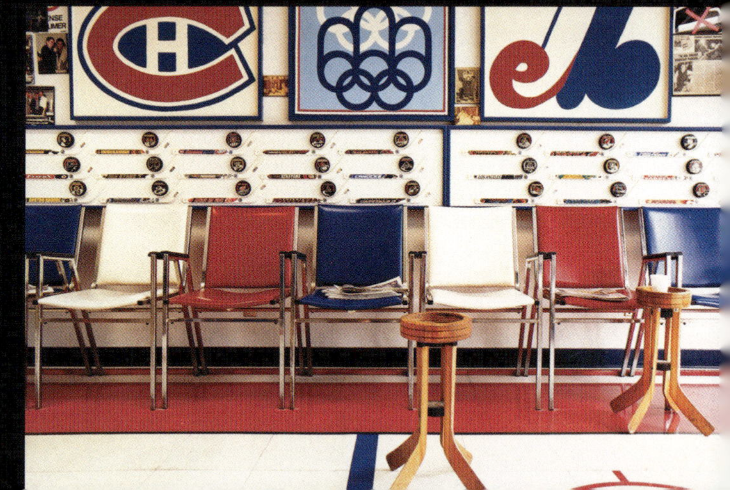

"**When I had my TV show**
we recorded six to seven shows a day in here, in the barbershop. Each show was a half-hour. I would do the interviews. The guest would arrive, sit in the barber chair and I would chat with him. There were no cuts in the filming, we continued the whole time, good, not good. We talked about this and that, alright. Then I would change shirts for my next guest so that it would look like another day. Sometimes I had time to change my pants too because I didn't do seven shows with the same pants... but let's say two shows, since they filmed mostly my top part.

The barbershop would stay open, we wouldn't close. We talked, we walked, we filmed as if nothing unusual was going on. As an interviewer, I asked the kind of questions that the guy at home could have asked. Some guys thought that I was an actor or comedian, not a barber."

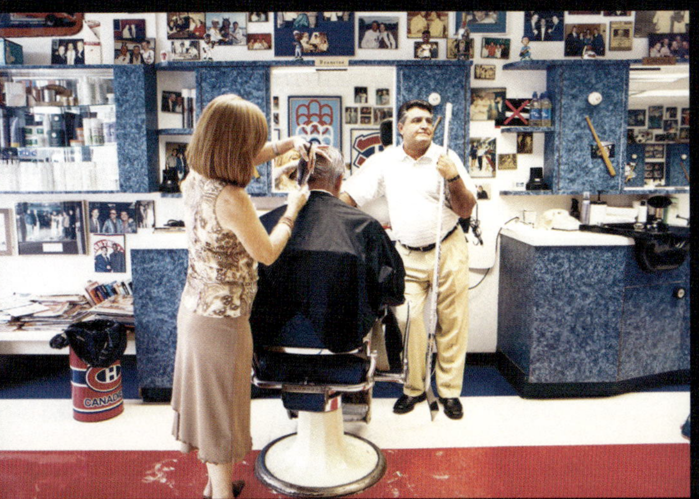

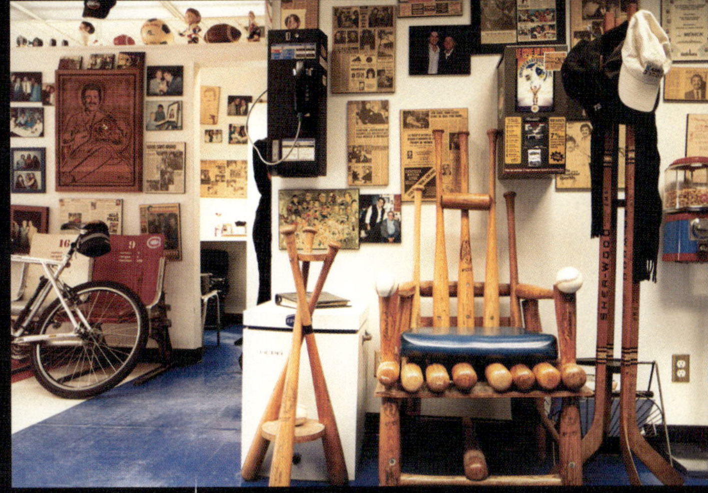

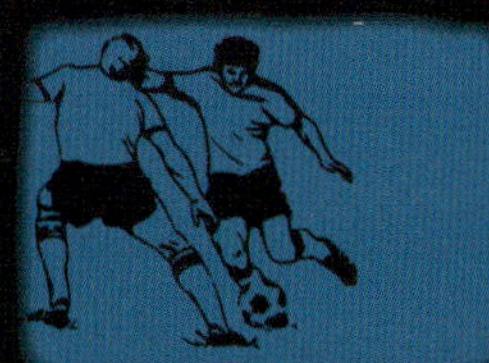

starring
Menick

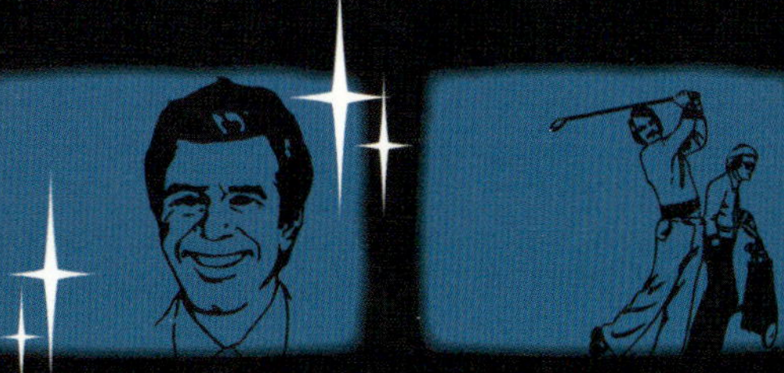

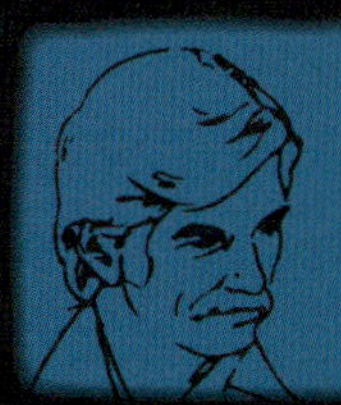

"MY BARBER POLE WAS STOLEN"

I had installed it myself up there with bolts. Long ones. At first I had put shorter bolts but then I put the longer ones and it was still stolen.

I hope the person who stole it was a barber because at least then it would be put to good use. If I were to see it somewhere I would recognise it. I had made it myself. I worked out the colours too. I took a Plexiglas cylinder and put a cover on top and on the bottom too.

Afterwards I took stickers in blue, red, and white. And voila! It sure was nice, but now it's less nice."

Jean-Guy

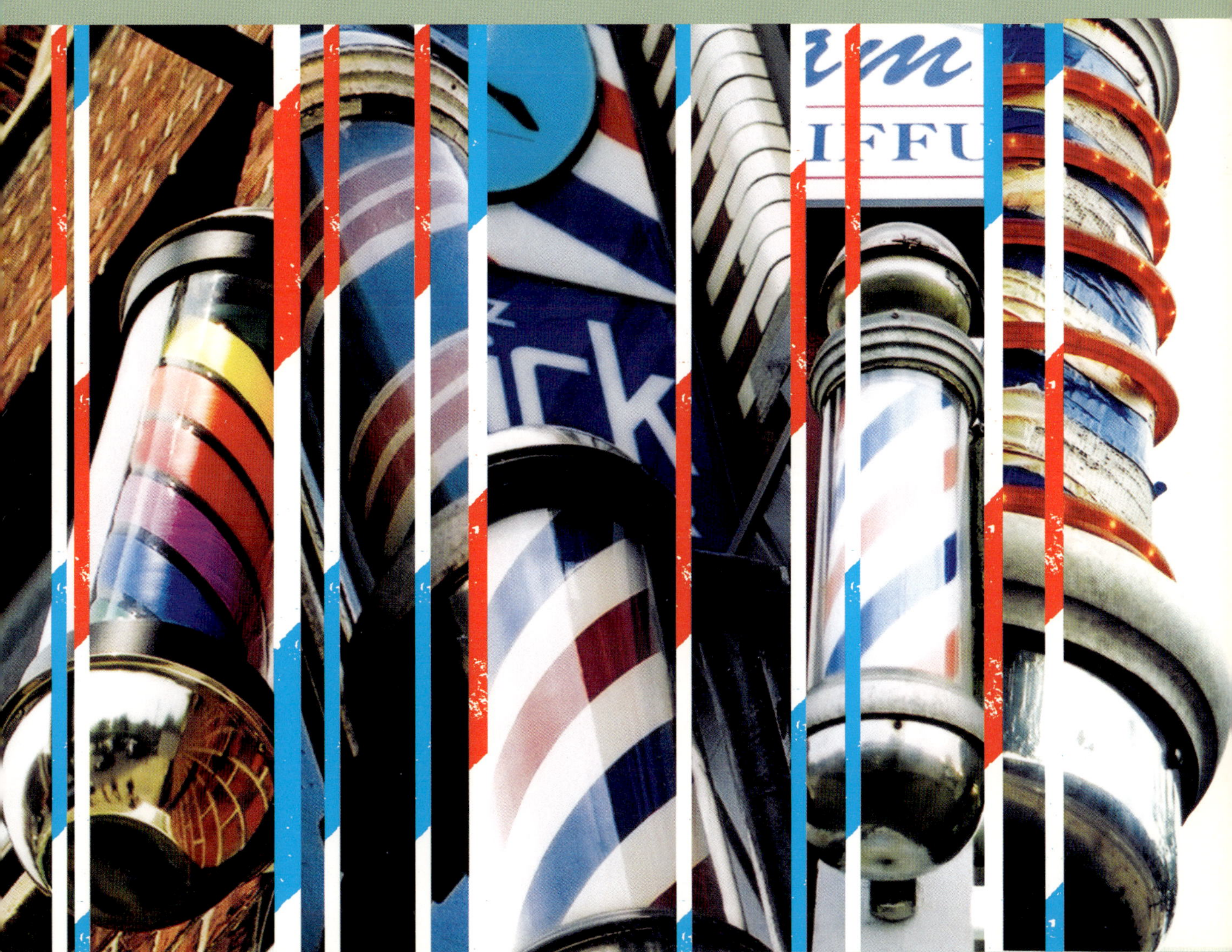

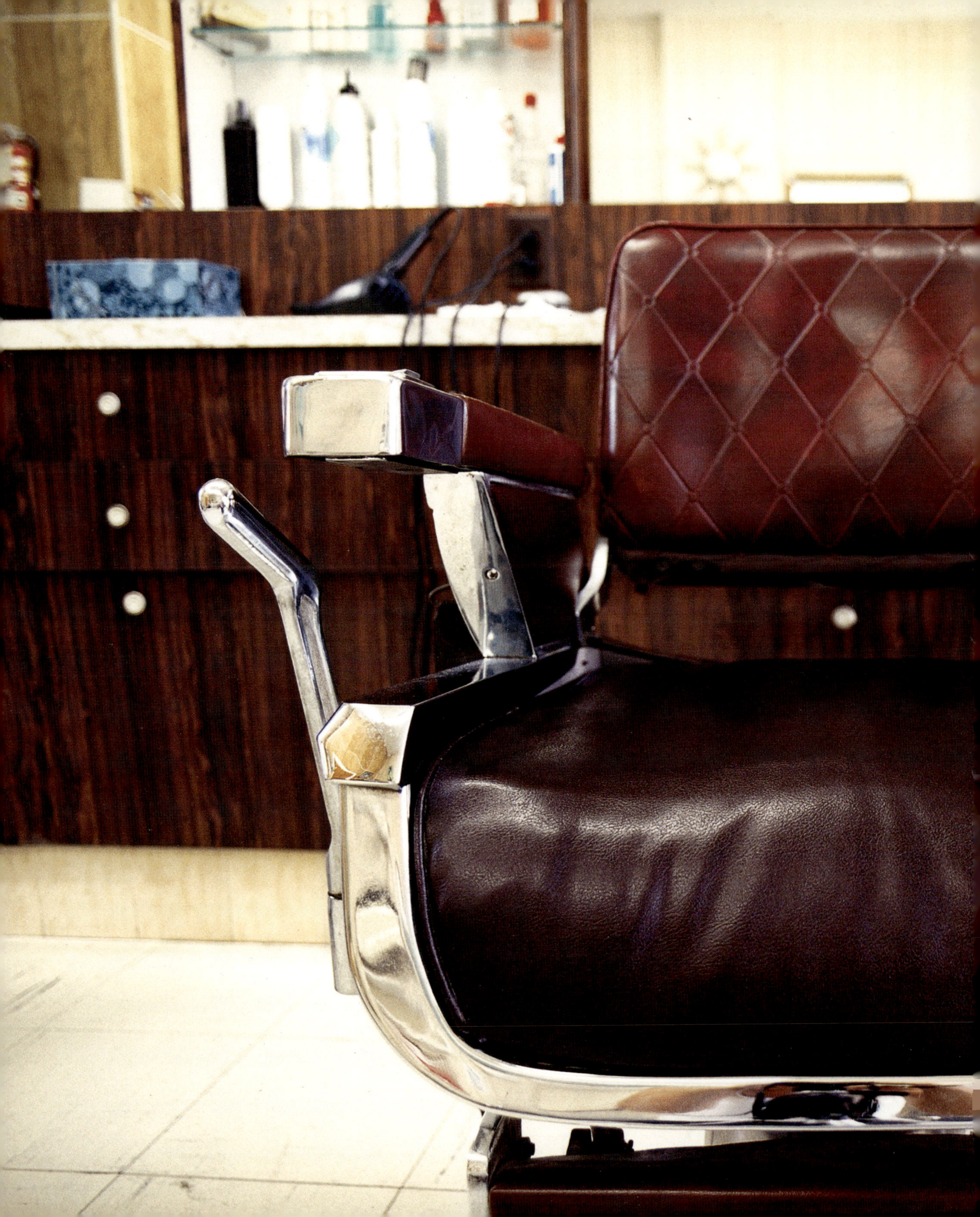

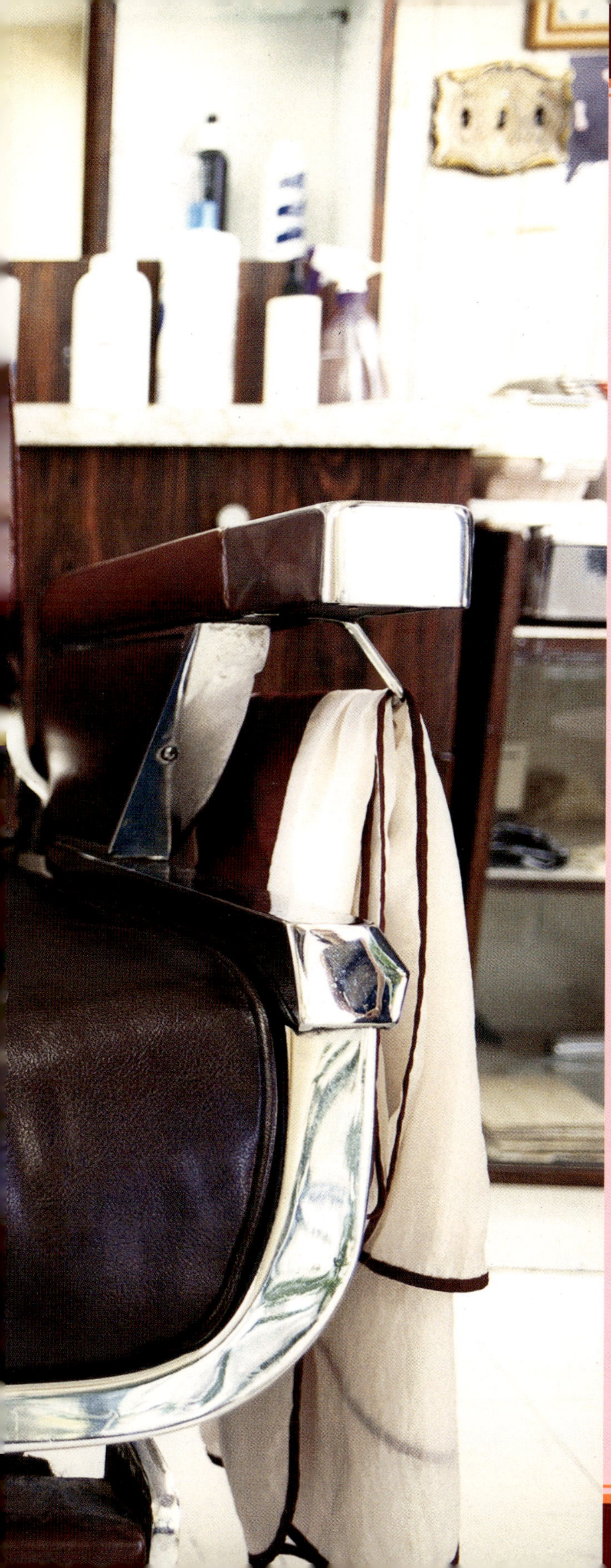

Barber:

"I've been working with these chairs for quite a few years."

Client:

"These, they have chrome in them. They don't make 'em like this anymore. It's like the cars, dammit. Cars nowadays have no chrome. They're all matte. They took away all the beauty of cars. And they charge more. Before, cars were nicer, with beautiful chrome. It was encouraging for the owners, they would upkeep them all the time. Today, nobody wants to maintain their cars... they're all matte!"

Barber:

"Let's say that they did it for the rust. Today they rust less. 'Cause they're in plastic or fiberglass."

Client:

"But that's like everything, rust. If you don't upkeep it, it will catch fast."

Barber:

"Yeah, but after five or six years it would get all stained."

Client:

"Exactly, they didn't upkeep it."

Barber:

"Let's say that even with the upkeep."

Client:

"Look at this, your chair here, there's no rust!"

Barber:

"That's different."

Client:

"It's chrome."

Barber:

"It's different chrome. There's chrome and there's chrome."

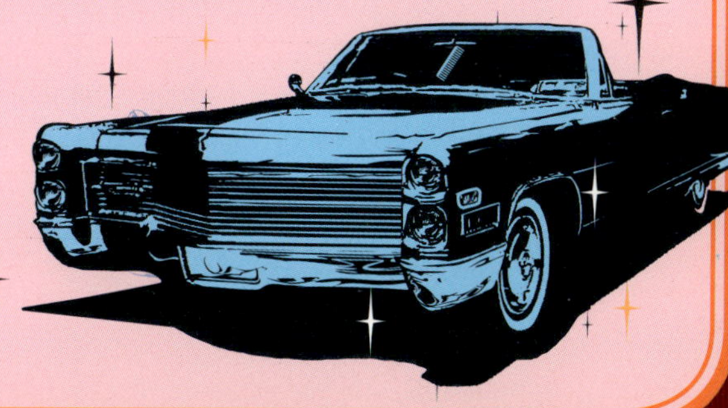

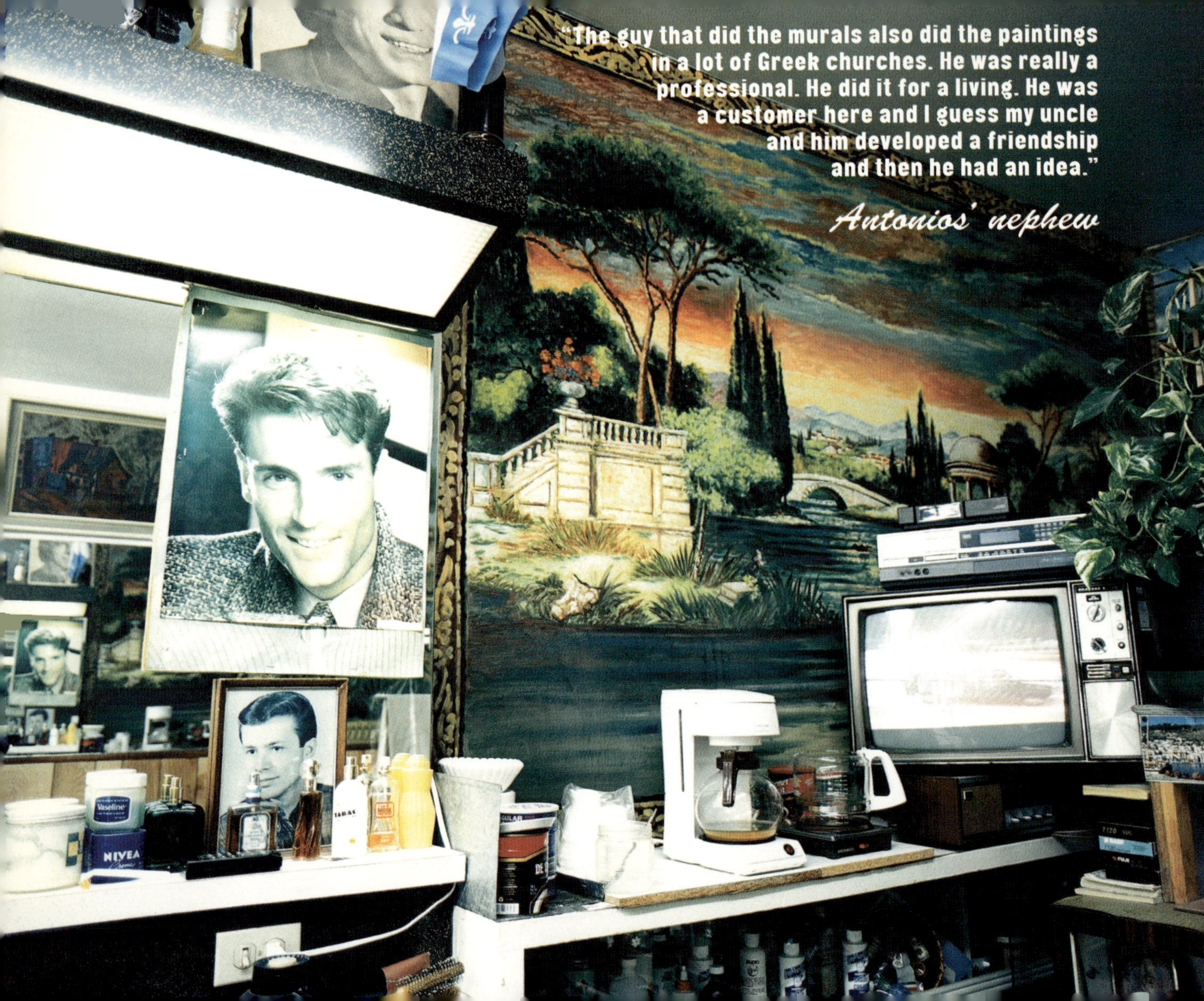

"The guy that did the murals also did the paintings in a lot of Greek churches. He was really a professional. He did it for a living. He was a customer here and I guess my uncle and him developed a friendship and then he had an idea."

Antonios' nephew

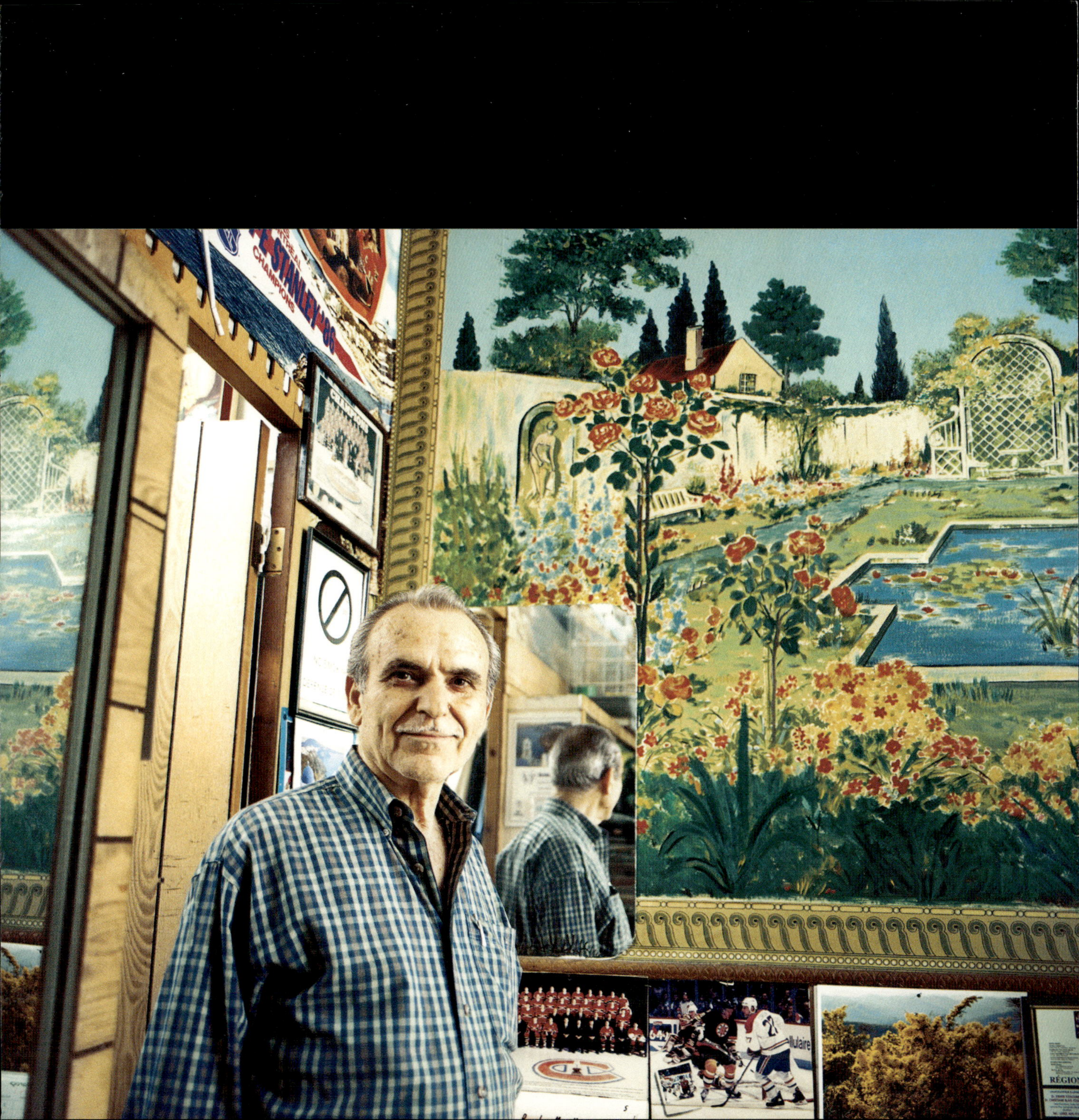
STANLEY '86
CHAMPIONS

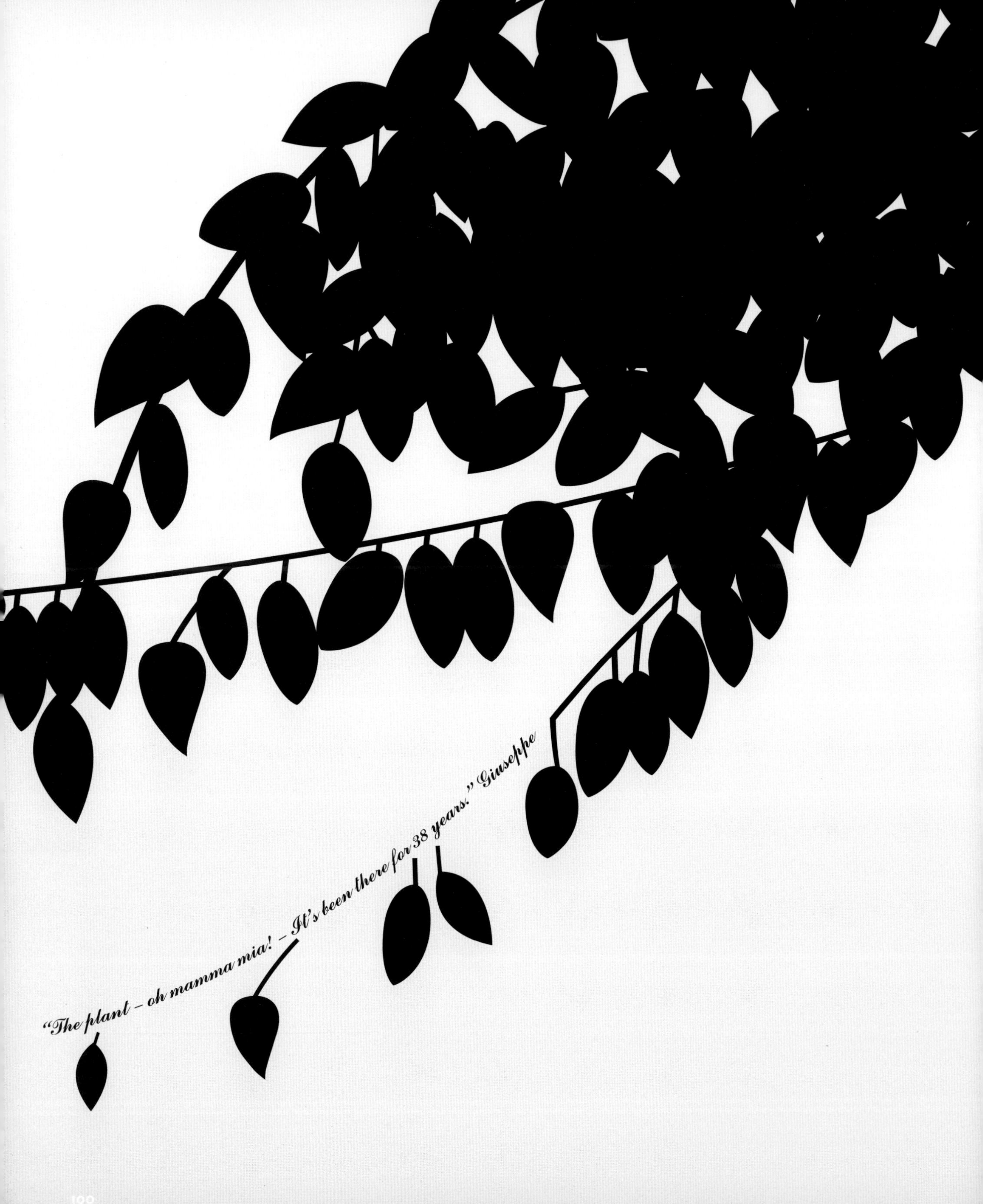
"The plant – oh mamma mia! – It's been there for 38 years." Giuseppe

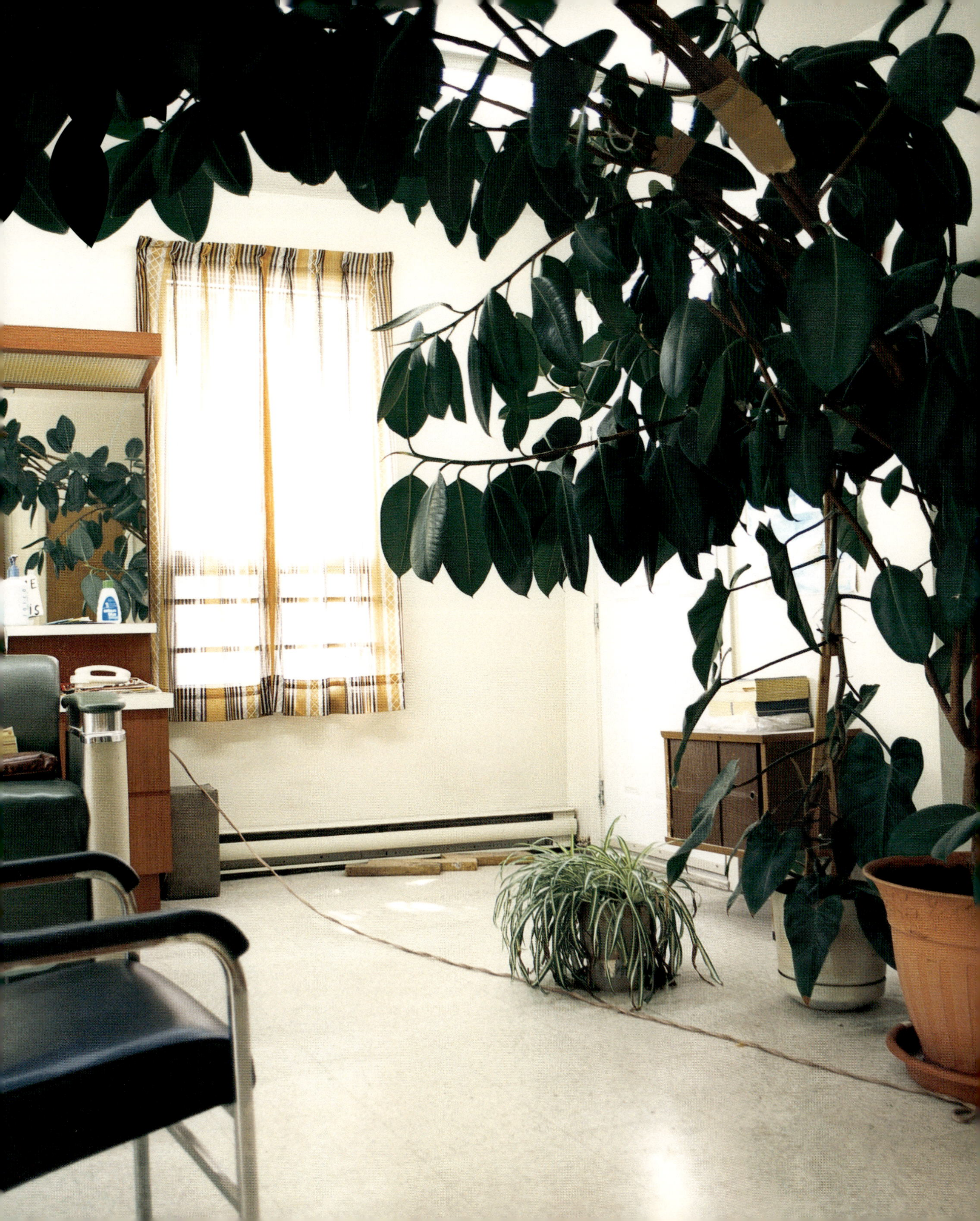

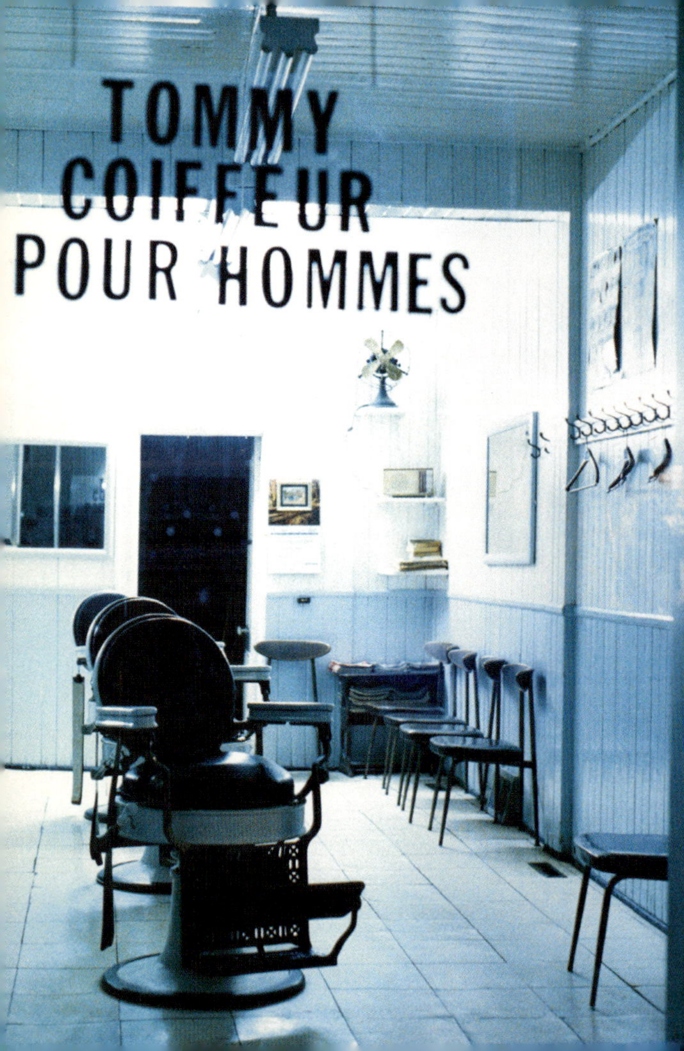

TOMMY
COIFFEUR
POUR HOMMES

"In 1967 I worked at a salon called The Monk's Tonsure. There were six barbers, all dressed up like monks. In the salon there were these big wood barrels. It was fun. I lasted two years there, then I bought my first Salon Bob. After that it was always Salon Bob.

Now I'm closing up shop. I wasn't supposed to close this year, it was supposed to be next year. I asked my son if he wanted to be a barber but he didn't want to. He's left-handed.

"When I arrived here with my one barber chair there was tons of room! So I bought some shelves... I put shelves everywhere. I sold stuff, antiques. If it hadn't been for the antiques, if I had just been a barber, I don't think I would have lasted."

Bob

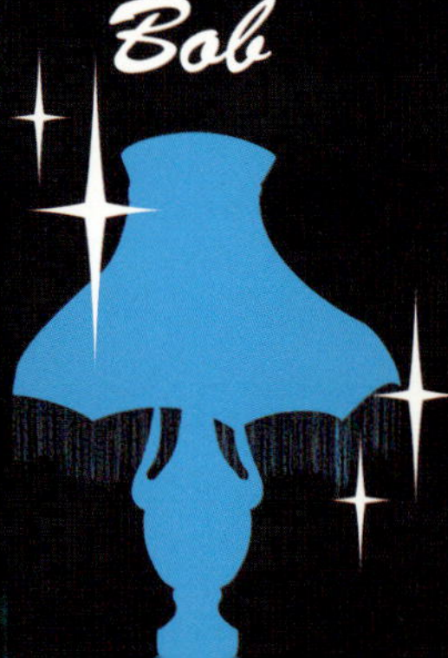

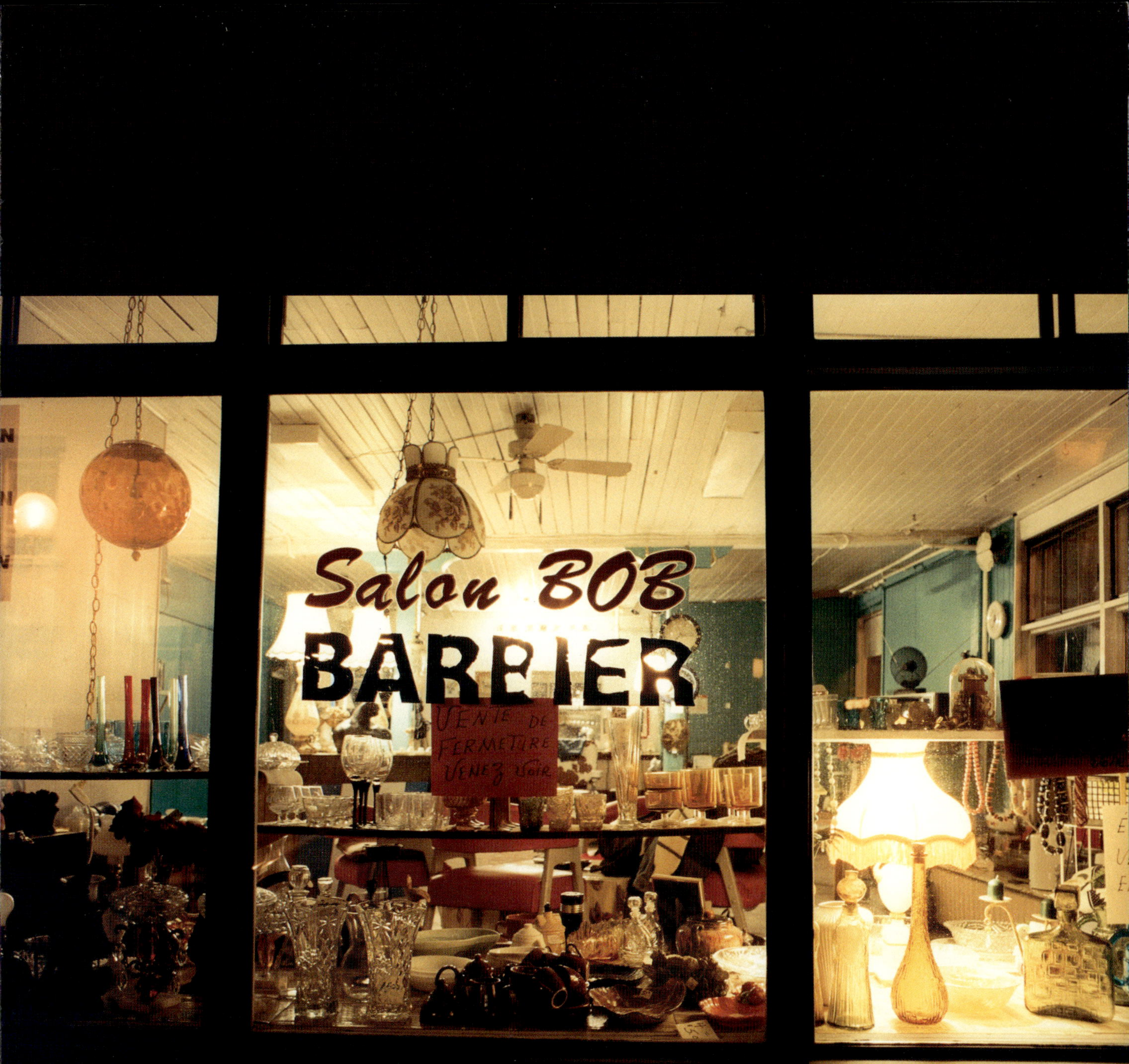

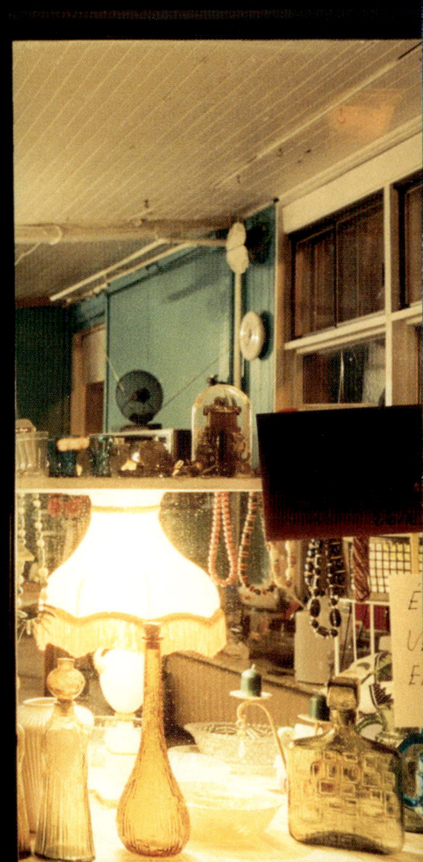
Salon BOB
BARBIER
VENTE DE
FERMETURE
VENEZ VOIR

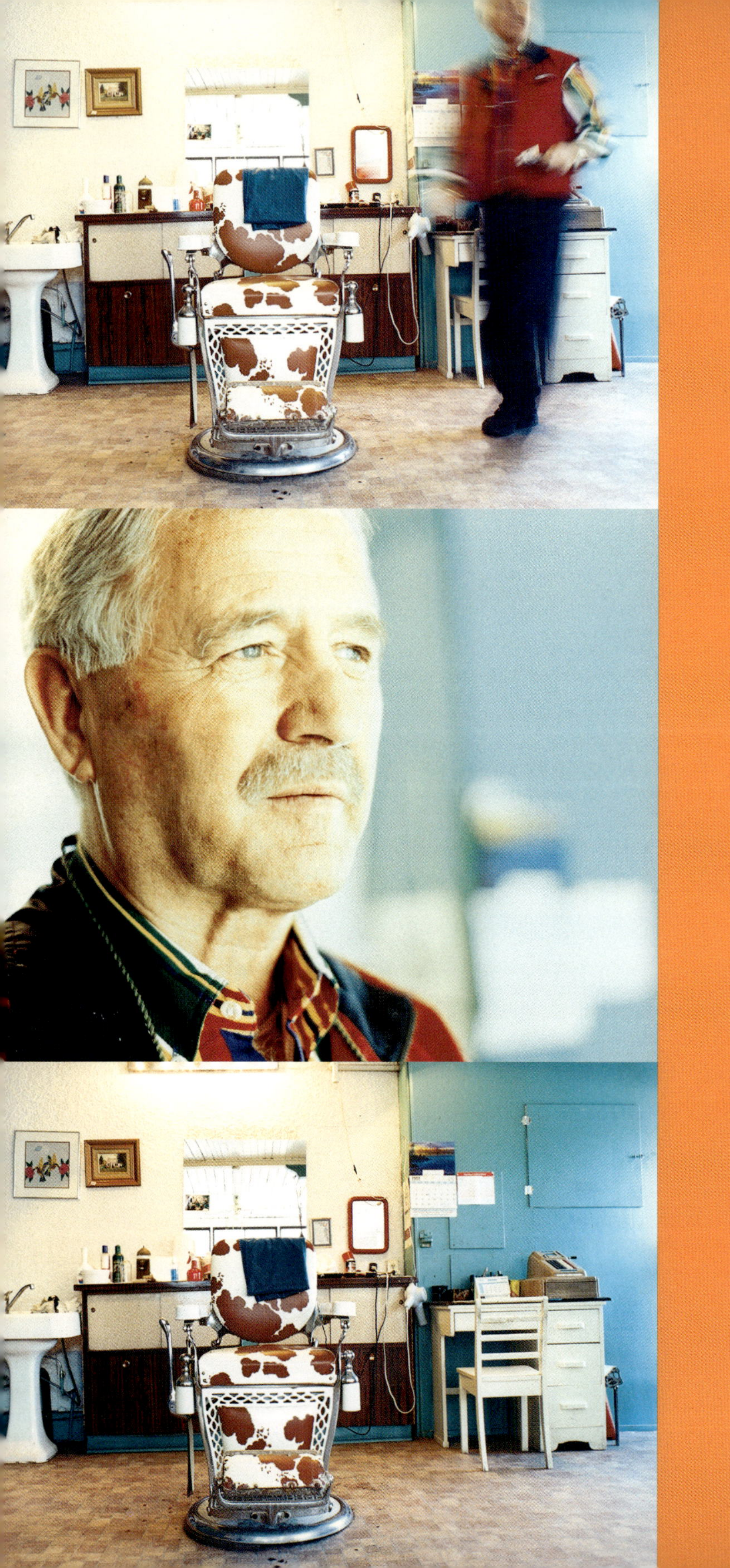

"The chair was orange before.
It didn't always have cowhide like that.
The cowhide is recent. It must be about two years old. One of my friends who works in leather came and did it for me.

Now it's sold,
it's going to a photo studio."

Bob

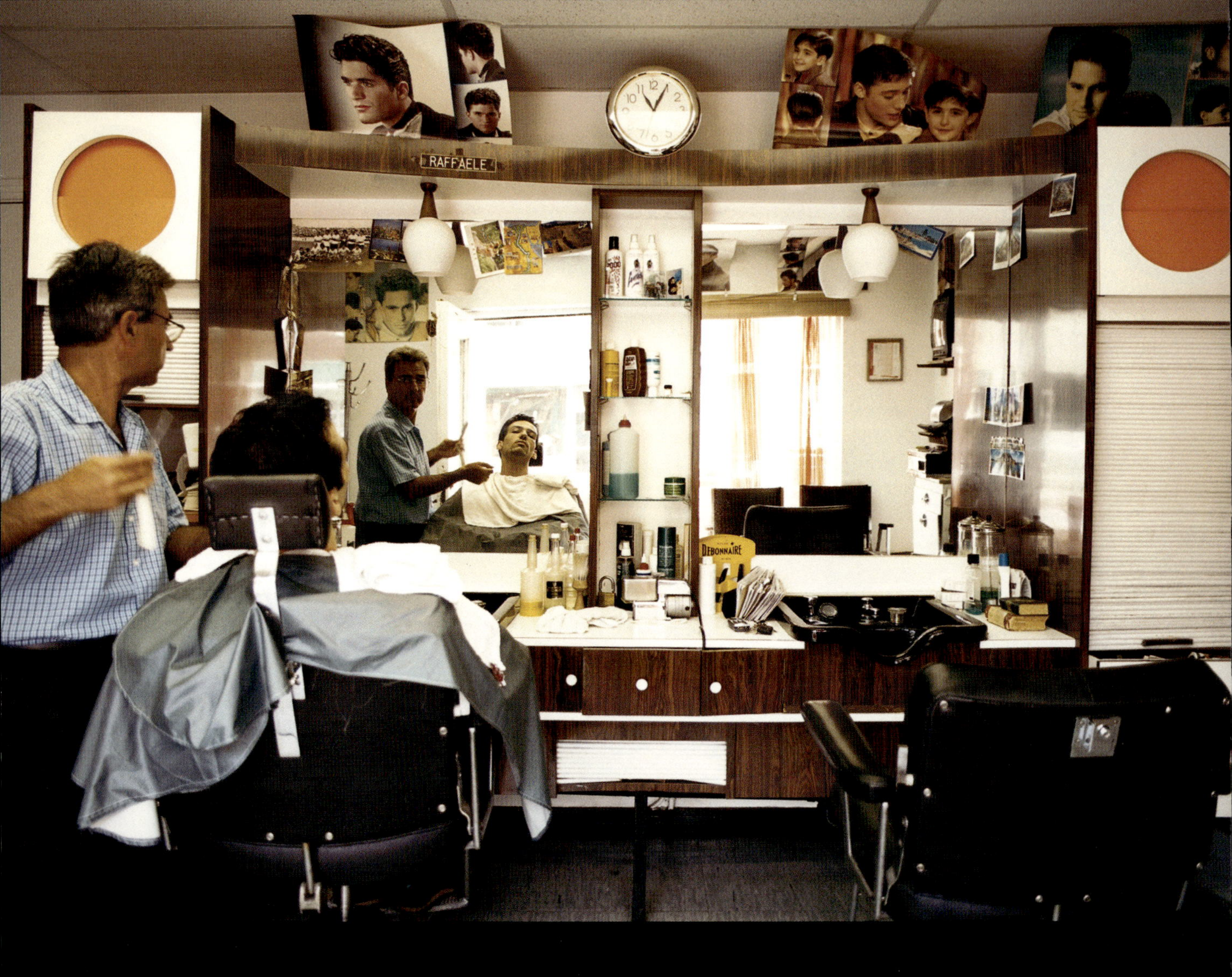
RAFFAELE
DEBONNAIRE

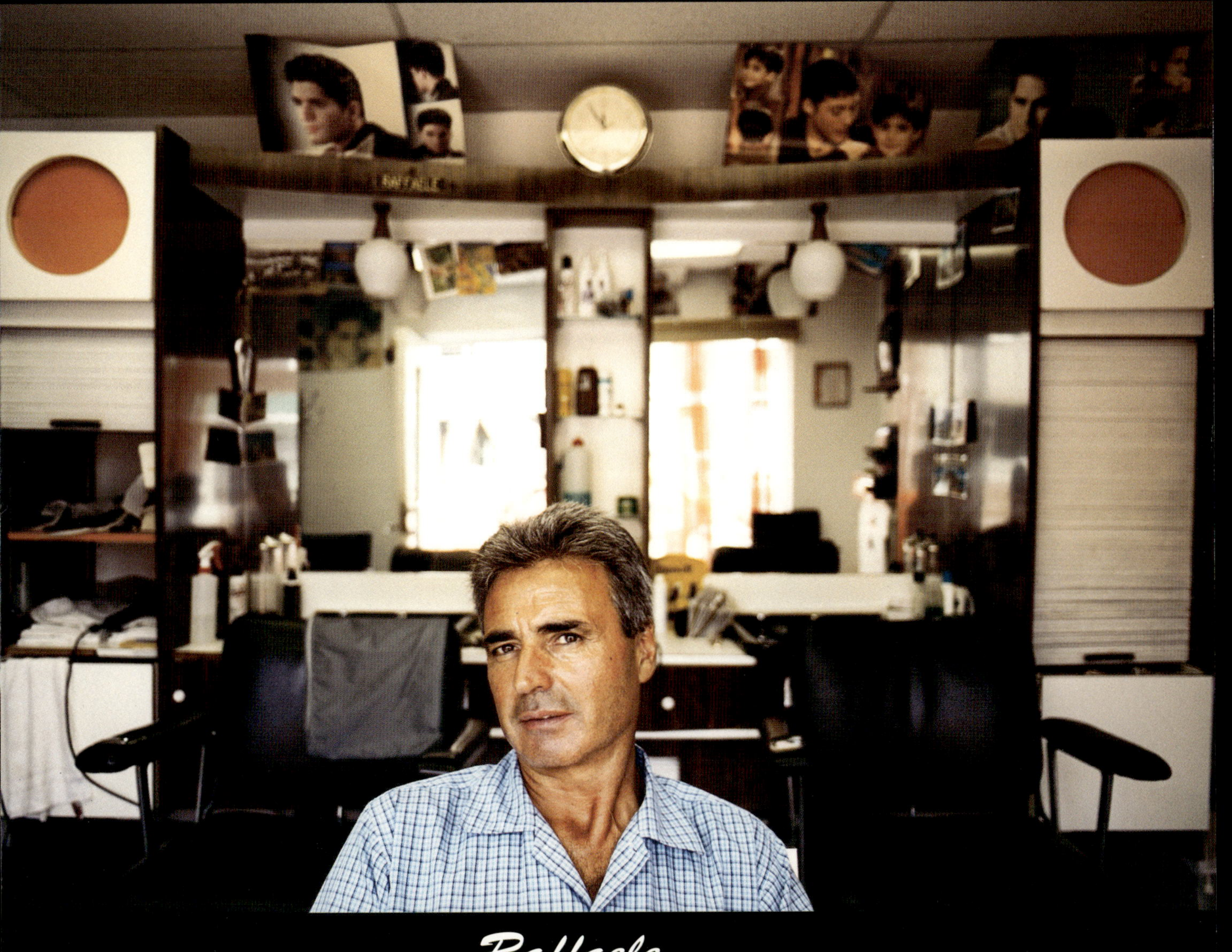

Raffaele

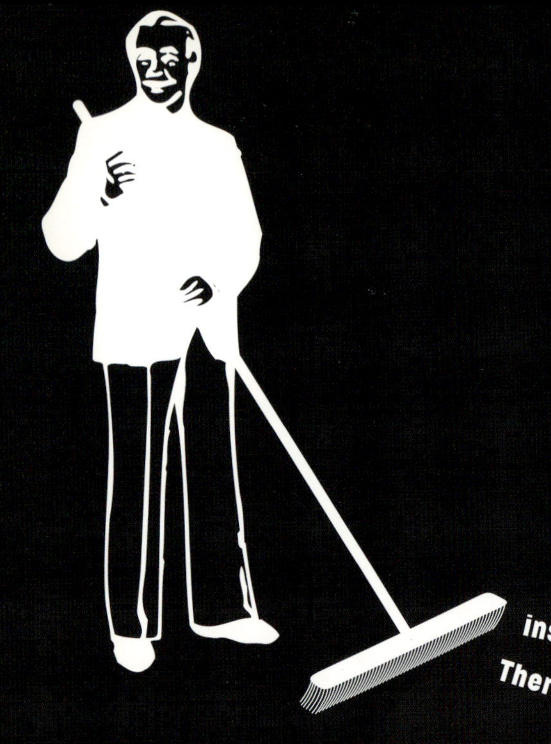

"I made a hole in the floor for us to sweep the hair into, instead of bending down every time to pick it up with the dustpan. There's a garbage bin underneath the floor attached to the ceiling in the basement. This shop isn't huge, try putting a garbage can in too! So by making holes like this – one for hair, one for empty soda cans, one for used towels – I made the place bigger."

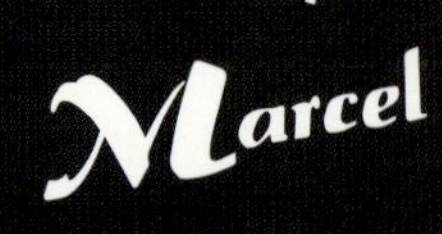

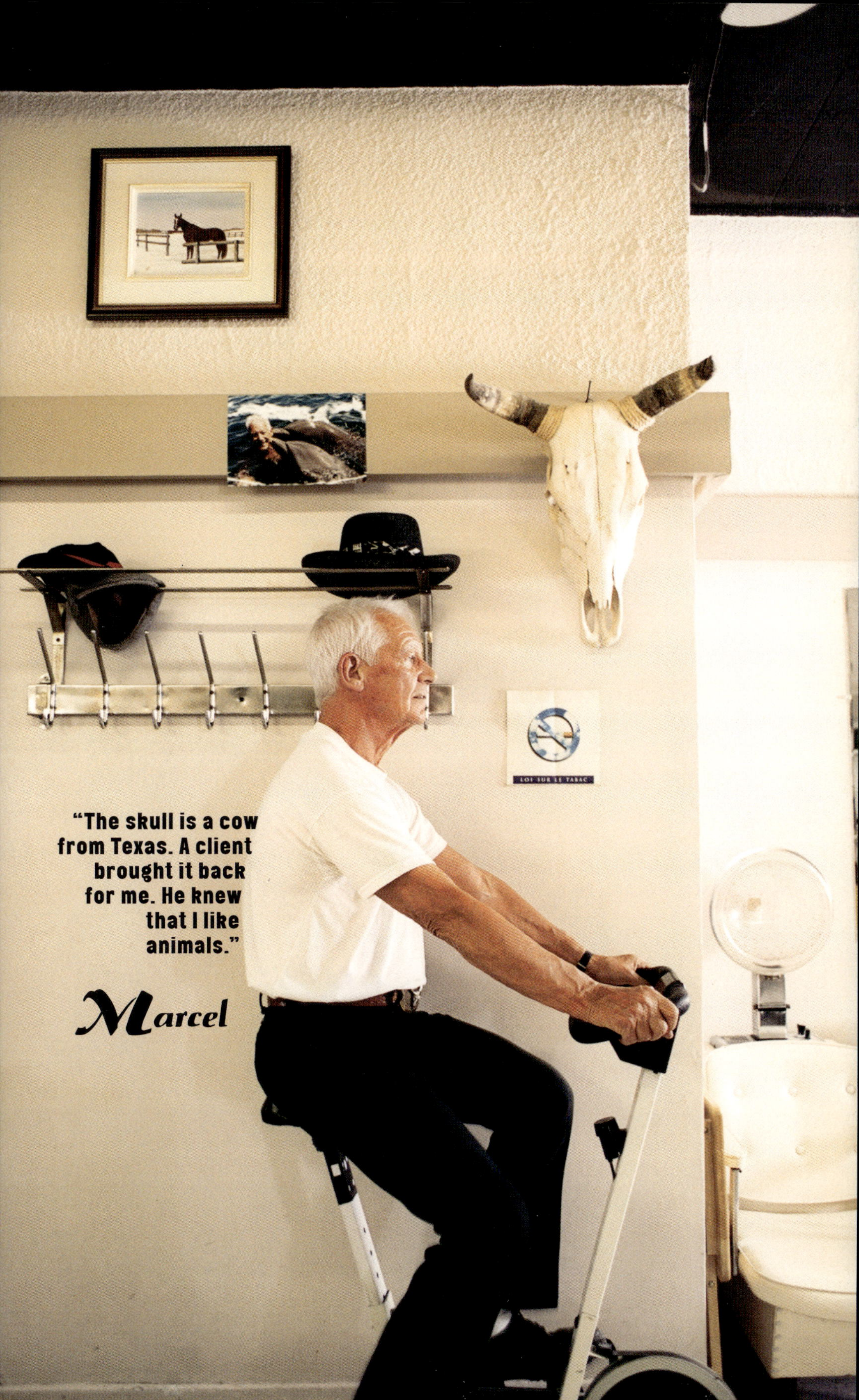

"The skull is a cow from Texas. A client brought it back for me. He knew that I like animals."

Marcel

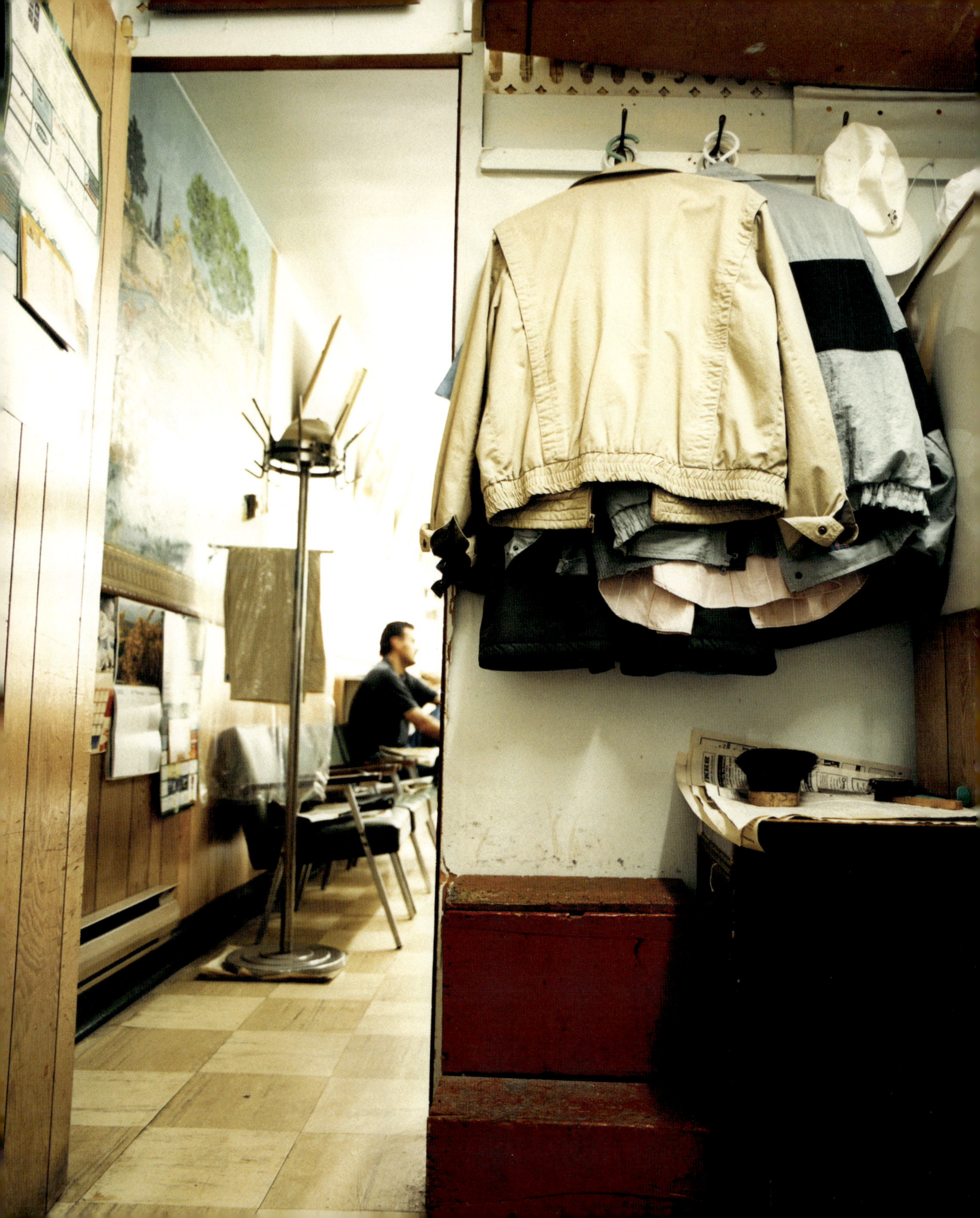

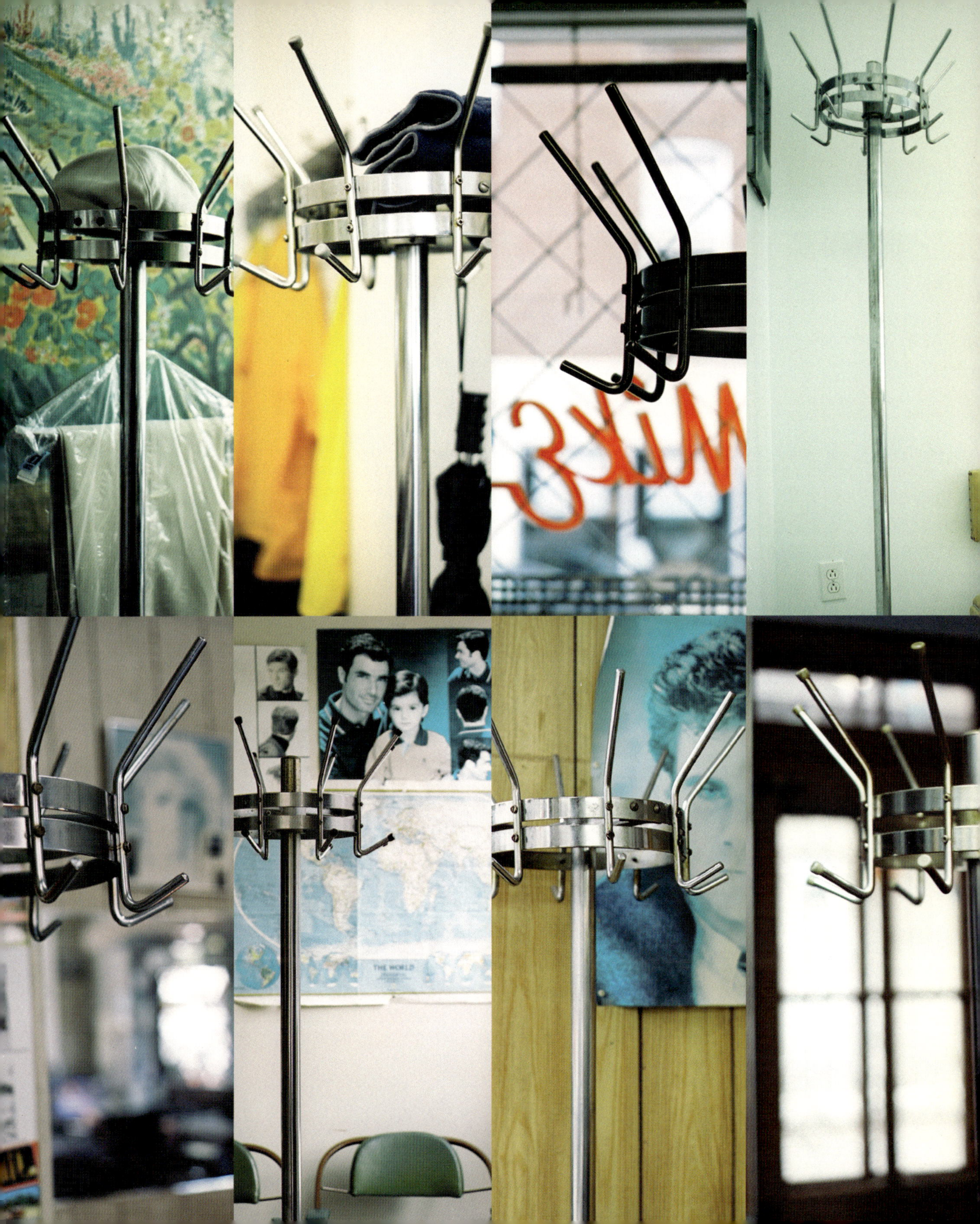
THE WORLD

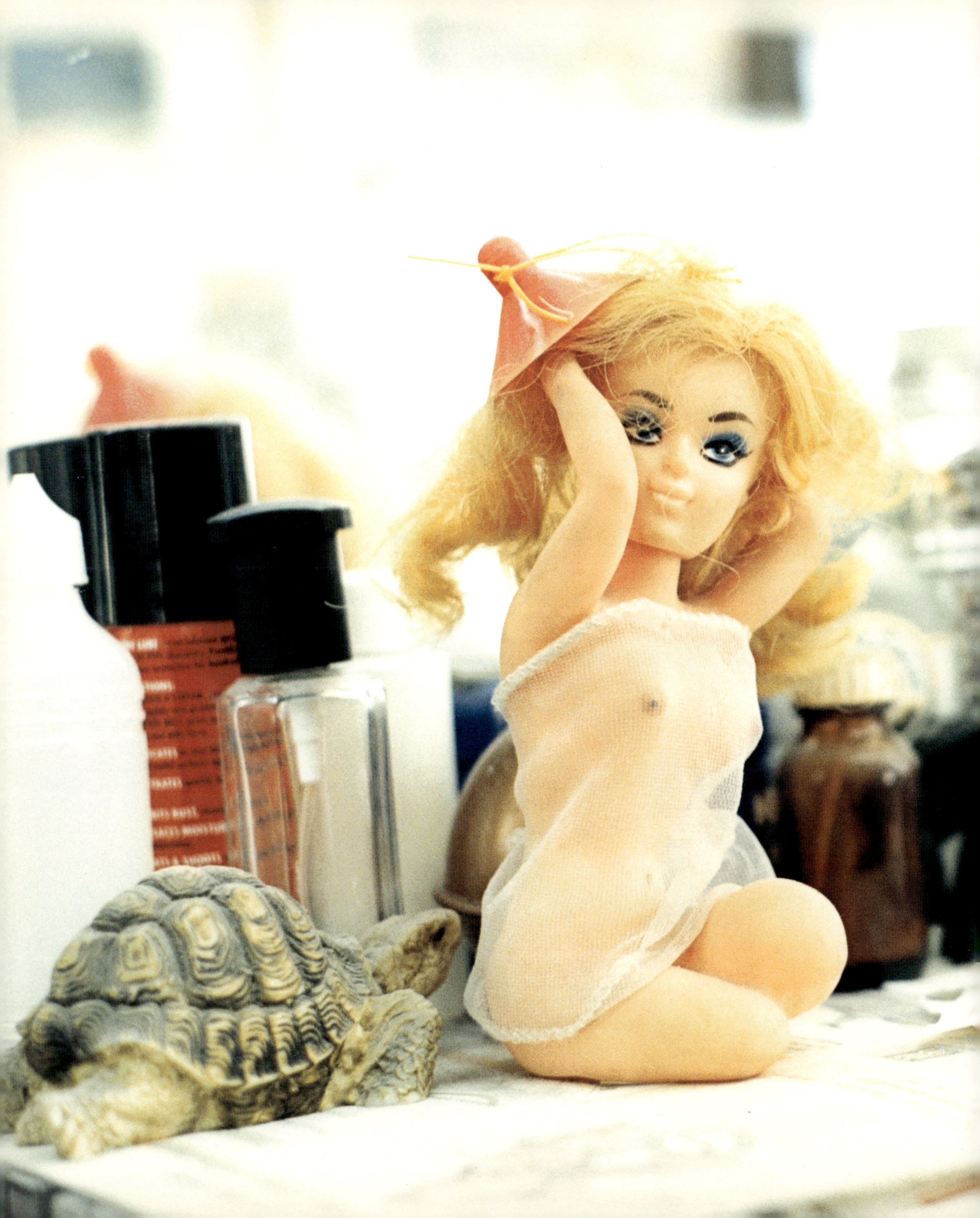

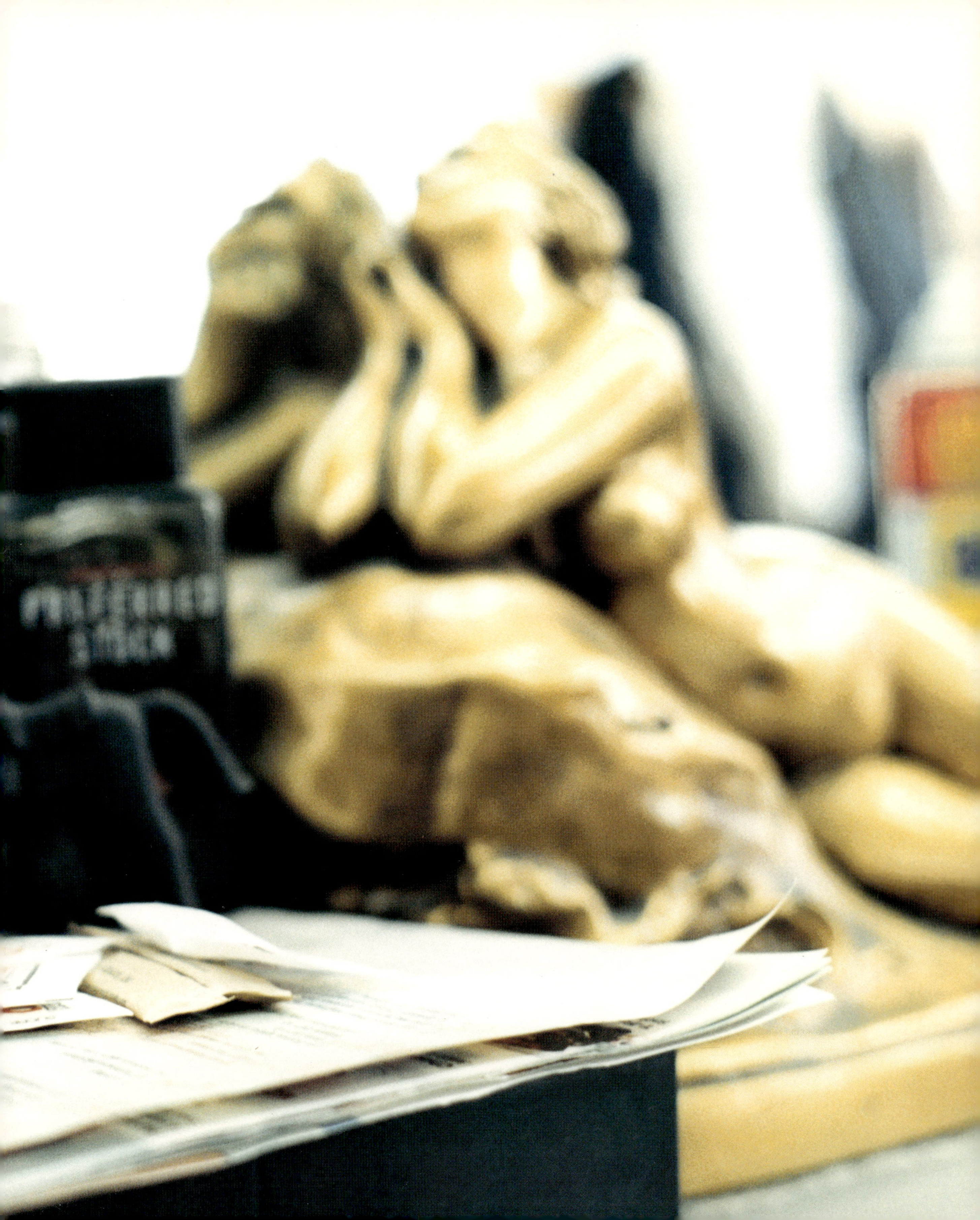

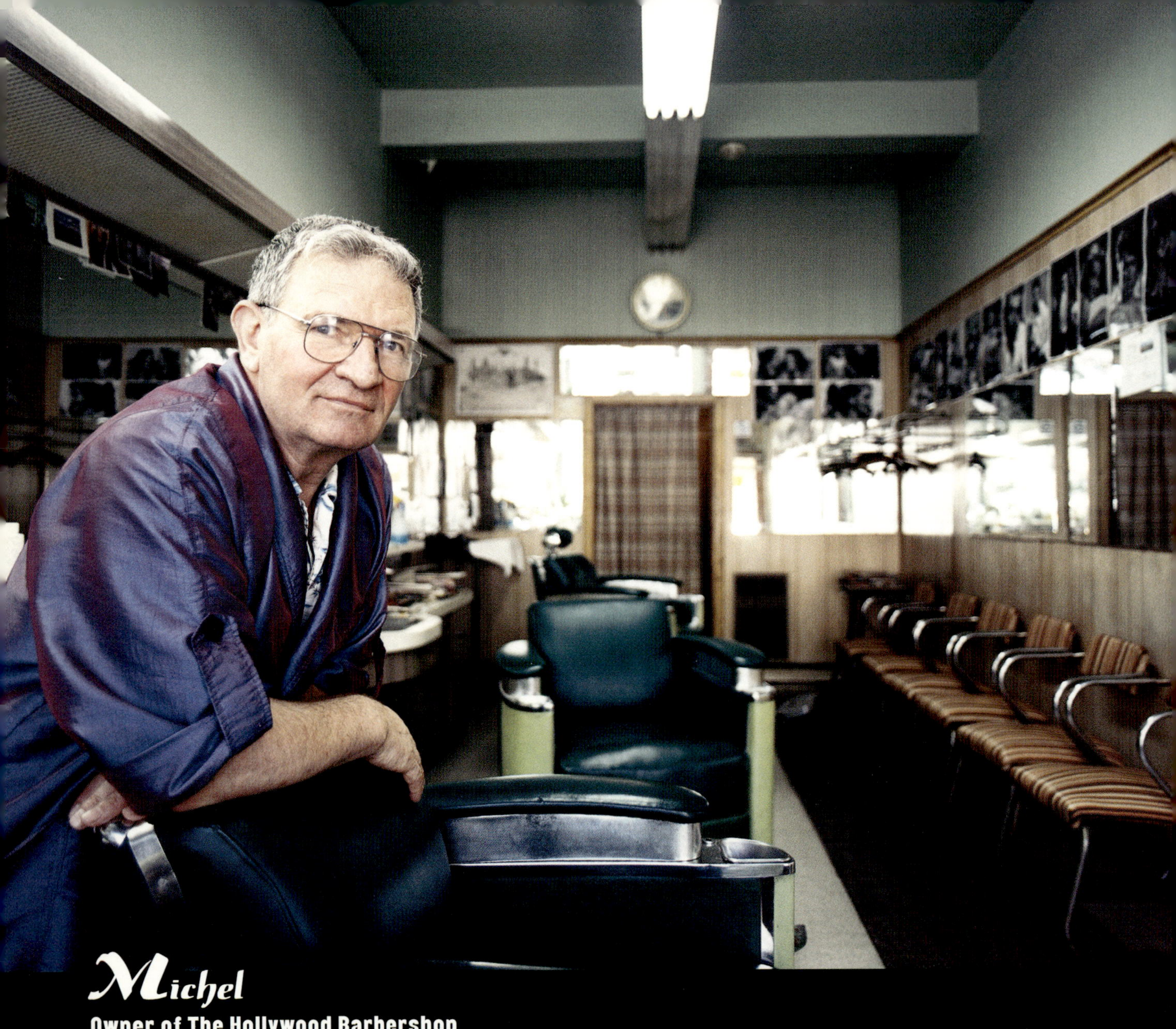

Michel

Owner of The Hollywood Barbershop
Knows the secret to grilling the perfect steak

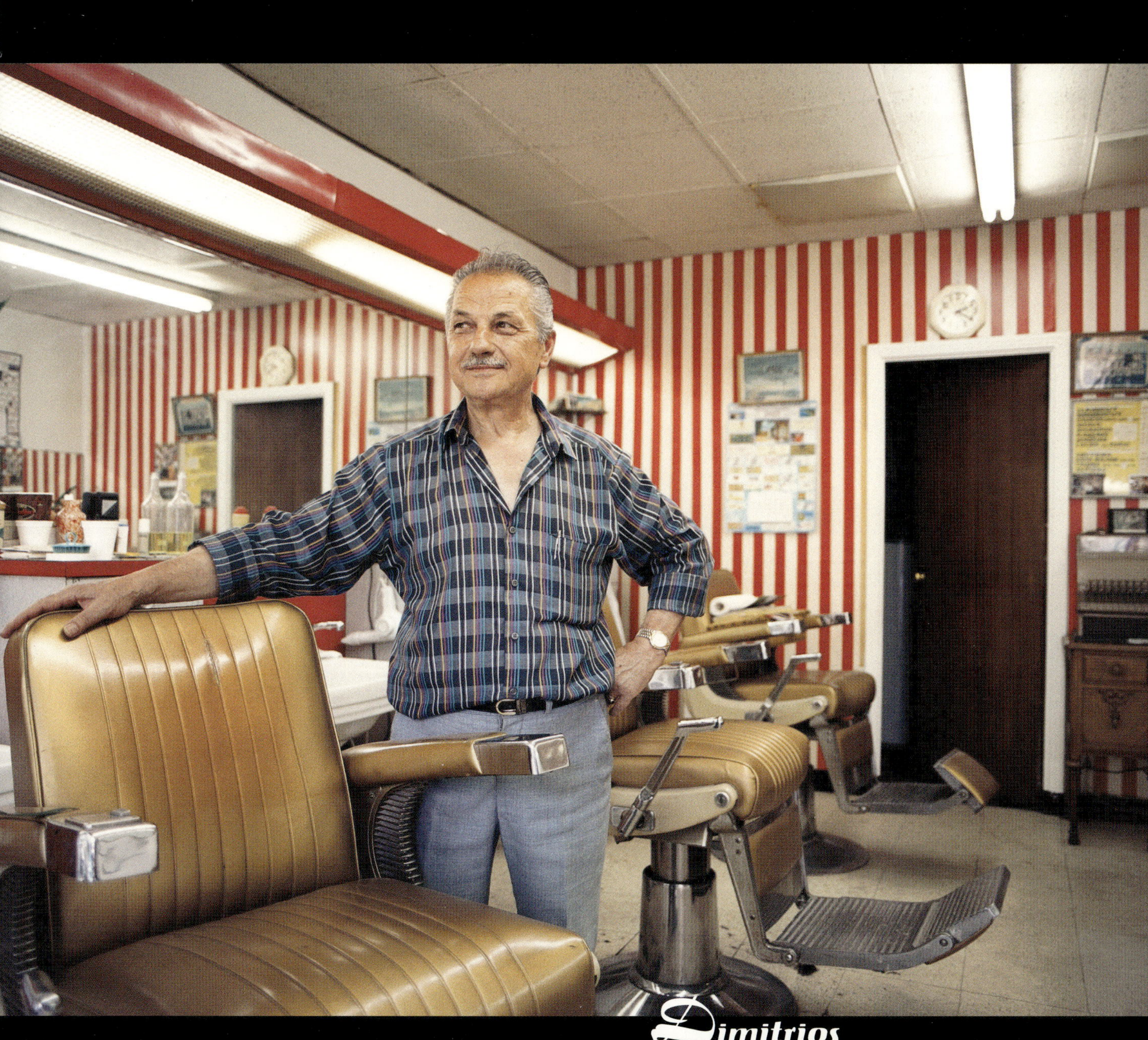

Dimitrios

Owner of Salon Athenes
Painted his barbershop with the stripes of his old soccer team from Greece

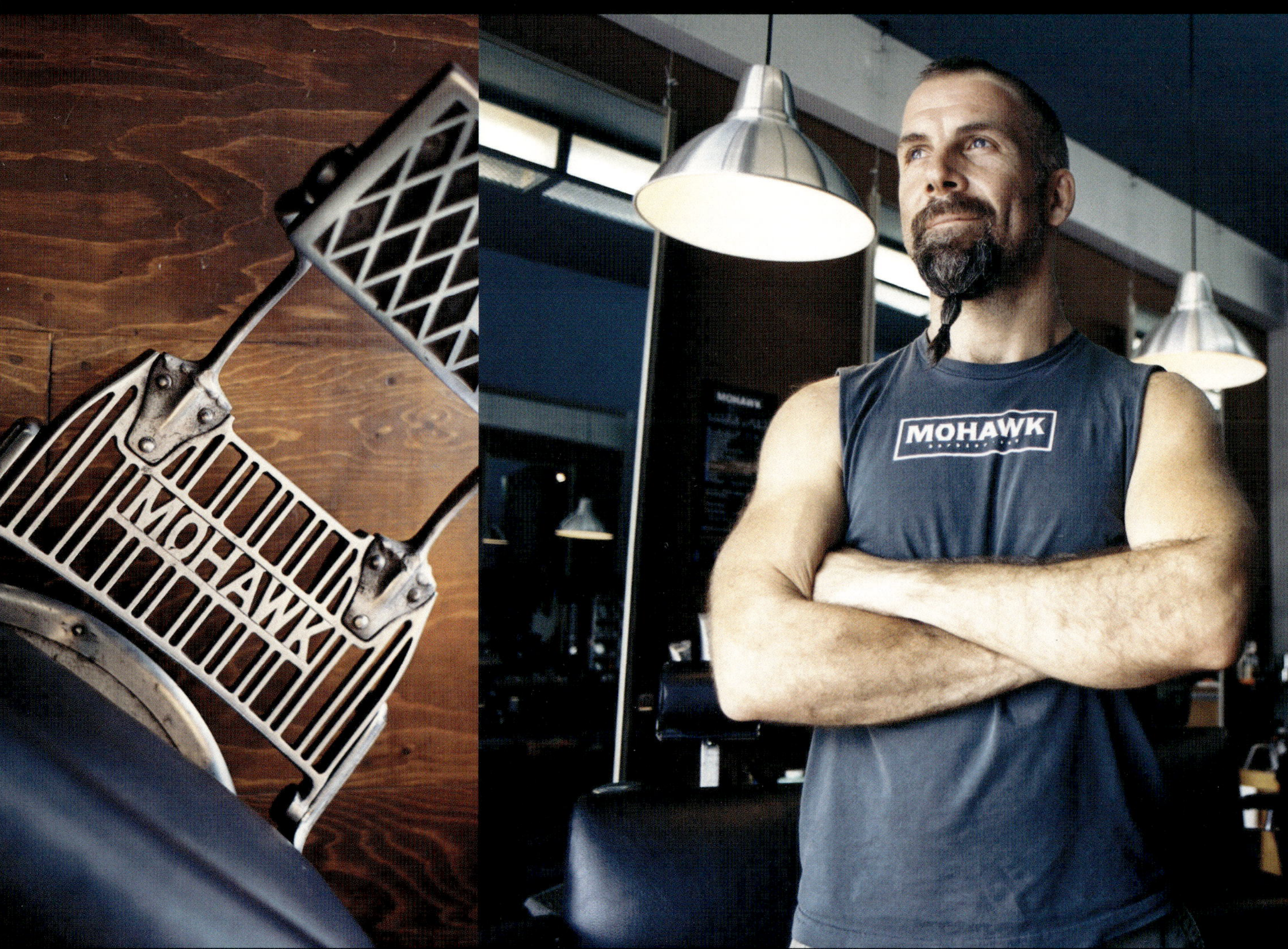

"When I was repairing my chairs I came up with the name for the barbershop. The brand of the chairs was Mohawk, it was a line of barber products in the 1950s and 1960s. The name was on the footstool part and I said: 'Oh my gosh! That's the name!' And what's more, I have a Mohawk. For sure the name makes it a bit 'underground'. If it was 'Angel Hair' the clientele would be different."

Jean-Marc

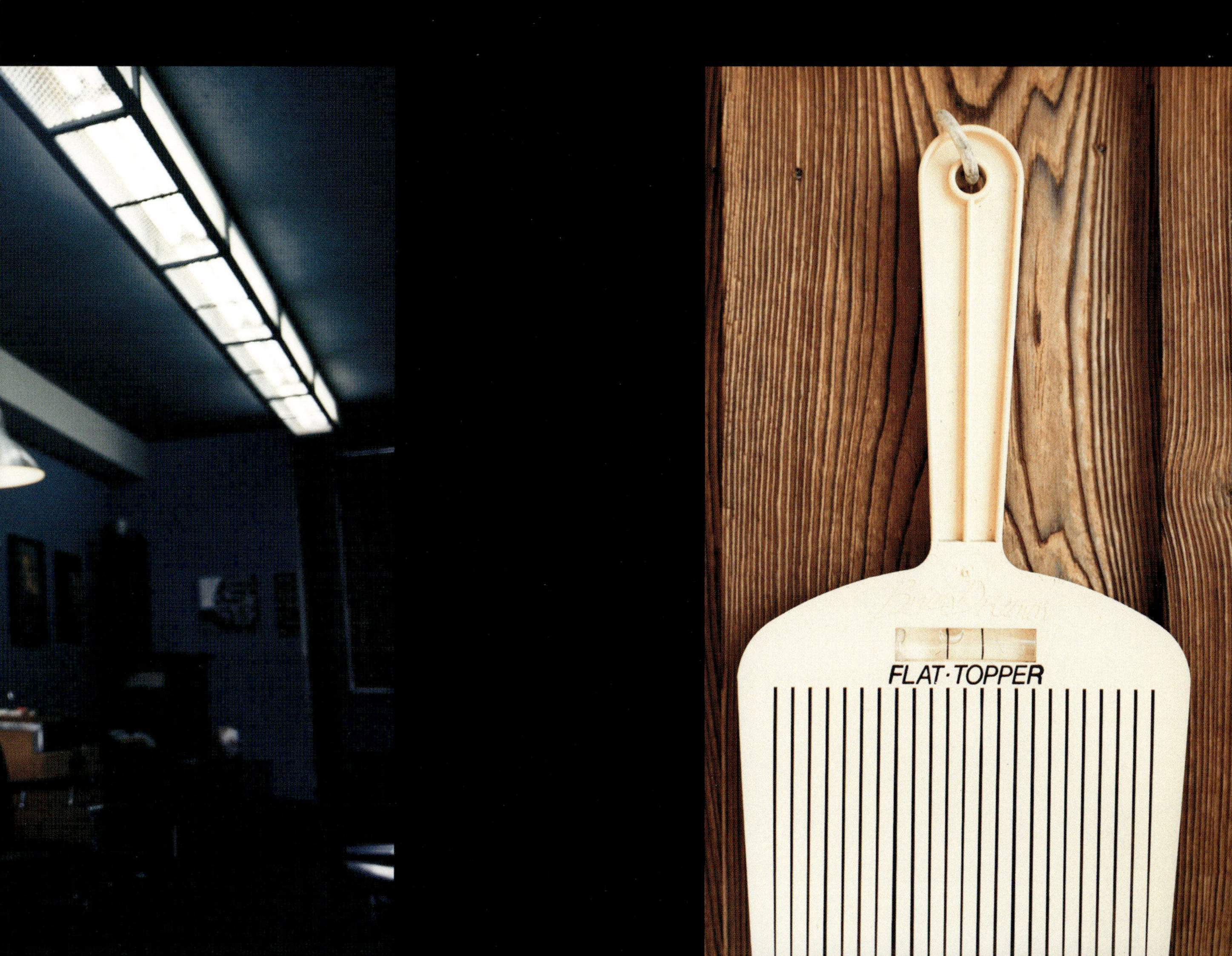
FLAT·TOPPER

THE BOXER JOE FRAZIER

CAME HERE ONCE TO GET HIS HAIR CUT.

★ AT THE TIME I HAD PICTURES UP OF ★

MOHAMMED ALI *and* JOE FRAZIER

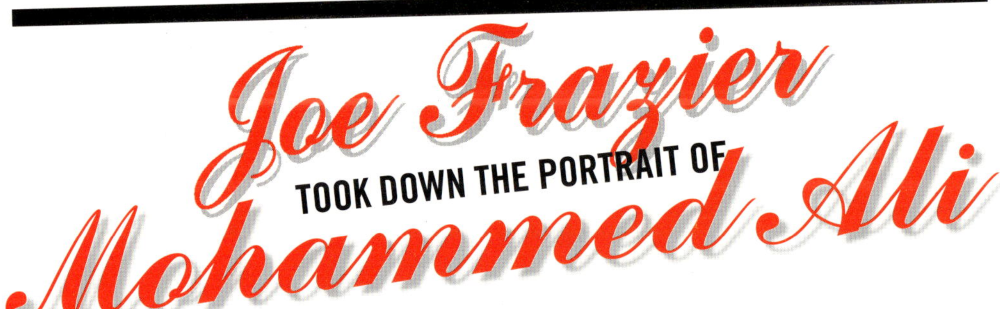

★ AND SAID: I'M THE CHAMPION ★

OF THE WORLD!

AND THEN I CUT HIS HAIR. NOW HIS PHOTO IS IN THE BATHROOM DOWNSTAIRS.

I DON'T KNOW WHERE THE PICTURE OF MOHAMMED ALI IS NOW.

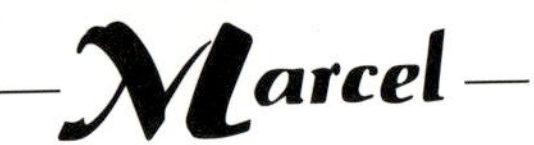

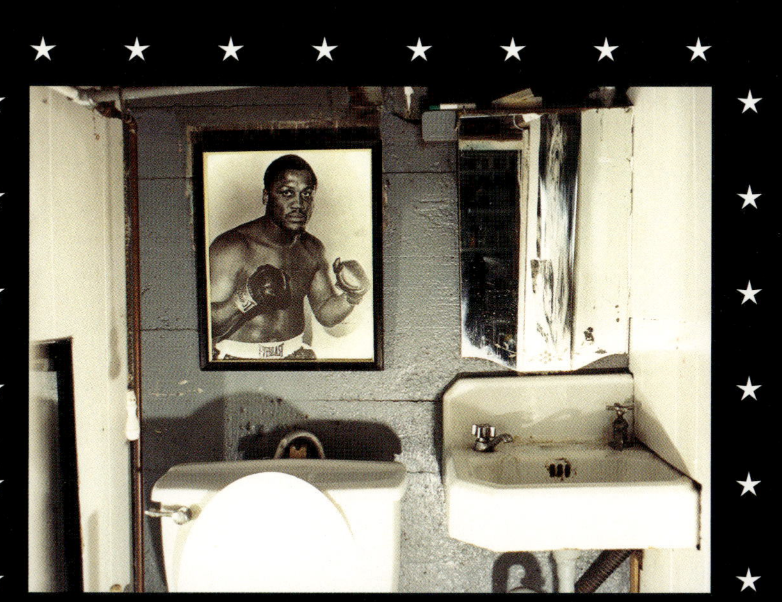

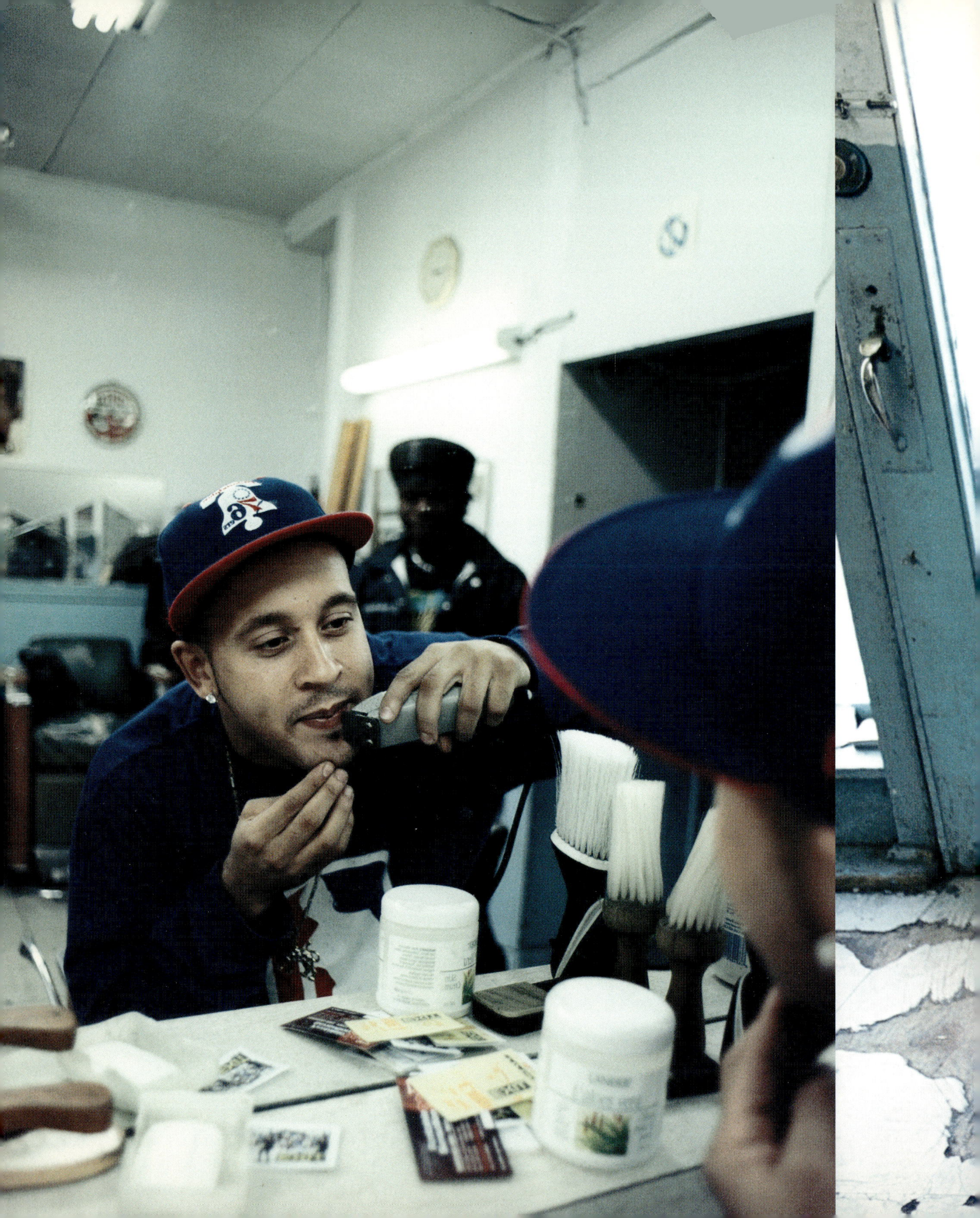

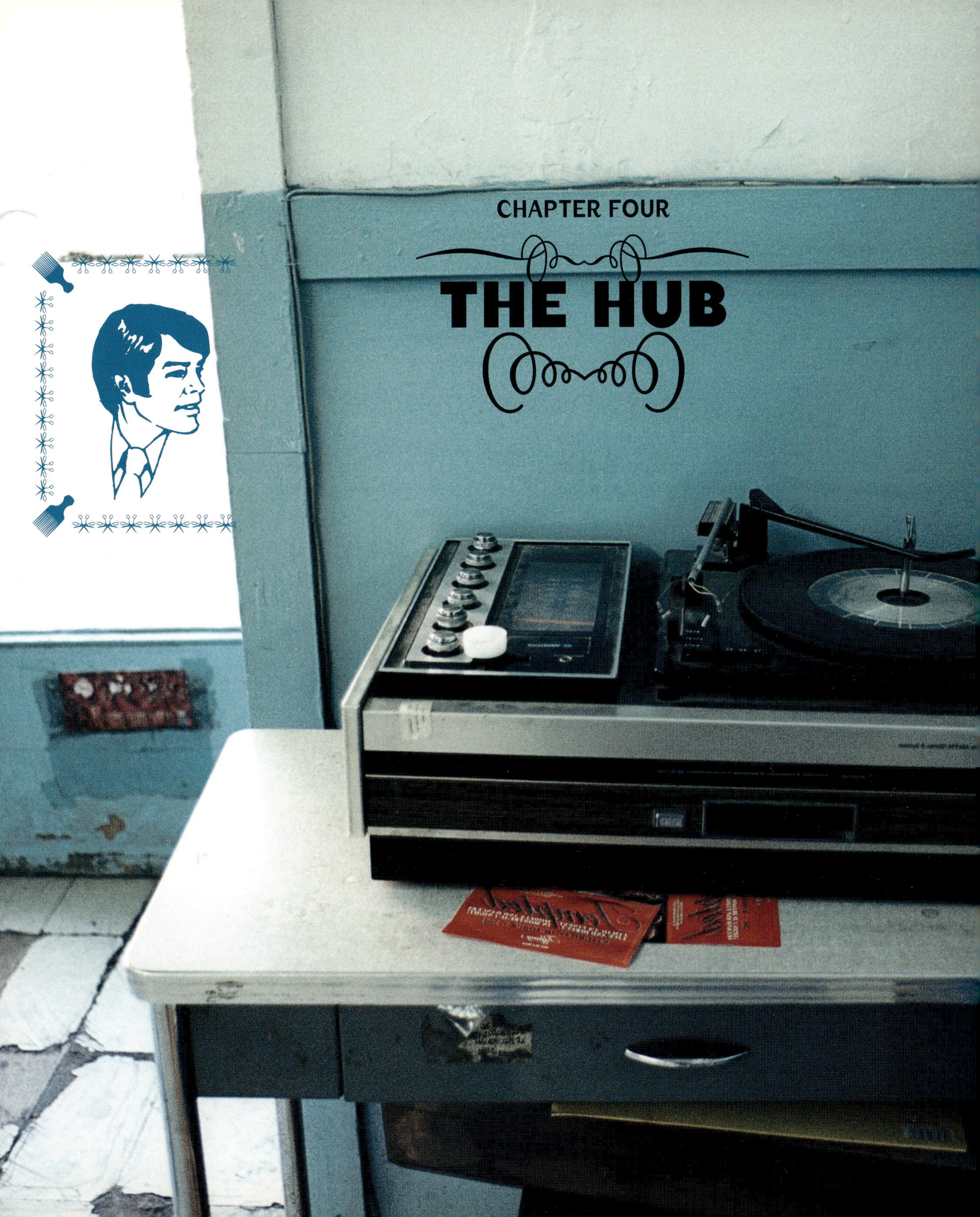

CHAPTER FOUR

THE HUB

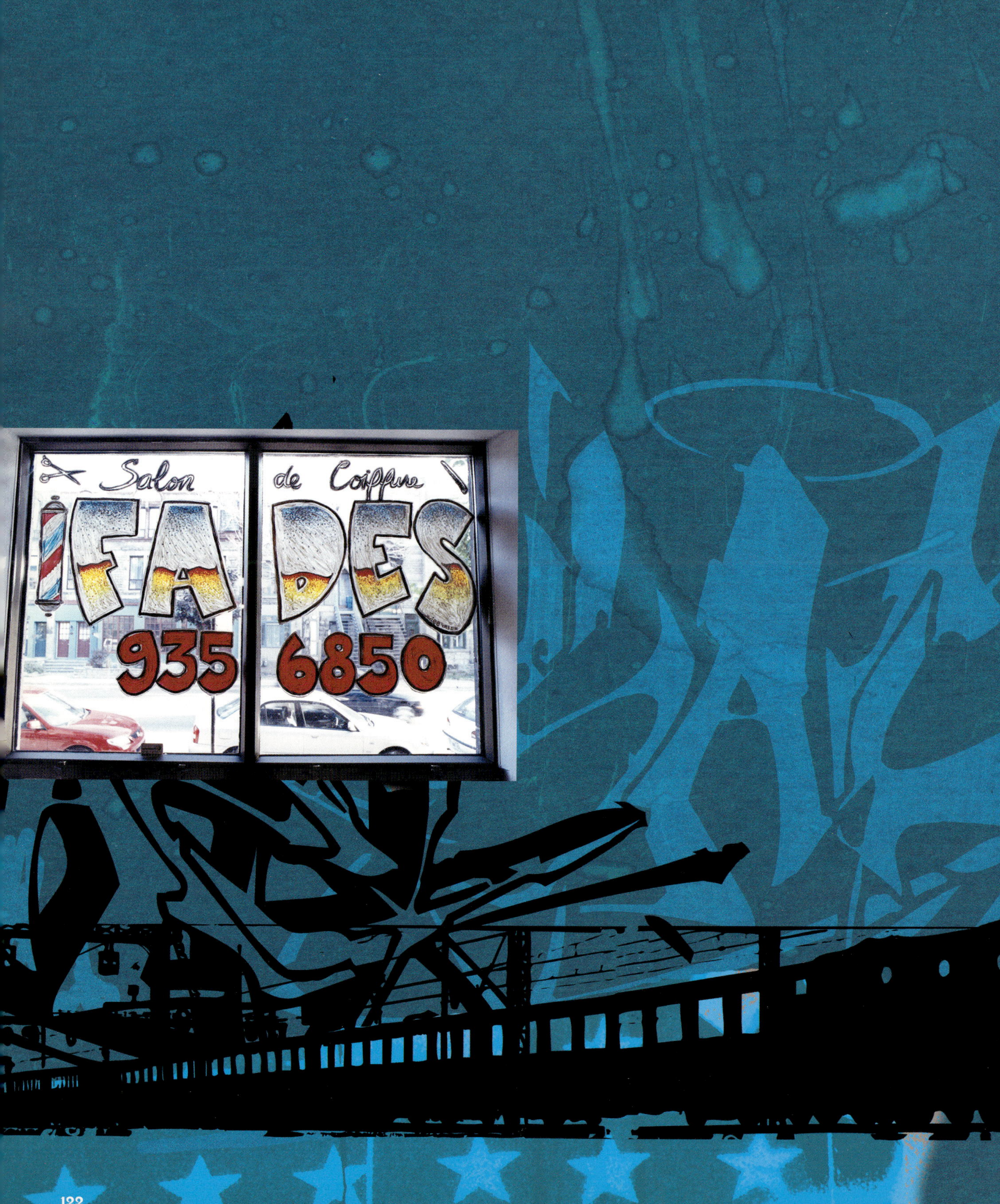
Salon de Coiffure
FADES
935 6850

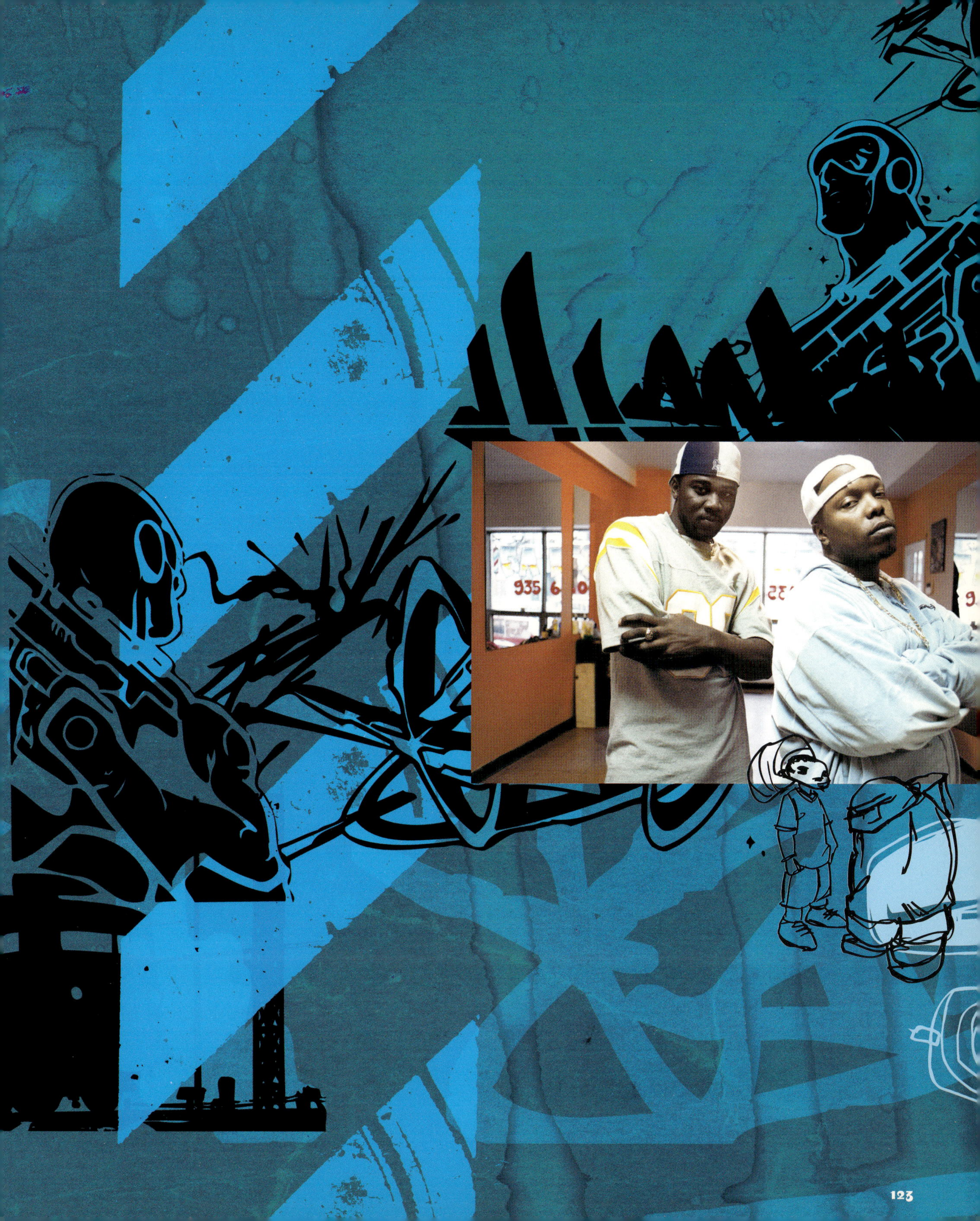

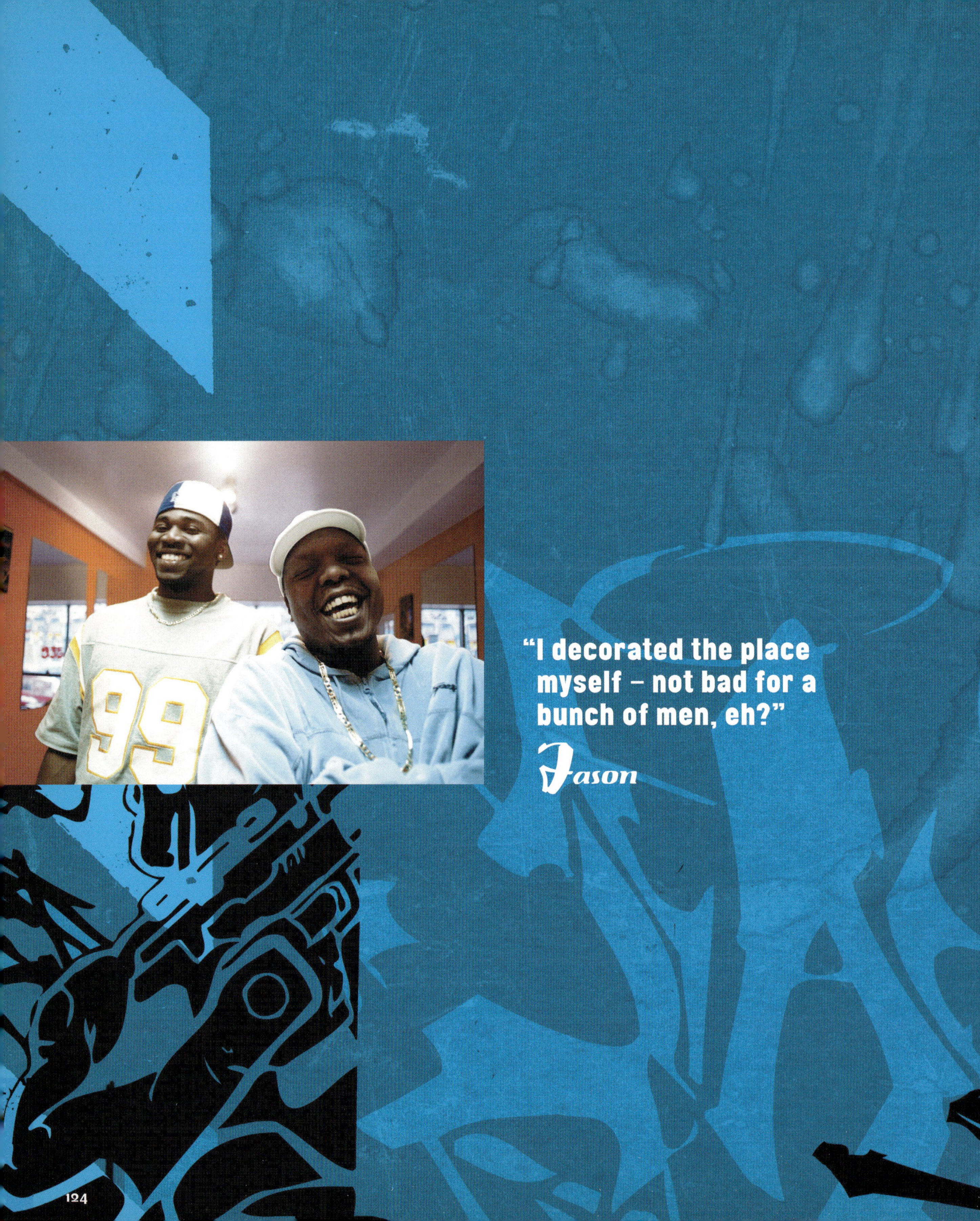

"I decorated the place myself – not bad for a bunch of men, eh?"

Jason

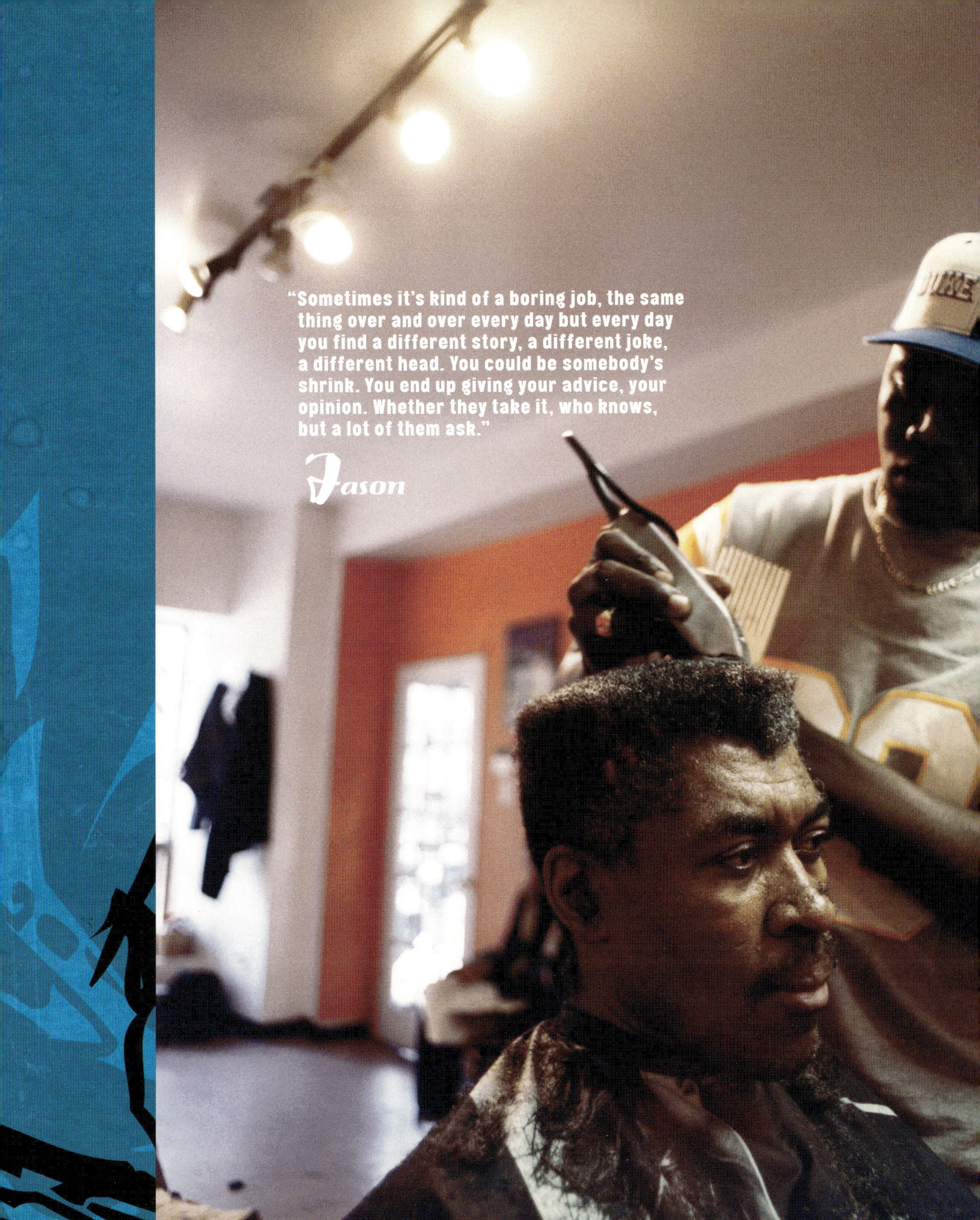
"Sometimes it's kind of a boring job, the same thing over and over every day but every day you find a different story, a different joke, a different head. You could be somebody's shrink. You end up giving your advice, your opinion. Whether they take it, who knows, but a lot of them ask."
Jason

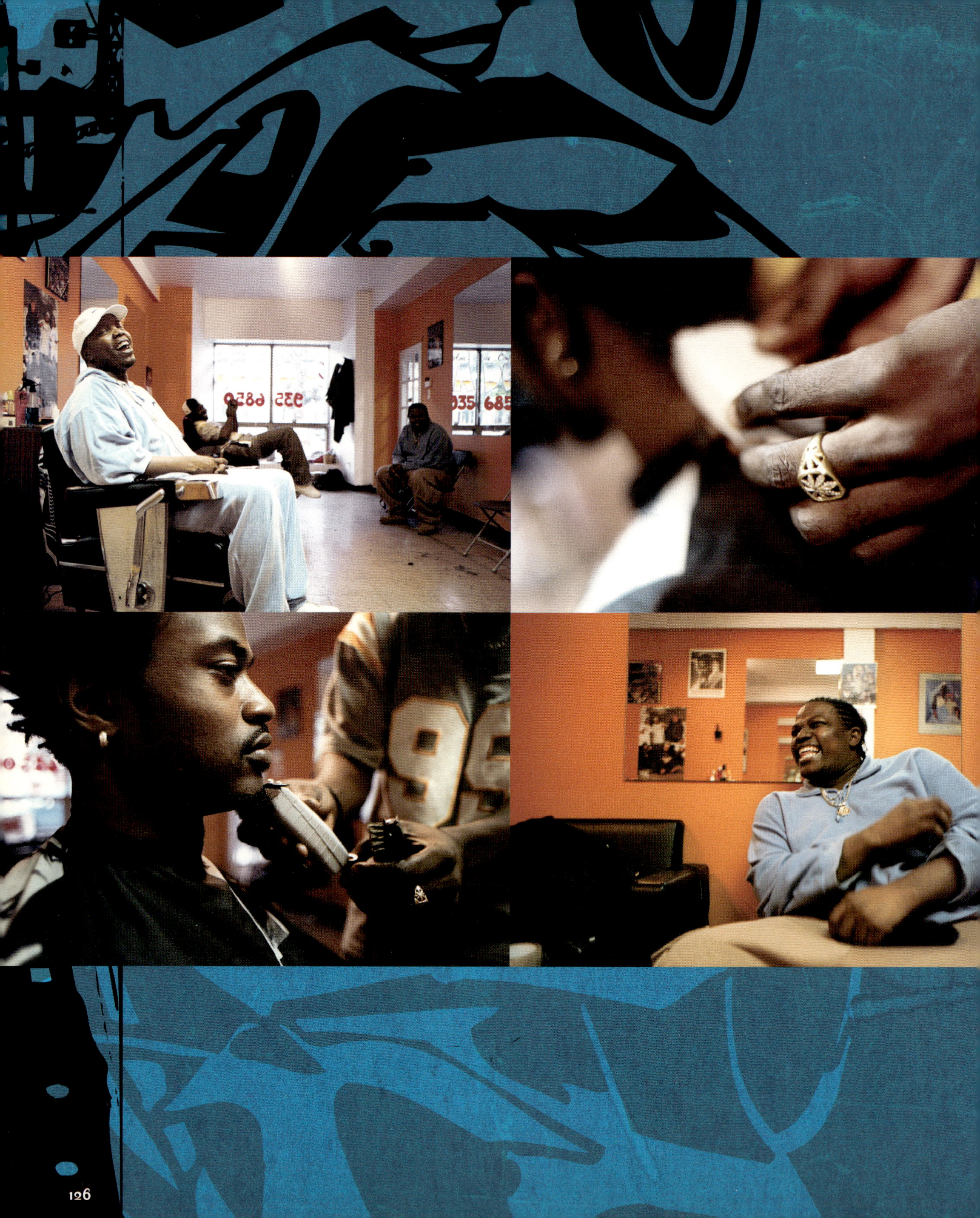

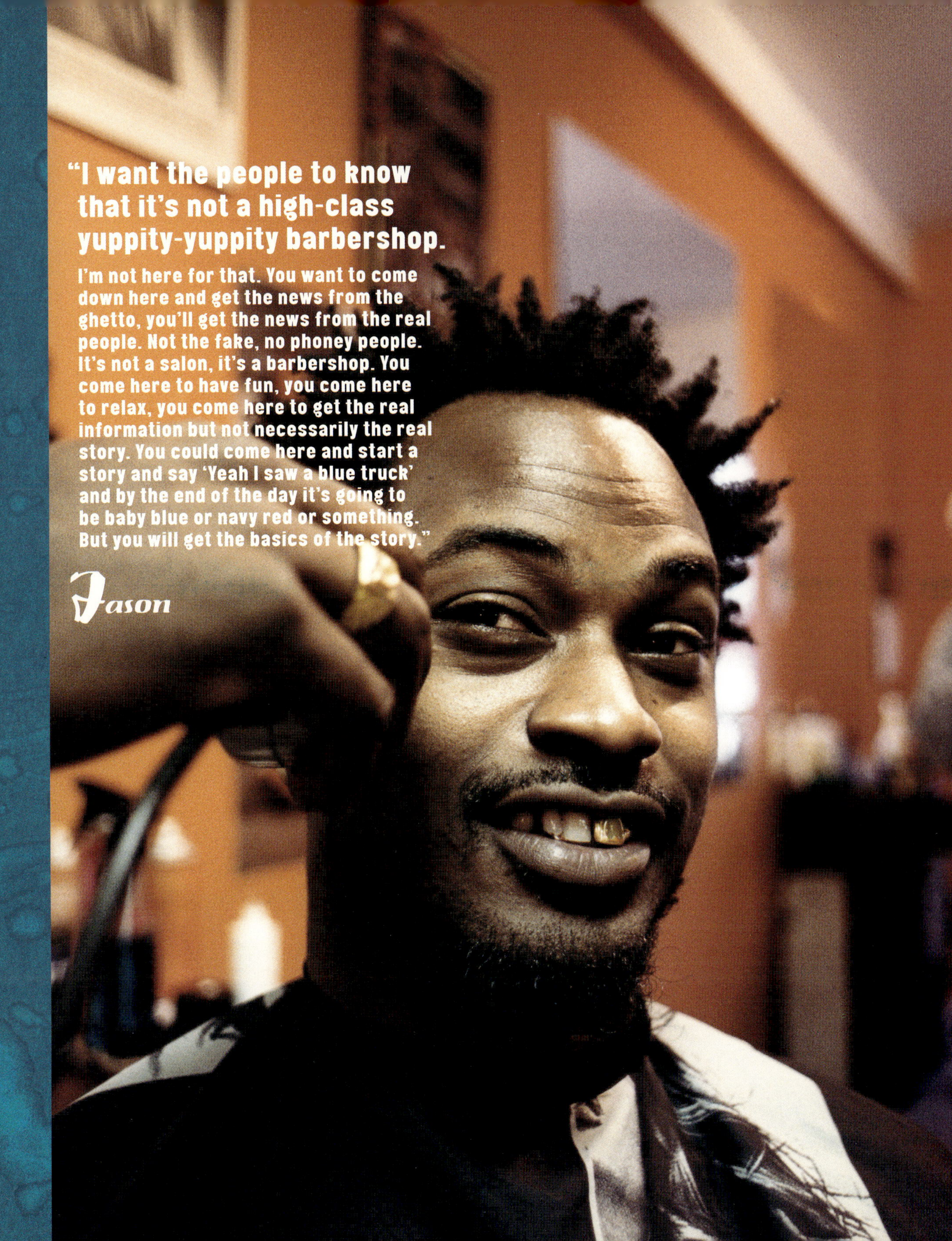
"I want the people to know that it's not a high-class yuppity-yuppity barbershop.
I'm not here for that. You want to come down here and get the news from the ghetto, you'll get the news from the real people. Not the fake, no phoney people. It's not a salon, it's a barbershop. You come here to have fun, you come here to relax, you come here to get the real information but not necessarily the real story. You could come here and start a story and say 'Yeah I saw a blue truck' and by the end of the day it's going to be baby blue or navy red or something. But you will get the basics of the story."
Jason

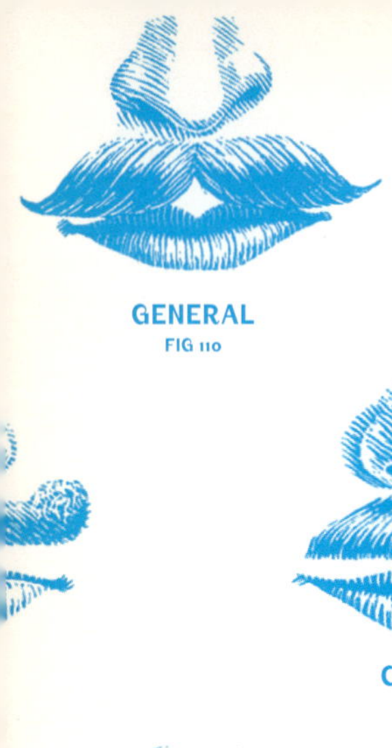

GENERAL
FIG 110

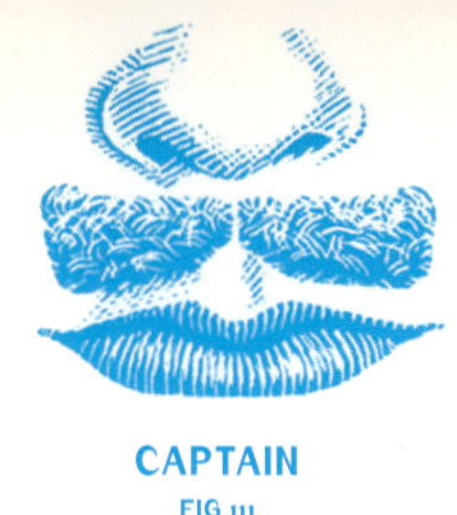

CAPTAIN
FIG 111

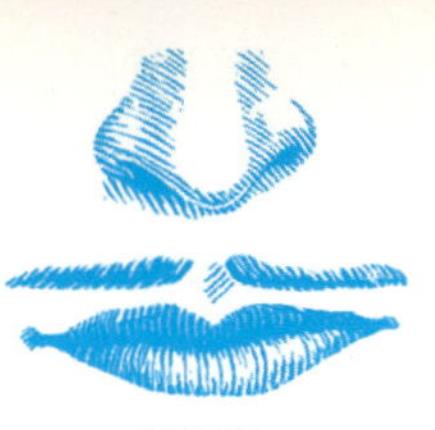

PUMA
FIG 112

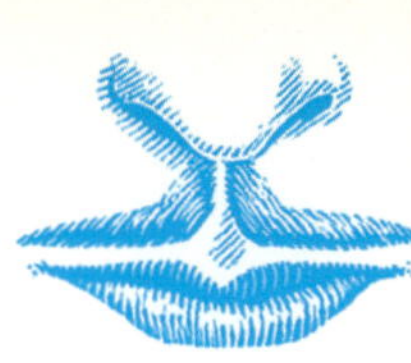

COLEMAN
FIG 113

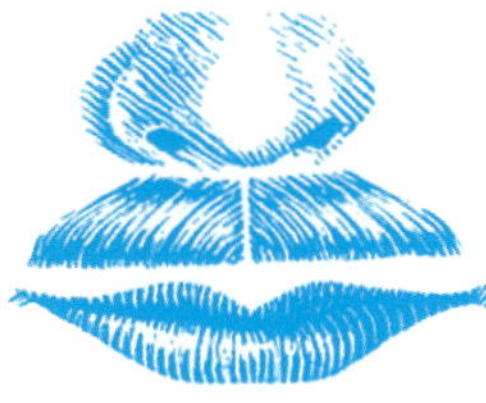

CONSORT
FIG 115

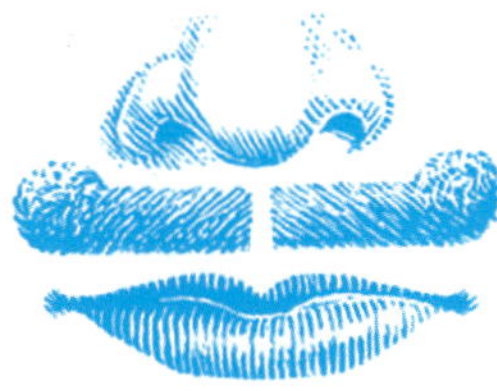

GUARDSMAN
FIG 116

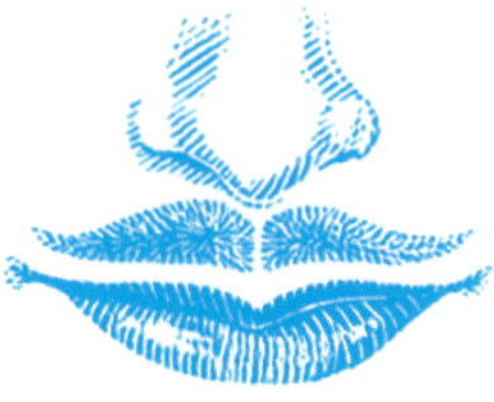

SHADOW
FIG 117

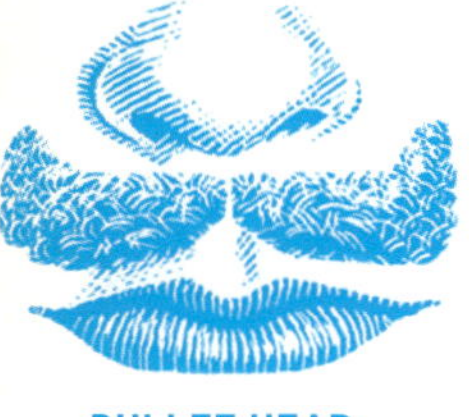

BULLET HEAD
FIG 120

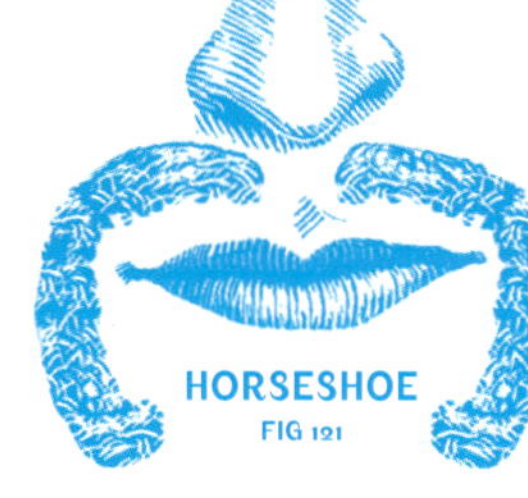

HORSESHOE
FIG 121

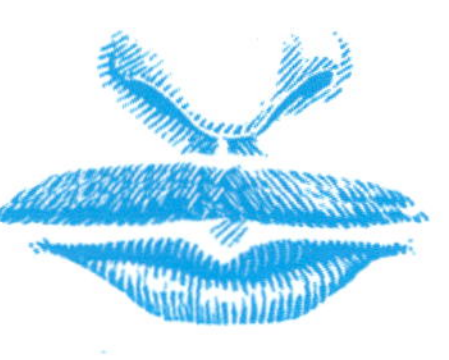

PAINTBRUSH
FIG 122

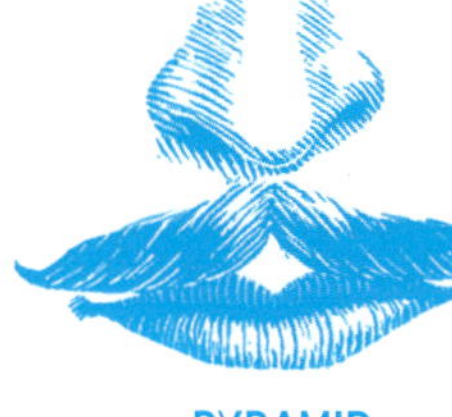

PYRAMID
FIG 123

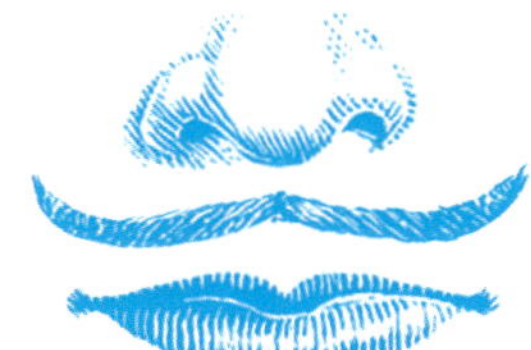

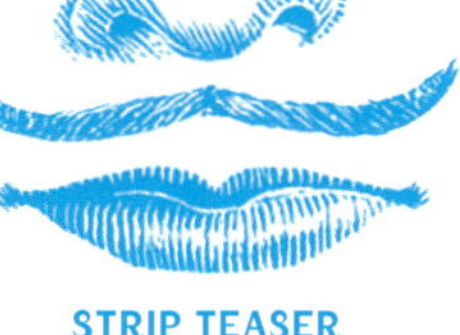

STRIP TEASER
FIG 125

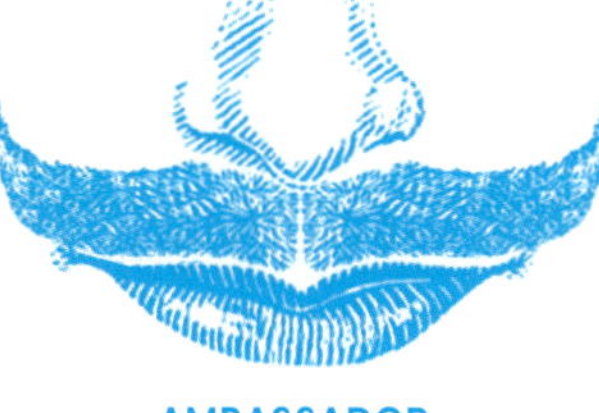

AMBASSADOR
FIG 126

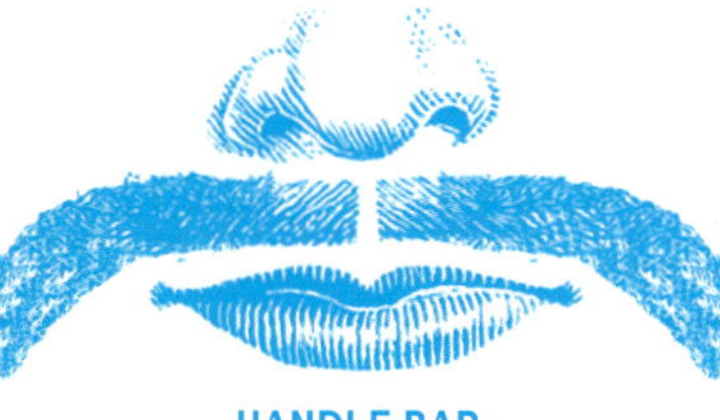

HANDLE BAR
FIG 127

HOWIE
FIG 135

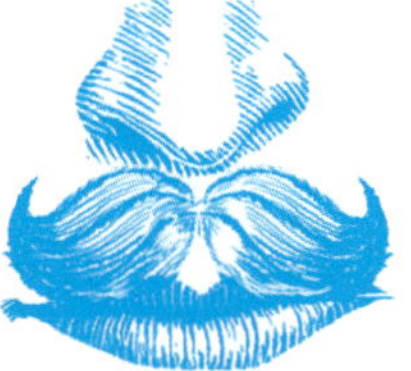

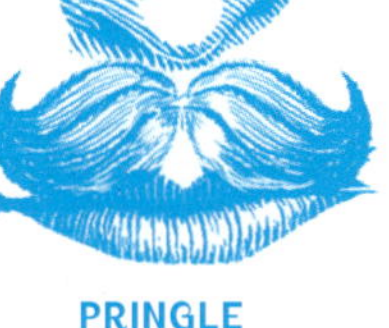

PRINGLE
FIG 136

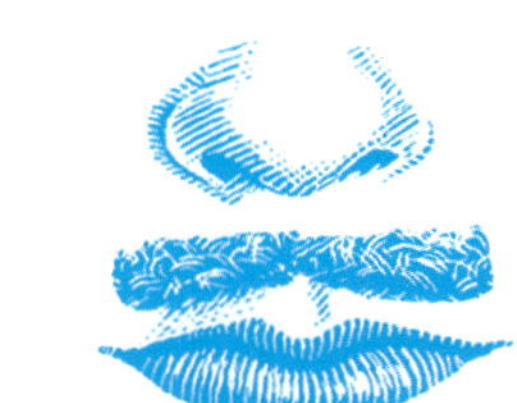

BOX CAR
FIG 137

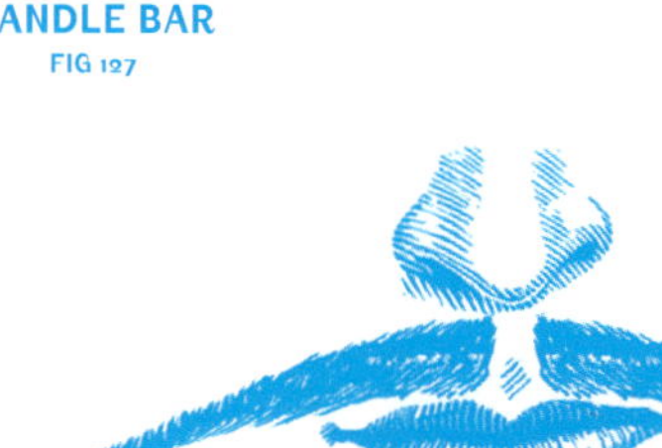

TURK
FIG 128

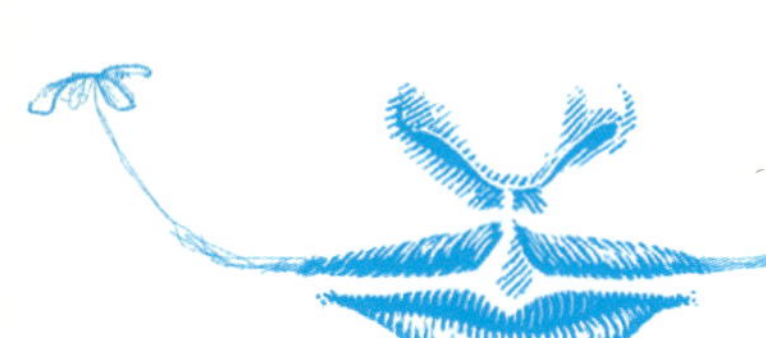

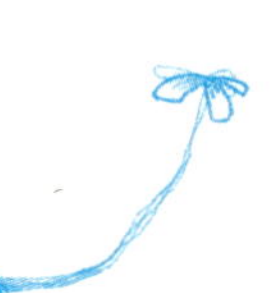

DALI
FIG 140

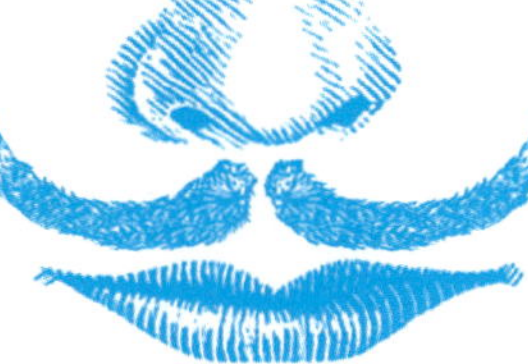

MISTLETOE
FIG 141

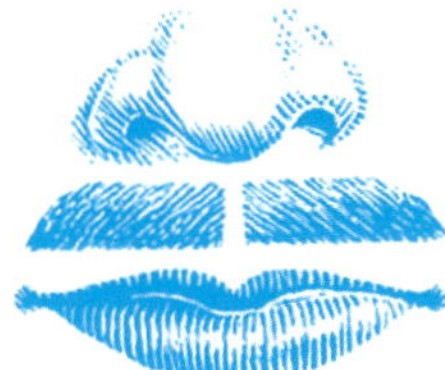

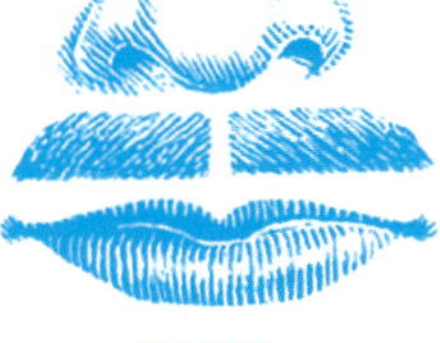

MAJOR
FIG 142

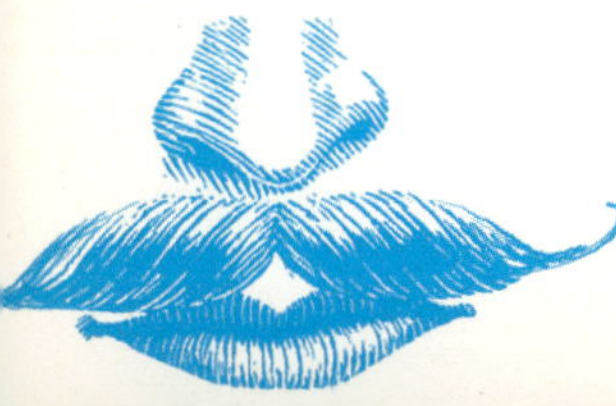

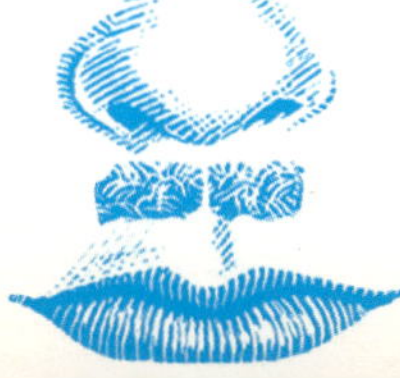

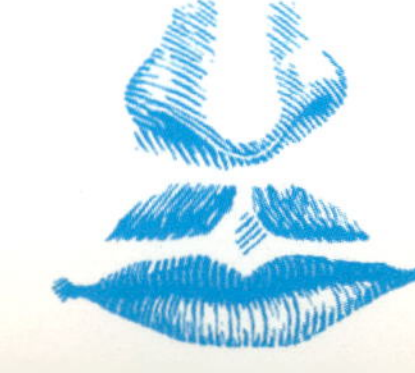

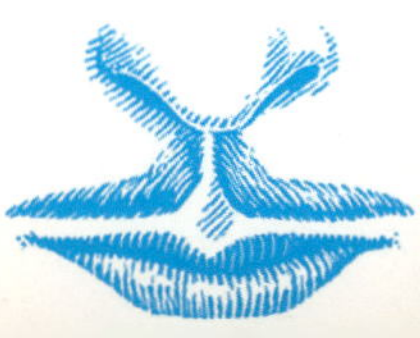

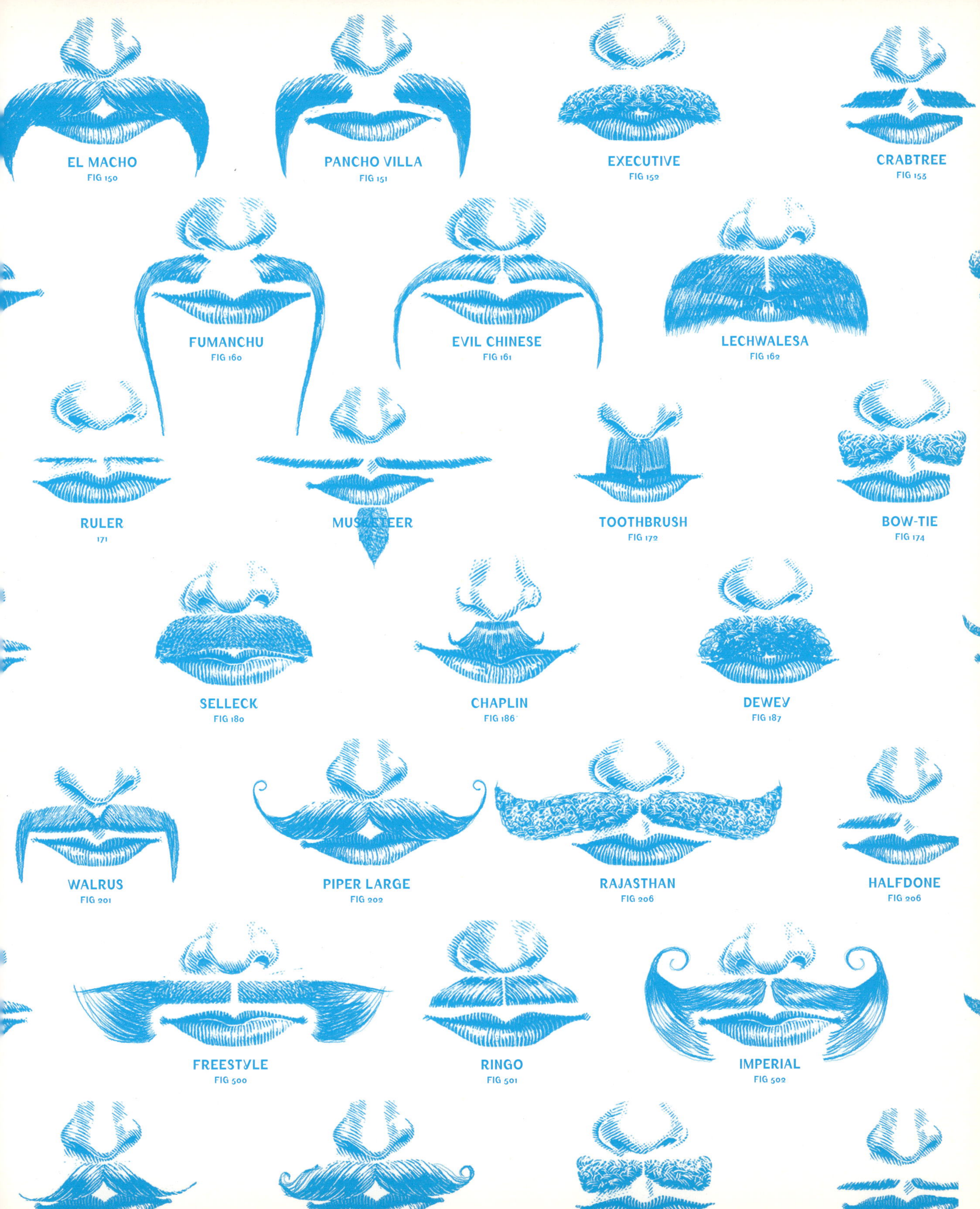
EL MACHO
FIG 150
PANCHO VILLA
FIG 151
EXECUTIVE
FIG 152
CRABTREE
FIG 153
FUMANCHU
FIG 160
EVIL CHINESE
FIG 161
LECHWALESA
FIG 162
RULER
171
MUS EER
TOOTHBRUSH
FIG 172
BOW-TIE
FIG 174
SELLECK
FIG 180
CHAPLIN
FIG 186
DEWEY
FIG 187
WALRUS
FIG 201
PIPER LARGE
FIG 202
RAJASTHAN
FIG 206
HALFDONE
FIG 206
FREESTYLE
FIG 500
RINGO
FIG 501
IMPERIAL
FIG 502

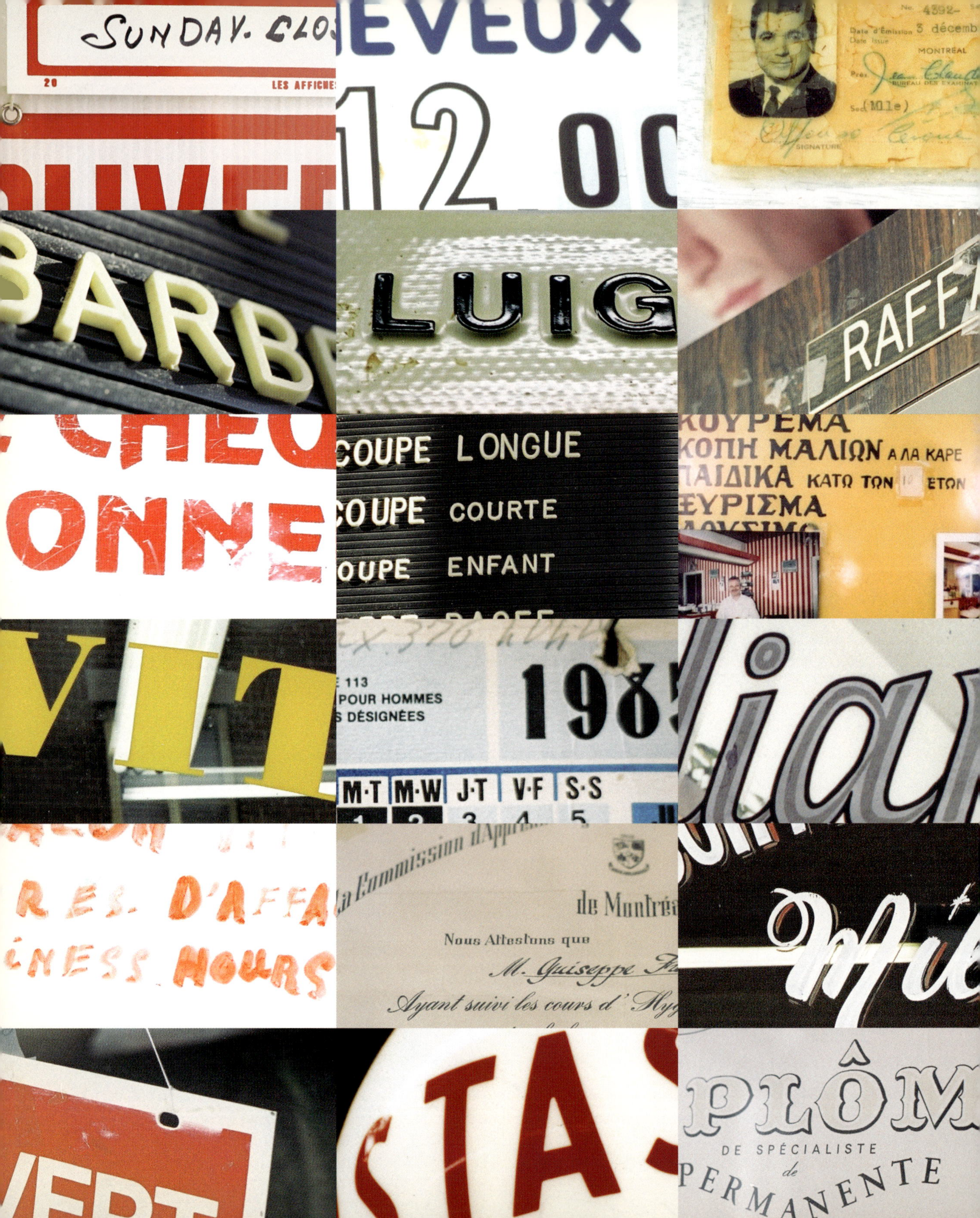

SUNDAY- CLO
20
LES AFFICHE
EVEUX
12 00
Date d'Émission 3 décemb
MONTRÉAL
BARB
LUIG
RAFF
ONNE
COUPE LONGUE
COUPE COURTE
OUPE ENFANT
ΚΟΥΡΕΜΑ
ΚΟΠΗ ΜΑΛΙΩΝ Α ΛΑ ΚΑΡΕ
ΑΙΔΙΚΑ ΚΑΤΩ ΤΩΝ 10 ΕΤΩΝ
ΞΥΡΙΣΜΑ
VIT
E 113
POUR HOMMES
S DÉSIGNÉES
198
M·T M·W J·T V·F S·S
lia
RES. D'AFFA
INESS HOURS
la Commission d'Appre
de Montréa
Nous Attestons que
M. Guiseppe F
Ayant suivi les cours d'Hy
VERT
STAS
PLÔM
DE SPÉCIALISTE
de
PERMANENTE

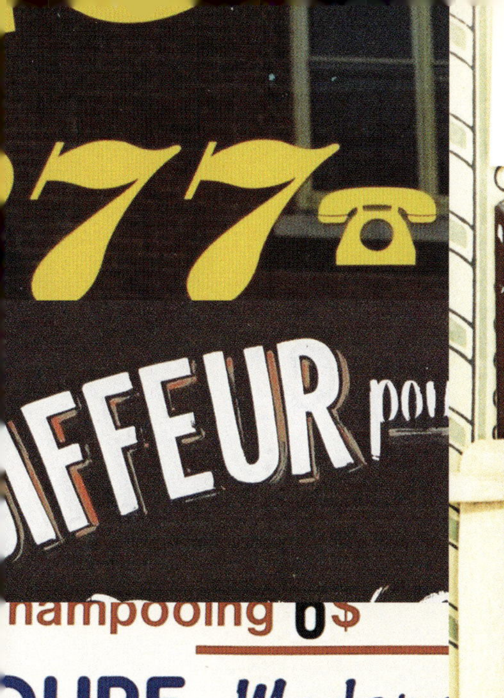

"On Friday nights, I used to give my keys over to the person who wanted to get the first haircut on Saturday morning. I would tell the guy: 'When you go in, just sit in the chair.' That way he was sure to be first. I have customers for whom it's like an obsession – they have to be the first ones in the morning. They're waiting at the door with their sandwich. Bacon, eggs, and cheese."

MARCEL

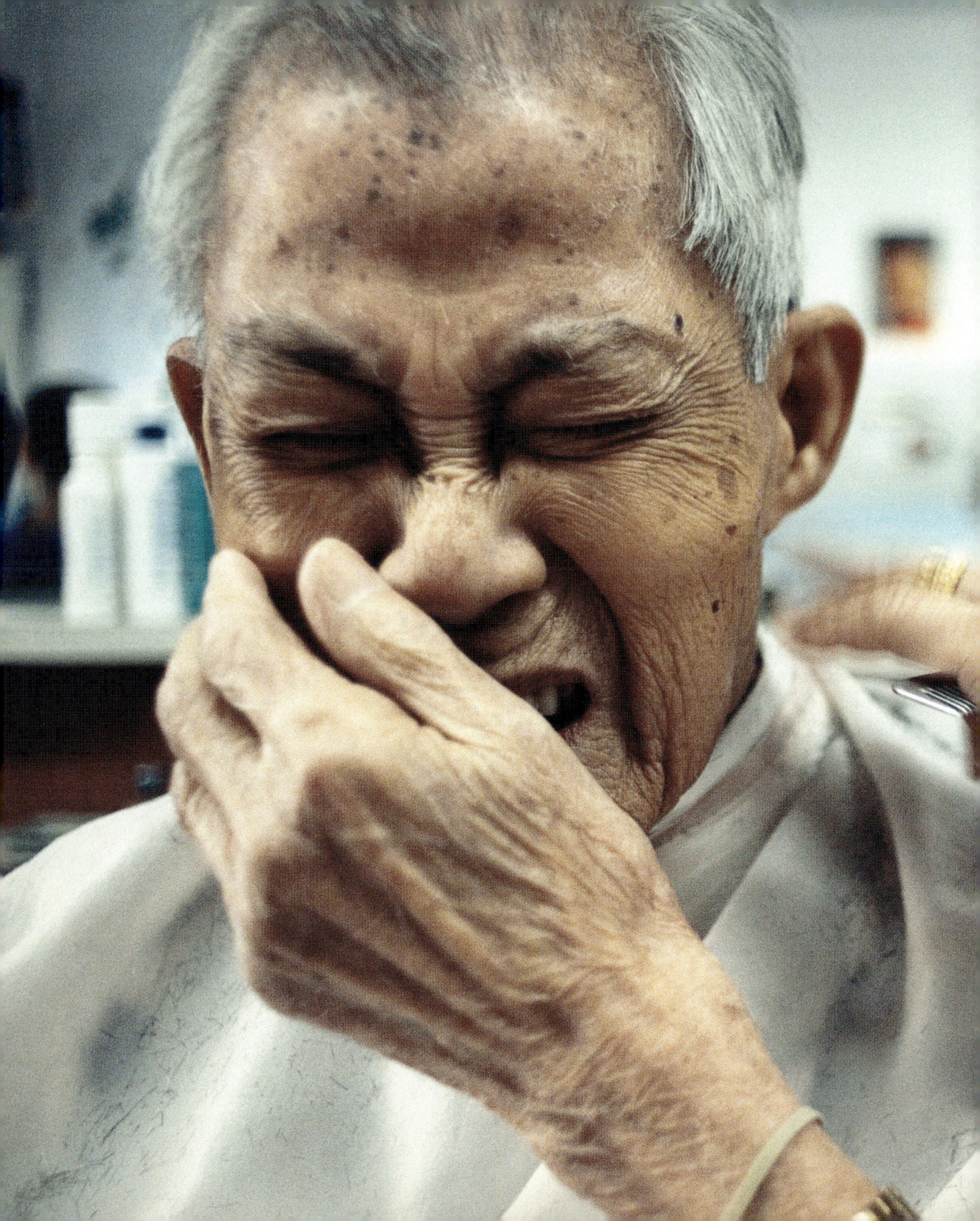

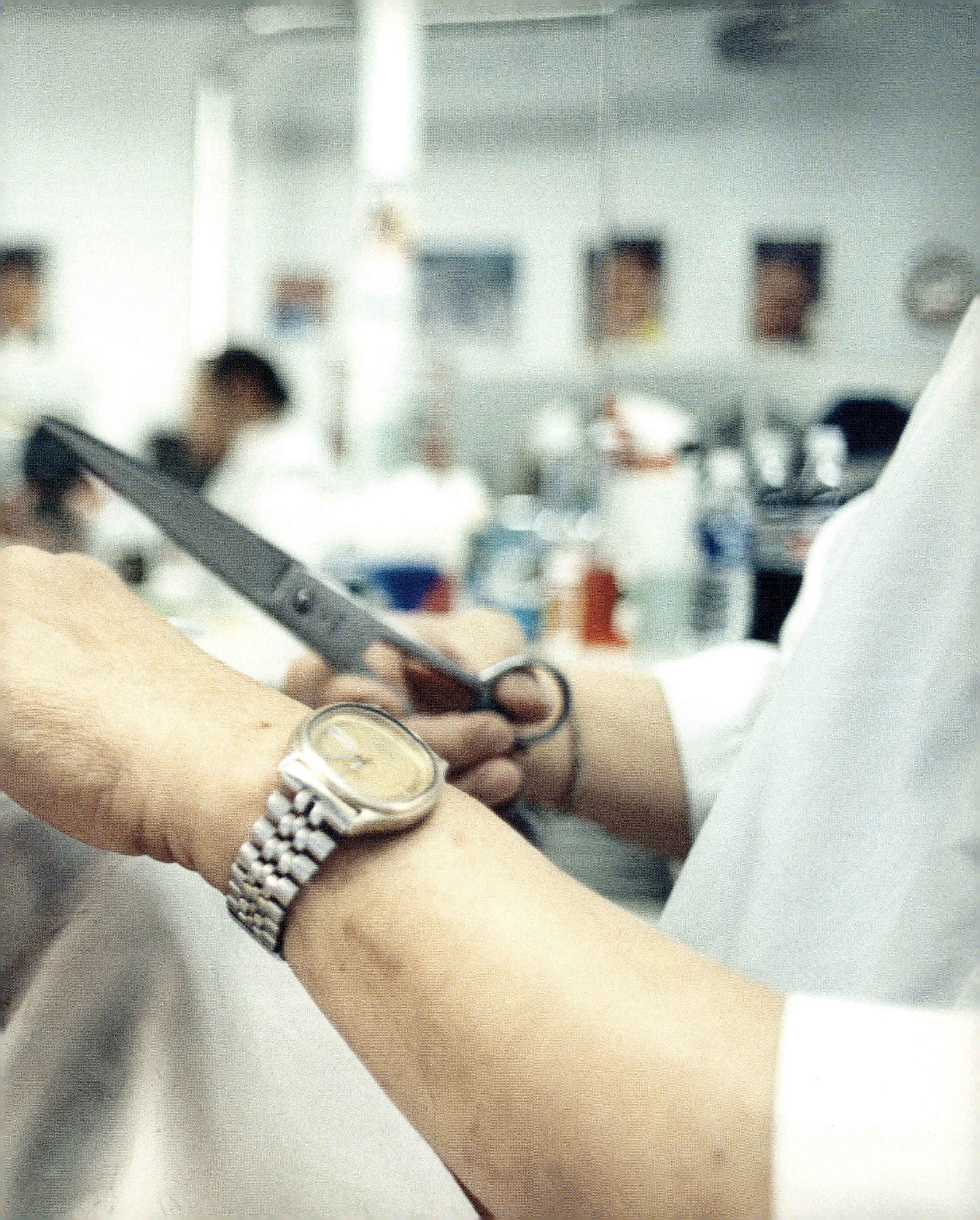

68% OF AUSTRALIANS have shifted away from the once-popular 2-in-1 shampoos to the two-step separate shampoo and conditioner method.

81% of Canadians believe that physical appearance can affect career advancement **AND 1 IN 8** respondents think that **hair is crucial to getting a job.**

There have been 39 U.S. elections since 2004 in which all the major candidates were clean-shaven. **FIVE U.S. PRESIDENTS have sported full beards,** and another four had moustaches.

A man's beard contains between **7,000 & 15,000 HAIRS.**

Women's hair is about **half the diameter of men's hair.**

A HAIR IS 70% EASIER TO CUT when soaked in warm water for two minutes.

In the United States in 1998, **$2 BILLION was spent on shampoo;** $1.4 billion on conditioner; $150 million on men's hair prod

60% OF WOMEN prefer men with hair.

IN 2003, 923,200 PEOPLE in the United States had laser hair removal, up 25% from the previous year.

Statistics show that men in the U.S. are spending more than **$4 BILLION A YEAR** on grooming products, such as [illegible] color and facial scrubs, driven by their desire to [illegible] feel their best.

"Sometimes it gets out of hand,

people talking about religion or politics, sometimes it just gets out of hand. Better we keep it to sports. Just sports. At least with sports you got your own opinion but there are statistics."

Jason

"Where I started, the salon was a small place in a small town.

It wasn't even a town, it was a village. At that time there was no radio, no television, no newspaper. So sometimes customers would come in who had traveled, maybe they had been out in the countryside, and so they would tell us everything that was going on there! My goodness, we were so clued up – we knew everything that was going on!"

Mike

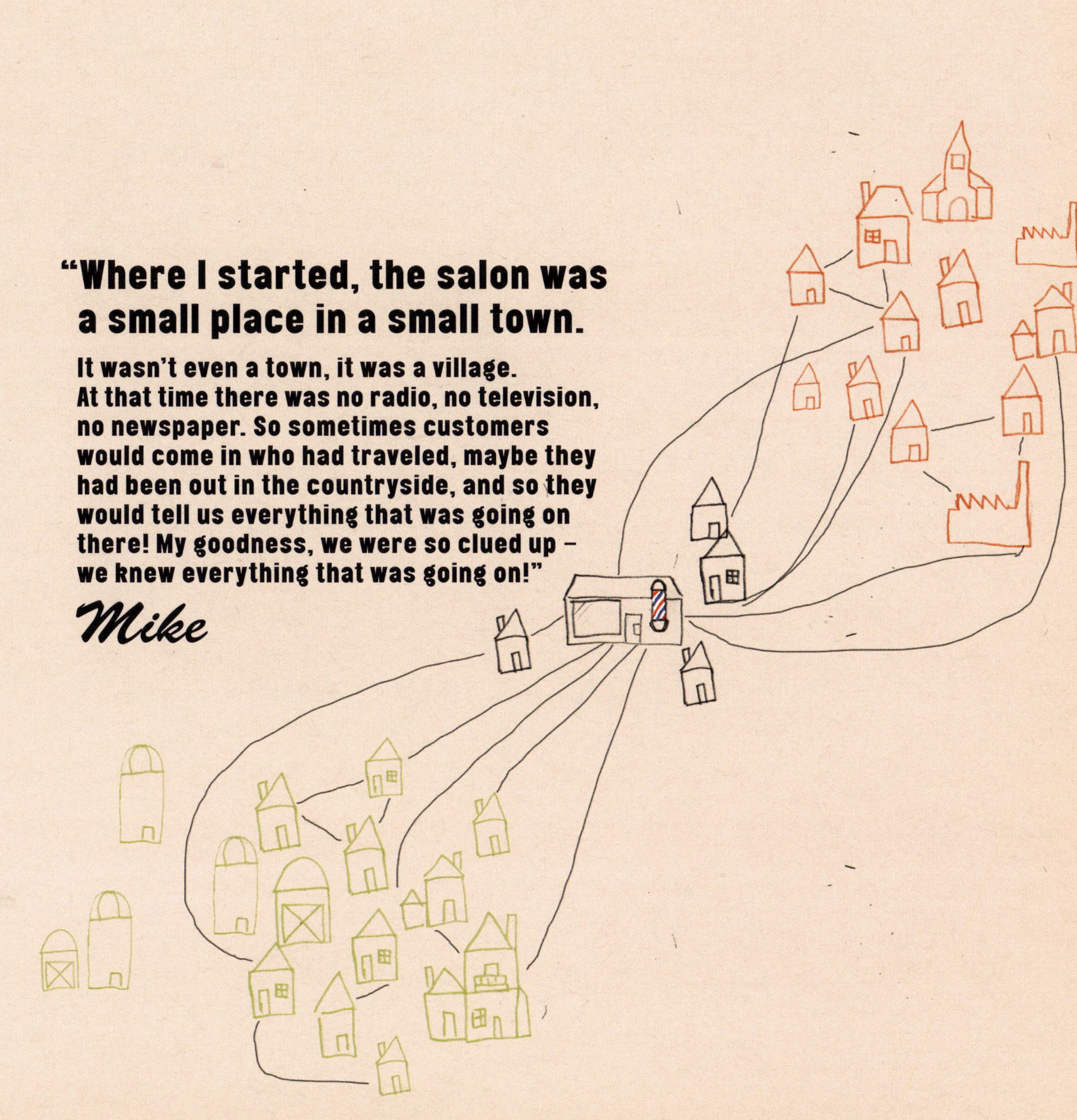

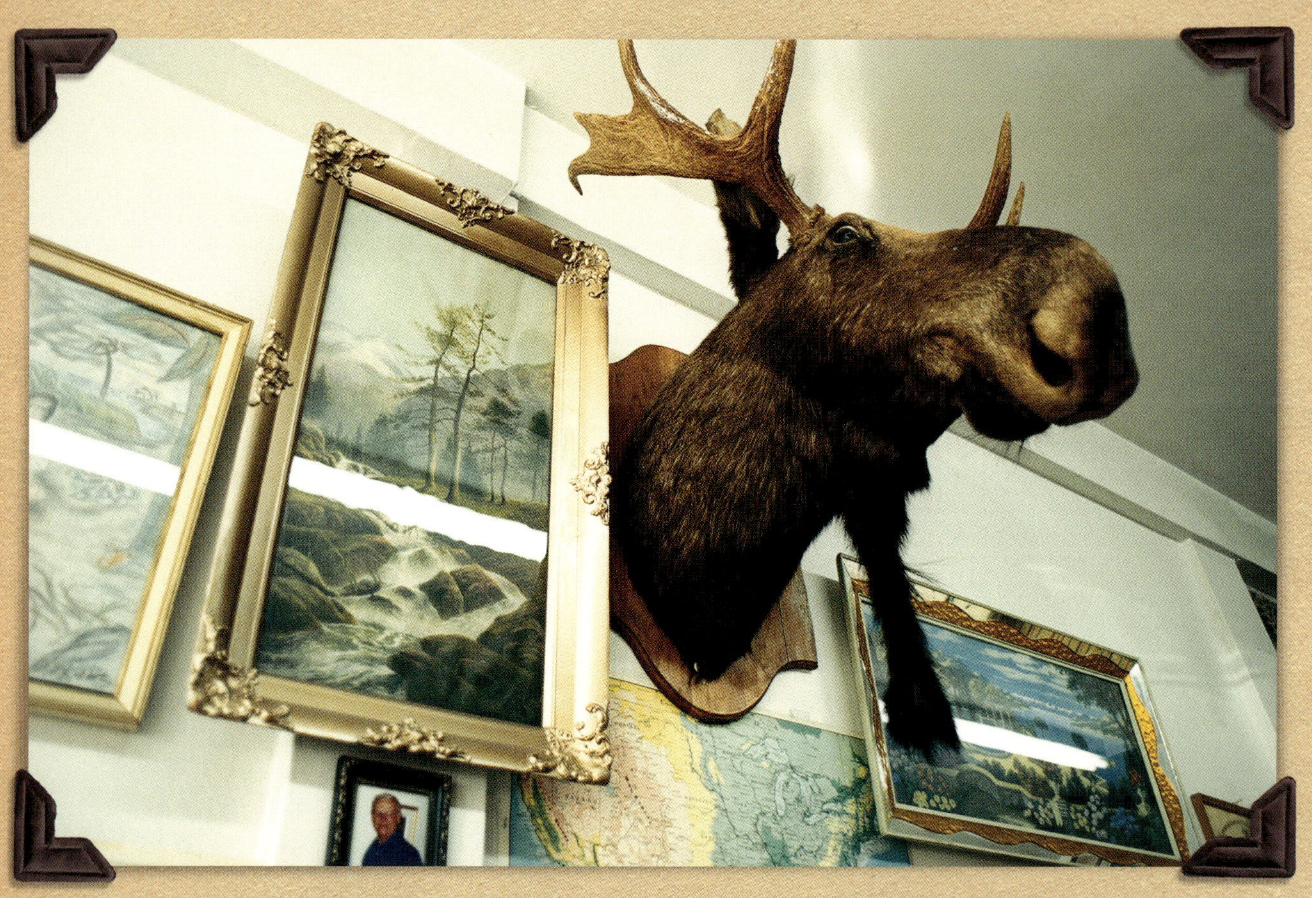

A Hunting Story

AS TOLD AT

SALON OUTREMONT

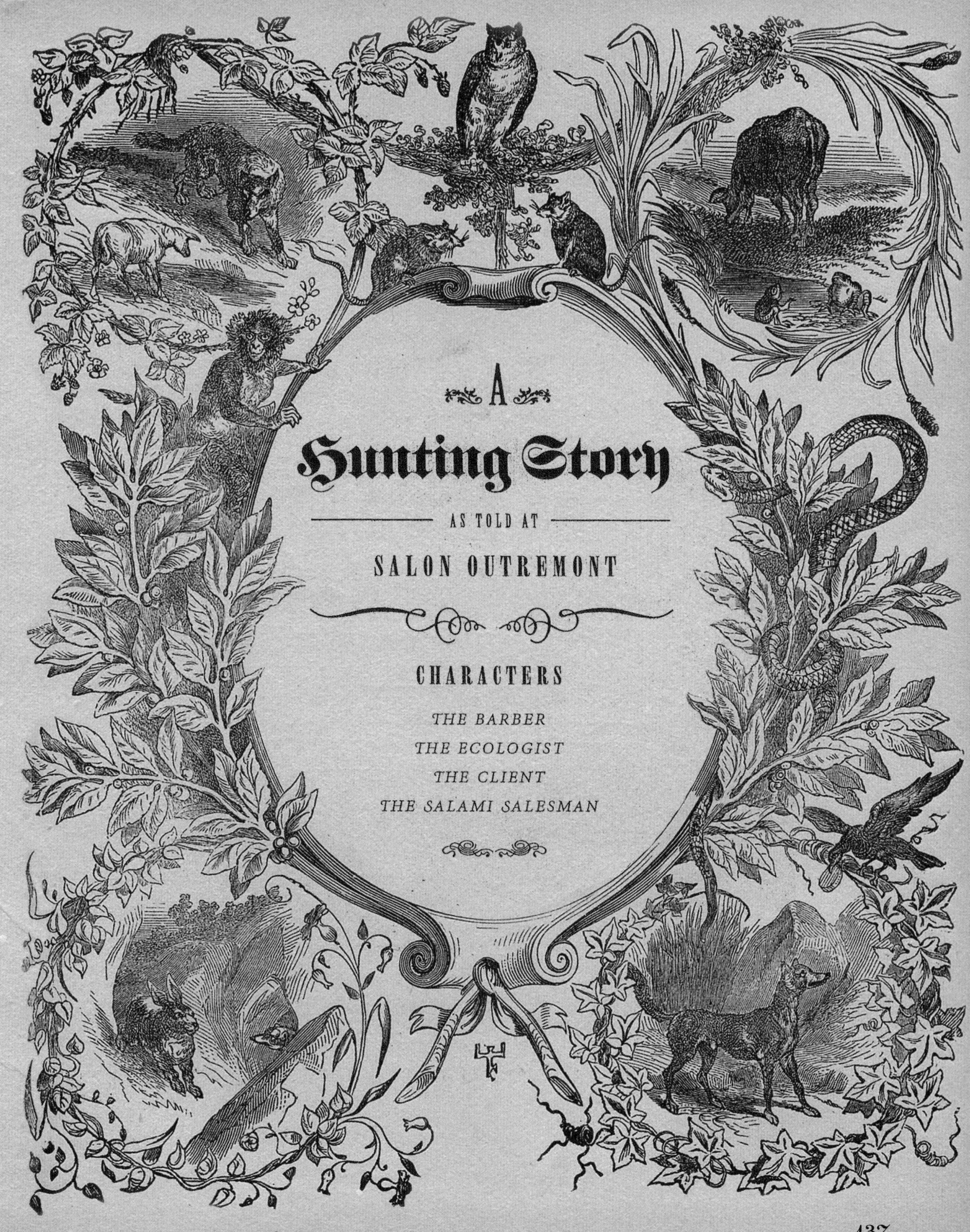

CHARACTERS

THE BARBER
THE ECOLOGIST
THE CLIENT
THE SALAMI SALESMAN

ACT ONE

THE BARBER
Most of the people who come here are hunters.

THE ECOLOGIST
Most of their stories are lies. A lot of stuff they say is bullshit. You can't believe all their stories. These are like fishermen's stories, a lot of lies. We're friends, though. But don't forget… all the hunters, I call them killers!

THE BARBER
It happens that this guy is a Greenpeace guy. He doesn't eat meat from any animal except the cow. He doesn't like the moose head on the wall.

THE ECOLOGIST
If I had the chance, I would smash everything! Because they go to hunt rabbits and instead of killing one or two, some of them come back with 40 or 50 rabbits taking them away from the other animals, like the foxes. So they disturb the ecosystem.

THE BARBER
Don't blame the hunters! It's a sport, ok!

THE CLIENT
I agree with the gentleman.

THE BARBER
I don't agree with the Greenpeace!

THE ECOLOGIST
Hunters disturb the ecosystem! And when I hear that one hunter kills another hunter, I say good!

THE BARBER
Relax, relax.

THE CLIENT
I agree with the gentleman.

THE BARBER
Never mind, there are very few who think like that.

THE CLIENT
Not a few, there are many of us.

THE BARBER
You blame the hunters because we have guns.

THE ECOLOGIST
No, it's not that. But you have that picture of the old fool who killed 50 rabbits. What for?

THE BARBER
That's an old story. You have no idea! You don't know about hunting!

THE ECOLOGIST
Those animals are there for the ecosystem. He doesn't have to kill 50 rabbits!
Kill two or three of them.

THE CLIENT
No, kill one. Just for the taste. Not a thousand.

THE BARBER
(to The Ecologist)
OK, so one guy thinks like you.

THE ECOLOGIST
Not one guy, many guys!

THE BARBER
You have the right to disagree, my friend. You're an ecologist.

THE ECOLOGIST
Why do you go and kill 50 rabbits, why?

THE BARBER
50 rabbits, they're not even in season now! Where are you going to get 50 rabbits?

THE ECOLOGIST
I'll show you the pictures of the guy with 50 rabbits. That's abuse. We speak the truth.
If I was able to avoid meat altogether, I would avoid it altogether. Because if you want to finish with the problems and diseases and all that, one of the most famous German doctors says 'Eat everything green.' Then you'll have no problem with the cancer. All the meat you eat, what is it?
It's all injected with everything.

THE BARBER
There's a guy here who sells salami, then why does he sell that if it's so bad?

THE ECOLOGIST
I don't care, that's my view, maybe some people think otherwise.

THE BARBER
Tell him to make salami with a vegetable!

THE SALAMI SALESMAN
I don't make the salamis, I sell them.

THE ECOLOGIST
For me, that's my view.

THE BARBER
He would be very happy to hear that Jimmy the barber was killed in the bush.
He's not going to bring flowers! He is going to be happy! He says no flowers for a hunter!
But barbers are like a bad cold, my friend, you can't get rid of them, you always find one of them!

INTERMISSION

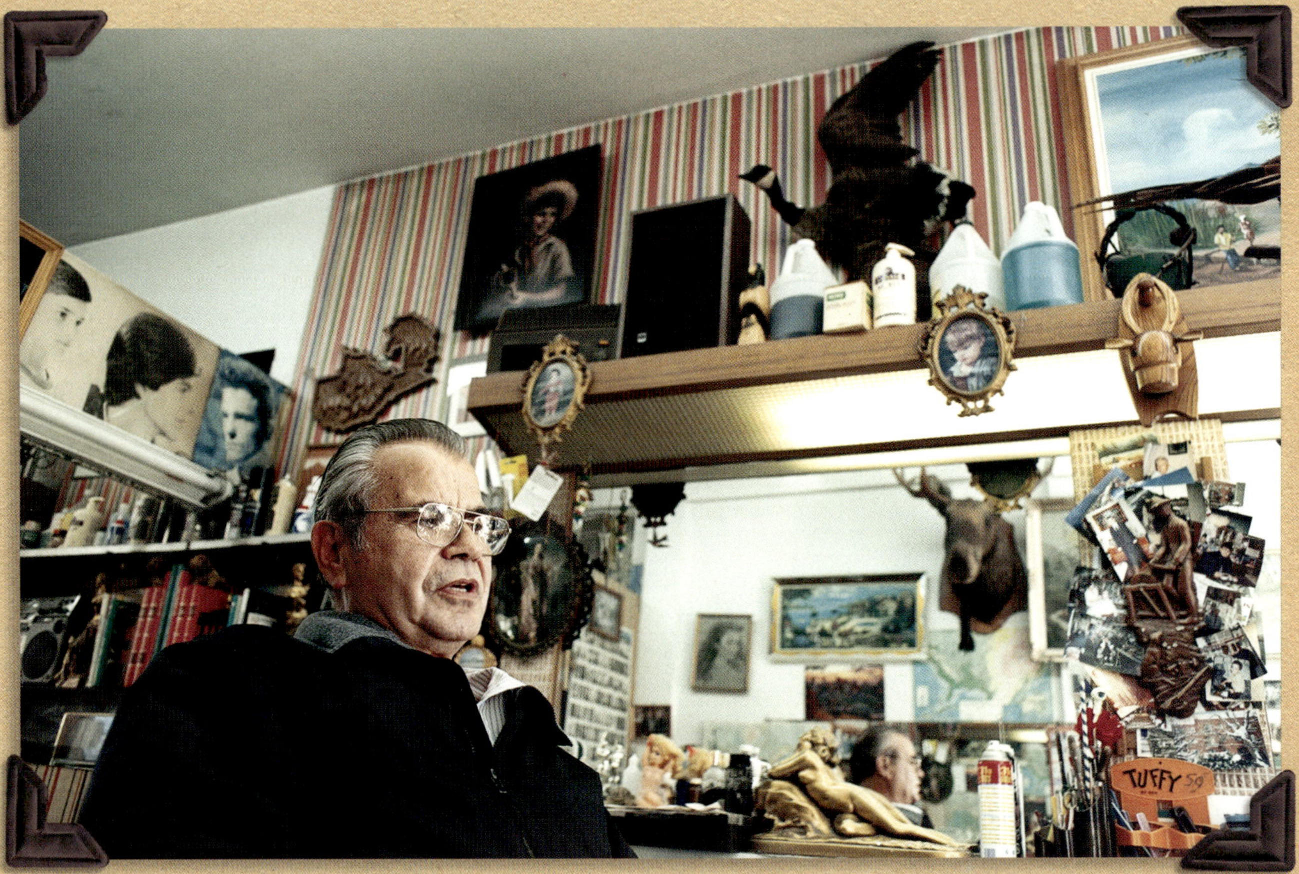

THE ECOLOGIST

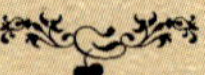

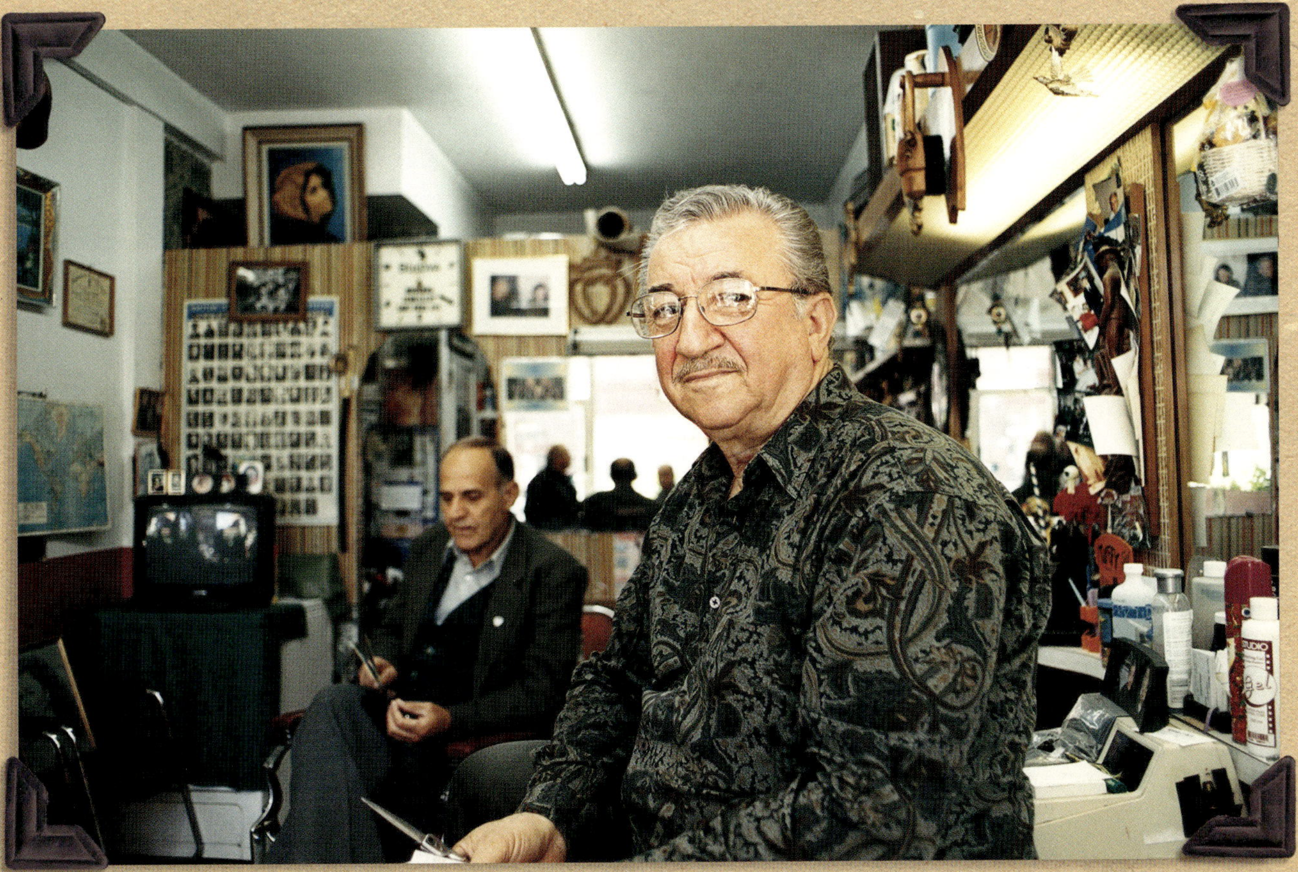

THE BARBER

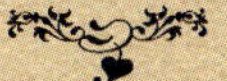

ACT TWO

THE BARBER
The biggest destroyers are animals themselves. The wolf kills more than the hunter.
It's proven by the system, it's not the hunter.

THE ECOLOGIST
That's not true! The animals kill what they need to eat and that's it. It's finished.
The humans' desires go beyond, you're not killing because you're hungry, you're killing for the sport.
So does that old fool who comes here.

THE BARBER
You call the hunters fools?

THE ECOLOGIST
So he comes and puts 50 rabbits on his Cadillac and drives around to show his friends.

THE BARBER
There were only seven! These are stories from 1963.
At that time, there were as many rabbits in Montreal as in Australia.
Today, you can't find 50 rabbits for all your life. You're too much, Mr. Ecologist.

THE ECOLOGIST
You guys want to take me in the woods and use me for target practice.
Do you remember that guy, the artist, somewhere in the Eastern Townships?
They mistook him for a moose and they killed him! He had white hair and a white beard.
He was about 65. He had long hair.

THE BARBER
He was an artist in Quebec.

THE ECOLOGIST
Every year, they put his picture in the paper on the anniversary of his death.

THE BARBER
Yeah, because he didn't get a haircut so he paid for it!

THE ECOLOGIST
I guarantee it was a barber who did that! Because he wasn't cutting his hair.
I told you, hunters are bad, but hunters combined with barbers are deadly!
Now I need a high blood-pressure pill.

The End

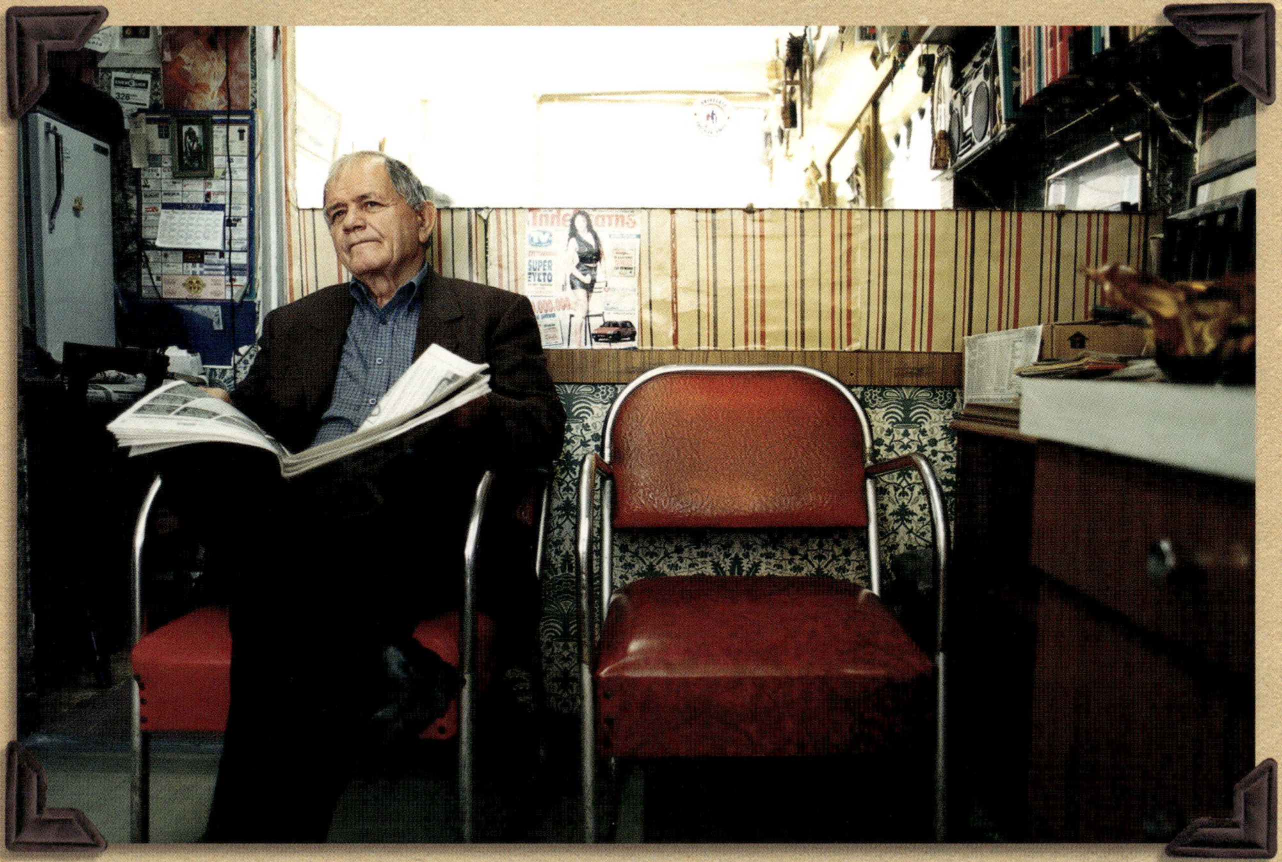

THE CLIENT

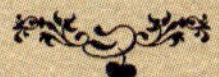

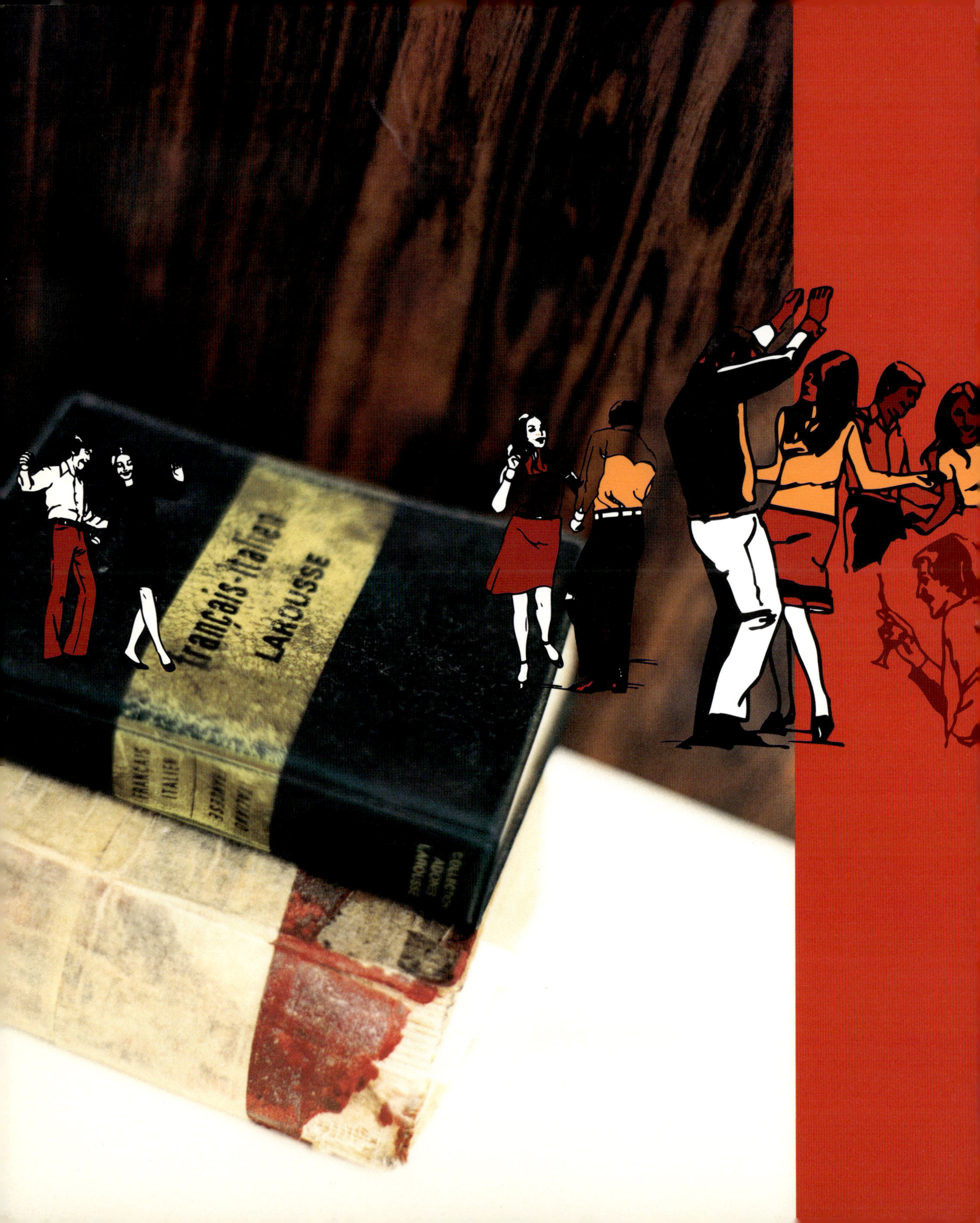
français-italien
LAROUSSE

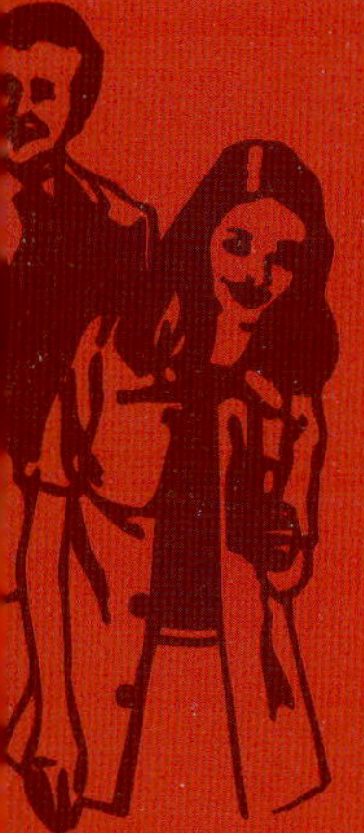

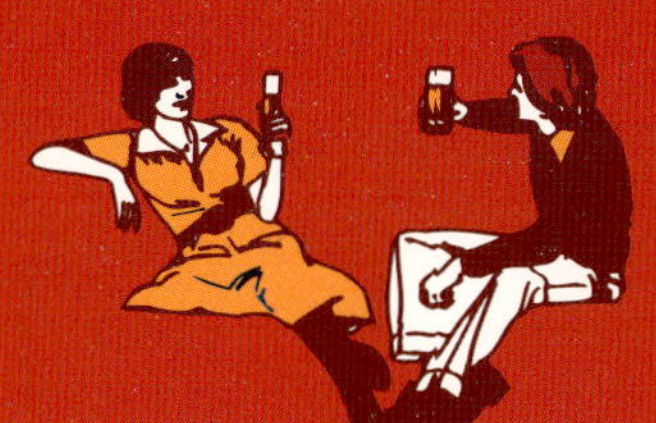

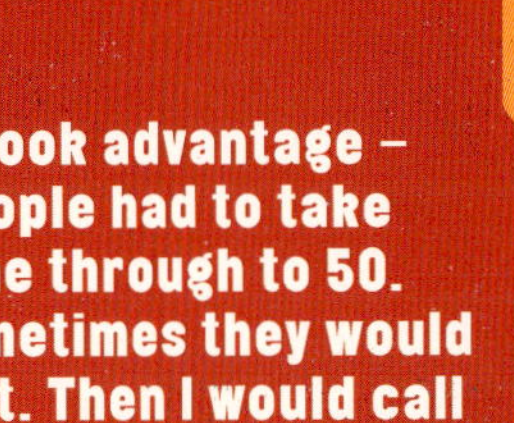

"When I came here,
I started to go out
with girls, dancing.
That's how I learnt
English.

Life is like that."

Giuseppe

"I bought the business when I was 17. I took advantage – it was really going well at the time. People had to take a number to get a haircut! Numbers one through to 50. The guys would take a number and sometimes they would go wait at the tavern across the street. Then I would call the tavern and say 'Hey, it's number 30!' and a guy would come running."

Marcel

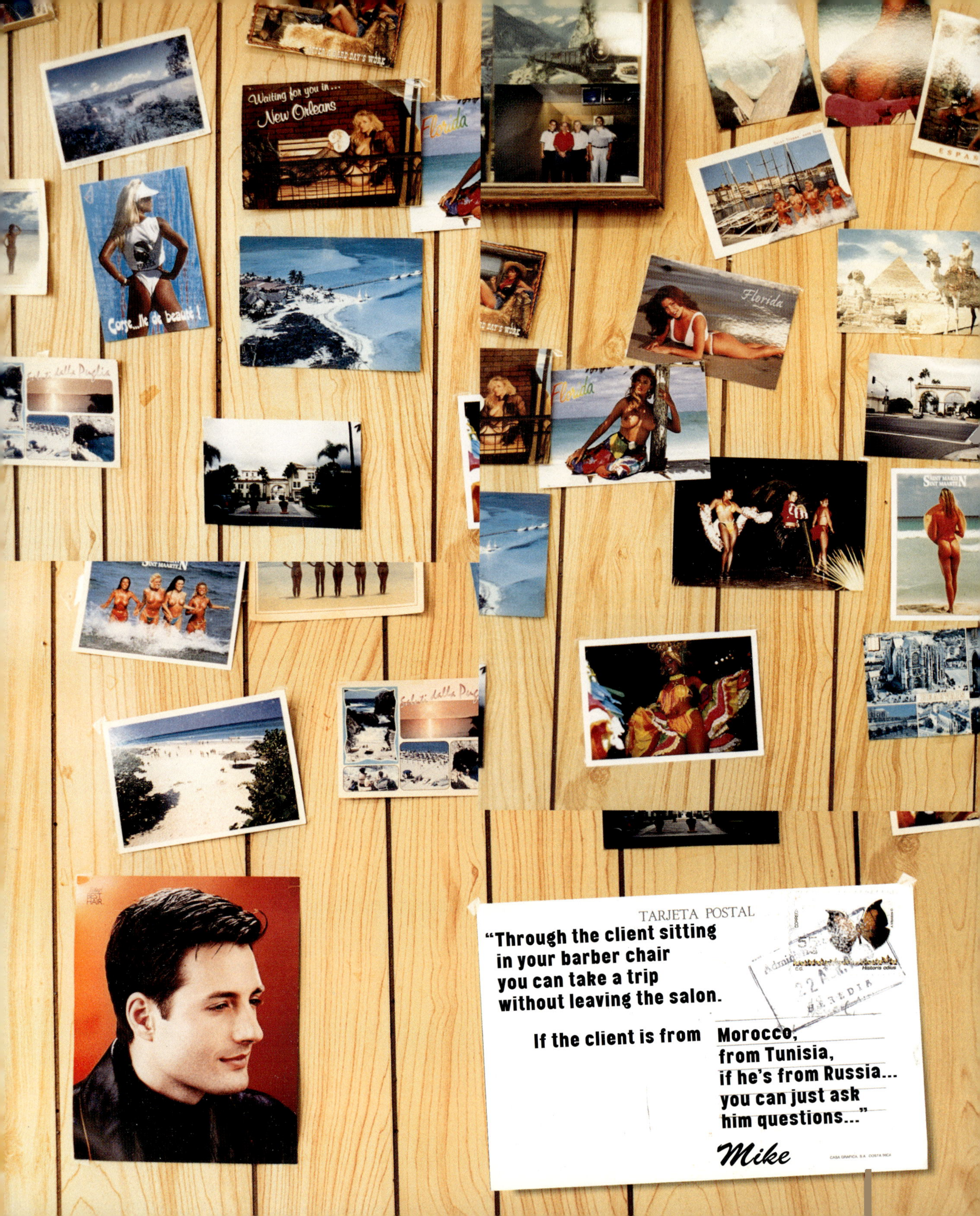
Waiting for you in...
New Orleans
Florida
Corse...Ile de beauté!
Saluti dalla Puglia
Florida
Florida
TARJETA POSTAL
"Through the client sitting
in your barber chair
you can take a trip
without leaving the salon.
If the client is from Morocco,
from Tunisia,
if he's from Russia...
you can just ask
him questions..."
Mike

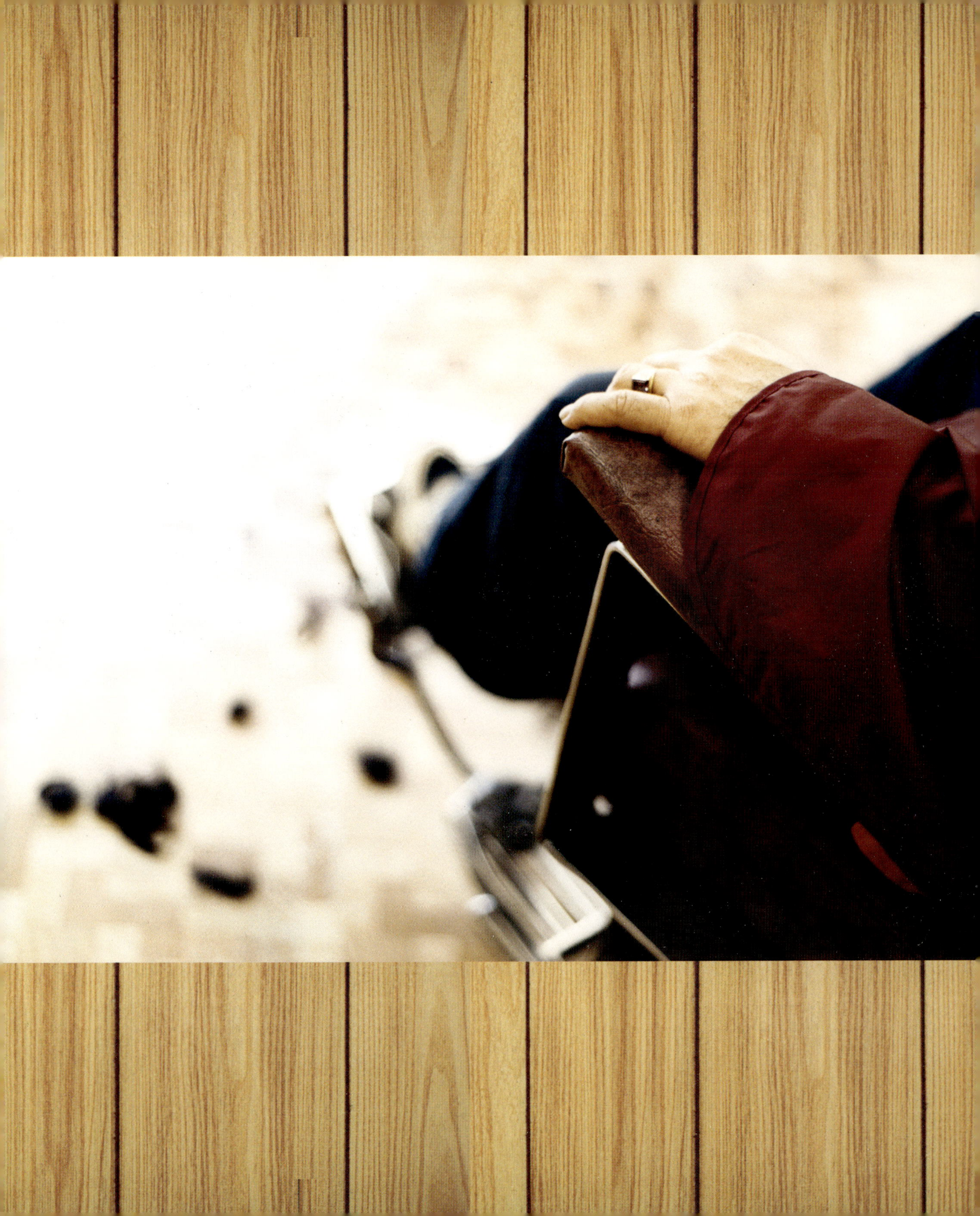

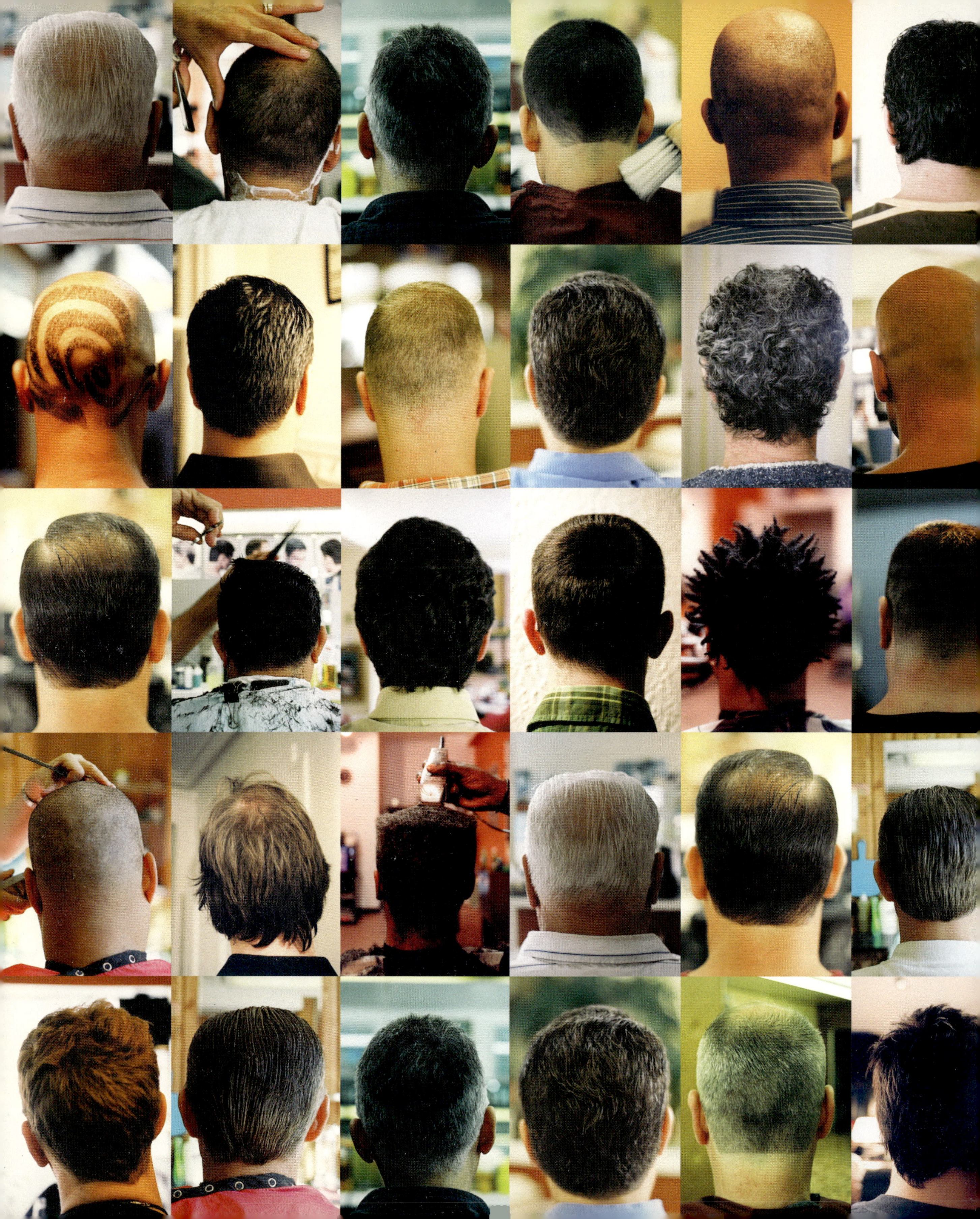

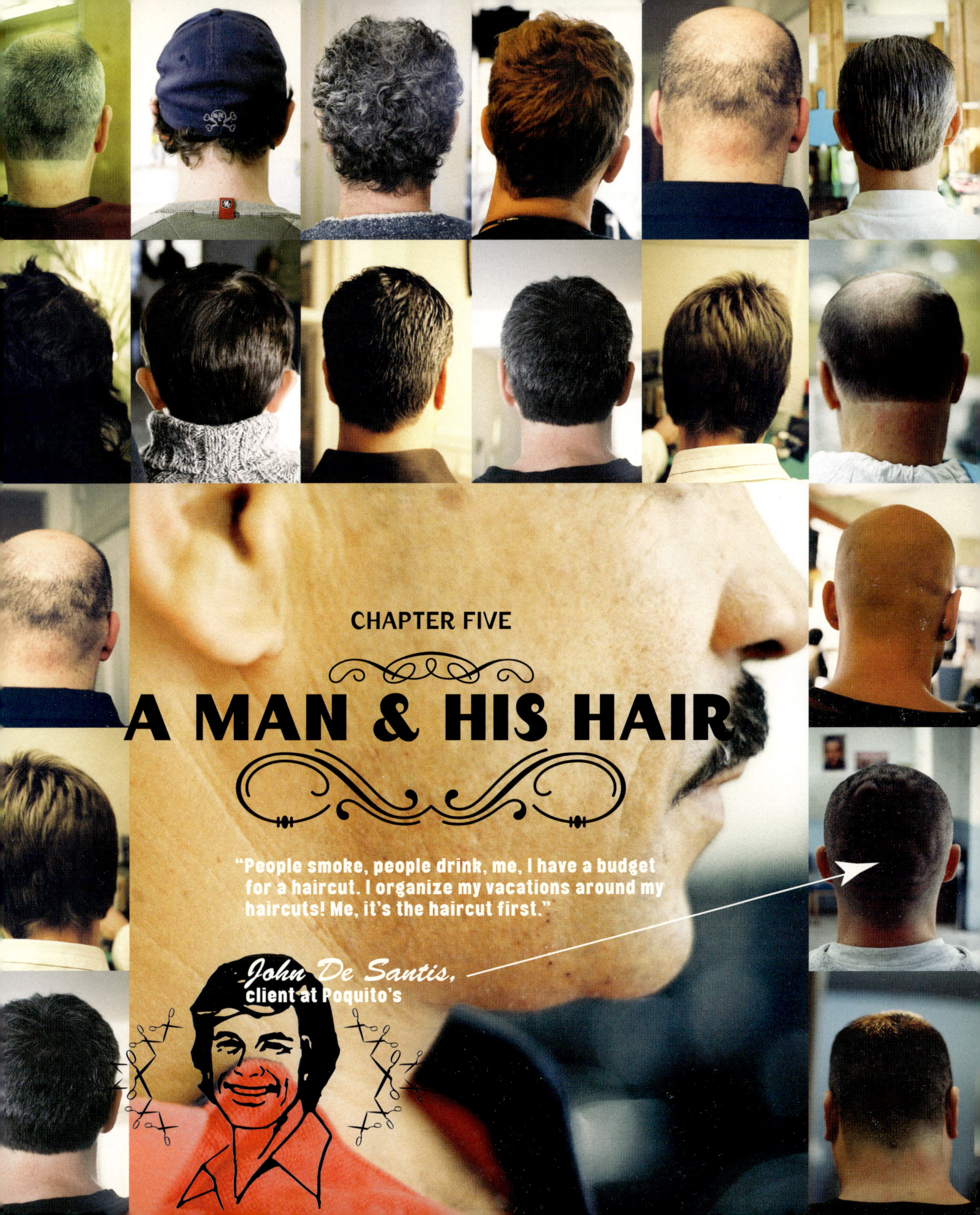
CHAPTER FIVE
A MAN & HIS HAIR
"People smoke, people drink, me, I have a budget for a haircut. I organize my vacations around my haircuts! Me, it's the haircut first."
John De Santis,
client at Poquito's

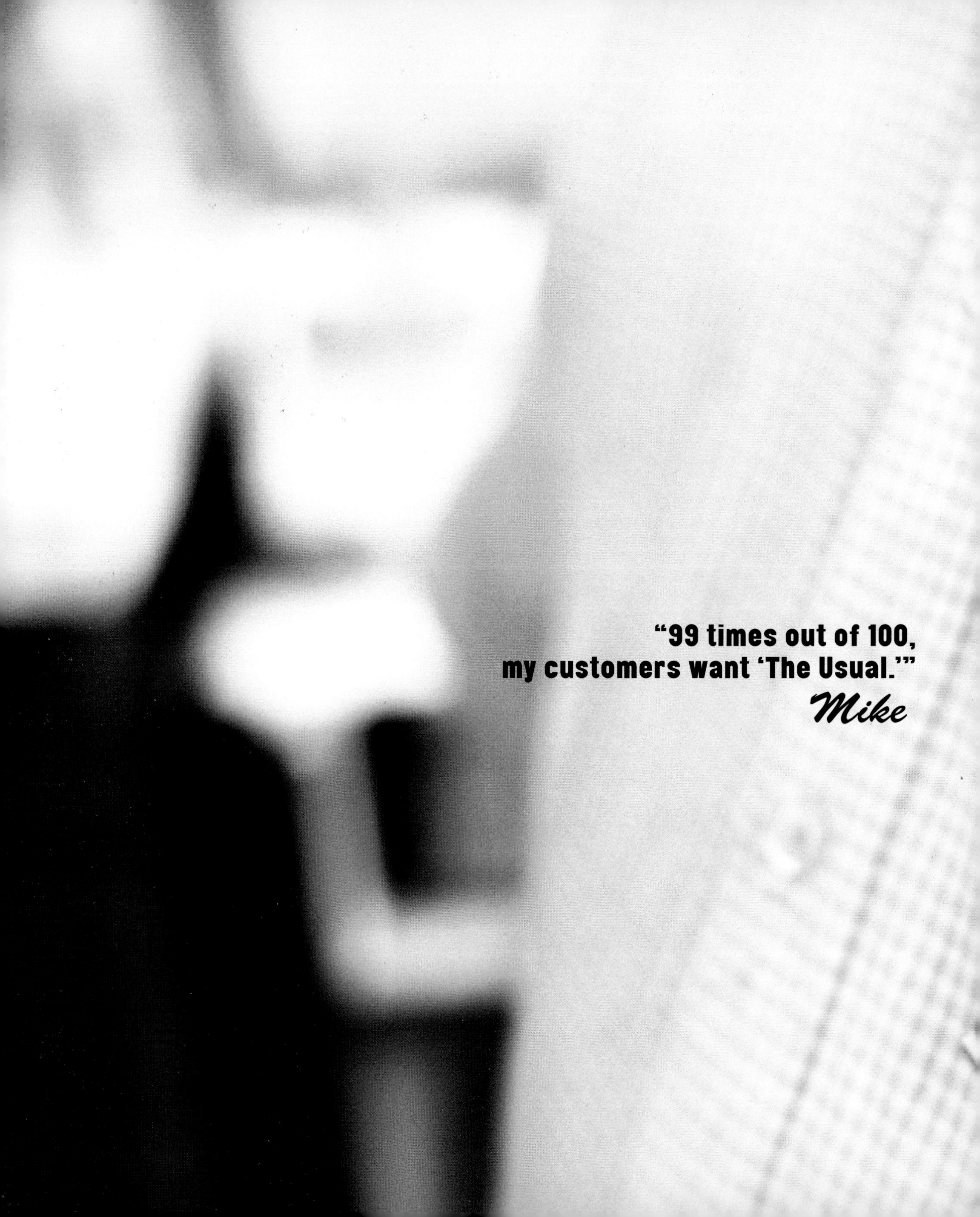

“99 times out of 100,
my customers want ‘The Usual.’”

Mike

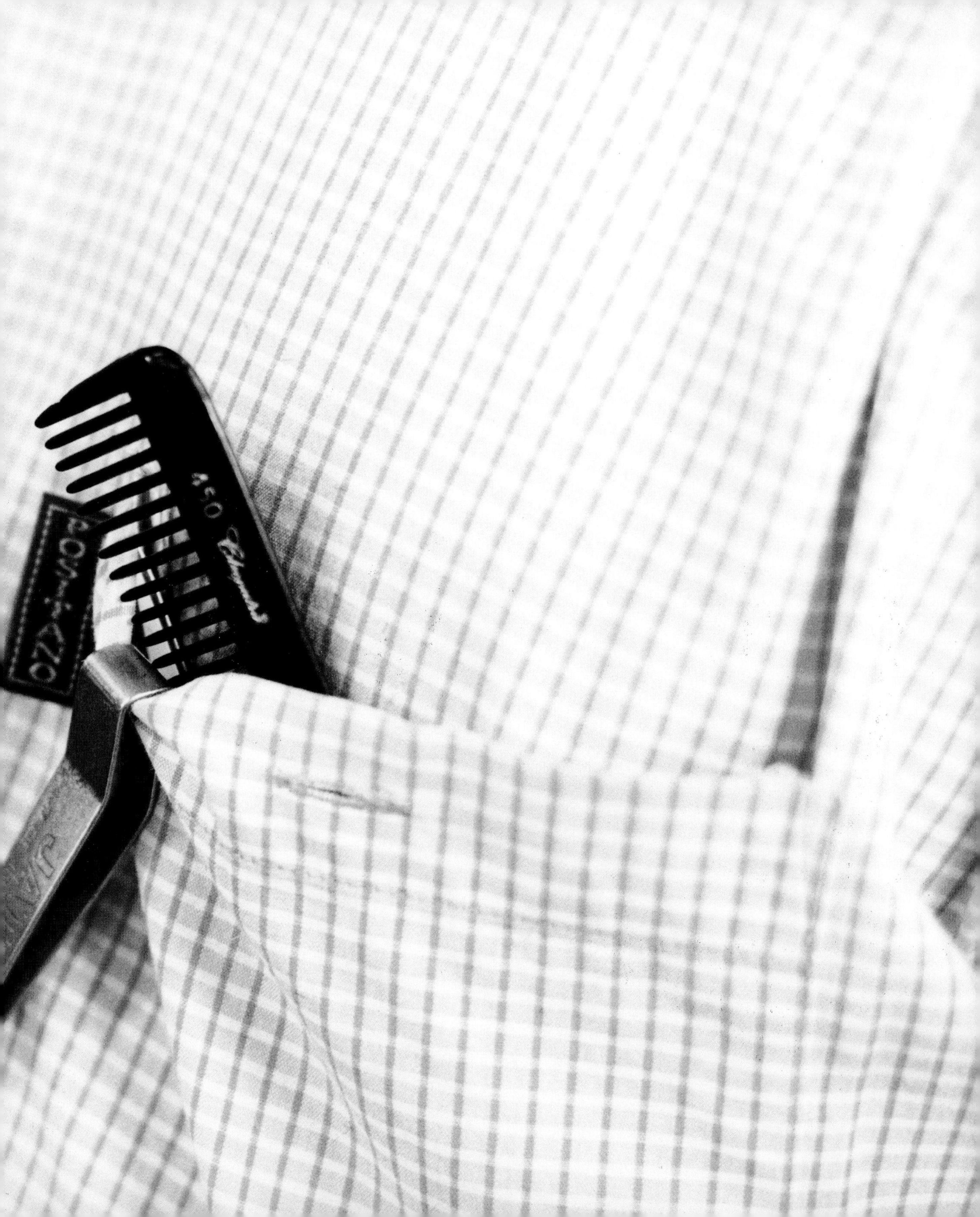
450

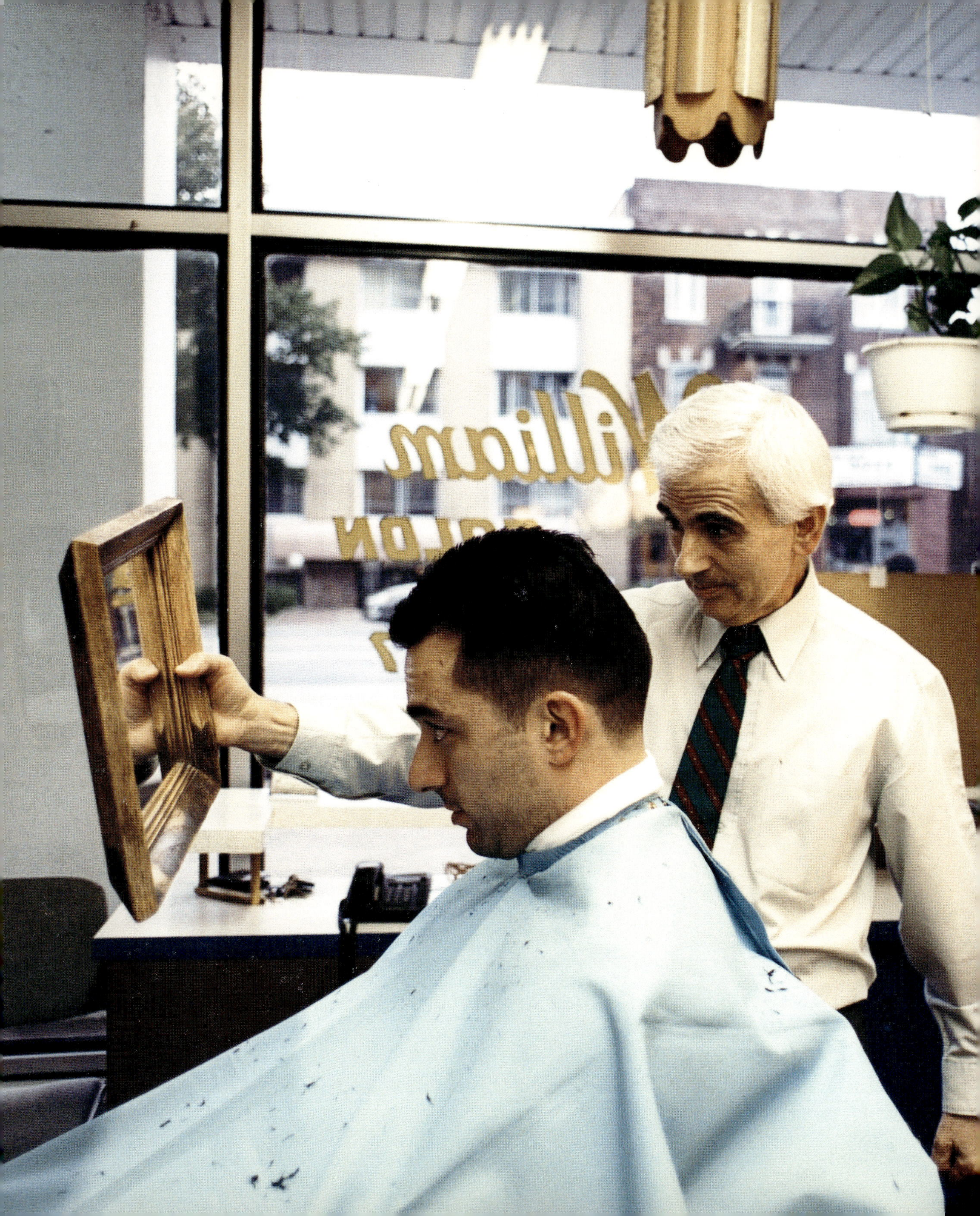

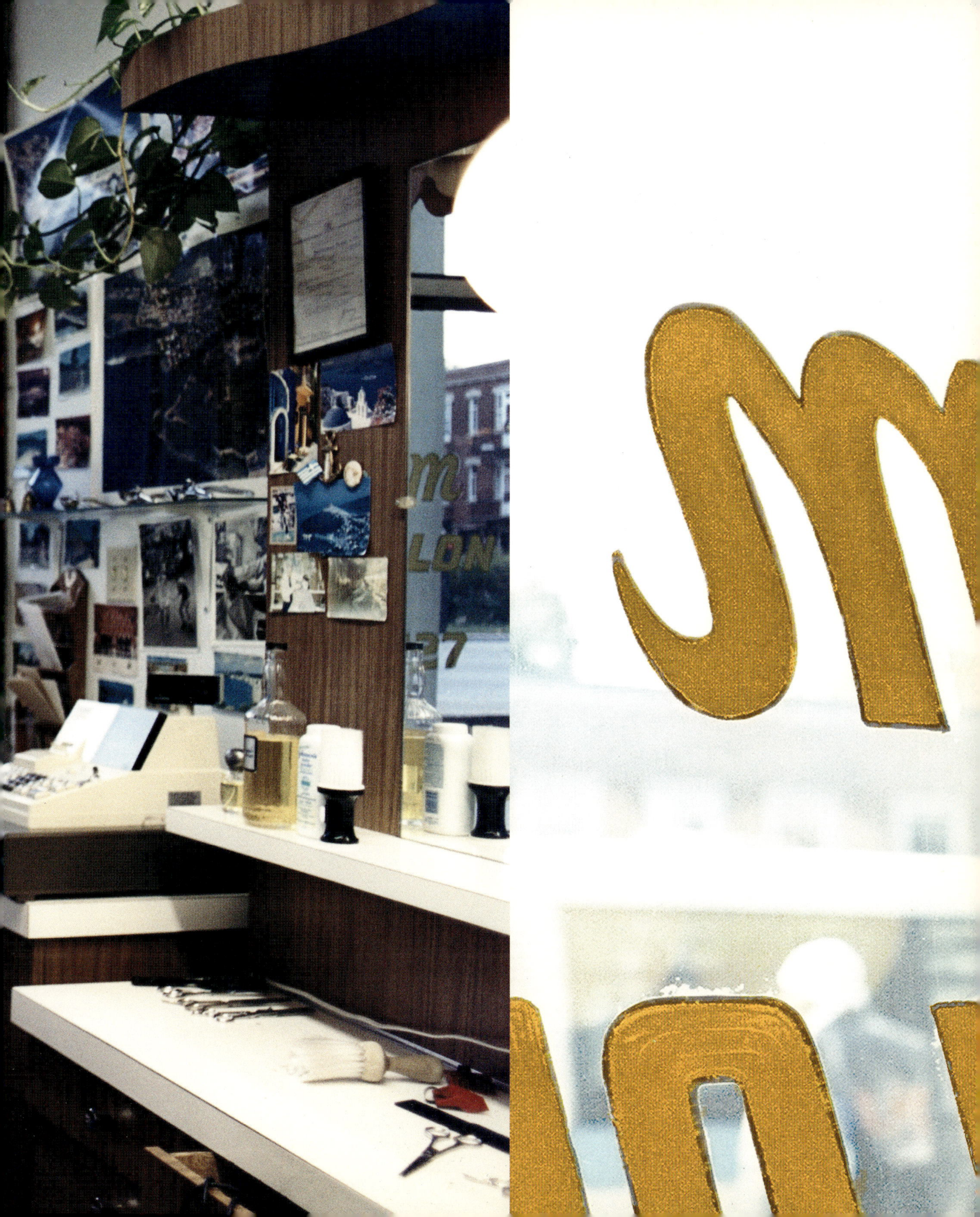
m
LON
27

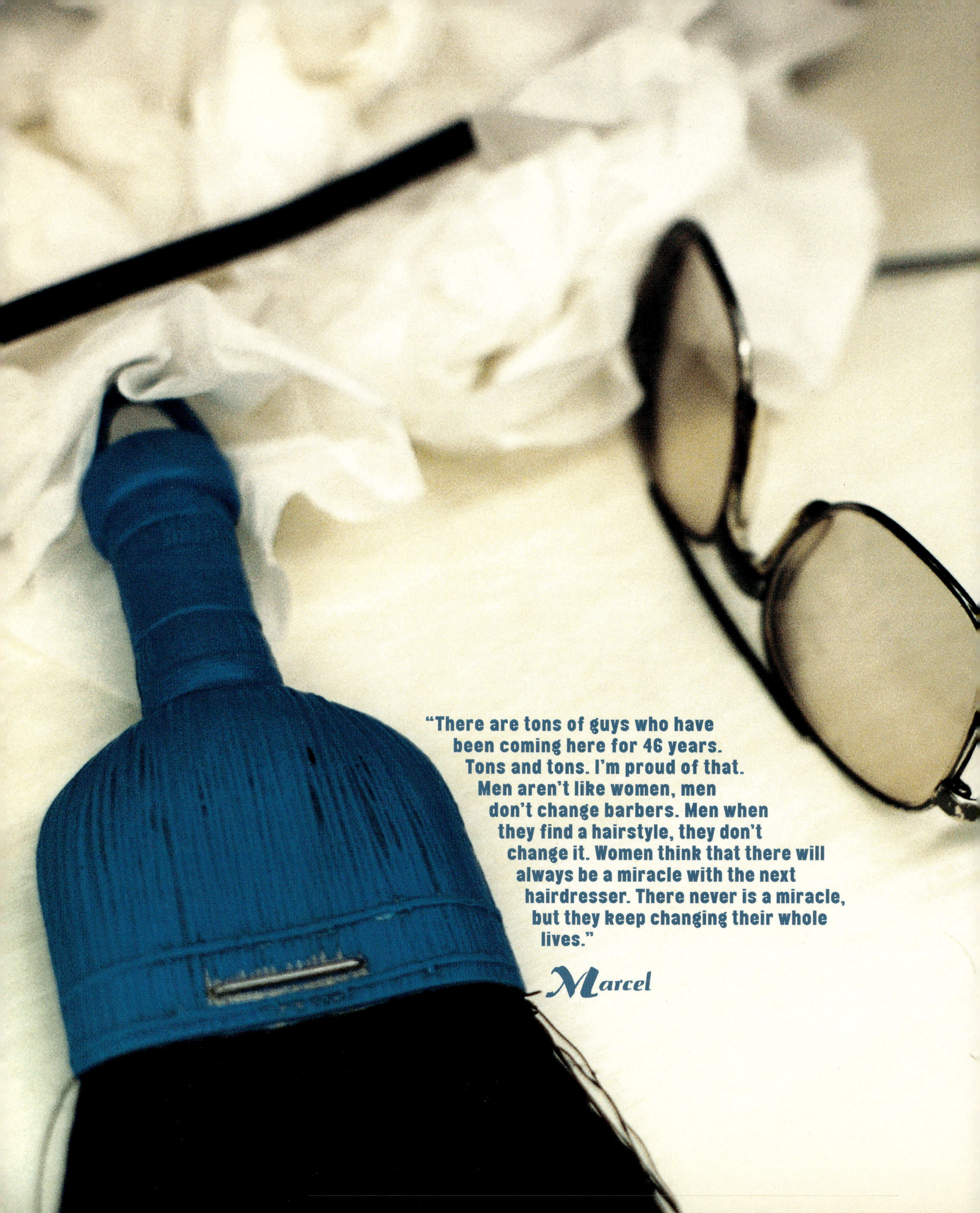
"There are tons of guys who have been coming here for 46 years. Tons and tons. I'm proud of that. Men aren't like women, men don't change barbers. Men when they find a hairstyle, they don't change it. Women think that there will always be a miracle with the next hairdresser. There never is a miracle, but they keep changing their whole lives."
Marcel

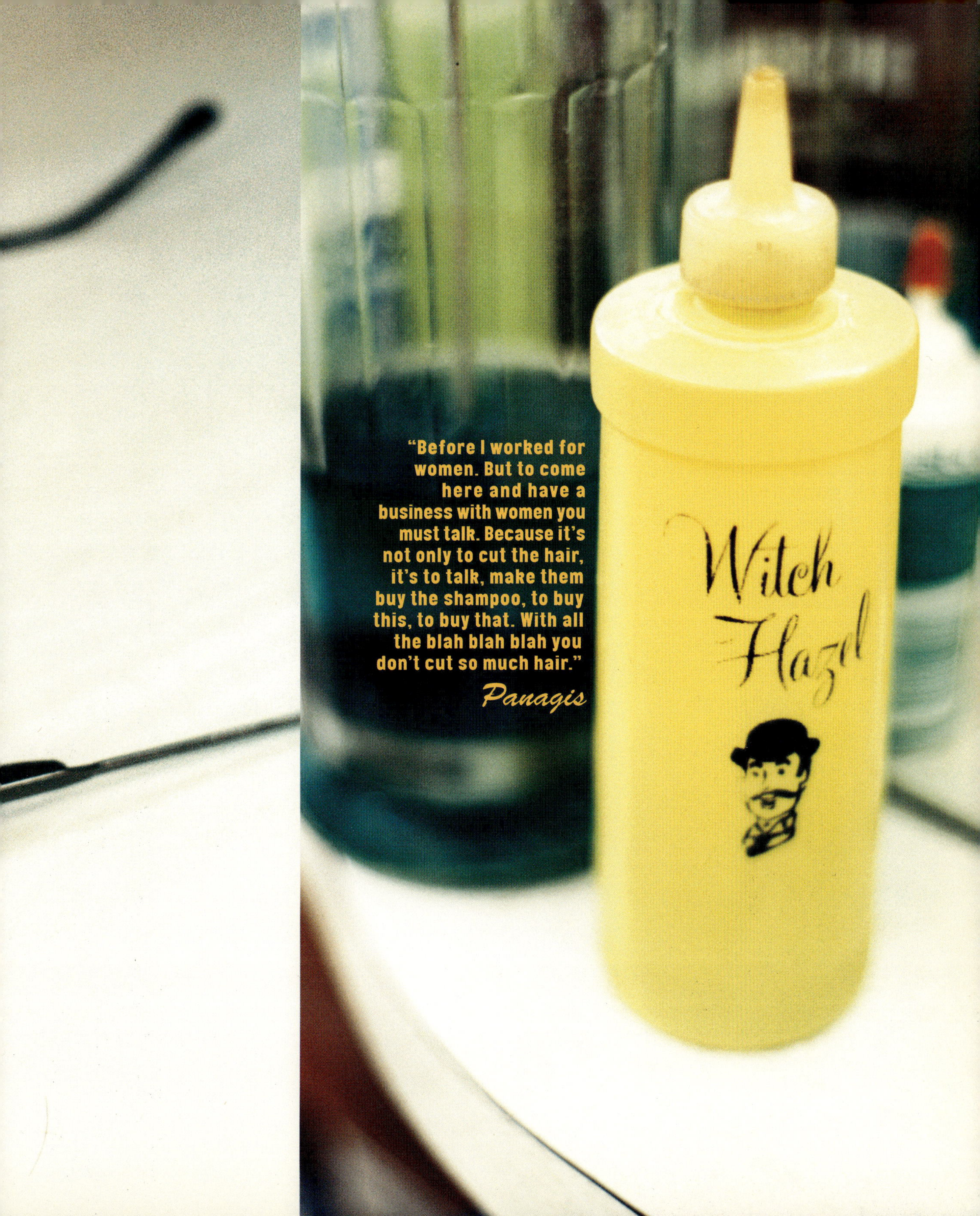

"Before I worked for women. But to come here and have a business with women you must talk. Because it's not only to cut the hair, it's to talk, make them buy the shampoo, to buy this, to buy that. With all the blah blah blah you don't cut so much hair."

Panagis

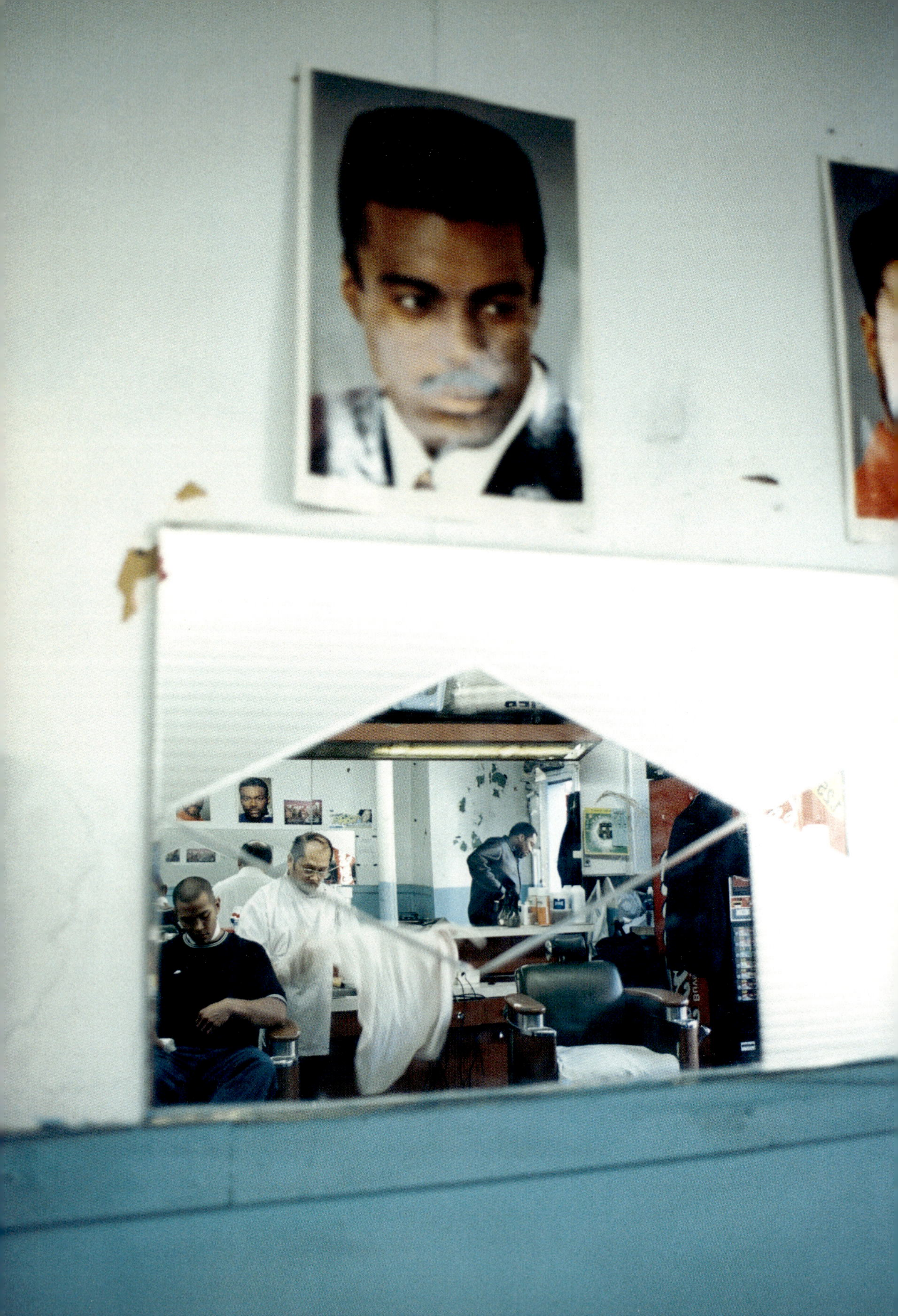

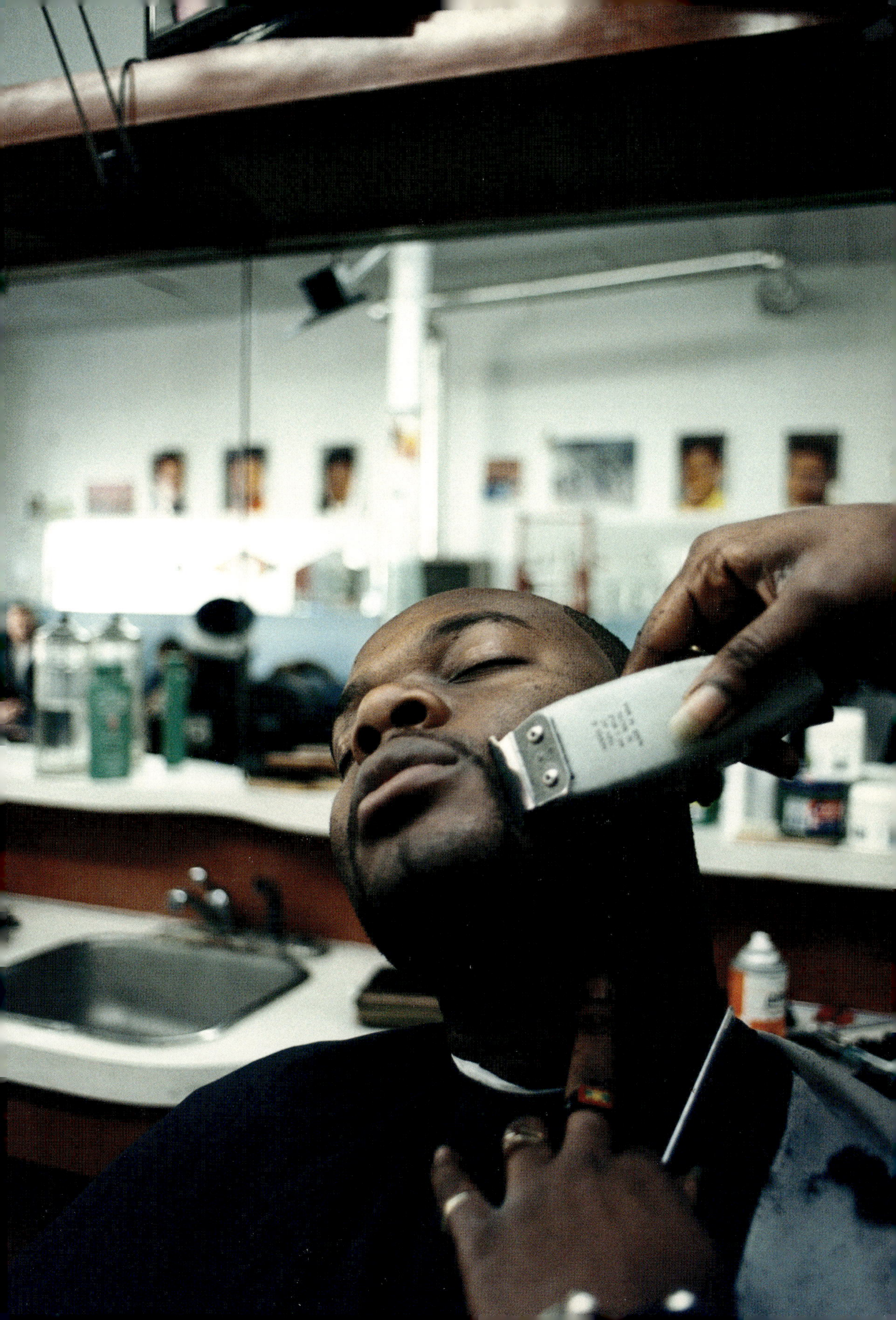

"I used to have a lot of clients who were firemen and policemen because I used to give them a special haircut – it was like two haircuts in one. For work, they had to have short hair but at the time it was more fashionable to have longer hair. I had a trick to make the longer hair presentable, so that they wouldn't get in trouble at the station. I would leave parts of the sideburn longer at the front. When they needed it to be short for work, they could tuck that hair behind their ears. Then when they would go out, they could pull the hair back in front of their ears and it would look longer. It was like two haircuts in one! It became really popular."

Marcel

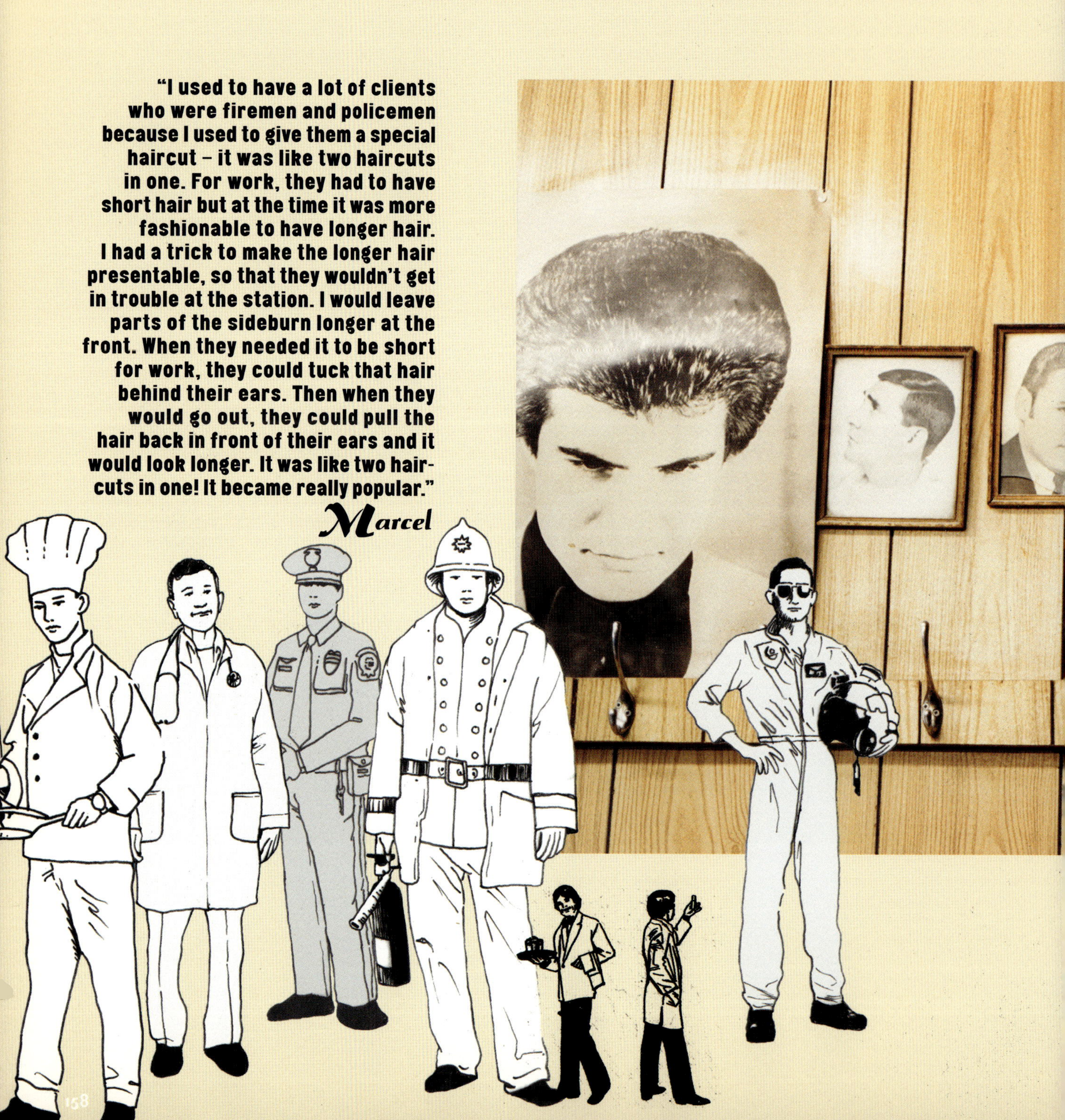

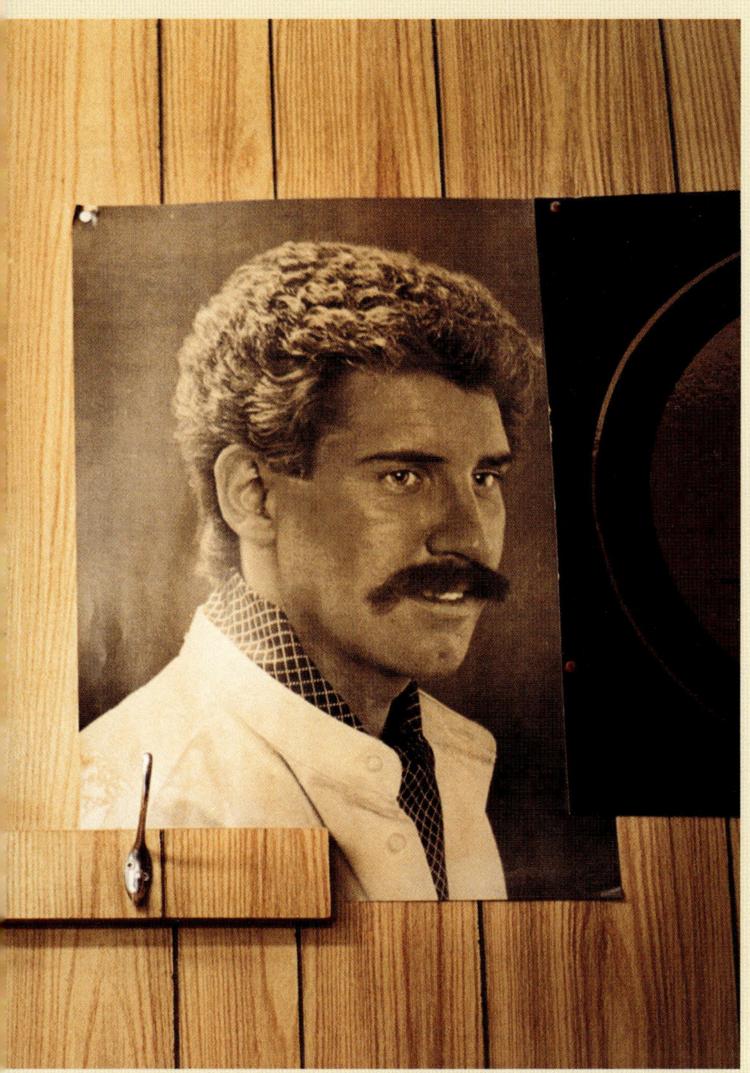

"The way to tell a good haircut isn't the day you get it cut, it's three or four days later. The way it grows, that's how you can tell."

John De Santis,
client at Poquito's

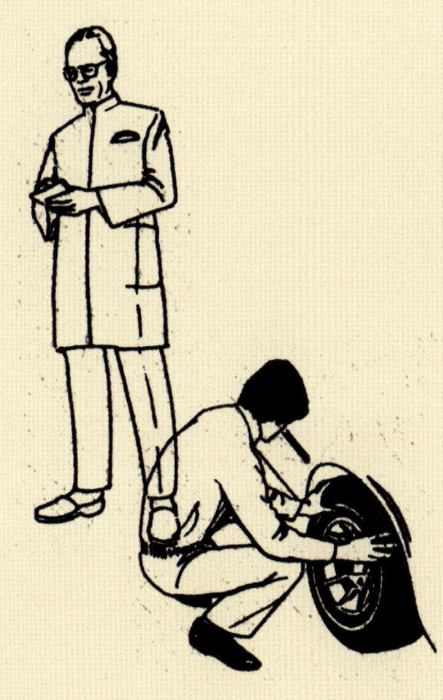

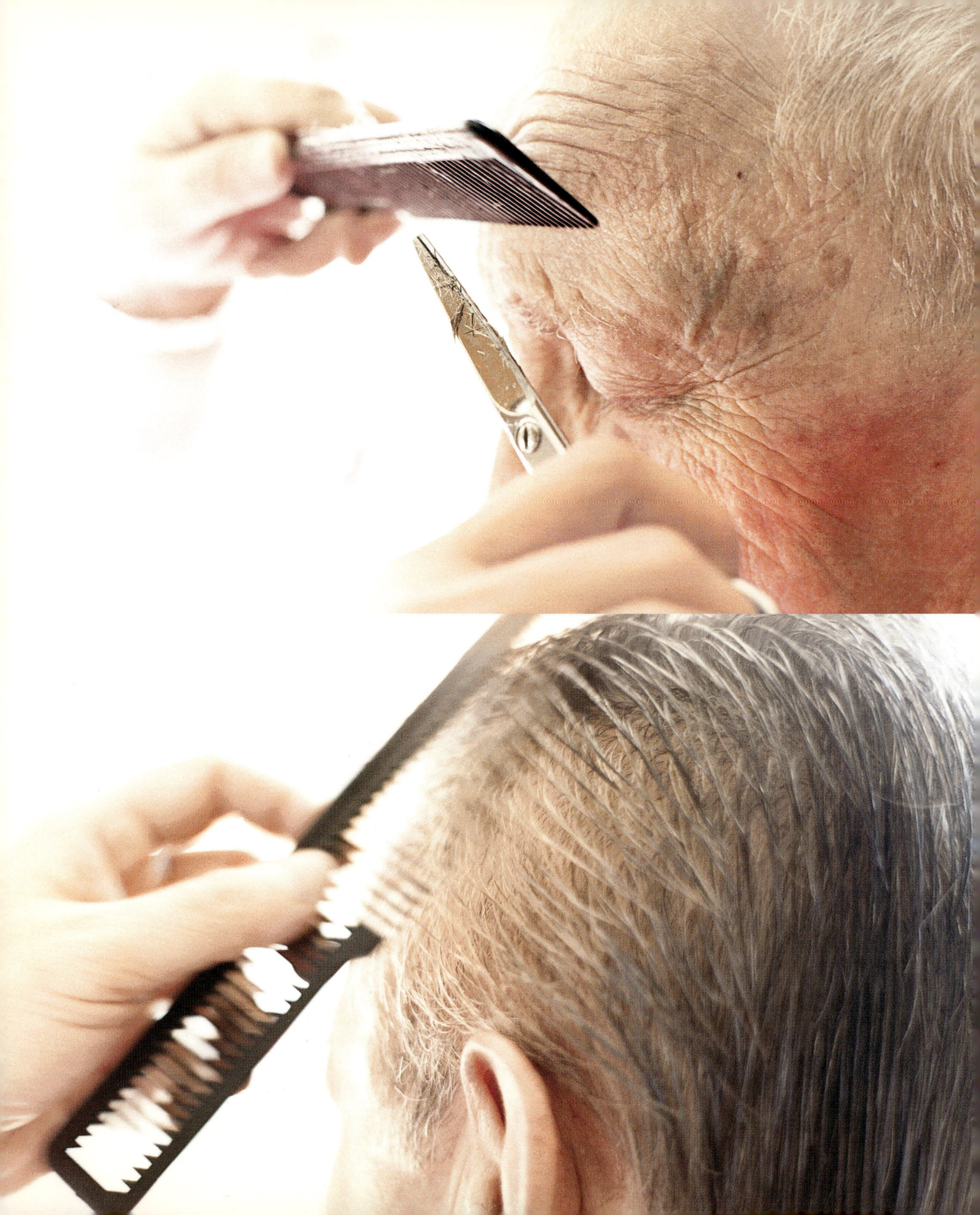

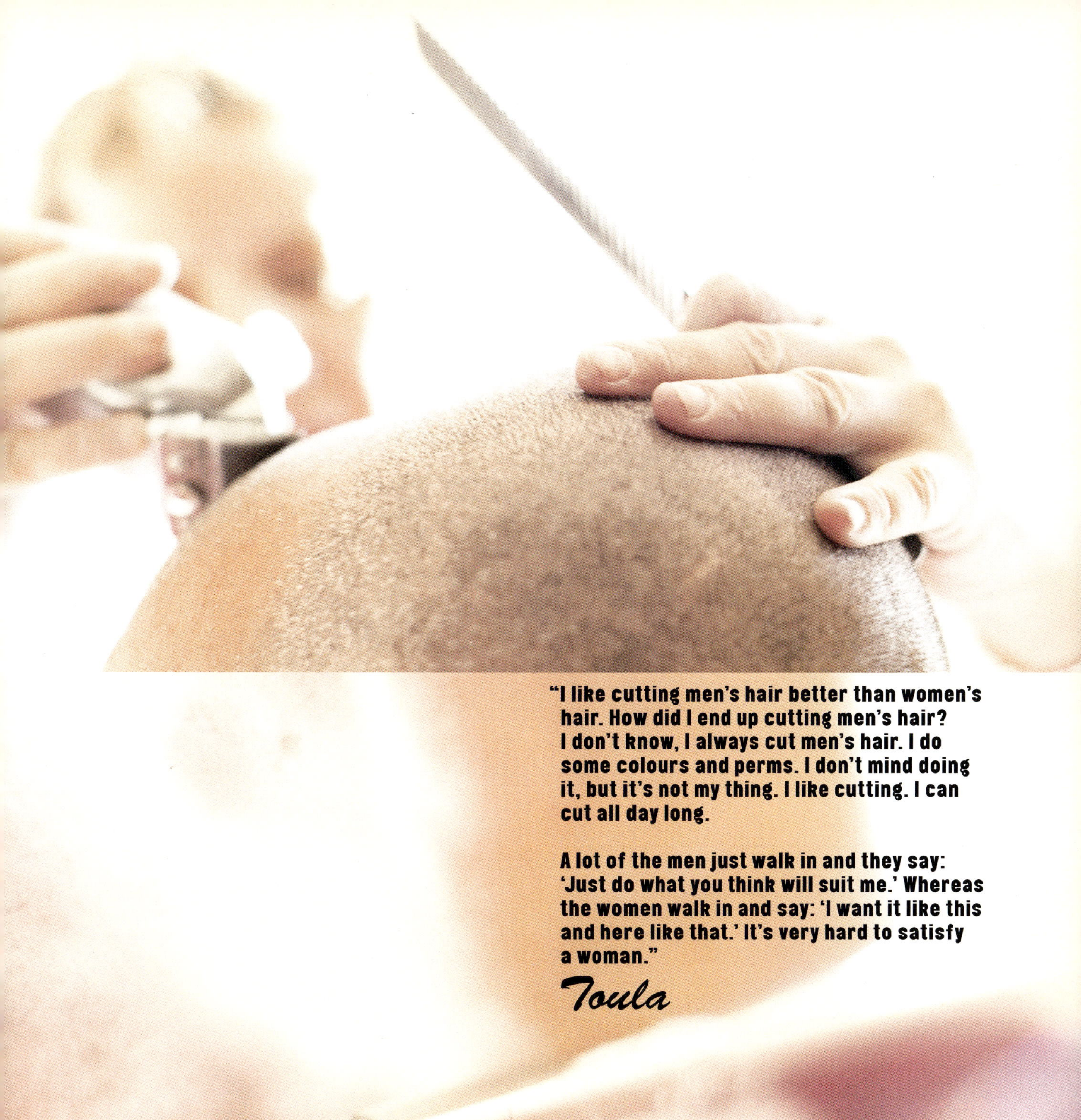

"I like cutting men's hair better than women's hair. How did I end up cutting men's hair? I don't know, I always cut men's hair. I do some colours and perms. I don't mind doing it, but it's not my thing. I like cutting. I can cut all day long.

A lot of the men just walk in and they say: 'Just do what you think will suit me.' Whereas the women walk in and say: 'I want it like this and here like that.' It's very hard to satisfy a woman."

Toula

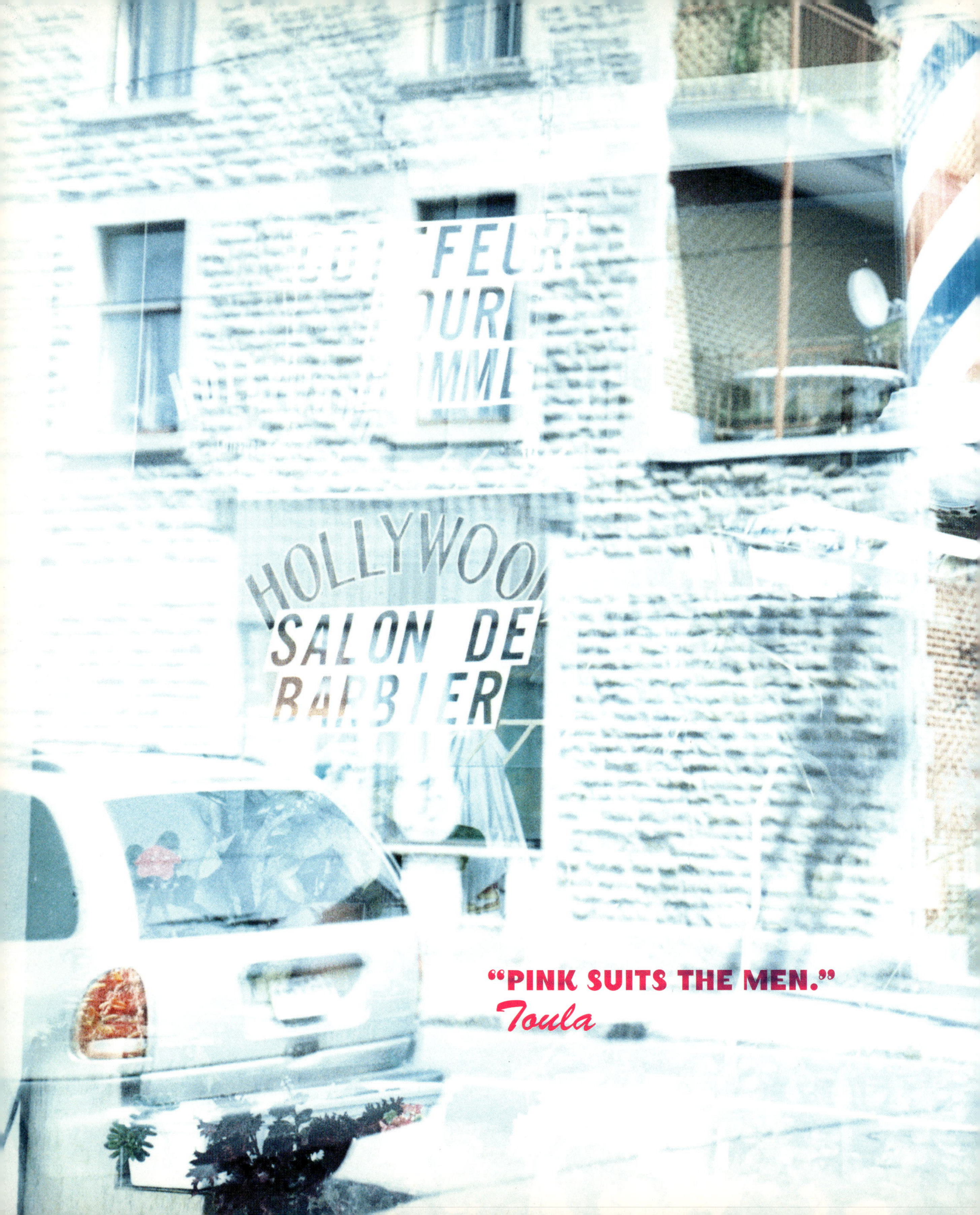

"PINK SUITS THE MEN."
Toula

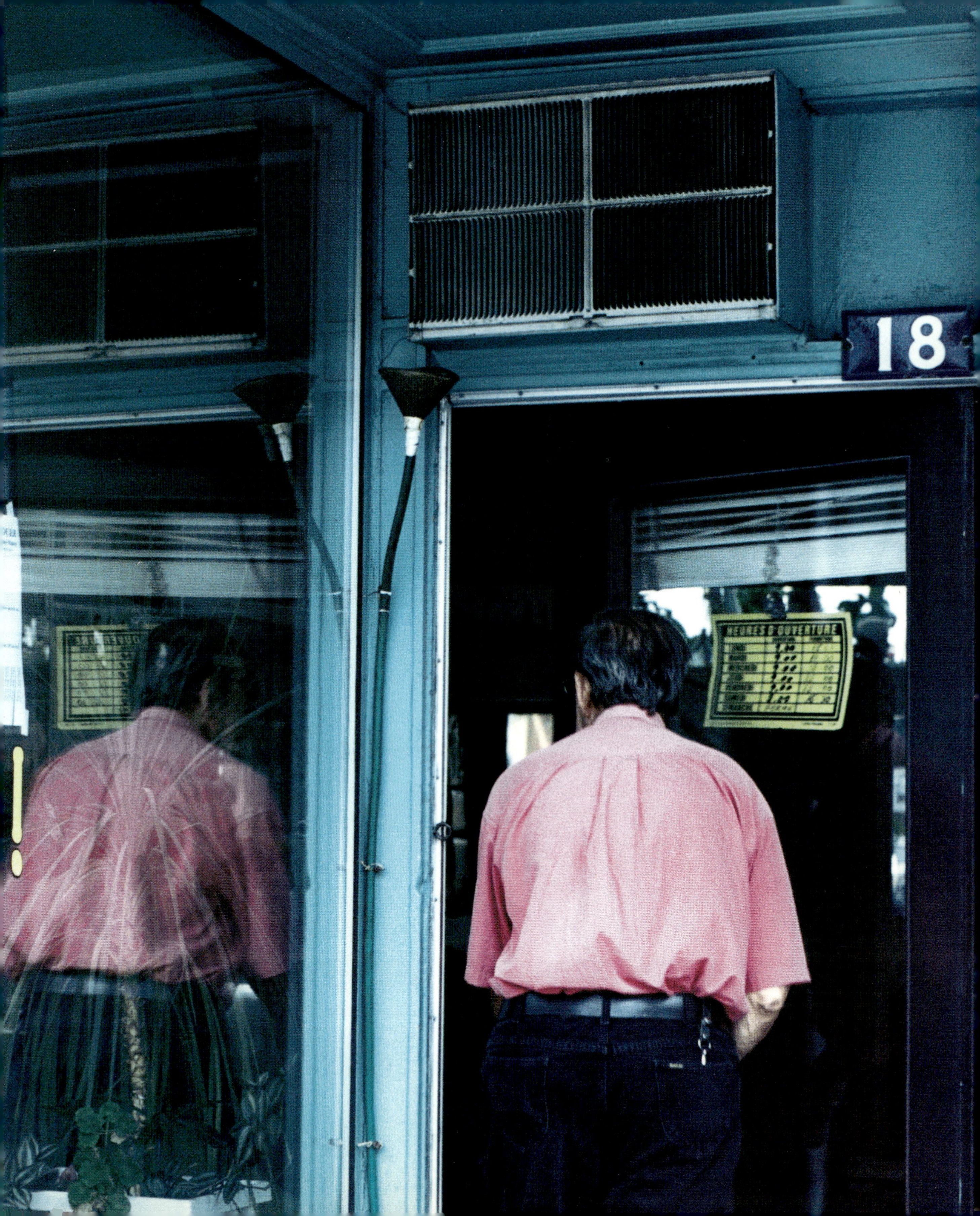
18
HEURES D'OUVERTURE

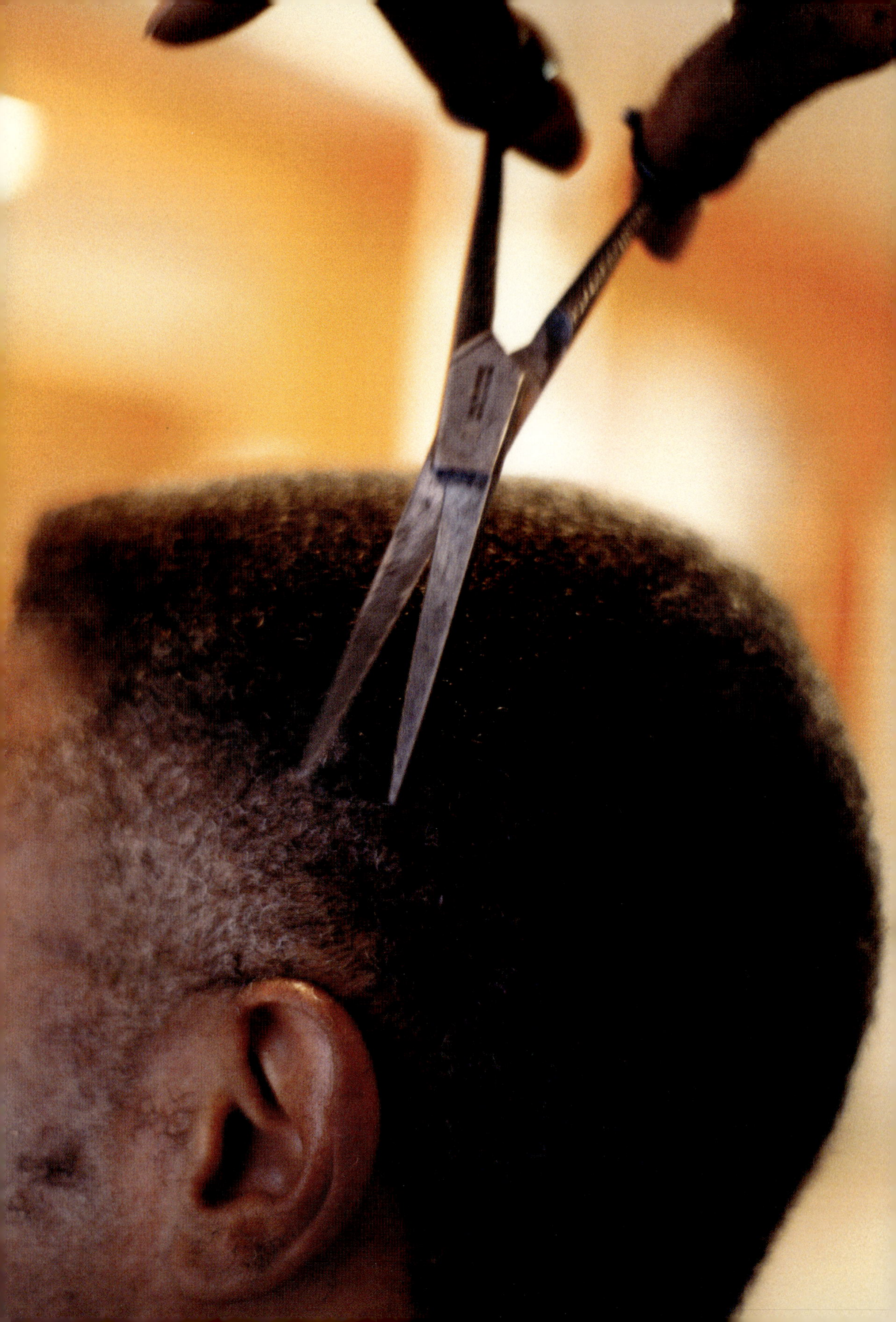

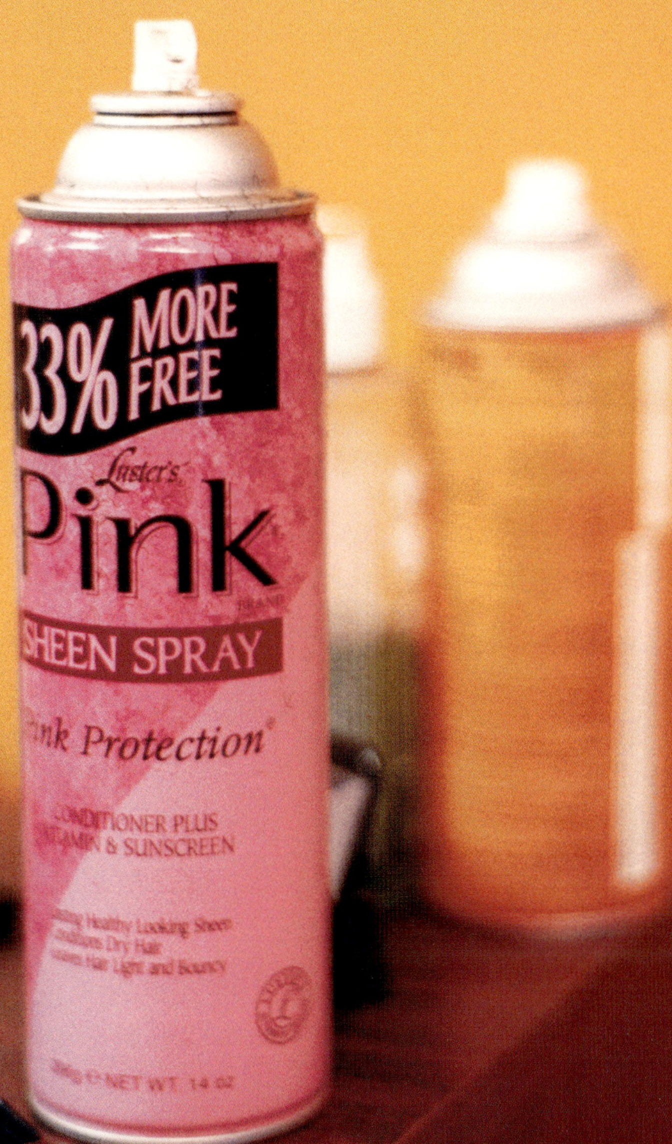
33% MORE FREE
Pink
SHEEN SPRAY

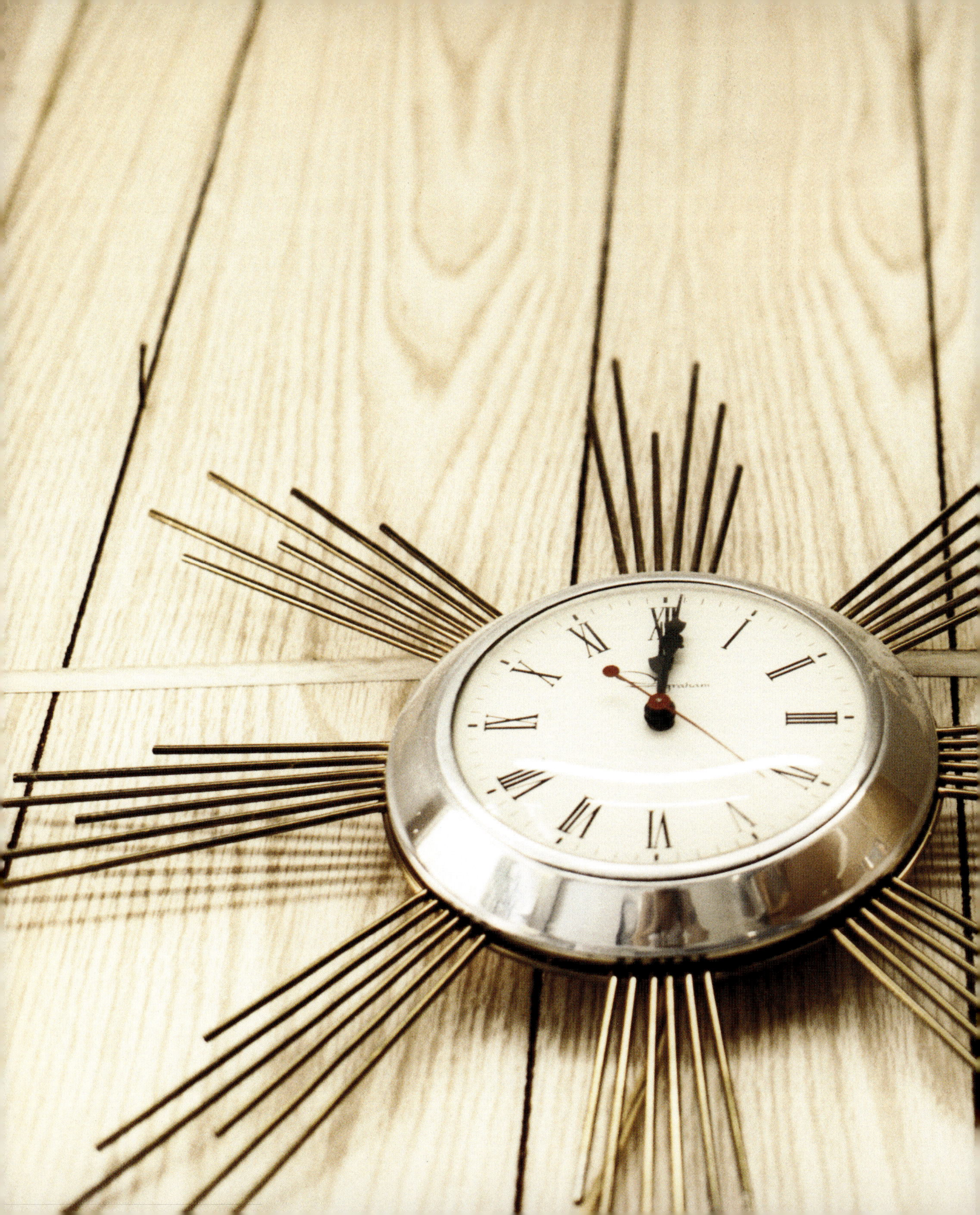

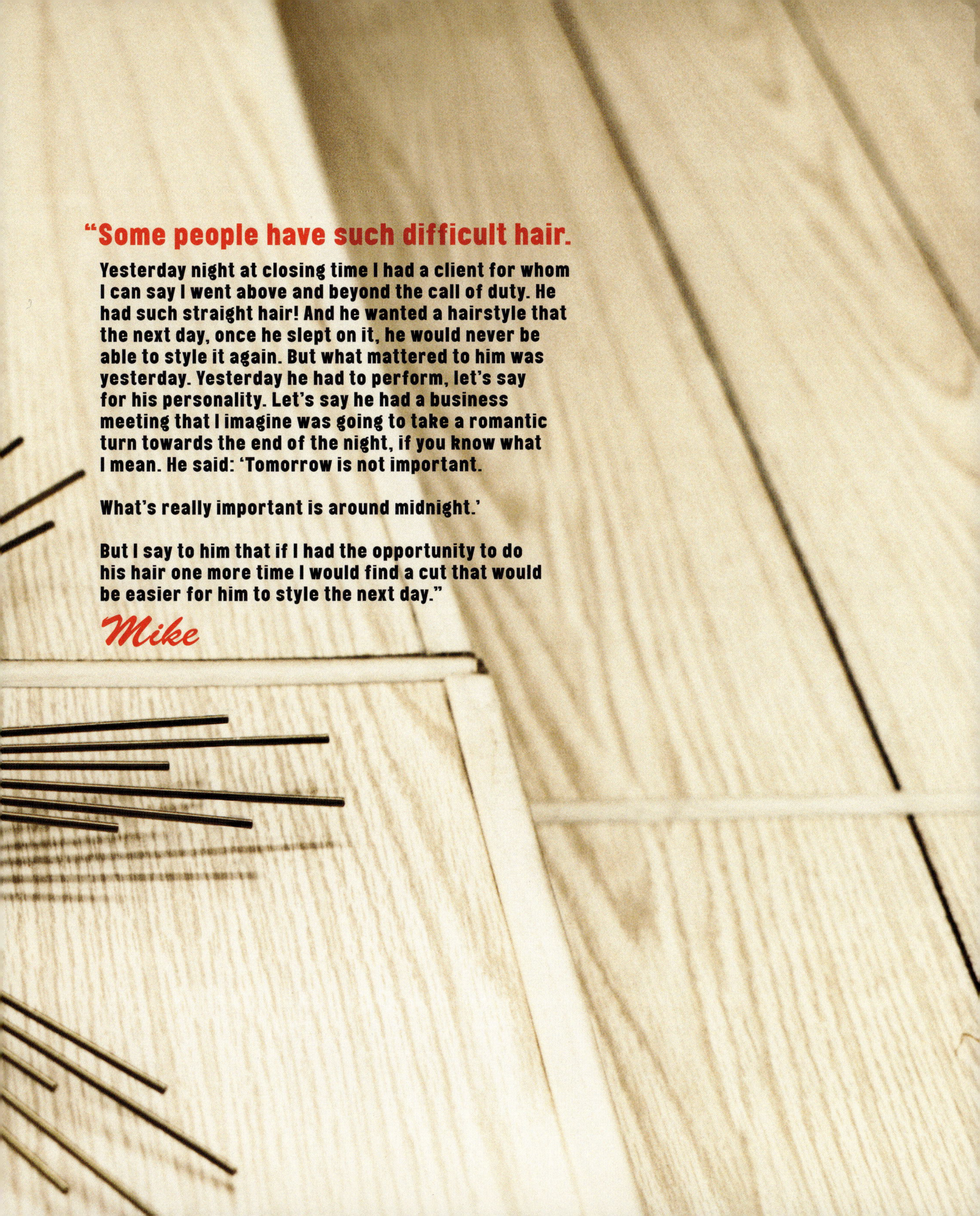

“Some people have such difficult hair.

Yesterday night at closing time I had a client for whom I can say I went above and beyond the call of duty. He had such straight hair! And he wanted a hairstyle that the next day, once he slept on it, he would never be able to style it again. But what mattered to him was yesterday. Yesterday he had to perform, let’s say for his personality. Let’s say he had a business meeting that I imagine was going to take a romantic turn towards the end of the night, if you know what I mean. He said: ‘Tomorrow is not important.

What’s really important is around midnight.’

But I say to him that if I had the opportunity to do his hair one more time I would find a cut that would be easier for him to style the next day.”

Mike

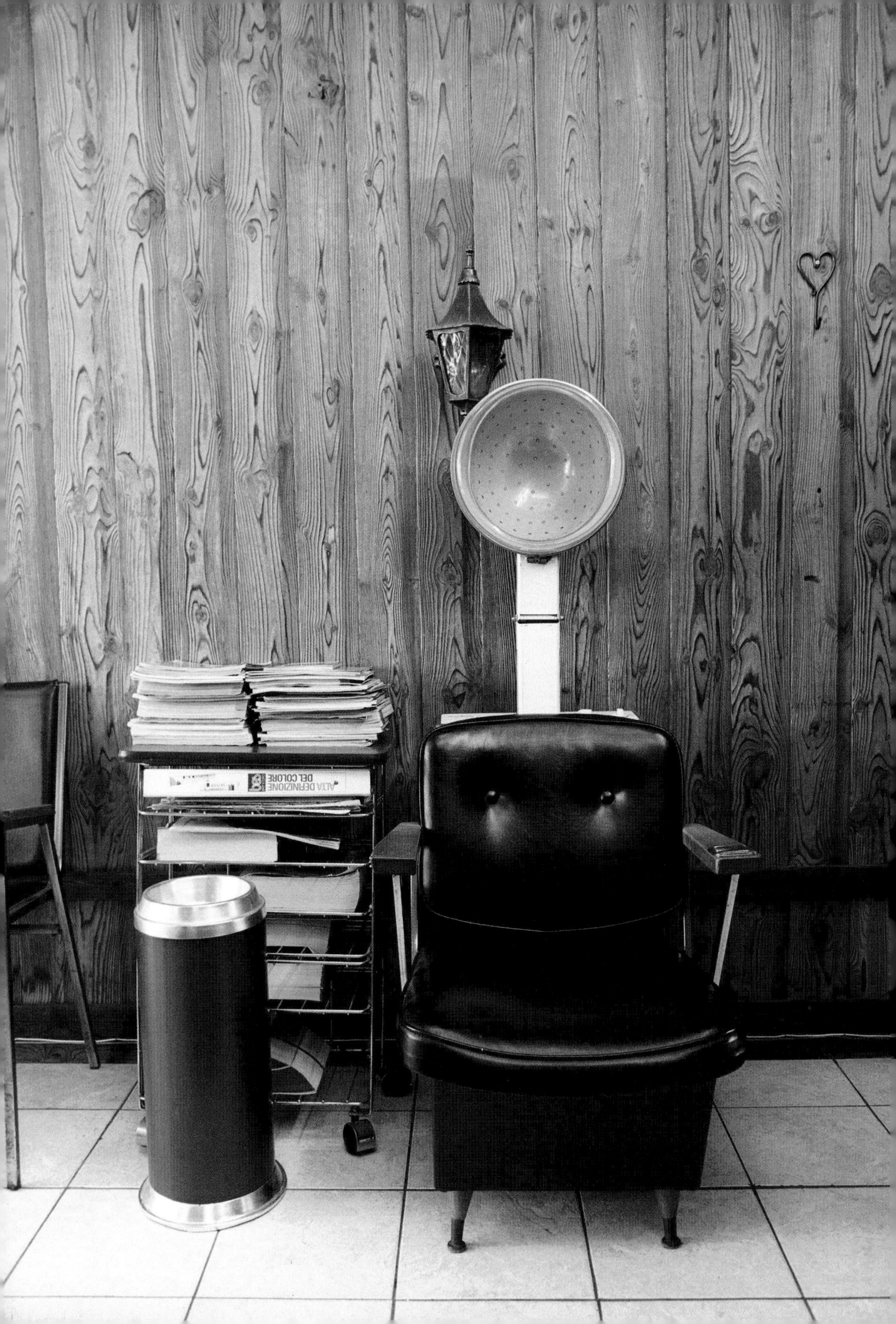
ALTA DEFINIZIONE
DEL COLORE

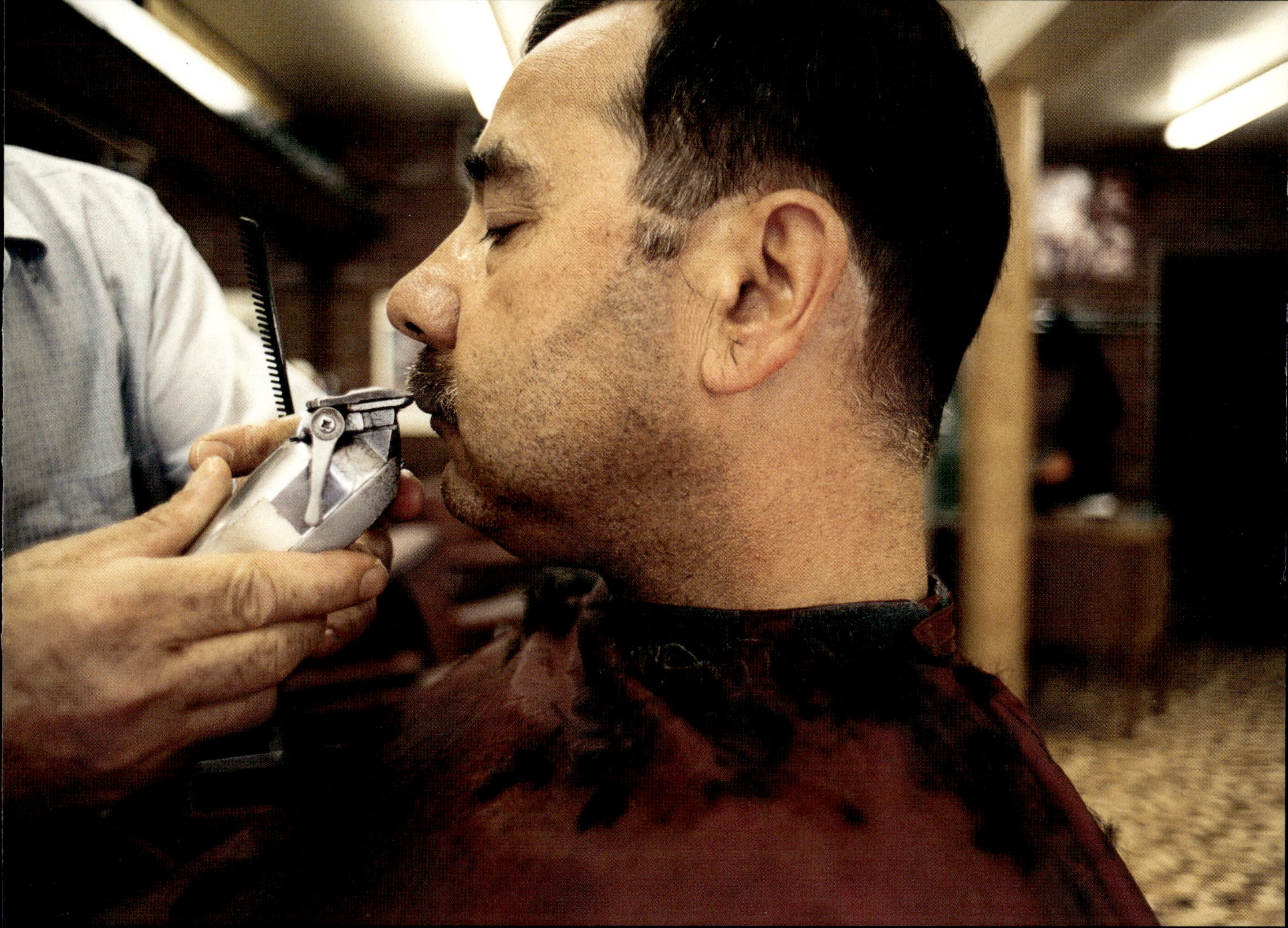

"Your secretary will say that you look better without a moustache, the waitress on the corner will tell you it looks better without, but your wife, she'll tell you that you looked better with your moustache."

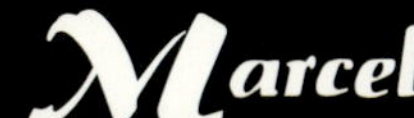

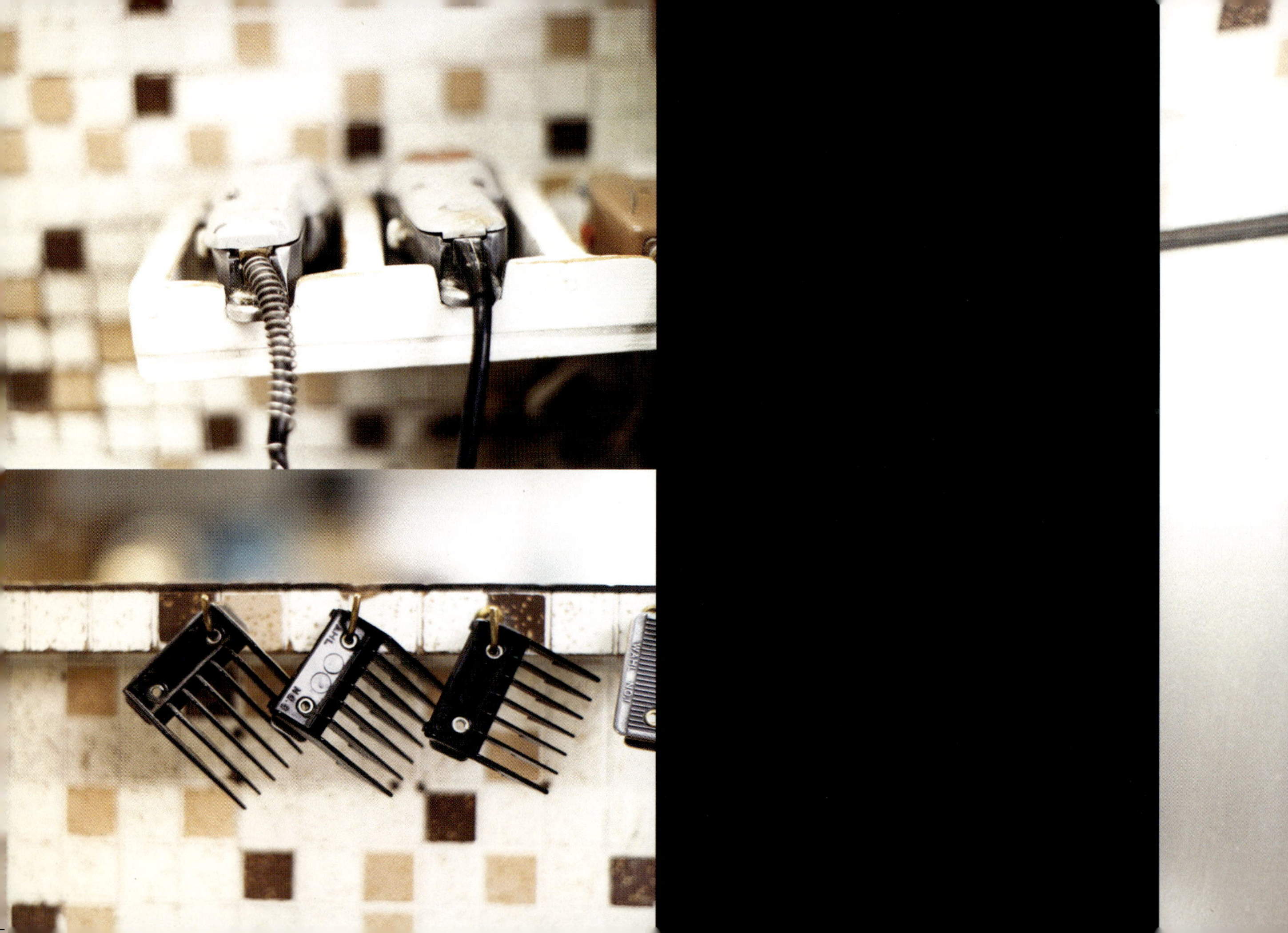

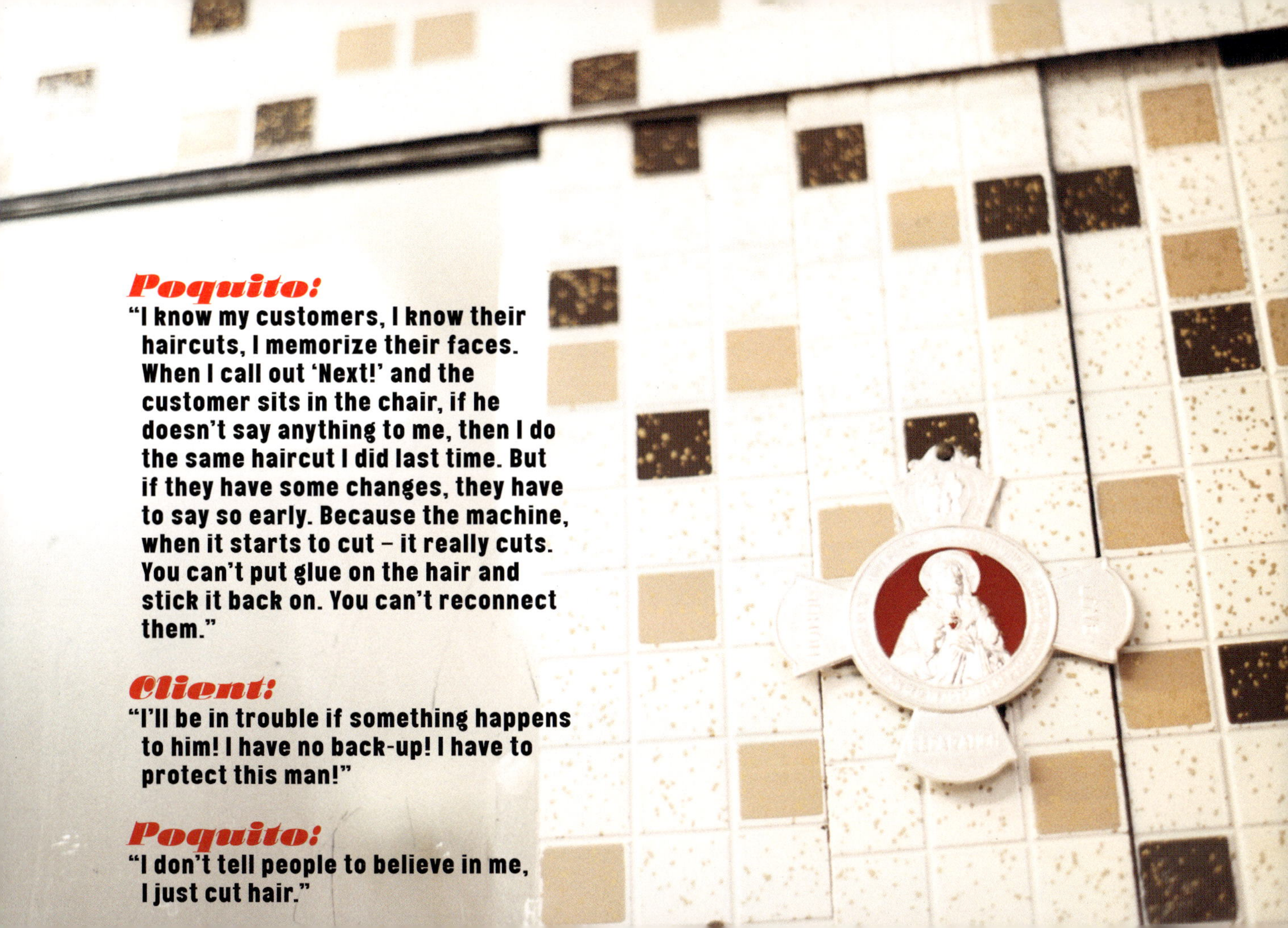

Poquito:

"I know my customers, I know their haircuts, I memorize their faces. When I call out 'Next!' and the customer sits in the chair, if he doesn't say anything to me, then I do the same haircut I did last time. But if they have some changes, they have to say so early. Because the machine, when it starts to cut – it really cuts. You can't put glue on the hair and stick it back on. You can't reconnect them."

Client:

"I'll be in trouble if something happens to him! I have no back-up! I have to protect this man!"

Poquito:

"I don't tell people to believe in me, I just cut hair."

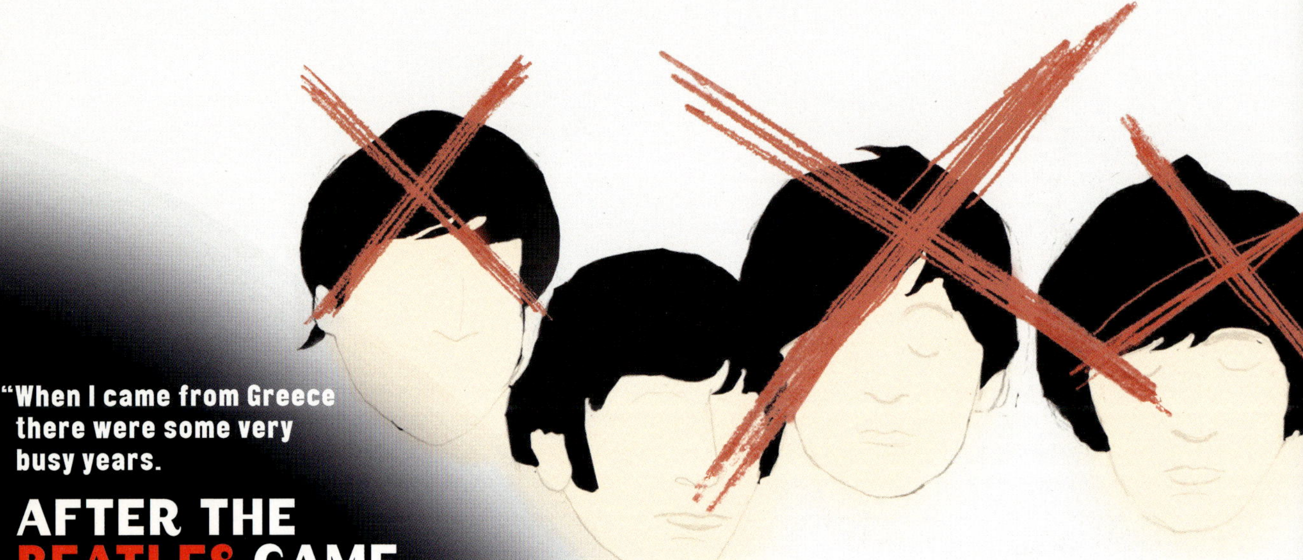

"When I came from Greece there were some very busy years.

AFTER THE BEATLES CAME WITH THE LONG HAIR BUSINESS SLOWED DOWN.

There used to be five to ten barbers in each barbershop. Now there are two, or three, or one. Before men used to get haircuts every two weeks and now they get haircuts every two months, three months, six months, one year. I know boys who have come here, they're 18 years old and they've never been in a barbershop before. They cut their hairs themselves.

Or their mothers cut it, I don't know."

Antonios

"Since January
I'm almost retired.
I reduced my days,

I'm closed Mondays. I'm going to reduce my hours even more and open later. I stay here to pass the time. I want to go, but my friends say: 'No, you can't close, you have to keep open.' One guy didn't like that I stayed open less, he asked why I'm closed on Monday and he got angry. He said: 'You have to reopen.' He has nowhere to go on Mondays."

Jimmy

Black Dog Publishing

Written by **Tally Abecassis**
Photographed by **Claudine Sauvé**
Designed by **Kuizin Studio**

Pages 4, 5, 26, 27, 63, 118, 119, 136-143
designed & illustrated by **Sébastien Bisson**
Pages 34, 35, 58, 100, 101, 158
designed & illustrated by **Tommy Doyle**
Pages 40, 135, 172, 173
designed & illustrated by **Jean-François Clermont**
Pages 123 illustrated by **Christine Battuz**
Pages 4, 8-15, 128, 129, 175 illustrations from ***The Art and Craft of Hairdressing,*** Pitman & Sons, 1964
Photos scanned by **PhotoSynthèse**
Printed in the European Union

Black Dog Publishing Limited
Unit 4.04 Tea Building
56 Shoreditch High Street
London E1 6JJ
T +44 (0)207613 1922
F +44 (0)207613 1944
E info@bdp.demon.co.uk
www.bdpworld.com

All opinions expressed within this publication are those of the author and not necessarily the publisher.

British Library Cataloguing-in-Publication Date.
A catalogue record for this book is available from the British Library.

ISBN 1 904772 14 5

MANY THANKS TO:

Tommy Doyle
Sébastien Bisson
Jean-Francois Clermont
For being so generous with their time and talent.

Marc, Geneviève, and Christine from Kuizin Studio
For throwing all their creative energy and organizational skills behind the book.

The entire staff of Black Dog, especially
Tahani, Duncan, Richard, and Catherine
For believing in the project and for being a support throughout.

Denis Rainville from PhotoSynthèse
For being such a colorful perfectionist.

Charmaine Lyn
Meghan Price
Marci Denesiuk
For their attentive reading skills and general enthusiasm.

Catherine Durand
Maryse Morin
Gabriel Jones

Elron Aluminum
For lending us such a stylish and functional car.
To the various cafes that made us hot drinks on our nights scouting barbershops on foot in the brutal Montreal winter.
La Fondation du maire de Montréal pour la jeunesse.
The Abecassis and Sauvé families and all our friends
For their encouragement.
David Mizraki for being a rock.

Special thanks to all the clients, regulars, hangers-on, and taxidermied mooseheads, but most of all to the inspiring barbers who were not afraid to let two girls into their shops to take hundreds of photos and dig up all their old stories.

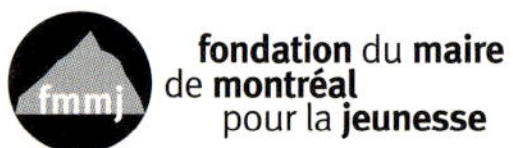

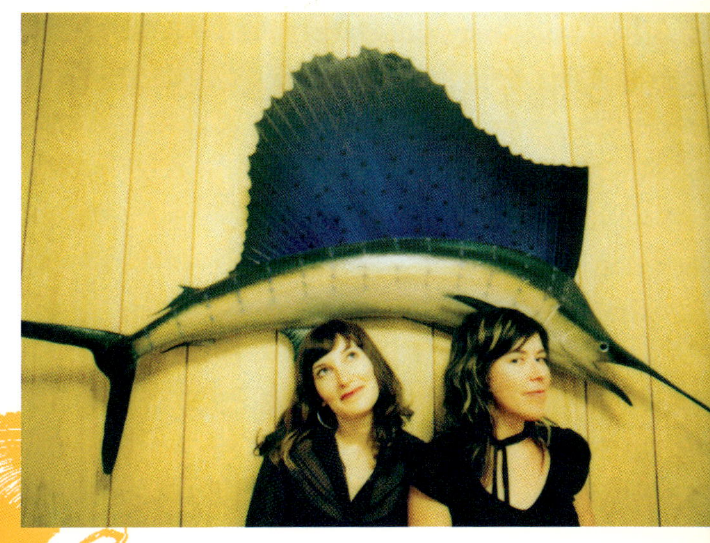

TALLY ABECASSIS

Tally Abecassis is a documentary filmmaker, writer, and radio producer. Her documentaries, which have been broadcast on television and screened in a variety of festivals, include *Warshaw on the Main*, *Lifelike*, and *Think Big*. In 2004, she won a national award for a radio program on childhood homes. Tally lives in Montreal with her husband, David.

CLAUDINE SAUVÉ

As a professional photographer and director of photography, Claudine Sauvé has completed a variety of fiction, documentary, and hybrid projects. She has won several Lux Grand Prize awards, recognizing the best professional photos in Quebec, most recently for a series from the *Barbershops* collection. Claudine lives in Montreal with her cat, Johnny Hairball.

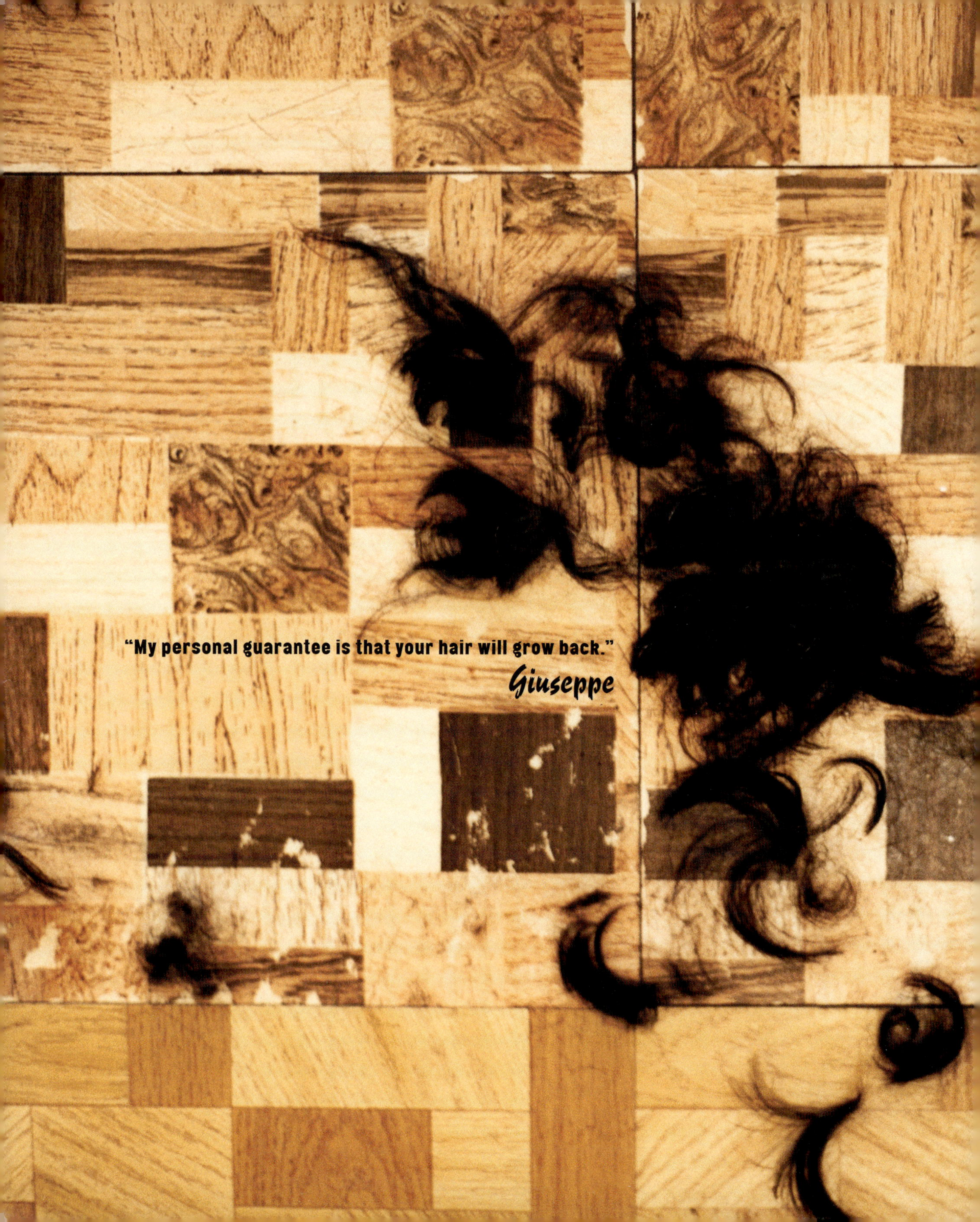

"My personal guarantee is that your hair will grow back."
Giuseppe